AF757092

THEORY AND APPLICATIONS OF MONTE CARLO SIMULATIONS

Edited by **Victor (Wai Kin) Chan**

Theory and Applications of Monte Carlo Simulations
http://dx.doi.org/10.5772/45892
Edited by Victor (Wai Kin) Chan

Contributors

Dragica Vasileska, Shaikh Ahmed, Mihail Nedjalkov, Rita Khanna, Mahdi Sadeghi, Pooneh Saidi, Claudio Tenreiro, Elshemey, Subhadip Raychaudhuri, Krasimir Kolev, Natalia D. Nikolova, Daniela Toneva-Zheynova, Kiril Tenekedjiev, Vladimir Elokhin, Wai Kin (Victor) Chan, Charles Malmborg, Masaaki Kijima, Ianik Plante, Paulo Guimarães Couto, Jailton Damasceno, Sérgio Pinheiro Oliveira

Published by InTech

Janeza Trdine 9, 51000 Rijeka, Croatia

Copyright © 2013 InTech

All chapters are distributed under the Creative Commons Attribution 3.0 license, which allows users to download, copy and build upon published articles even for commercial purposes, as long as the author and publisher are properly credited, which ensures maximum dissemination and a wider impact of our publications. However, users who aim to disseminate and distribute copies of this book as a whole must not seek monetary compensation for such service (excluded InTech representatives and agreed collaborations). After this work has been published by InTech, authors have the right to republish it, in whole or part, in any publication of which they are the author, and to make other personal use of the work. Any republication, referencing or personal use of the work must explicitly identify the original source.

Notice

Statements and opinions expressed in the chapters are these of the individual contributors and not necessarily those of the editors or publisher. No responsibility is accepted for the accuracy of information contained in the published chapters. The publisher assumes no responsibility for any damage or injury to persons or property arising out of the use of any materials, instructions, methods or ideas contained in the book.

Publishing Process Manager Iva Simcic
Technical Editor InTech DTP team
Cover InTech Design team

Additional hard copies can be obtained from orders@intechopen.com

Theory and Applications of Monte Carlo Simulations, Edited by Victor (Wai Kin) Chan
p. cm.
ISBN 978-953-51-1012-5

We are IntechOpen,
the world's leading publisher of
Open Access books
Built by scientists, for scientists

4,000+
Open access books available

116,000+
International authors and editors

120M+
Downloads

151
Countries delivered to

Our authors are among the
Top 1%
most cited scientists

12.2%
Contributors from top 500 universities

BOOK CITATION INDEX
CLARIVATE ANALYTICS
INDEXED
WEB OF SCIENCE™

Selection of our books indexed in the Book Citation Index
in Web of Science™ Core Collection (BKCI)

Interested in publishing with us?
Contact book.department@intechopen.com

Numbers displayed above are based on latest data collected.
For more information visit www.intechopen.com

For EU product safety concerns:
IN TECH d.o.o., Prolaz Marije Krucifikse Kozulić 3, 51000 Rijeka, Croatia,
info@intechopen.com or visit our website at intechopen.com.

Meet the editor

Dr. Wai Kin (Victor) Chan is an Associate Professor of the Department of Industrial and Systems Engineering at the Rensselaer Polytechnic Institute (RPI), Troy, NY. He received a Ph.D. degree in industrial engineering and operations research from the University of California, Berkeley in 2005. Dr. Chan has published papers in Operations Research, ACM TOMACS, INFORMS Journal of Service Science, IEEE Transactions, International Journal of Production Research, and Artificial Intelligence Review. Dr. Chan is a recipient of the Pritsker thesis award, the NSF CAREER Award, the IEEE CASE Best Paper Awards, and the INFORMS Service Science Best Paper Award. Dr. Chan serves and has served as a program co-chair of the 2013 Industrial and System Engineering Research Conference, editor of the IEEE Conference on Automation Science and Engineering, associate editor of the IIE Transactions, and track chair of the Winter Simulation Conference. Dr. Chan is a member of INFORMS, IIE, IEEE, and Alpha Pi Mu.

Contents

Preface

The objective of this book is to introduce recent advances and state-of-the-art applications of Monte Carlo Simulation (MCS) in various fields. MCS is a class of statistical methods for performance analysis and decision making based on taking random samples from underlying systems or problems to draw inferences or estimations.

Let us make an analogy by using the structure of an umbrella to define and exemplify the position of this book within the fields of science and engineering. Imagine that one can place MCS at the centerpoint of an umbrella and define the tip of each spoke as one engineering or science discipline: this book lays out the various applications of MCS with a goal of sparking innovative exercises of MCS across fields.

Despite the excitement that MCS spurs, MCS is not impeccable due to criticisms about leaking a rigorous theoretical foundation—if the umbrella analogy is made again, then one can say that "this umbrella" is only half-way open. This book attempts to open "this umbrella" a bit more by showing evidence of recent advances in MCS.

To get a glimpse at this book, Chapter 1 deals with an important question in experimental studies: how to fit a theoretical distribution to a set of experimental data. In many cases, dependence within datasets invalidates standard approaches. Chapter 1 describes an MCS procedure for fitting distributions to datasets and testing goodness-of-fit in terms of statistical significance. This MCS procedure is applied in charactering fibrin structure.

MCS is a potential alternative to traditional methods for measuring uncertainty. Chapter 2 exemplifies such a potential in the domain of metrology. This chapter shows that MCS can overcome the limitations of traditional methods and work well on a wide range of applications. MCS has been extensively used in the area of finance. Chapter 3 presents various stochastic models for simulating fractional Brownian motion. Both exact and approximate methods are discussed. For unfamiliar readers, this chapter can be a good introduction to these stochastic models and their simulation using MCS. MCS has been a popular approach in optimization. Chapter 4 presents an MCS procedure to solving dynamic line layout problems. The line layout problem is a facility design problem. It concerns with how to optimally allocate space to a set of work centers within a facility such that the total intra traffic flow among the work centers is minimized. This problem is a difficult optimization problem. This chapter presents a simple MCS approach to solve this problem efficiently.

MCS has been one major performance analysis approach in semiconductor manufacturing. Chapter 5 deals with improving the MCS technique used for Nanoscale MOSFETs. It introduces three event biasing techniques and demonstrates how they can improve statistical estimations and facilitate the computation of characteristics of these devices. Chapter 6 describes the use of MCS in the ensembles of polyaromatic hydrocarbons. It also provides an introduction to MCS and its performance in the field of materials. Chapter 7 discusses variance reduction techniques for MCS in nuclear engineering. Variance reduction techniques are frequently used in various studies to improve estimation accuracy and computational efficiency. This chapter first highlights estimation errors and accuracy issues, and then introduces the use of variance reduction techniques in mitigating these problems. Chapter 8 presents experimental results and the use of MCS in the formation of self-oscillations and chemical waves in CO oxidation reaction. Chapter 9 introduces the sampling of the Green's function and describes how to apply it to one, two, and three dimensional problems in particle diffusion. Two applications are presented: the simulation of ligands molecules near a plane membrane and the simulation of partially diffusion-controlled chemical reactions. Simulation results and future applications are also discussed. Chapter 10 reviews the applications of MCS in biophysics and biology with a focus on kinetic MCS. A comprehensive list of references for the applications of MCS in biophysics and biology is also provided. Chapter 11 demonstrates how MCS can improve healthcare practices. It describes the use of MCS in helping to detect breast cancer lumps without excision.

This book unifies knowledge of MCS from aforementioned diverse fields to make a coherent text to facilitate research and new applications of MCS.

Having a background in industrial engineering and operations research, I found it useful to see the different usages of MCS in other fields. Methods and techniques that other researchers used to apply MCS in their fields shed light on my research on optimization and also provide me with new insights and ideas about how to better utilize MCS in my field. Indeed, with the increasing complexity of nowadays systems, borrowing ideas from other fields has become one means to breaking through obstacles and making great discoveries. A researcher with his/her eyes open in related knowledge happening in other fields is more likely to succeed than one who does not.

I hope that this book can help shape our understanding of MCS and spark new ideas for novel and better usages of MCS.

As an editor, I would like to thank all contributing authors of this book. Their work is a valuable contribution to Monte Carlo Simulation research and applications. I am also grateful to InTech for their support in editing this book, in particular, Ms. Iva Simcic and Ms. Ana Nikolic for their publishing and editorial assistance.

Victor (Wai Kin) Chan, Ph.D.
Associate Professor
Department of Industrial and Systems Engineering
Rensselaer Polytechnic Institute
Troy, NY
USA

Chapter 1

Monte Carlo Statistical Tests for Identity of Theoretical and Empirical Distributions of Experimental Data

Natalia D. Nikolova, Daniela Toneva-Zheynova, Krasimir Kolev and Kiril Tenekedjiev

Additional information is available at the end of the chapter

http://dx.doi.org/10.5772/53049

1. Introduction

Often experimental work requires analysis of many datasets derived in a similar way. For each dataset it is possible to find a specific theoretical distribution that describes best the sample. A basic assumption in this type of work is that if the mechanism (experiment) to generate the samples is the same, then the distribution type that describes the datasets will also be the same [1]. In that case, the difference between the sets will be captured not through changing the type of the distribution, but through changes in its parameters. There are some advantages in finding whether a type of theoretical distribution that fits several datasets exists. At first, it improves the fit because the assumptions concerning the mechanism underlying the experiment can be verified against several datasets. Secondly, it is possible to investigate how the variation of the input parameters influences the parameters of the theoretical distribution. In some experiments it might be proven that the differences in the input conditions lead to qualitative change of the fitted distributions (i.e. change of the type of the distribution). In other cases the variation of the input conditions may lead only to quantitative changes in the output (i.e. changes in the parameters of the distribution). Then it is of importance to investigate the statistical significance of the quantitative differences, i.e. to compare the statistical difference of the distribution parameters. In some cases it may not be possible to find a single type of distribution that fits all datasets. A possible option in these cases is to construct empirical distributions according to known techniques [2], and investigate whether the differences are statistically significant. In any case, proving that the observed difference between theoretical, or between empirical distributions, are not statistically significant allows merging datasets and operating on larger amount of data, which is a prerequisite for higher precision of the statistical results. This task is similar to testing for stability in regression analysis [3].

INTECH
open science | open minds

© 2013 The Author(s). Licensee InTech. This chapter is distributed under the terms of the Creative Commons Attribution License http://creativecommons.org/licenses/by/3.0), which permits unrestricted use, distribution, and reproduction in any medium, provided the original work is properly cited.

Formulating three separate tasks, this chapter solves the problem of identifying an appropriate distribution type that fits several one-dimensional (1-D) datasets and testing the statistical significance of the observed differences in the empirical and in the fitted distributions for each pair of samples. The first task (Task 1) aims at identifying a type of 1-D theoretical distribution that fits best the samples in several datasets by altering its parameters. The second task (Task 2) is to test the statistical significance of the difference between two empirical distributions of a pair of 1-D datasets. The third task (Task 3) is to test the statistical significance of the difference between two fitted distributions of the same type over two arbitrary datasets.

Task 2 can be performed independently of the existence of a theoretical distribution fit valid for all samples. Therefore, comparing and eventually merging pairs of samples will always be possible. This task requires comparing two independent discontinuous (stair-case) empirical cumulative distribution functions (CDF). It is a standard problem and the approach here is based on a symmetric variant of the Kolmogorov-Smirnov test [4] called the Kuiper two-sample test, which essentially performs an estimate of the closeness of a pair of independent stair-case CDFs by finding the maximum positive and the maximum negative deviation between the two [5]. The distribution of the test statistics is known and the p value of the test can be readily estimated.

Tasks 1 and 3 introduce the novel elements of this chapter. Task 1 searches for a type of theoretical distribution (out of an enumerated list of distributions) which fits best multiple datasets by varying its specific parameter values. The performance of a distribution fit is assessed through four criteria, namely the Akaike Information Criterion (AIC) [6], the Bayesian Information Criterion (BIC) [7], the average and the minimal p value of a distribution fit to all datasets. Since the datasets contain random measurements, the values of the parameters for each acquired fit in Task 1 are random, too. That is why it is necessary to check whether the differences are statistically significant, for each pair of datasets. If not, then both theoretical fits are identical and the samples may be merged. In Task 1 the distribution of the Kuiper statistic cannot be calculated in a closed form, because the problem is to compare an empirical distribution with its own fit and the independence is violated. A distribution of the Kuiper statistic in Task 3 cannot be estimated in close form either, because here one has to compare two analytical distributions, but not two stair-case CDFs. For that reason the distributions of the Kuiper statistic in Tasks 1 and 3 are constructed via a Monte Carlo simulation procedures, which in Tasks 1 is based on Bootstrap [8].

The described approach is illustrated with practical applications for the characterization of the fibrin structure in natural and experimental thrombi evaluated with scanning electron microscopy (SEM).

2. Theoretical setup

The approach considers N 1-D datasets $\chi^i=\left(x_1^i, x_2^i, \ldots, x_{n_i}^i\right)$, for i=1,2,…,N. The data set χ^i contains n_i>64 sorted positive samples ($0<x_1^i\leq x_2^i\leq\ldots\leq x_{n_i}^i$) of a given random quantity under equal conditions. The datasets contain samples of the same random quantity, but under slightly different conditions.

The procedure assumes that M types of 1-D theoretical distributions are analyzed. Each of them has a probability density function $PDF_j(x, \vec{p}_j)$, a cumulative distribution function $CDF_j(x, \vec{p}_j)$, and an inverse cumulative distribution function $invCDF_j(P, \vec{p}_j)$, for j=1, 2, ..., M. Each of these functions depends on n_j^p-dimensional parameter vectors $\vec{p}_j$ (for j=1, 2, ..., M), dependent on the type of theoretical distribution.

2.1. Task 1 – Theoretical solution

The empirical cumulative distribution function $CDF_e^i(.)$ is initially linearly approximated over (n_i+1) nodes as (n_i-1) internal nodes $CDF_e^i(x_k^i/2+x_{k+1}^i/2)=k/n_i$ for k=1,2,...,n_i–1 and two external nodes $CDF_e^i(x_1^i-\Delta_d^i)=0$ and $CDF_e^i(x_{n_i}^i+\Delta_u^i)=1$, where $\Delta_d^i=\min(x_1^i, (x_{16}^i-x_1^i)/30)$ and $\Delta_u^i=(x_{n_i}^i-x_{n_i-15}^i)/30$ are the halves of mean inter-sample intervals in the lower and upper ends of the dataset χ^i. This is the most frequent case when the sample values are positive and the lower external node will never be with a negative abscissa because $(x_1^i-\Delta_d^i)\geq 0$. If both negative and positive sample values are acceptable then $\Delta_d^i=(x_{16}^i-x_1^i)/30$ and $\Delta_u^i=(x_{n_i}^i-x_{n_i-15}^i)/30$. Of course if all the sample values have to be negative then $\Delta_d^i=(x_{16}^i-x_1^i)/30$ and $\Delta_u^i=\min(-x_{n_i}^i, (x_{n_i}^i-x_{n_i-15}^i)/30)$. In that rare case the upper external node will never be with positive abscissa because $(x_{n_i}^i+\Delta_u^i)\leq 0$.

It is convenient to introduce "before-first" $x_0^i=x_1^i-2\Delta_d^i$ and "after-last" $x_{n_i+1}^i=x_{n_i}^i+2\Delta_u^i$ samples. When for some k=1,2,...,n_i and for p>1 it is true that $x_{k-1}^i<x_k^i=x_{k+1}^i=x_{k+2}^i=...=x_{k+p}^i<x_{k+p+1}^i$, then the initial approximation of $CDF_e^i(.)$ contains a vertical segment of p nodes. In that case the p nodes on that segment are replaced by a single node in the middle of the vertical segment $CDF_e^i(x_k^i)=(k+p/2-1/2)/n_i$. The described two-step procedure [2] results in a strictly increasing function $CDF_e^i(.)$ in the closed interval $[x_1^i-\Delta_d^i; x_{n_i}^i+\Delta_u^i]$. That is why it is possible to introduce $invCDF_e^i(.)$ with the domain [0; 1] as the inverse function of $CDF_e^i(.)$ in $[x_1^i-\Delta_d^i; x_{n_i}^i+\Delta_u^i]$. The median and the interquartile range of the empirical distribution can be estimated from $invCDF_e^i(.)$, whereas the mean and the standard deviation are easily estimated directly from the dataset χ^i:

- mean: $mean_e^i=\frac{1}{n_i}\sum_{k=1}^{n_i} x_k^i$
- median: $med_e^i=invCDF_e^i(0.5)$
- standard deviation: $std_e^i=\sqrt{\frac{1}{n_i-1}\sum_{k=1}^{n_i}\left(x_k^i-mean_e^i\right)^2}$;
- inter-quartile range: $iqr_e^i=invCDF_e^i(0.75)-invCDF_e^i(0.25)$.

The non-zero part of the empirical density $PDF_e^i(.)$ is determined in the closed interval $\left[x_1^i - \Delta_d^i; x_{n_i}^i + \Delta_u^i\right]$ as a histogram with bins of equal area (each bin has equal product of density and span of data). The number of bins b_i is selected as the minimal from the Scott [9], Sturges [10] and Freedman-Diaconis [11] suggestions: $b_i = \min\{b_i^{Sc}, b_i^{St}, b_i^{FD}\}$, where $b_i^{Sc} = fl\left(0.2865\left(x_{n_i}^i - x_1^i\right)\sqrt[3]{n_i} / std_e^i\right)$, $b_i^{St} = fl\left(1 + log_2(n_i)\right)$, and $b_i^{FD} = fl\left(0.5\left(x_{n_i}^i - x_1^i\right)\sqrt[3]{n_i} / iqr_e^i\right)$. In the last three formulae, $fl(y)$ stands for the greatest whole number less or equal to y. The lower and upper margins of the k-th bin $m_{d,k}^i$ and $m_{u,k}^i$ are determined as quantiles $(k-1)/b_i$ and k/b_i respectively: $m_{d,k}^i = invCDF_e^i(k/b_i - 1/b_i)$ and $m_{u,k}^i = invCDF_e^i(k/b_i)$. The density of the kth bin is determined as $PDF_e^i(x) = b_i^{-1} / \left(m_{u,k}^i - m_{d,k}^i\right)$. The described procedure [2] results in a histogram, where the relative error of the worst $PDF_e^i(.)$ estimate is minimal from all possible splitting of the samples into b_i bins. This is so because the PDF estimate of a bin is found as the probability that the random variable would have a value in that bin divided to the bin's width. This probability is estimated as the relative frequency to have a data point in that bin at the given data set. The closer to zero that frequency is the worse it has been estimated. That is why the worst PDF estimate is at the bin that contains the least number of data points. Since for the proposed distribution each bin contains equal number of data points, any other division to the same number of bins would result in having a bin with less data points. Hence, the relative error of its PDF estimate would be worse.

The improper integral $\int_{-\infty}^{x} PDF_e^i(x)dx$ of the density is a smoothened version of $CDF_e^i(.)$ linearly approximated over (b_i+1) nodes: $\left(invCDF_e^i(k/b_i); k/b_i\right)$ for k=0, 1, 2, …, b_i.

If the samples are distributed with density $PDF_j(x, \vec{p}_j)$, then the likelihood of the dataset χ^i is $L_j^i(\vec{p}_j) = \prod_{k=1}^{n_i} PDF_j(x_k^i, \vec{p}_j)$. The maximum likelihood estimates (MLEs) of $\vec{p}_j$ are determined as those $\vec{p}'^i_j$, which maximize $L_j^i(\vec{p}_j)$, that is $\vec{p}'^i_j = \arg\left\{\max_{\vec{p}_j}\left[L_j^i(\vec{p}_j)\right]\right\}$. The numerical characteristics of the jth theoretical distribution fitted to the dataset χ^i are calculated as:

- mean: $mean_j^i = \int_{-\infty}^{+\infty} x.PDF_j\left(x, \vec{p}'^i_j\right)dx$
- median: $med_j^i = invCDF_j\left(0.5, \vec{p}'^i_j\right)$
- mode: $mode_j^i = \arg\left\{\max_x\left[PDF_j(x, \vec{p}_j)\right]\right\}$
- standard deviation: $std_j^i = \sqrt[2]{\int_{-\infty}^{+\infty}\left(x - mean_j^i\right)^2 PDF_j\left(x, \vec{p}'^i_j\right)dx}$;

- inter-quartile range: $iqr_j^i = invCDF_j\left(0.75, \vec{p}^i_j\right) - invCDF_j\left(0.25, \vec{p}^i_j\right)$.

The quality of the fit can be assessed using a statistical hypothesis test. The null hypothesis H_0 is that $CDF_e^i(x)$ is equal to $CDF_j\left(x, \vec{p}^i_j\right)$, which means that the sample χ^i is drawn from $CDF_j\left(x, \vec{p}^i_j\right)$. The alternative hypothesis H_1 is that $CDF_e^i(x)$ is different from $CDF_j\left(x, \vec{p}^i_j\right)$, which means that the fit is not good. The Kuiper statistic V_j^i [12] is a suitable measure for the goodness-of-fit of the theoretical cumulative distribution functions $CDF_j\left(x, \vec{p}^i_j\right)$ to the dataset χ^i:

$$V_j^i = \max_x\left\{CDF_e^i(x) - CDF_j\left(x, \vec{p}^i_j\right)\right\} + \max_x\left\{CDF_j\left(x, \vec{p}^i_j\right) - CDF_e^i(x)\right\}. \quad (1)$$

The theoretical Kuiper's distribution is derived just for the case of two independent staircase distributions, but not for continuous distribution fitted to the data of another [5]. That is why the distribution of V from (1), if H_0 is true, should be estimated by a Monte Carlo procedure. The main idea is that if the dataset $\chi^i = \left(x_1^i, x_2^i, \ldots, x_{n_i}^i\right)$ is distributed in compliance with the 1-D theoretical distributions of type j, then its PDF would be very close to its estimate $PDF_j\left(x, \vec{p}^i_j\right)$, and so each synthetic dataset generated from $PDF_j\left(x, \vec{p}^i_j\right)$ would produce Kuiper statistics according to (1), which would be close to zero [1].

The algorithm of the proposed procedure is the following:

1. Construct the empirical cumulative distribution function $CDF_e^i(x)$ describing the data in χ^i.
2. Find the MLE of the parameters for the distributions of type j fitting χ^i as $\vec{p}^i_j = \arg\left\{\max_{\vec{p}_j}\left[\prod_{k=1}^{n_i} PDF_j\left(x_k^i, \vec{p}_j\right)\right]\right\}$.
3. Build the fitted cumulative distribution function $CDF_j\left(x, \vec{p}^i_j\right)$ describing χ^i.
4. Calculate the actual Kuiper statistic V_j^i according to (1).
5. Repeat for $r=1,2,\ldots, n^{MC}$ (in fact use n^{MC} simulation cycles):
    a. generate a synthetic dataset $\chi_r^{i,syn} = \left\{x_{1,r}^{i,syn}, x_{2,r}^{i,syn}, \ldots, x_{n_i,r}^{i,syn}\right\}$ from the fitted cumulative distribution function $CDF_j\left(x, \vec{p}^i_j\right)$. The dataset $\chi_r^{i,syn}$ contains n_i sorted samples $\left(x_{1,r}^{i,syn} \le x_{2,r}^{i,syn} \le \ldots \le x_{n_i,r}^{i,syn}\right)$;
    b. construct the synthetic empirical distribution function $CDF_{e,r}^{i,syn}(x)$ describing the data in $\chi_r^{i,syn}$;
    c. find the MLE of the parameters for the distributions of type j fitting $\chi_r^{i,syn}$ as

$$\vec{p}^{\,i,syn}_{j,r} = \arg\left\{\max_{\vec{p}_j}\left[\prod_{k=1}^{n_i} PDF_j\left(x^{i,syn}_{k,r}, \vec{p}_j\right)\right]\right\};$$

d. build the theoretical distribution function $CDF^{syn}_{j,r}\left(x, \vec{p}^{\,i,syn}_{j,r}\right)$ describing $\chi^{i,syn}_r$;

e. estimate the rth instance of the synthetic Kuiper statistic as $V^{i,syn}_{j,r} = \max_x\left\{CDF^{i,syn}_{e,r}(x) - CDF^{syn}_{j,r}\left(x, \vec{p}^{\,i,syn}_{j,r}\right)\right\} + \max_x\left\{CDF^{syn}_{j,r}\left(x, \vec{p}^{\,i,syn}_{j,r}\right) - CDF^{i,syn}_{e,r}(x)\right\}$.

6. The p-value $P^{fit,i}_{value,j}$ of the statistical test (the probability to reject a true hypothesis H_0 that the jth type theoretical distribution fits well to the samples in dataset χ^i) is estimated as the frequency of generating synthetic Kuiper statistic greater than the actual Kuiper statistic V^i_j from step 4:

$$P^{fit,i}_{value,j} = \frac{1}{n^{mc}} \sum_{\substack{r=1 \\ V^i_j < V^{i,syn}_{j,r}}}^{n^{mc}} 1 \tag{2}$$

In fact, (2) is the sum of the indicator function of the crisp set, defined as all synthetic datasets with a Kuiper statistic greater than V^i_j.

The performance of each theoretical distribution should be assessed according to its goodness-of-fit measures to the N datasets simultaneously. If a given theoretical distribution cannot be fitted even to one of the datasets, then that theoretical distribution has to be discarded from further consideration. The other theoretical distributions have to be ranked according to their ability to describe all datasets. One basic and three auxiliary criteria are useful in the required ranking.

The basic criterion is the minimal p-value of the theoretical distribution fits to the N datasets:

$$min P^{fit}_{value,j} = \min\left\{P^{fit,1}_{value,j}, P^{fit,2}_{value,j}, \ldots, P^{fit,N}_{value,j}\right\}, \; for \;\; j=1, 2, \ldots, M. \tag{3}$$

The first auxiliary criterion is the average of the p-values of the theoretical distribution fits to the N datasets:

$$mean P^{fit}_{value,j} = \frac{1}{N}\sum_{j=1}^{N} P^{fit,i}_{value,j}, \;\; for \; j=1, \; 2, \; .., \; M. \tag{4}$$

The second and the third auxiliary criteria are the AIC-Akaike Information Criterion [6] and the BIC-Bayesian Information Criterion [7], which corrects the negative log-likelihoods with the number of the assessed parameters:

$$AIC_j = -2\sum_{i=1}^{N} \log\left(L_j^i(\vec{p}^i_j)\right) + 2\log\left(N.n_j^p\right) = \\ = -2\sum_{i=1}^{N}\sum_{j=1}^{M} \log PDF_j\left(x_k^i, \vec{p}^i_j\right) + 2\log\left(N.n_j^p\right) \tag{5}$$

$$BIC_j = -2\sum_{i=1}^{N} \log\left(L_j^i(\vec{p}^i_j)\right) + 2\log\left(N.n_j^p\right).\log\left(\sum_{i=1}^{M} n_i\right) = \\ = -2\sum_{i=1}^{N}\sum_{j=1}^{M} \log PDF_j\left(x_k^i, \vec{p}^i_j\right) + 2\log\left(N.n_j^p\right).\log\left(\sum_{i=1}^{M} n_i\right) \tag{6}$$

for j=1,2,..,M. The best theoretical distribution type should have maximal values for $minP^{fit}_{value,\,j}$ and $meanP^{fit}_{value,\,j}$, whereas its values for AIC_j and BIC_j should be minimal. On top, the best theoretical distribution type should have $minP^{fit}_{value,\,j}>0.05$, otherwise no theoretical distribution from the initial M types fits properly to the N datasets.

That solves the problem for selecting the best theoretical distribution type for fitting the samples in the N datasets.

2.2. Task 2 – Theoretical solution

The second problem is the estimation of the statistical significance of the difference between two datasets. It is equivalent to calculating the p-value of a statistical hypothesis test, where the null hypothesis H_0 is that the samples of χ^{i1} and χ^{i2} are drawn from the same underlying continuous population, and the alternative hypothesis H_1 is that the samples of χ^{i1} and χ^{i2} are drawn from different underlying continuous populations. The two-sample asymptotic Kuiper test is designed exactly for that problem, because χ^{i1} and χ^{i2} are independently drawn datasets. That is why "staircase" empirical cumulative distribution functions [13] are built from the two datasets χ^{i1} and χ^{i2}:

$$CDF^i_{sce}(x) = \sum_{\substack{k=1 \\ x_k^i \le x}}^{n_i} 1/n_i, \quad \text{for } i \in \{i1,\, i2\}. \tag{7}$$

The "staircase" empirical $CDF^i_{sce}(.)$ is a discontinuous version of the already defined empirical $CDF^i_e(.)$. The Kuiper statistic $V^{i1,i2}$ [12] is a measure for the closeness of the two 'staircase' empirical cumulative distribution functions $CDF^{i1}_{sce}(.)$ and $CDF^{i2}_{sce}(.)$:

$$V^{i1,i2} = \max_x\left\{CDF^{i1}_{sce}(x) - CDF^{i2}_{sce}(x)\right\} + \max_x\left\{CDF^{i2}_{sce}(x) - CDF^{i1}_{sce}(x)\right\} \tag{8}$$

The distribution of the test statics $V^{i1,i2}$ is known and the p-value of the two tail statistical test with null hypothesis H_0, that the samples in χ^{i1} and in χ^{i2} result in the same 'staircase' empirical cumulative distribution functions is estimated as a series [5] according to formulae (9) and (10).

The algorithm for the theoretical solution of Task 2 is straightforward:

1. Construct the "staircase" empirical cumulative distribution function describing the data in χ^{i1} as $CDF_{sce}^{i1}(x) = \sum_{\substack{k=1 \\ x_k^{i1} \le x}}^{n_{i1}} 1/n_{i1}$.

2. Construct the "staircase" empirical cumulative distribution function describing the data in χ^{i2} as $CDF_{sce}^{i2}(x) = \sum_{\substack{k=1 \\ x_k^{i2} \le x}}^{n_{i2}} 1/n_{i2}$.

3. Calculate the actual Kuiper statistic $V^{i1,i2}$ according to (8).

4. The p-value of the statistical test (the probability to reject a true null hypothesis H_0) is estimated as:

$$P_{value,e}^{i1,i2} = 2\sum_{j=1}^{+\infty} \left(4j^2\lambda^2 - 1\right) e^{-2j^2\lambda^2} \tag{9}$$

where

$$\lambda = \frac{1}{V^{i1,i2}} \left(\sqrt{\frac{n_{i1}n_{i2}}{n_{i1} + n_{i2}}} + 0.155 + 0.24\sqrt{\frac{n_{i1} + n_{i2}}{n_{i1}n_{i2}}} \right) \tag{10}$$

If $P_{value,e}^{i1,i2} < 0.05$ the hypothesis H_0 is rejected.

2.3. Task 3 – Theoretical solution

The last problem is to test the statistical significance of the difference between two fitted distributions of the same type. This type most often would be the best type of theoretical distribution, which was identified in the first problem, but the test is valid for any type. The problem is equivalent to calculating the p-value of statistical hypothesis test, where the null hypothesis H_0 is that the theoretical distribution $CDF_j\left(x, \vec{p}_j^{\,i1}\right)$ and $CDF_j\left(x, \vec{p}_j^{\,i2}\right)$ fitted to the datasets χ^{i1} and χ^{i2} are identical, and the alternative hypothesis H_1 is that $CDF_j\left(x, \vec{p}_j^{\,i1}\right)$ and $CDF_j\left(x, \vec{p}_j^{\,i2}\right)$ are not identical.

The test statistic again is the Kuiper one $V_j^{i1,i2}$:

$$V_j^{i1,i2}=\max_x\left\{CDF_j\left(x,\vec{p}_j^{i1}\right)-CDF_j\left(x,\vec{p}_j^{i2}\right)\right\}+\max_x\left\{CDF_j\left(x,\vec{p}_j^{i2}\right)-CDF_j\left(x,\vec{p}_j^{i1}\right)\right\}. \tag{11}$$

As it has already been mentioned the theoretical Kuiper's distribution is derived just for the case of two independent staircase distributions, but not for the case of two independent continuous cumulative distribution functions. That is why the distribution of V from (11), if H_0 is true, should be estimated by a Monte Carlo procedure. The main idea is that if H_0 is true, then $CDF_j\left(x,\vec{p}_j^{i1}\right)$ and $CDF_j\left(x,\vec{p}_j^{i2}\right)$ should be identical to the merged distribution $CDF_j\left(x,\vec{p}_j^{i1+i2}\right)$, fitted to the merged dataset χ^{i1+i2} formed by merging the samples of χ^{i1} and χ^{i2} [1].

The algorithm of the proposed procedure is the following:

1. Find the MLE of the parameters for the distributions of type j fitting χ^{i1} as $\vec{p}_j^{i1}=\arg\left\{\max_{\vec{p}_j}\left[\prod_{k=1}^{n_{i1}}PDF_j\left(x_k^{i1},\vec{p}_j\right)\right]\right\}$.
2. Build the fitted cumulative distribution function $CDF_j\left(x,\vec{p}_j^{i1}\right)$ describing χ^{i1}.
3. Find the MLE of the parameters for the distributions of type j fitting χ^{i2} as $\vec{p}_j^{i2}=\arg\left\{\max_{\vec{p}_j}\left[\prod_{k=1}^{n_{i2}}PDF_j\left(x_k^{i2},\vec{p}_j\right)\right]\right\}$.
4. Build the fitted cumulative distribution function $CDF_j\left(x,\vec{p}_j^{i2}\right)$ describing χ^{i2}.
5. Calculate the actual Kuiper statistic $V_j^{i1,i2}$ according to (11).
6. Merge the samples χ^{i1} and χ^{i2}, and form the merged data set χ^{i1+i2}.
7. Find the MLE of the parameters for the distributions of type j fitting χ^{i1+i2} as $\vec{p}_j^{i1+i2}=\arg\left\{\max_{\vec{p}_j}\left[\prod_{k=1}^{n_{i1}}PDF_j\left(x_k^{i1},\vec{p}_j\right)\prod_{k=1}^{n_{i2}}PDF_j\left(x_k^{i2},\vec{p}_j\right)\right]\right\}$.
8. Fit the merged fitted cumulative distribution function $CDF_j\left(x,\vec{p}_j^{i1+i2}\right)$ to χ^{i1+i2}.
9. Repeat for r=1,2,..., n^{MC} (in fact use n^{MC} simulation cycles):
   a. a. generate a synthetic dataset $\chi_r^{i1,syn}=\left\{x_{1,r}^{i1,syn},x_{2,r}^{i1,syn},\ldots,x_{n_{i1},r}^{i1,syn}\right\}$ from the fitted cumulative distribution function $CDF_j\left(x,\vec{p}_j^{i1+i2}\right)$;
   b. b. find the MLE of the parameters for the distributions of type j fitting $\chi_r^{i1,syn}$ as

      $$\vec{p}_{j,r}^{i1,syn}=\arg\left\{\max_{\vec{p}_j}\left[\prod_{k=1}^{n_{i1}}PDF_j\left(x_{k,r}^{i1,syn},\vec{p}_j\right)\right]\right\};$$
   c. c. build the theoretical distribution function $CDF_{j,r}^{syn}\left(x,\vec{p}_{j,r}^{i1,syn}\right)$ describing $\chi_r^{i1,syn}$;

d. d. generate a synthetic dataset $\chi_r^{i2,syn} = \left\{ x_{1,r}^{i2,syn}, x_{2,r}^{i2,syn}, \ldots, x_{n_{i2},r}^{i2,syn} \right\}$ from the fitted cumulative distribution function $CDF_j\left(x, \vec{p}_j^{i1+i2}\right)$;

e. e. find the MLE of the parameters for the distributions of type j fitting $\chi_r^{i2,syn}$ as

$$\vec{p}_{j,r}^{i2,syn} = \arg\left\{ \max_{\vec{p}_j} \left[\prod_{k=1}^{n_{i2}} PDF_j\left(x_{k,r}^{i2,syn}, \vec{p}_j\right) \right] \right\};$$

f. f. build the theoretical distribution function $CDF_{j,r}^{syn}\left(x, \vec{p}_{j,r}^{i2,syn}\right)$ describing $\chi_r^{i2,syn}$;

g. g. estimate the rth instance of the synthetic Kuiper statistic as:

$$V_{j,r}^{i1,i2,syn} = \max_x \left\{ CDF_{j,r}^{syn}\left(x, \vec{p}_{j,r}^{i1,syn}\right) - CDF_{j,r}^{syn}\left(x, \vec{p}_{j,r}^{i2,syn}\right) \right\} +$$
$$+ \max_x \left\{ CDF_{j,r}^{syn}\left(x, \vec{p}_{j,r}^{i2,syn}\right) - CDF_{j,r}^{syn}\left(x, \vec{p}_{j,r}^{i1,syn}\right) \right\}.$$

10. The p-value $P_{value,j}^{i1,i2}$ of the statistical test (the probability to reject a true hypothesis H_0 that the jth type theoretical distribution function $CDF_j\left(x, \vec{p}_j^{i1}\right)$ and $CDF_j\left(x, \vec{p}_j^{i2}\right)$ are identical) is estimated as the frequency of generating synthetic Kuiper statistic greater than the actual Kuiper statistic $V_j^{i1,i2}$ from step 5:

$$P_{value,j}^{i1,i2} = \frac{1}{n^{mc}} \sum_{\substack{r=1 \\ V_j^{i1,i2} < V_{j,r}^{i1,i2,syn}}}^{n^{mc}} 1 \qquad (12)$$

Formula (12), similar to (2), is the sum of the indicator function of the crisp set, defined as all synthetic dataset pairs with a Kuiper statistic greater than $V_j^{i1,i2}$.

If $P_{value,j}^{i1,i2} < 0.05$ the hypothesis H_0 is rejected.

3. Software

A platform of program functions, written in MATLAB environment, is created to execute the statistical procedures from the previous section. At present the platform allows users to test the fit of 11 types of distributions on the datasets. A description of the parameters and PDF of the embodied distribution types is given in Table 1 [14, 15]. The platform also permits the user to add optional types of distribution.

The platform contains several main program functions. The function *set_distribution* contains the information about the 11 distributions, particularly their names, and the links to the functions that operate with the selected distribution type. Also, the function permits the inclusion of new distribution type. In that case, the necessary information the user must provide as input is the procedures to find the CDF, PDF, the maximum likelihood measure, the negative log-likelihood, the mean and variance and the methods of generating random arrays from the given distribution type. The function also determines the screen output for each type of distribution.

	Beta distribution		**Lognormal distribution**
Parameters	$\alpha>0, \beta>0$	Parameters	$\mu \in (-\infty; +\infty), \sigma>0,$
Support	$x \in [0; 1]$	Support	$x \in [0; +\infty)$
PDF	$f(x; \alpha, \beta) = \frac{x^{\alpha-1}(1-x)^{\beta-1}}{B(\alpha, \beta)}$, where $B(\alpha, \beta)$ is a beta function	PDF	$f(x; \mu, \sigma) = \frac{1}{x\sigma\sqrt{2\pi}} e^{-\frac{(\ln(x)-\mu)^2}{2\sigma^2}}$
	Exponential distribution		**Normal distribution**
Parameters	$\lambda>0$	Parameters	$\mu, \sigma>0$
Support	$x \in [0; +\infty)$	Support	$x \in (-\infty; +\infty)$
PDF	$f(x; \lambda) = \begin{cases} \lambda e^{-\lambda x} & \text{for } x \geq 0 \\ 0 & \text{for } x<0 \end{cases}$	PDF	$f(x; \mu, \sigma) = \frac{1}{\sigma\sqrt{2\pi}} e^{-\frac{(x-\mu)^2}{2\sigma^2}}$
	Extreme value distribution		**Rayleigh distribution**
Parameters	$\alpha, \beta \neq 0$	Parameters	$\sigma>0$
Support	$x \in (-\infty; +\infty)$	Support	$x \in [0; +\infty)$
PDF	$f(x; \alpha, \beta) = \frac{e^{[(\alpha-x)/\beta]-e^{(\alpha-x)/\beta}}}{\beta}$	PDF	$f(x; \sigma) = \frac{1}{\sigma^2} \times \left[x \exp\left(\frac{-x^2}{2\sigma^2}\right)\right]$
	Gamma distribution		**Uniform distribution**
Parameters	$k>0, \theta>0$	Parameters	$a, b \in (-\infty; +\infty)$
Support	$x \in [0; +\infty)$	Support	$a \leq x \leq b$
PDF	$f(x; k, \theta) = x^{k-1} \frac{e^{-x/\theta}}{\theta^k \Gamma(k)}$, where $\Gamma(k)$ is a gamma function	PDF	$f(x; a, b) = \begin{cases} \frac{1}{b-a} & \text{for } a \leq x \leq b \\ 0 & \text{for } x<a \text{ or } x>b \end{cases}$
	Generalized extreme value distribution		**Weibull distribution**
Parameters	$\mu \in (-\infty; +\infty), \sigma \in (0; +\infty), \xi \in (-\infty; +\infty)$	Parameters	$\lambda>0, k>0$
Support	$x>\mu-\sigma/\xi \quad (\xi>0), x<\mu-\sigma/\xi \quad (\xi<0),$ $x \in (-\infty; +\infty) \quad (\xi=0)$	Support	$x \in [0; +\infty)$
PDF	$\frac{1}{\sigma}(1+\xi z)^{-1/\xi-1} e^{-(1+\xi z)-1/\xi}$ where $z = \frac{x-\mu}{\sigma}$	PDF	$f(x; \lambda, k) = \begin{cases} \frac{k}{\lambda}\left(\frac{x}{\lambda}\right)^{k-1} e^{-(x/\lambda)^k} & \text{for } x \geq 0 \\ 0 & \text{for } x<0 \end{cases}$
	Generalized Pareto distribution		
Parameters	$x_m>0, k>0$		
Support	$x \in [x_m; +\infty)$		
PDF	$f(x; x_m, k) = \frac{k x_m^k}{x^{k+1}}$		

Table 1. Parameters, support and formula for the PDF of the eleven types of theoretical distributions embodied into the MATLAB platform

The program function *kutest2* performs a two-sample Kuiper test to determine if the independent random datasets are drawn from the same underlying continuous population, i.e. it solves Task 2 (see section 2.2) (to check whether two different datasets are drawn from the same general population).

Another key function is *fitdata*. It constructs the fit of each theoretical distribution over each dataset, evaluates the quality of the fits, and gives their parameters. It also checks whether two distributions of one type fitted to two different arbitrary datasets are identical. In other words, this function is associated with Task 1 and 3 (see sections 2.1 and 2.2). To execute the Kuiper test the function calls *kutest*. Finally, the program function *plot_print_data* provides the on-screen results from the statistical analysis and plots figures containing the pair of distributions that are analyzed. The developed software is available free of charge upon request from the authors provided proper citation is done in subsequent publications.

4. Source of experimental data for analysis

The statistical procedures and the program platform introduced in this chapter are implemented in an example focusing on the morphometric evaluation of the effects of thrombin concentration on fibrin structure. Fibrin is a biopolymer formed from the blood-borne fibrinogen by an enzyme (thrombin) activated in the damaged tissue at sites of blood vessel wall injury to prevent bleeding. Following regeneration of the integrity of the blood vessel wall, the fibrin gel is dissolved to restore normal blood flow, but the efficiency of the dissolution strongly depends on the structure of the fibrin clots. The purpose of the evaluation is to establish any differences in the density of the branching points of the fibrin network related to the activity of the clotting enzyme (thrombin), the concentration of which is expected to vary in a broad range under physiological conditions.

For the purpose of the experiment, fibrin is prepared on glass slides in total volume of 100 μl by clotting 2 mg/ml fibrinogen (dissolved in different buffers) by varying concentrations of thrombin for 1 h at 37 °C in moisture chamber. The thrombin concentrations in the experiments vary in the range 0.3 – 10 U/ml, whereas the two buffers used are: 1) buffer1 – 25 mM Na-phosphate pH 7.4 buffer containing 75 mM NaCl; 2) buffer2 - 10 mM N-(2-Hydroxyethyl) piperazine-N'-(2-ethanesulfonic acid) (abbreviated as HEPES) pH 7.4 buffer containing 150 mM NaCl. At the end of the clotting time the fibrins are washed in 3 ml 100 mM Na-cacodilate pH 7.2 buffer and fixated with 1% glutaraldehyde in the same buffer for 10 min. Thereafter the fibrins are dried in a series of ethanol dilutions (20 – 96 %), 1:1 mixture of 96 %(v/v) ethanol/acetone and pure acetone followed by critical point drying with CO2 in E3000 Critical Point Drying Apparatus (Quorum Technologies, Newhaven, UK). The dry samples are examined in Zeiss Evo40 scanning electron microscope (Carl Zeiss, Jena, Germany) and images are taken at an indicated magnification. A total of 12 dry samples of fibrins are elaborated in this fashion, each having a given combination of thrombin concentration and buffer. Electron microscope images are taken for each dry sample (one of the analyzed dry samples of fibrins is presented in Fig. 1). Some main parameters of the 12 collected datasets are given in Table 2.

An automated procedure is elaborated in MATLAB environment (embodied into the program function *find_distance.m*) to measure lengths of fibrin strands (i.e. sections between two branching points in the fibrin network) from the SEM images. The procedure takes the file name of the fibrin image (see Fig. 1) and the planned number of measurements as input. Each file contains the fibrin image with legend at the bottom part, which gives the scale, the time the image was taken, etc.

The first step requires setting of the scale. A prompt appears, asking the user to type the numerical value of the length of the scale in μm. Then the image appears on screen and a red line has to be moved and resized to fit the scale (Fig. 2a and 2b). The third step requires a red rectangle to be placed over the actual image of the fibrin for selection of the region of interest (Fig. 2c). With this, the preparations of the image are done, and the user can start taking the desired number of measurements for the distances between adjacent nodes (Fig. 2d).

Using this approach 12 datasets containing measurements of lengths between branching points of fibrin have been collected (Table 2) and the three statistical tasks described above are executed over these datasets.

Datasets	N	$mean_e$	med_e	std_e	iqr_e	Thrombin concentration	Buffer
DS1	274	0.9736	0.8121	0.5179	0.6160	1.0	buffer1
DS2	68	1.023	0.9374	0.5708	0.7615	10.0	buffer1
DS3	200	1.048	0.8748	0.6590	0.6469	4.0	buffer1
DS4	276	1.002	0.9003	0.4785	0.5970	0.5	buffer1
DS5	212	0.6848	0.6368	0.3155	0.4030	1.0	buffer2
DS6	300	0.1220	0.1265	0.04399	0.05560	1.2	buffer2
DS7	285	0.7802	0.7379	0.3253	0.4301	2.5	buffer2
DS8	277	0.9870	0.9326	0.4399	0.5702	0.6	buffer2
DS9	200	0.5575	0.5284	0.2328	0.2830	0.3	buffer1
DS10	301	0.7568	0.6555	0.3805	0.4491	0.6	buffer1
DS11	301	0.7875	0.7560	0.3425	0.4776	1.2	buffer1
DS12	307	0.65000	0.5962	0.2590	0.3250	2.5	buffer1

Table 2. Distance between branching points of fibrin fibers. Sample size (N), mean ($mean_e$ in μm), median (med_e in μ m), standard deviation (std_e), inter-quartile range (iqr_e, in μm) of the empirical distributions over the 12 datasets for different thrombin concentrations (in U/ml) and buffers are presented

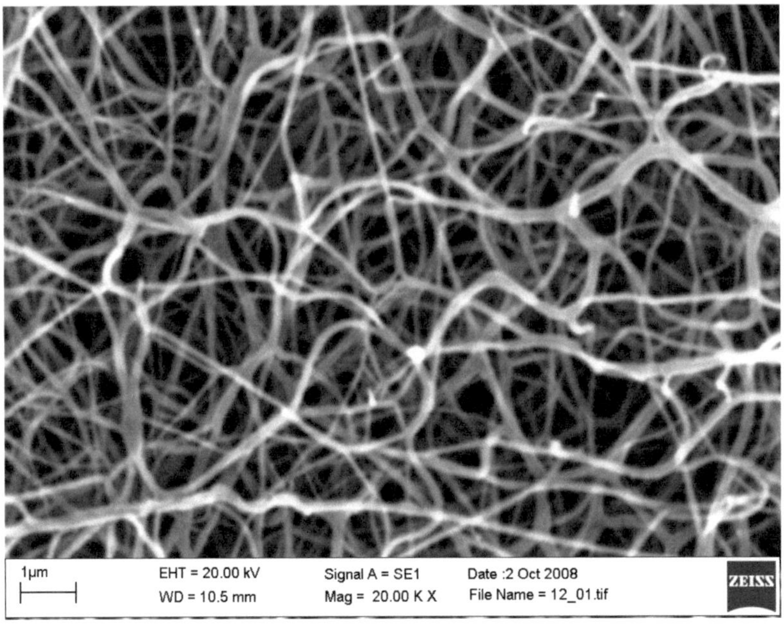

Figure 1. SEM image of fibrin used for morphometric analysis

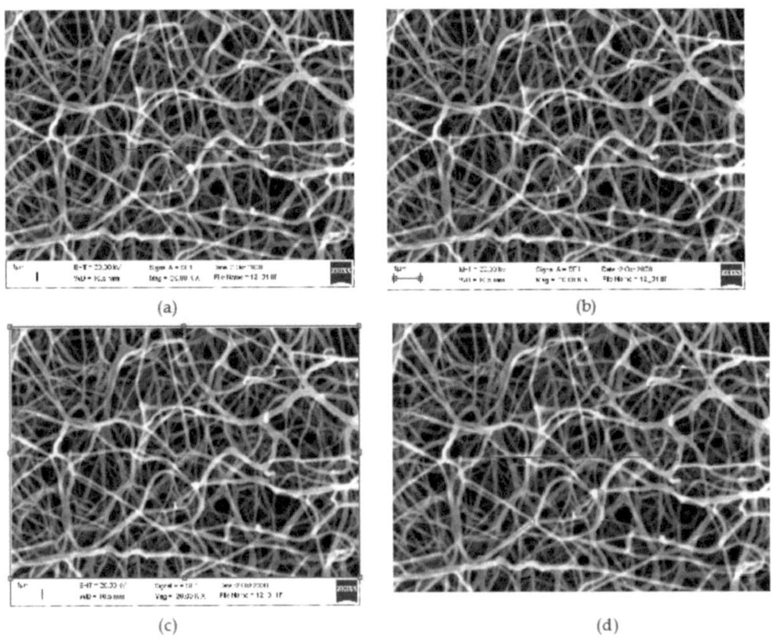

Figure 2. Steps of the automated procedure for measuring distances between branching points in fibrin. Panels *a* and *b*: scaling. Panel c: selection of region of interest. Panel d: taking a measurement

4.1. Task 1 – Finding a common distribution fit

A total of 11 types of distributions (Table 1) are tested over the datasets, and the criteria (3)-(6) are evaluated. The Kuiper statistic's distribution is constructed with 1000 Monte Carlo simulation cycles. Table 3 presents the results regarding the distribution fits, where only the maximal values for $minP_{value, j}^{fit}$ and $meanP_{value, j}^{fit}$, along with the minimal values for AIC_j and BIC_j across the datasets are given. The results allow ruling out the beta and the uniform distributions. The output of the former is NaN (not-a-number) since it does not apply to values of $x \notin [0; 1]$. The latter has the lowest values of (3) and (4), and the highest of (5) and (6), i.e. it is the worst fit. The types of distributions worth using are mostly the lognormal distribution (having the lowest AIC and BIC), and the generalized extreme value (having the highest possible $meanP_{value, j}^{fit}$). Figure 3 presents 4 of the 11 distribution fits to DS4. Similar graphical output is generated for all other datasets and for all distribution types.

Distribution type	1	2	3	4	5	6
AIC	NaN	3.705e+3	3.035e+3	8.078e+2	7.887e+2	1.633e+3
BIC	NaN	3.873e+3	3.371e+3	1.144e+3	1.293e+3	2.137e+3
$minP_{value}^{fit}$	**5.490e–1**	*0*	*0*	5.000e–3	1.020e–1	*0*
$meanP_{value}^{fit}$	NaN	*0*	*0*	5.914e–1	**6.978e–1**	7.500e–4
Distribution type	7	8	9	10	11	
AIC	**7.847e+2**	1.444e+3	1.288e+3	*3.755e+3*	1.080e+3	
BIC	**1.121e+3**	1.781e+3	1.457e+3	*4.092e+3*	1.416e+3	
$minP_{value}^{fit}$	8.200e–2	*0*	*0*	*0*	*0*	
$meanP_{value}^{fit}$	5.756e–1	2.592e–2	8.083e–2	*0*	1.118e–1	

Legend: The numbers of the distribution types stand for the following: 1- beta, 2 – exponential, 3 – extreme value, 4- gamma, 5 - generalized extreme value, 6 – generalized Pareto; 7 – lognormal, 8 – normal, 9 – Rayleigh, 10 – uniform, 11 – Weibull

Table 3. Values of the criteria used to evaluate the goodness-of-fit of 11 types of distributions over the datasets with 1000 Monte Carlo simulation cycles. The table contains the maximal values for $minP_{value,j}^{fit}$ and $meanP_{value,j}^{fit}$, and the minimal values for AIC_j and BIC_j across the datasets for each distribution type. The bold and the italic values are the best one and the worst one achieved for a given criterion, respectively.

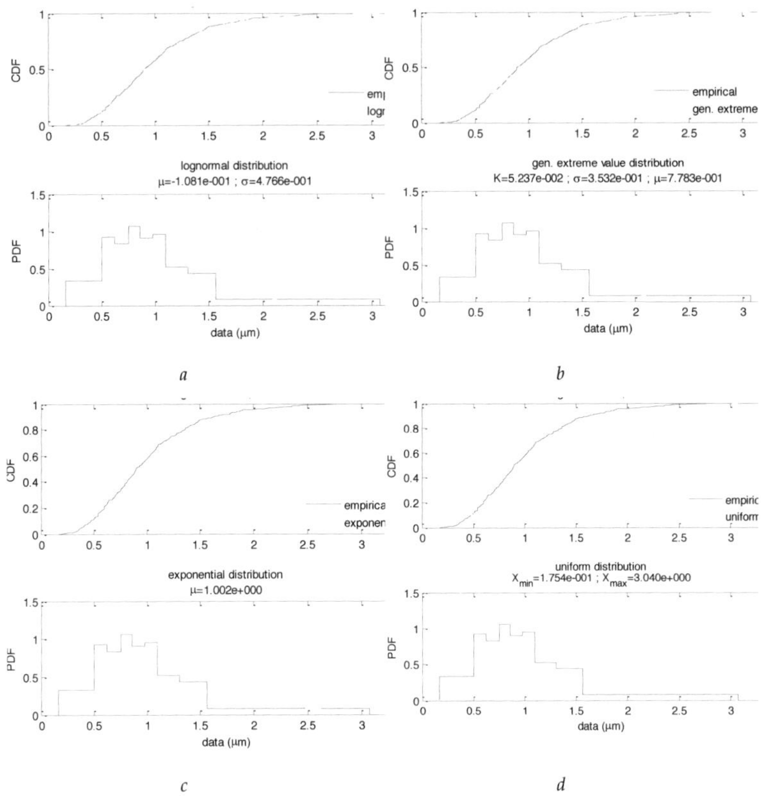

Figure 3. Graphical results from the fit of the lognormal (a), generalized extreme value (b), exponential (c), and uniform (d) distributions over DS4 (where μ, σ, X_{min}, X_{max}, k are the parameters of the theoretical distributions from Table 1)

4.2. Task 2 – Identity of empirical distributions

Table 4 contains the p-value calculated according to (9) for all pairs of distributions. The bolded values indicate the pairs, where the null hypothesis fails to be rejected and it is possible to assume that those datasets are drawn from the same general population. The results show that it is possible to merge the following datasets: 1) DS1, DS2, DS3, D4 and DS8; 2) DS7, DS10, and DS11; 3) DS5 and DS12. All other combinations (except DS5 and DS10) are not allowed and may give misleading results in a further statistical analysis, since the samples are not drawn from the same general population. Figure 4a presents the stair-case distributions over DS4 (with $mean_e^4$=1.002, med_e^4=0.9003, std_e^4=0.4785, iqr_e^4=0.5970) and DS9 (with $mean_e^9$=0.5575, med_e^9 =0.5284, std_e^9=0.2328, iqr_e^9=0.2830). The Kuiper statistic for identity of the empirical distributions, calculated according to (8), is $V^{4,9}$=0.5005, whereas according to (9) $P_{value,e}^{4,9}$=2.024e–24<0.05. Therefore the null hypothesis is rejected, which is also evident from the graphical output. In the same fashion, Figure 4b presents the stair-case distributions over DS1 (with $mean_e^1$

http://dx.doi.org/10.5772/53049

=0.9736, med_e^1=0.8121, std_e^1=0.5179, iqr_e^1=0.6160) and DS4. The Kuiper statistic for identity of the empirical distributions, calculated according to (8), is $V^{1,4}$=0.1242, whereas according to (9) $P_{value,e}^{1,4}$=0.1957>0.05. Therefore the null hypothesis fails to be rejected, which is also confirmed by the graphical output.

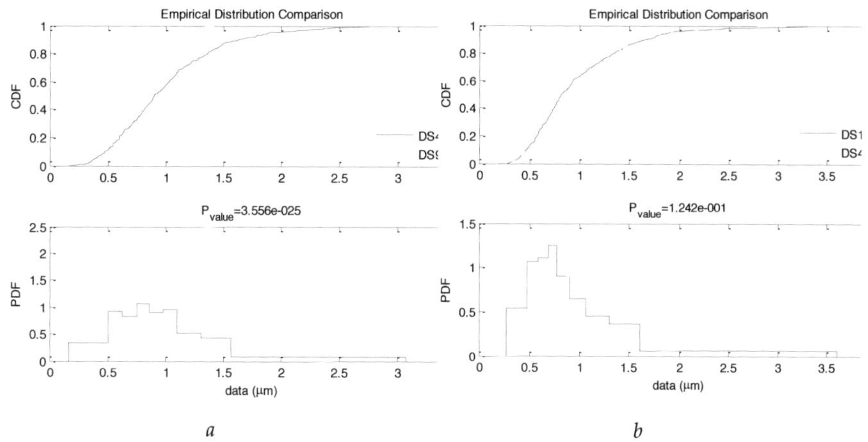

Figure 4. Comparison of the stair-case empirical distributions over DS4 and DS9 (a) and over DS1 and DS4 (b)

Datasets	DS1	DS2	DS3	DS4	DS5	DS6	DS7	DS8	DS9	DS10	DS11	DS12
DS1	1.00e+00	**3.81e-01**	**6.18e-01**	**1.96e-01**	5.80e-06	8.88e-125	3.46e-03	**5.21e-02**	4.57e-19	1.73e-04	1.89e-02	2.59e-10
DS2	**3.81e-01**	1.00e+00	**6.77e-01**	**6.11e-01**	1.94e-05	5.13e-44	2.13e-03	**2.92e-01**	1.71e-09	7.17e-04	5.34e-03	3.96e-08
DS3	**6.18e-01**	**6.77e-01**	1.00e+00	**2.01e-01**	1.46e-07	1.84e-101	6.94e-05	**1.47e-01**	1.79e-20	5.05e-06	1.55e-03	1.53e-12
DS4	**1.96e-01**	**6.11e-01**	**2.01e-01**	1.00e+00	5.47e-11	1.73e-123	5.14e-05	**8.57e-01**	2.02e-24	9.34e-08	3.50e-05	2.02e-17
DS5	5.80e-06	1.94e-05	1.46e-07	5.47e-11	1.00e+00	2.61e-100	9.67e-03	1.59e-11	6.68e-04	**2.32e-01**	1.65e-02	**1.52e-01**
DS6	8.88e-125	5.13e-44	1.84e-101	1.73e-123	2.61e-100	1.00e+00	7.45e-124	1.69e-125	3.14e-94	7.35e-125	9.98e-126	1.75e-124
DS7	3.46e-03	2.13e-03	6.94e-05	5.14e-05	9.67e-03	7.45e-124	1.00e+00	9.53e-05	7.13e-11	**1.64e-01**	**4.59e-01**	2.49e-05
DS8	**5.21e-02**	**2.92e-01**	**1.47e-01**	**8.57e-01**	1.59e-11	1.69e-125	9.53e-05	1.00e+00	1.04e-25	1.19e-08	6.36e-06	8.47e-19
DS9	4.57e-19	1.71e-09	1.79e-20	2.02e-24	6.68e-04	3.14e-94	7.13e-11	1.04e-25	1.00e+00	3.48e-06	6.05e-12	4.64e-03
DS10	1.73e-04	7.17e-04	5.05e-06	9.34e-08	**2.32e-01**	7.35e-125	**1.64e-01**	1.19e-08	3.48e-06	1.00e+00	**1.55e-01**	9.18e-03
DS11	1.89e-03	5.34e-03	1.55e-03	3.50e-05	1.65e-02	9.98e-126	**4.59e-01**	6.36e-06	6.05e-12	1.55e-01	1.00e+00	2.06e-04
DS12	2.59e-10	3.96e-08	1.53e-12	2.02e-17	**1.52e-01**	1.75e-124	2.49e-05	8.47e-19	4.64e-03	9.18e-03	2.06e-04	1.00e+00

Table 4. P-values of the statistical test for identity of stair-case distributions on pairs of datasets. The values on the main diagonal are shaded. The bold values are those that exceed 0.05, i.e. indicate the pairs of datasets whose stair-case distributions are identical.

4.3. Task 3 – Identity of fitted distributions

As concluded in task 1, the lognormal distribution provides possibly the best fit to the 12 datasets. Table 5 contains the p-values calculated according to (12) for the lognormal distribution fitted to the datasets with 1000 Monte Carlo simulation cycles. The bold values indicate the pairs, where the null hypothesis fails to be rejected and it is possible to assume that the distribution fits are identical. The results show that the lognormal fits to the following datasets are identical: 1) DS1, DS2, DS3, and DS4; 2) DS1, DS4, and DS8; 3) DS7, DS10, and DS11; 4) DS5 and DS10; 5) DS5 and DS12. These results correlate with the identity of the empirical distribution. Figure 5a presents the fitted lognormal distribution over DS4 (with μ= –0.1081, σ=0.4766, $mean_7^4$=1.005, med_7^4=0.8975, mode_7^4=0.7169, std_7^4=0.5077, iqr_7^4dy=0.5870) and DS9 (with μ= –0.6694, σ=0.4181, $mean_7^9$=0.5587, med_7^9=0.5120, mode_7^9 =0.4322, std_7^9=0.2442, iqr_7^9=0.2926). The Kuiper statistic for identity of the fits, calculated according to (11), is $V_7^{4,9}$=0.4671, whereas according to (12), $P_{value,7}^{4,9}$=0<0.05. Therefore the null hypothesis is rejected, which is also evident from the graphical output. In the same fashion, Fig. 5b presents the lognormal distribution fit over DS1 (with μ= –1477, σ=0.4843, $mean_7^1$=0.9701, med_7^1=0.8627, mode_7^1=0.6758, std_7^1=0.4988, iqr_7^1=0.5737) and DS4. The Kuiper statistic for identity of the fits, calculated according to (11), is $V_7^{1,4}$=0.03288, whereas according to (12), $P_{value,7}^{1,4}$=0.5580>0.05. Therefore the null hypothesis fails to be rejected, which is also evident from the graphical output.

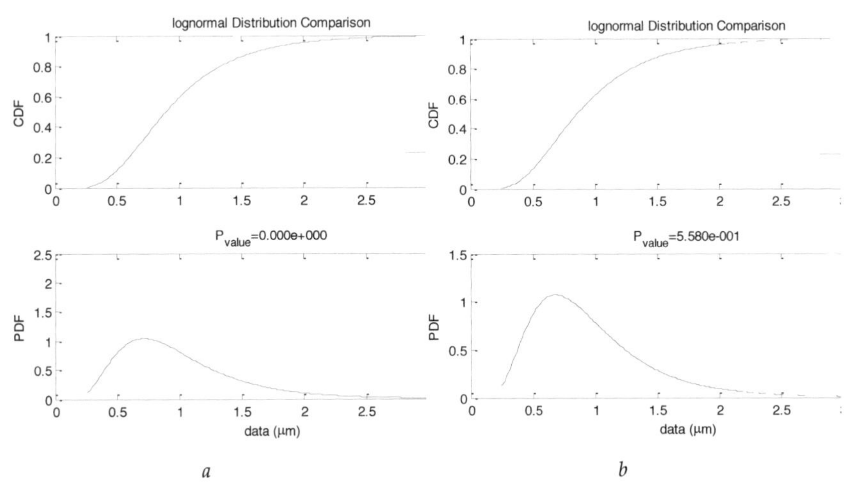

Figure 5. Comparison of the lognormal distribution fits over DS4 and DS9 (a) and over DS1 and DS4 (b)

http://dx.doi.org/10.5772/53049

Datasets	DS1	DS2	DS3	DS4	DS5	DS6	DS7	DS8	DS9	DS10	DS11	DS12
DS1	1.00	**1.39e–1**	**1.90e–1**	**5.58e–1**	0.00	0.00	0.00	**3.49e–1**	0.00	0.00	0.00	0.00
DS2	**1.39e–1**	1.00	**6.37e–1**	**1.05e–1**	0.00	0.00	0.00	3.40e–2	0.00	0.00	1.00e–3	0.00
DS3	**1.90e–1**	**6.37e–1**	1.00	**2.01e–1**	0.00	0.00	0.00	3.20e–2	0.00	0.00	0.00	0.00
DS4	**5.58e–1**	**1.05e–1**	**2.01e–1**	1.00	0.00	0.00	0.00	**6.65e–1**	0.00	0.00	0.00	0.00
DS5	0.00	0.00	0.00	0.00	1.00	0.00	1.00e–3	0.00	0.00	**5.70e–2**	1.00e–3	**5.10e–2**
DS6	0.00	0.00	0.00	0.00	0.00	1.00	0.00	0.00	0.00	0.00	0.00	0.00
DS7	0.00	0.00	0.00	0.00	1.00e–3	0.00	1.00	0.00	0.00	**8.70e–2**	**7.90e–1**	0.00
DS8	**3.49e–1**	3.40e–2	3.20e–2	**6.65e–1**	0.00	0.00	0.00	1.00	0.00	0.00	0.00	0.00
DS9	0.00	0.00	0.00	0.00	0.00	0.00	0.00	0.00	1.00	0.00	0.00	0.00
DS10	0.00	0.00	0.00	0.00	**5.70e–2**	0.00	**8.70e–2**	0.00	0.00	1.00	**1.86e–1**	0.00
DS11	0.00	1.00e–3	0.00	0.00	1.00e–3	0.00	**7.90e–1**	0.00	0.00	**1.86e–1**	1.00	0.00
DS12	0.00	0.00	0.00	0.00	**5.10e–2**	0.00	0.00	0.00	0.00	0.00	0.00	1.00

Table 5. P-values of the statistical test that the lognormal fitted distributions over two datasets are identical. The values on the main diagonal are shaded. The bold values indicate the distribution fit pairs that may be assumed as identical.

The statistical procedures described above have been successfully applied for the solution of important medical problems [16; 17]. At first we could prove the role of mechanical forces in the organization of the final architecture of the fibrin network. Our *ex vivo* exploration of the ultrastructure of fibrin at different locations of surgically removed thrombi evidenced gross differences in the fiber diameter and pore area of the fibrin network resulting from shear forces acting in circulation (Fig. 6). *In vitro* fibrin structures were also generated and their equivalence with the *in vivo* fibrin architecture was proven using the distribution analysis described in this chapter (Fig. 7). Stretching changed the arrangement of the fibers (Fig. 7A) to a pattern similar to the one observed on the surface of thrombi (Fig. 6A); both the median fiber diameter and the pore area of the fibrins decreased 2-3-fold and the distribution of these morphometric parameters became more homogeneous (Fig. 7B). Thus, following this verification of the experimental model ultrastructure, the *in vitro* fibrin clots could be used for the convenient evaluation of these structures with respect to their chemical stability and resistance to enzymatic degradation [16].

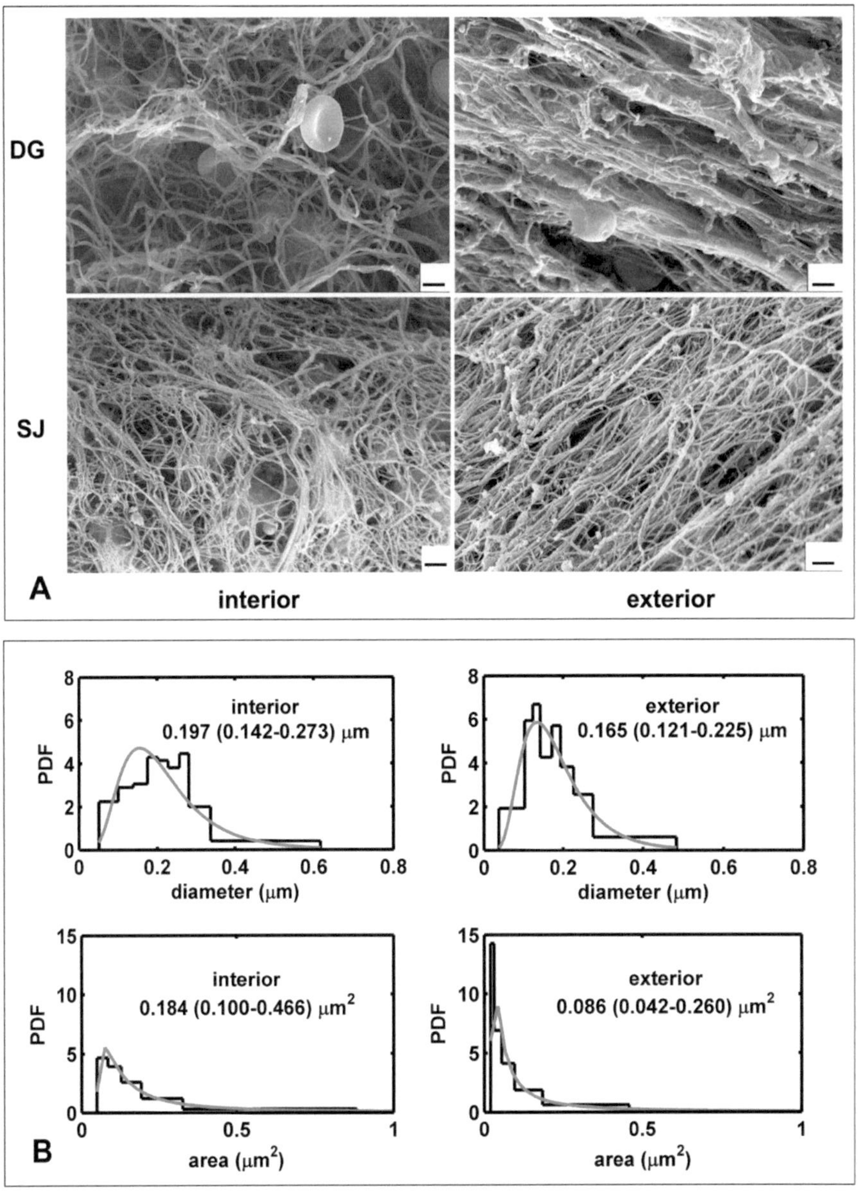

Figure 6. Fibrin structure on the surface and in the core of thrombi. A. Following thrombectomy thrombi were washed, fixed and dehydrated. SEM images were taken from the surface and transverse section of the same thrombus sample, scale bar = 2 μm. DG: a thrombus from popliteal artery, SJ: a thrombus from aorto-bifemoral by-pass Dacron graft. B. Fiber diameter (upper graphs) and fibrin pore area (lower graphs) were measured from the SEM images of the DG thrombus shown in A using the algorithms described in this chapter. The graphs present the probability density function (PDF) of the empirical distribution (black histogram) and the fitted theoretical distribution (grey curves). The numbers under the location of the observed fibrin structure show the median, as well as the bottom and the top quartile values (in brackets) of the fitted theoretical distributions (lognormal for fiber diameter and generalized extreme value for area). The figure is reproduced from Ref. [16].

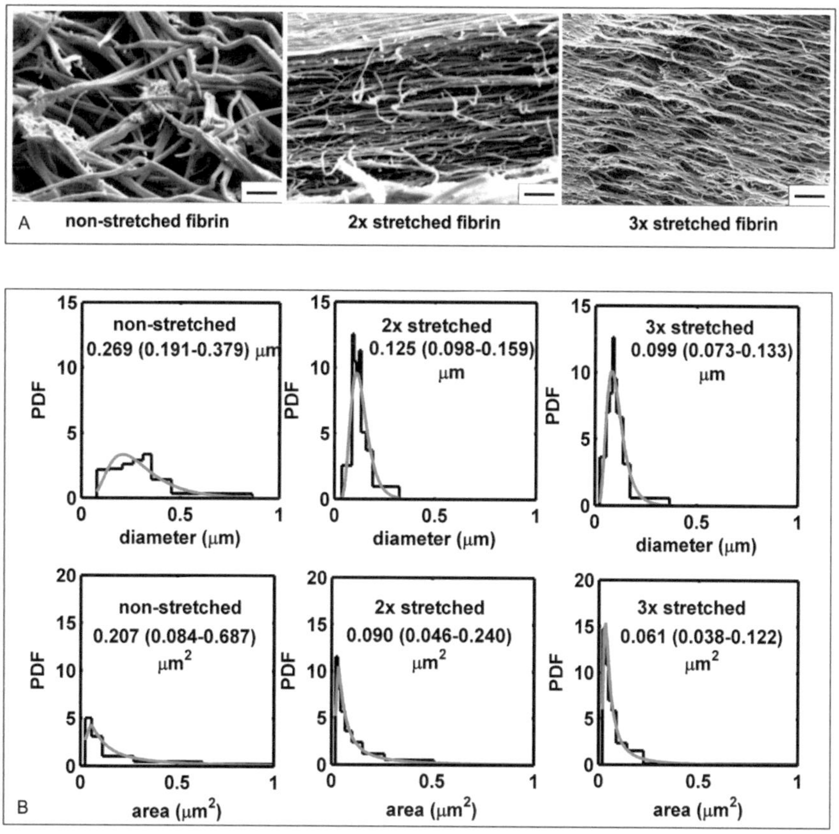

Figure 7. Changes in fibrin network structure caused by mechanical stretching. A. SEM images of fibrin clots fixed with glutaraldehyde before stretching or following 2-and 3-fold stretching as indicated, scale bar = 2 μm. B. Fiber diameter (upper graphs) and fibrin pore area (lower graphs) were measured from the SEM images illustrated in A using the algorithms described in this chapter. The graphs present the probability density function (PDF) of the empiric distribution (black histogram) and the fitted theoretical distribution (grey curves). The numbers under the fibrin type show the median, as well as the bottom and the top quartile values (in brackets) of the fitted theoretical distributions (lognormal for fiber diameter and generalized extreme value for area). The figure is reproduced from Ref. [16].

Application of the described distribution analysis allowed identification of the effect of red blood cells (RBCs) on the structure of fibrin [17]. The presence of RBCs at the time of fibrin formation causes a decrease in the fiber diameter (Fig. 8) based on a specific interaction between fibrinogen and a cell surface receptor. The specificity of this effect could be proven partially by the sensitivity of the changes in the distribution parameters to the presence of a drug (eptifibatide) that blocks the RBC receptor for fibrinogen (compare the median and interquartile range values for the experimental fibrins in the presence and absence of the drug illustrated in Fig. 8). It is noteworthy that the type of distribution was not changed by the drug, only its parameters were modified. This example underscores the applicability of the designed procedure for testing of statistical hypotheses in situations when subtle quantitative biological and pharmacological effects are at issue.

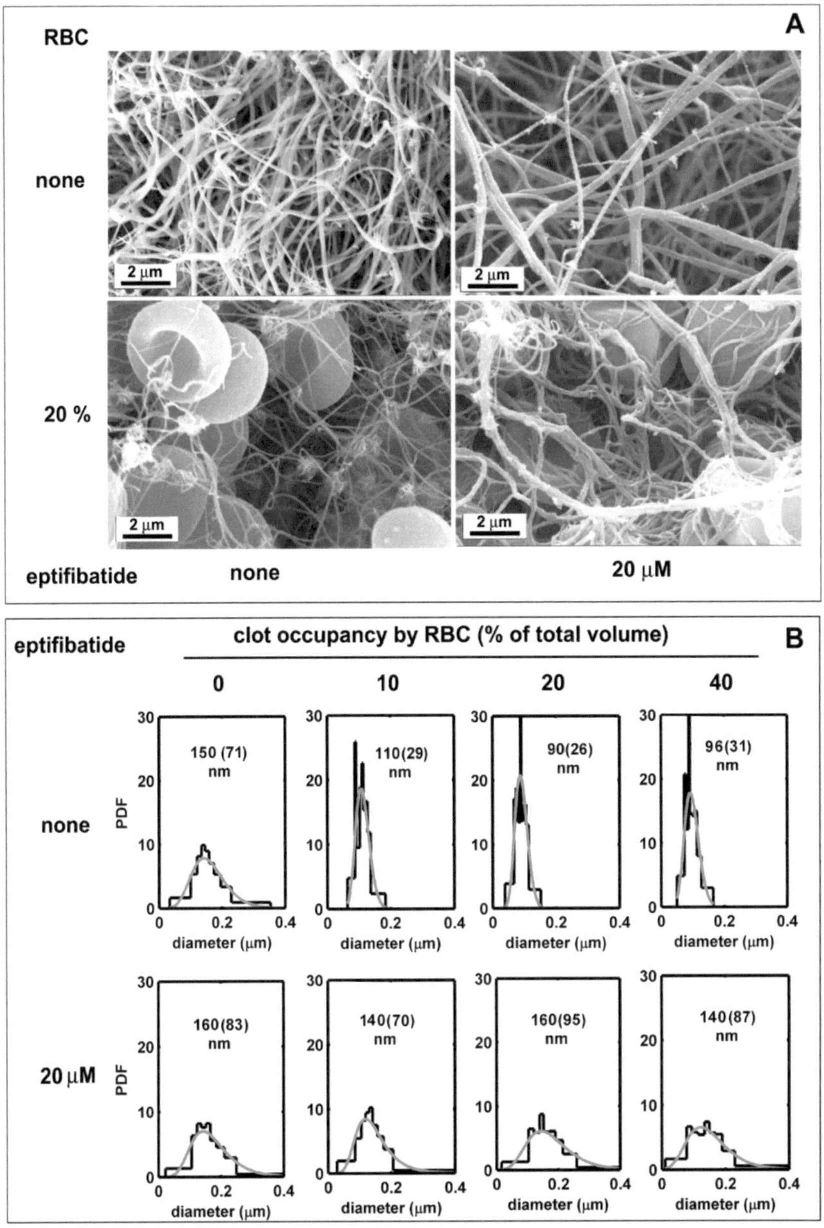

Figure 8. Changes. in the fibrin network structure caused by red blood cells and eptifibatide. The SEM images in Panel A illustrate the fibrin structure in clots of identical volume and fibrinogen content in the absence or presence of 20 % RBC. Panel B shows fiber diameter measured from the SEM images for a range of RBC-occupancy in the same clot model. Probability density functions (PDF) of the empirical distribution (black histogram) and the fitted lognormal theoretical distribution (grey curves) are presented with indication of the median and the interquartile range (in brackets) of the fitted theoretical distributions. In the presence of RBC the parameters of the fitted distributions of the eptifibatide-free and eptifibatide-treated fibers differ at $p<0.001$ level (for the RBC-free fibrins the eptifibatide-related difference is not significant, $p>0.05$). The figure is reproduced from Ref. [17].

http://dx.doi.org/10.5772/53049

5. Discussion and conclusions

This chapter addressed the problem of identifying a single type of theoretical distribution that fits to different datasets by altering its parameters. The identification of such type of distribution is a prerequisite for comparing the results, performing interpolation and extrapolation over the data, and studying the dependence between the input parameters (e.g. initial conditions of an experiment) and the distribution parameters. Additionally, the procedures included hypothesis tests addressing the identity of empirical (stair-case) and of fitted distributions. In the case of empirical distributions, the failure to reject the null hypothesis proves that samples come from one and the same general population. In the case of fitted distributions, the failure to reject the null hypothesis proves that although parameters are random (as the fits are also based on random data), the differences are not statistically significant. The implementation of the procedures is facilitated by the creation of a platform in MATLAB that executes the necessary calculation and evaluation procedures.

Some parts of the three problems analyzed in this chapter may be solved using similar methods or software tools different from the MATLAB procedures described in section 3. Some software packages solve the task of choosing the best distribution type to fit the data [18, 19]. The appropriateness of the fit is defined by the goodness-of-fit metrics, which may be selected by the user. The Kolmogorov-Smirnov statistics is recommended for the case of samples with continuous variables, but strictly speaking the analytical Kolmogorov-Smirnov distribution should not be used to calculate the p-value in case any of the parameters has been calculated on the basis of the sample as explicitly stated in [19]. Its widespread application, however, is based on the fact that it is the most conservative, i.e. the probability to reject the null hypothesis is lower compared to the other goodness-of-fit criteria. Some available tools [20] also use analytical expressions to calculate the p-value of the Kolmogorov-Smirnov test in the case of a sample that is normally distributed, exponentially distributed or extreme-value distributed [21, 22]. Those formulae are applied in the *lillietest* MATLAB function from the Statistical toolbox, where Monte-Carlo simulation is conducted for the other distributions. It is recommended to use Monte-Carlo simulation even for the three aforementioned distributions in case any of the parameters has been derived from the sample. Some applications calculate a goodness-of-fit metrics of a single sample as a Kuiper statistics (e.g. in the awkwardly spelled *kupiertest* MATLAB function of [23]) and the p-value is calculated analytically. The main drawback of that program is that the user must guarantee that the parameters of the theoretical distribution have not been calculated from the sample. Other available applications offer single-sample Kuiper test (e.g. *v.test* function in [24]) or single- and two-sample Kuiper tests (e.g. *KuiperTest* function in [25]), which use Monte-Carlo simulation. The results of the functions *v.test* and *KuiperTest* are quite similar to those presented in this chapter, the main difference being our better approximation of the empirical distribution with a linear function, rather than with a histogram. Our approach to calculate p-values with Monte-Carlo simulation stems from the previously recognized fact that "…if one or more parameters have to be estimated, the standard tables for the Kuiper test are no longer valid …" [26]. Similar concepts have been proposed by others too [27].

An advantage of the method applied by us is that the Kuiper statistics is very sensitive to discrepancies at the tails of the distribution, unlike the Kolmogorov-Smirnov statistics, whereas at the same time it does not need to distribute the data into bins, as it is for the chi-square statistics. Another advantage is that the method is very suitable for circular probability distributions [23, 24], because it is invariant to the starting point where cyclic variations are observed in the sample. In addition it is easily generalized for multi-dimensional cases [25].

A limitation of our method is that it cannot be used for discrete variables [25], whereas the Kolmogorov-Smirnov test could be easily modified for the discrete case. The second drawback is that if the data are not *i.i.d.* (independent and identically distributed), then all Bootstrap and Monte-Carlo simulations give wrong results. In that case, the null hypothesis is rejected even if true, but this is an issue with all Monte-Carlo approaches. Some graphical and analytical possibilities to test the *i.i.d.* assumption are described in [19].

Further extension of the statistical procedures proposed in this chapter may focus on the inclusion of additional statistical tests evaluating the quality of the fits and the identity of the distributions. The simulation procedures in Task 3 may be modified to use Bootstrap, because this method relies on fewer assumptions about the underlying process and the associated measurement error [28]. Other theoretical distribution types could also be included in the program platform, especially those that can interpret different behaviour of the data around the mean and at the tails. Finally, further research could focus on new areas (e.g. economics, finance, management, other natural sciences) to implement the described procedures.

Acknowledgements

This. research is funded by the Hungarian Scientific Research Fund OTKA 83023. The authors wish to thank Imre Varju from the Department of Medical Biochemistry, Semmelweis University, Budapest, Hungary for collecting the datasets with length measurements, and Laszlo Szabo from the Chemical Research Center, Hungarian Academy of Sciences, Budapest, Hungary for taking the SEM images.

Author details

Natalia D. Nikolova[1], Daniela Toneva-Zheynova[2], Krasimir Kolev[3] and Kiril Tenekedjiev[1]

*Address all correspondence to: Kolev.Krasimir@med.semmelweis-univ.hu

1 Department of Information Technologies, N. Vaptsarov Naval Academy, Varna, Bulgaria

2 Department of Environmental Management, Technical University – Varna, Varna, Bulgaria

3 Department of Medical Biochemistry, Semmelweis University, Budapest, Hungary

References

[1] Nikolova ND, Toneva D, Tenekedjieva A-M. Statistical Procedures for Finding Distribution Fits over Datasets with Applications in Biochemistry. Bioautomation 2009; 13(2) 27-44.

[2] Tenekedjiev K, Dimitrakiev D, Nikolova ND. Building Frequentist Distribution of Continuous Random Variables. Machine Mechanics 2002; 47 164-168,

[3] Gujarati DN. Basic Econometrics, Third Edition. USA: McGraw-Hill, pp. 15-318; 1995

[4] Knuth DE. The Art of Computer Programming, Vol. 2: Seminumerical Algorithms, 3rd ed. Reading, MA: Addison-Wesley, pp. 45-52; 1998.

[5] Press W, Flannery B, Teukolsky S, Vetterling W. Numerical Recipes in FORTRAN: The Art of Scientific Computing 2nd ed. England: Cambridge University Press, pp. 620-622; (1992).

[6] Burnham KP, Anderson DR. Model Selection and Inference: A Practical Information-Theoretic Approach. Springer, pp. 60-64; 2002.

[7] Schwarz G. Estimating the Dimension of a Model. Annals of Statistic 1974; 6 461-464.

[8] Politis D. Computer-intensive Methods in Statistical Analysis. IEEE Signal Processing Magazine 1998; 15(1) 39-55.

[9] Scott DW. On Optimal and Data-based Histograms, Biometrika 1979; 66 605-610.

[10] Sturges HA. The Choice of a Class Interval. J.Am.Stat.Assoc. 1926; 21 65-66.

[11] Freedman D, Diaconis P. On the Histogram as a Density Estimator: L_2 Theory, Zeitschrift fur Wahrscheinlichkeitstheorie und verwandte Gebiete 1981; 57 453–476.

[12] Kuiper NH. Tests Concerning Random Points on a Circle. Proceedings of the Koninklijke Nederlandse Akademie van Wetenshappen 1962; A(63) 38-47.

[13] The MathWorks. Statistical ToolboxTM 7.0 User's Guide. USA: the MathWorks Inc.; 2008.

[14] Finch SR. Extreme Value Constants. England: Cambridge University Press, pp. 363-367; 2003.

[15] Hanke JE, Reitsch AG. Understanding Business Statistics. USA: Irwin, pp. 165-198; 1991.

[16] Varjú I, Sótonyi P, Machovich R, Szabó L, Tenekedjiev T, Silva M, Longstaff C, Kolev K. Hindered Dissolution of Fibrin Formed under Mechanical Stress. J Thromb Haemost 2011; 9 979-986.

[17] Wohner N, Sótonyi P, Machovich R, Szabó L, Tenekedjiev K, Silva MMCG, Longstaff C, Kolev K. Lytic Resistance of Fibrin Containing Red Blood Cells. Arterioscl Thromb Vasc Biol 2011; 31 2306-2313.

[18] Palisade Corporation. Guide to Using @RISK – Risk Analysis and Simulation Add-in for Microsoft Excel, Version 4.5. USA: Palisade Corporation; (2004).

[19] Geer Mountain Software Corporation Inc. Stat::Fit - Version 2. USA: Geer Mountain Software Corporation Inc.; (2001).

[20] The MathWorks. Statistics Toolbox Software – User's Guide: Version 8.0. USA: The MathWorks; (2012).

[21] Lilliefors HW. On the Kolmogorov-Smirnov Test for Normality with Mean and Variance Unknown. J.Am.Stat.Assoc.: 1967; 62 399-402

[22] Lilliefors HW. On the Kolmogorov-Smirnov Test for the Exponential Distribution with Mean Unknown. J.Am.Stat.Assoc: 1969; 64 387-389.

[23] Mossi D. Single Sample Kupier Goodness-Of-Fit Hypothesis Test. (2005) http://www.mathworks.com/matlabcentral/fileexchange/8717-kupiertest

[24] Venables WN, Smith DM, the R Core Team. An Introduction to R. USA: R Core Team; (2012).

[25] Weisstein EW. Kuiper Statistic. From MathWorld--A Wolfram Web Resource, http://mathworld.wolfram.com/KuiperStatistic.html, retrieved 2012 September

[26] Louter AS, Koerts J. On the Kuiper Test for Normality with Mean and Variance Unknown. Statistica Neerlandica 1970; 24 83–87.

[27] Paltani S. Searching for Periods in X-ray Observations using Kuiper's Test. Application to the ROSAT PSPC Archive. Astronomy and Astrophysics: 2004; 420 789-797.

[28] Efron B, Tibshirani RJ. An Introduction to the Bootstrap. USA: Chapman &Hall, pp. 45-59; 1993;

Chapter 2

Monte Carlo Simulations Applied to Uncertainty in Measurement

Paulo Roberto Guimarães Couto,
Jailton Carreteiro Damasceno and
Sérgio Pinheiro de Oliveira

Additional information is available at the end of the chapter

http://dx.doi.org/10.5772/53014

1. Introduction

Metrology is the science that covers all theoretical and practical concepts involved in a measurement, which when applied are able to provide results with appropriate accuracy and metrological reliability to a given measurement process. In any area in which a decision is made from a measurement result, all attention is critical to the metrological concepts involved. For example, the control panels of an aircraft are composed by several instruments that must be calibrated to perform measurements with metrological traceability and reliability, influencing the decisions that the pilot will make during the flight. In this way, it is clear that concepts involving metrology and reliability of measurements must be well established and harmonized to provide reliability and quality for products and services.

In the last two decades, basic documents for the international harmonization of metrological and laboratorial aspects have been prepared by international organizations. Adoption of these documents helps the evolution and dynamics of the globalization of markets. The ISO IEC 17025:2005 standard [1], for example, describes harmonized policies and procedures for testing and calibration laboratories. The International Vocabulary of Metrology (VIM - JCGM 200:2012) presents all the terms and concepts involved in the field of metrology [2]. The JCGM 100:2008 guide (Evaluation of measurement data – Guide to the expression of uncertainty in measurement) provides guidelines on the estimation of uncertainty in measurement [3]. Finally, the JCGM 101:2008 guide (Evaluation of measurement data – Supplement 1 to the "Guide to the expression of uncertainty in measurement" – Propagation of distributions using a Monte Carlo method) is responsible to give practical guidance on the application of Monte Carlo simulations to the estimation of uncertainty [4].

INTECH
open science | open minds

© 2013 The Author(s). Licensee InTech. This chapter is distributed under the terms of the Creative Commons Attribution License http://creativecommons.org/licenses/by/3.0), which permits unrestricted use, distribution, and reproduction in any medium, provided the original work is properly cited.

Measurement uncertainty is a quantitative indication of the quality of measurement results, without which they could not be compared between themselves, with specified reference values or to a standard. According to the context of globalization of markets, it is necessary to adopt a universal procedure for estimating uncertainty of measurements, in view of the need for comparability of results between nations and for a mutual recognition in metrology. The harmonization in this field is very well accomplished by the JCGM 100:2008. This document provides a full set of tools to treat different situations and processes of measurement. Estimation of uncertainty, as presented by the JCGM 100:2008, is based on the law of propagation of uncertainty (LPU). This methodology has been successfully applied for several years worldwide for a range of different measurements processes.

The LPU however do not represent the most complete methodology for the estimation of uncertainties in all cases and measurements systems. This is because LPU contains a few approximations and consequently propagates only the main parameters of the probability distributions of influence. Such limitations include for example the linearization of the measurement model and the approximation of the probability distribution of the resulting quantity (or measurand) by a Student's t-distribution using a calculated effective degrees of freedom.

Due to these limitations of the JCGM 100:2008, the use of Monte Carlo method for the propagation of the full probability distributions has been recently addressed in the supplement JCGM 101:2008. In this way, it is possible to cover a broader range of measurement problems that could not be handled by using the LPU alone. The JCGM 101:2008 provides especial guidance on the application of Monte Carlo simulations to metrological situations, recommending a few algorithms that best suit its use when estimating uncertainties in metrology.

2. Terminology and basic concepts

In order to advance in the field of metrology, a few important concepts should be presented. These are basic concepts that can be found on the International Vocabulary of Metrology (VIM) and are explained below.

Quantity. "Property of a phenomenon, body, or substance, where the property has a magnitude that can be expressed as a number and a reference". For example, when a cube is observed, some of its properties such as its volume and mass are quantities which can be expressed by a number and a measurement unit.

Measurand. "Quantity intended to be measured". In the example given above, the volume or mass of the cube can be considered as measurands.

True quantity value. "Quantity value consistent with the definition of a quantity". In practice, a true quantity value is considered unknowable, unless in the special case of a fundamental quantity. In the case of the cube example, its exact (or true) volume or mass cannot be determined in practice.

http://dx.doi.org/10.5772/53014

Measured quantity value. "Quantity value representing a measurement result". This is the quantity value that is measured in practice, being represented as a measurement result. The volume or mass of a cube can be measured by available measurement techniques.

Measurement result. "Set of quantity values being attributed to a measurand together with any other available relevant information". A measurement result is generally expressed as a single measured quantity value and an associated measurement uncertainty. The result of measuring the mass of a cube is represented by a measurement result: 131.0 g ± 0.2 g, for example.

Measurement uncertainty. "Non-negative parameter characterizing the dispersion of the quantity values being attributed to a measurand, based on the information used". Since the true value of a measurement result cannot be determined, any result of a measurement is only an approximation (or estimate) of the value of a measurand. Thus, the complete representation of the value of such a measurement must include this factor of doubt, which is translated by its measurement uncertainty. In the example given above, the measurement uncertainty associated with the measured quantity value of 131.0 g for the mass of the cube is 0.2 g.

Coverage interval. "Interval containing the set of true quantity values of a measurand with a stated probability, based on the information available". This parameter provides limits within which the true quantity values may be found with a determined probability (coverage probability). So for the cube example, there could be 95% probability of finding the true value of the mass within the interval of 130.8 g to 131.2 g.

3. The GUM approach on estimation of uncertainties

As a conclusion from the definitions and discussion presented above, it is clear that the estimation of measurement uncertainties is a fundamental process for the quality of every measurement. In order to harmonize this process for every laboratory, ISO (International Organization for Standardization) and BIPM (Bureau International des Poids et Mesures) gathered efforts to create a guide on the expression of uncertainty in measurement. This guide was published as an ISO standard – ISO/IEC Guide 98-3 "Uncertainty of measurement - Part 3: Guide to the expression of uncertainty in measurement" (GUM) – and as a JCGM (Joint Committee for Guides in Metrology) guide (JCGM 100:2008). This document provides complete guidance and references on how to treat common situations on metrology and how to deal with uncertainties.

The methodology presented by the GUM can be summarized in the following main steps:

a. Definition of the measurand and input sources.

It must be clear to the experimenter what exactly is the measurand, that is, which quantity will be the final object of the measurement. In addition, one must identify all the variables that directly or indirectly influence the determination of the measurand. These variables are known as the input sources. For example, Equation 1 shows a measurand y as a function of four different input sources: x_1, x_2, x_3 and x_4.

$$y = f(x_1, x_2, x_3, x_4) \tag{1}$$

b. Modeling.

In this step, the measurement procedure should be modeled in order to have the measurand as a result of all the input sources. For example, the measurand y in Equation 1 could be modeled as in Equation 2.

$$y = \frac{x_1(x_2 + x_3)}{x_4^2} \tag{2}$$

Construction of a cause-effect diagram helps the experimenter to visualize the modeling process. This is a critical phase, as it defines how the input sources impact the measurand. A well defined model certainly allows a more realistic estimation of uncertainty, which will include all the sources that impact the measurand.

c. Estimation of the uncertainties of input sources.

This phase is also of great importance. Here, uncertainties for all the input sources will be estimated. According to the GUM, uncertainties can be classified in two main types: Type A, which deals with sources of uncertainties from statistical analysis, such as the standard deviation obtained in a repeatability study; and Type B, which are determined from any other source of information, such as a calibration certificate or obtained from limits deduced from personal experience.

Type A uncertainties from repeatability studies are estimated by the GUM as the standard deviation of the mean obtained from the repeated measurements. For example, the uncertainty $u(x)$ due to repeatability of a set of n measurements of the quantity x can be expressed by $s(\bar{x})$ as follows:

$$u(x) = s(\bar{x}) = \frac{s(x)}{\sqrt{n}} \tag{3}$$

where $\bar{x}$ is the mean value of the repeated measurements, $s(x)$ is its standard deviation and $s(\bar{x})$ is the standard deviation of the mean.

Also, it is important to note that the estimation of uncertainties of the Type B input sources must be based on careful analysis of observations or in an accurate scientific judgment, using all available information about the measurement procedure.

d. Propagation of uncertainties.

The GUM uncertainty framework is based on the law of propagation of uncertainties (LPU). This methodology is derived from a set of approximations to simplify the calculations and is valid for a wide range of models.

According to the LPU approach, propagation of uncertainties is made by expanding the measurand model in a Taylor series and simplifying the expression by considering only the first order terms. This approximation is viable as uncertainties are very small numbers compared with the values of their corresponding quantities. In this way, treatment of a model where the measurand y is expressed as a function of N variables $x_1,\ldots, x_N$ (Equation 4), leads to a general expression for propagation of uncertainties (Equation 5).

$$y=f(x_1,\ \ldots,\ x_N) \tag{4}$$

$$u_y^2=\sum_{i=1}^{N}\left(\frac{\partial f}{\partial x_i}\right)^2 u_{x_i}^2+2\sum_{i=1}^{N-1}\sum_{j=i+1}^{N}\left(\frac{\partial f}{\partial x_i}\right)\left(\frac{\partial f}{\partial x_j}\right)\mathrm{cov}(x_i,\ x_j) \tag{5}$$

where u_y is the combined standard uncertainty for the measurand y and u_{x_i} is the uncertainty for the ith input quantity. The second term of Equation 5 is related to the correlation between the input quantities. If there is no supposed correlation between them, Equation 5 can be further simplified as:

$$u_y^2=\sum_{i=1}^{N}\left(\frac{\partial f}{\partial x_i}\right)^2 u_{x_i}^2 \tag{6}$$

e. Evaluation of the expanded uncertainty.

The result provided by Equation 6 corresponds to an interval that contains only one standard deviation (or approx. 68.2% of the measurements). In order to have a better level of confidence for the result, the GUM approach expands this interval by assuming a Student's t-distribution for the measurand. The effective degrees of freedom ν_{eff} for the t-distribution can be estimated by using the Welch-Satterthwaite formula (Equation 7).

$$\nu_{\text{eff}}=\frac{u_y^4}{\sum_{i=1}^{N}\frac{u_{x_i}^4}{\nu_{x_i}}} \tag{7}$$

where ν_{x_i} is the degrees of freedom for the ith input quantity.

The expanded uncertainty is then evaluated by multiplying the combined standard uncertainty by a coverage factor k that expands it to a coverage interval delimited by a t-distribution with a chosen level of confidence (Equation 8).

$$U_y=ku_y \tag{8}$$

4. The GUM limitations

As mentioned before, the approach to estimate measurement uncertainties using the law of propagation of uncertainties presented by the GUM is based on some assumptions, that are not always valid. These assumptions are:

- The model used for calculating the measurand must have insignificant non-linearity. When the model presents strong elements of non-linearity, the approximation made by truncation of the first term in the Taylor series used by the GUM approach may not be enough to correctly estimate the uncertainty output.
- Validity of the central limit theorem, which states that the convolution of a large number of distributions has a resulting normal distribution. Thus, it is assumed that the probability distribution of the output is approximately normal and can be represented by a t-distribution. In some real cases, this resulting distribution may have an asymmetric behavior or does not tend to a normal distribution, invalidating the approach of the central limit theorem.
- After obtaining the standard uncertainty by using the law of propagation of uncertainties, the GUM approach uses the Welch-Satterthwaite formula to obtain the effective degrees of freedom, necessary to calculate the expanded uncertainty. The analytical evaluation of the effective degrees of freedom is still an unsolved problem [5], and therefore not always adequate.

In addition, the GUM approach may not be valid when one or more of the input sources are much larger than the others, or when the distributions of the input quantities are not symmetric. The GUM methodology may also not be appropriate when the order of magnitude of the estimate of the output quantity and the associated standard uncertainty are approximately the same.

In order to overcome these limitations, methods relying on the propagation of distributions have been applied to metrology. This methodology carries more information than the simple propagation of uncertainties and generally provides results closer to reality. Propagation of distributions involves the convolution of the probability distributions of the input quantities, which can be accomplished in three ways: a) analytical integration, b) numerical integration or c) by numerical simulation using Monte Carlo methods. The GUM Supplement 1 (or JCGM 101:2008) provides basic guidelines for using the Monte Carlo simulation for the propagation of distributions in metrology. It is presented as a fast and robust alternative method for cases where the GUM approach fails. This method provides reliable results for a wider range of measurement models as compared to the GUM approach.

5. Monte Carlo simulation applied to metrology

The Monte Carlo methodology as presented by the GUM Supplement 1 involves the propagation of the distributions of the input sources of uncertainty by using the model to provide the distribution of the output. This process is illustrated in Figure 1 in comparison with the propagation of uncertainties used by the GUM.

http://dx.doi.org/10.5772/53014

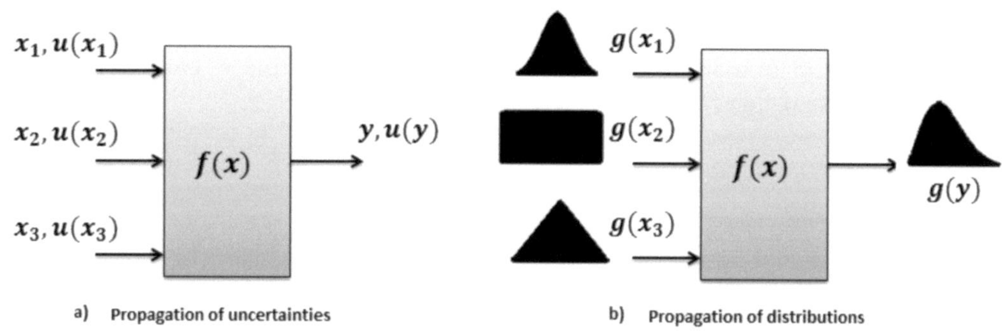

Figure 1. Illustrations of the methodologies of a) propagation of uncertainties, where x_1, x_2 and x_3 are input quantities, $u(x_1)$, $u(x_2)$ and $u(x_3)$ are their respective uncertainties and y and $u(y)$ are the measurand and its uncertainty, respectively; and b) propagation of distributions, where $g(x_1)$, $g(x_2)$ and $g(x_3)$ are the distribution functions of the input quantities and $g(y)$ is the distribution function of the measurand

Figure 1a) shows an illustration representing the propagation of uncertainties. In this case, three input quantities are presented x_1, x_2 and x_3 along with their respective uncertainties $u(x_1)$, $u(x_2)$ and $u(x_3)$. As can be noted, only the main moments (expectation and standard deviation) of the input quantities are used in the propagation and thus a certain amount of information is lost. When propagating distributions however, see Figure 1b), no approximations are made and the whole information contained on the input distributions are propagated to the output.

The GUM Supplement 1 provides a sequence of steps to be followed similarly as to what is done in the GUM:

a. definition of the measurand and input quantities;

b. modeling;

c. estimation of the probability density functions (PDFs) for the input quantities;

d. setup and run the Monte Carlo simulation;

e. summarizing and expression of the results.

The steps (a) and (b) are exactly the same as described in the GUM. Step (c) now involves the selection of the most appropriate probability density functions (or PDFs) for each of the input quantities. In this case, the maximum entropy principle used in the Bayesian theory can be applied in the sense one should consider the most generic distribution for the level of information that is known about the input source. In other words, one should select a PDF that does not transmit more information than that which is known. As an example, if the only information available on an input source is a maximum and a minimum limits, a uniform PDF should be used.

After all the input PDFs have been defined, a number of Monte Carlo trials should be selected – step (d). Generally, the greater the number of simulation trials, the greater the convergence of the results. This number can be chosen *a priori* or by using an adaptive methodology. When choosing *a priori* trials, the GUM Supplement 1 recommends the selection of a number M of trials, according to the following general rule, in order to provide a reasonable representation of the expected result:

$$M > \frac{10^4}{1 - p} \tag{9}$$

where $100p\%$ is the selected coverage probability. So for example, when the chosen coverage probability is 95%, $p=0.95$ and M should be at least higher than 200,000.

The adaptive methodology involves the selection of a condition to check after each trial for the stabilization of the results of interest. The results of interest in this case are the expectation (or mean) and the standard deviation of the output quantity and the endpoints of the chosen interval. According to the GUM Supplement 1, a result is considered to be stabilized if twice the standard deviation associated with it is less than the numerical tolerance associated with the standard deviation of the output quantity.

The numerical tolerance of an uncertainty, or standard deviation, can be obtained by expressing the standard uncertainty as $c \times 10^l$, where c is an integer with a number of digits equal to the number of significant digits of the standard uncertainty and l is an integer. Then the numerical tolerance δ is expressed as:

$$\delta = \frac{1}{2} 10^l \tag{10}$$

The next step after setting M is to run the simulation itself. Despite the advantages discussed for the Monte Carlo numerical methodology for estimating measurement uncertainties, one of the main requirements for a reliable simulation is to have a good pseudo-random number generator. In this way, the GUM Supplement 1 recommends the use of the enhanced Wichmann-Hill algorithm [6].

Simulations can easily be setup to run even on low cost personal computers. Generally, a simulation for an average model with 200,000 iterations, which would generate reasonable results for a coverage probability of 95%, runs in a few minutes only, depending on the software and hardware used. In this way, computational costs are usually not a major issue.

The last stage is to summarize and express the results. According to the GUM Supplement 1, the following parameters should be reported as results: a) an estimate of the output quantity, taken as the average of the values generated for it; b) the standard uncertainty, taken as the standard deviation of these generated values; c) the chosen coverage probability (usually 95%); and d) the endpoints corresponding to the selected coverage interval.

The selection of this coverage interval should be done by determining: i) the probabilistically symmetric coverage interval, in the case of a resulting symmetric PDF for the output quantity; ii) the shortest $100p\%$ coverage interval, when the output PDF is asymmetrical.

http://dx.doi.org/10.5772/53014

6. Case studies: Fuel cell efficiency

In order to better understand the application of Monte Carlo simulations on the estimation of measurement uncertainty, some case studies will be presented and discussed along this chapter. The first example to be shown concerns the estimation of the real efficiency of a fuel cell. As discussed before, the first steps are to define the measurand and the input sources, as well as a model associated with them.

Fuel cells are electrochemical devices that produce electrical energy using hydrogen gas as fuel [7]. The energy production is a consequence of the chemical reaction of a proton with oxygen gas yielding water as output. There is also the generation of heat as a byproduct which could be used in cogeneration energy processes enhancing the overall energy efficiency. Two kinds of fuel cells are most used currently: PEMFC (proton exchange membrane fuel cell) and SOFC (oxide solid fuel cell). The former is used in low temperature applications (around 80 °C) and the last is used in the high temperature range (near 1000 °C).

One of the most important parameters to be controlled and measured in a fuel cell is its energy efficiency. To do so, it is necessary to know both the energy produced by the cell and the energy generated by the chemical reaction. The thermodynamic efficiency of a fuel cell can be calculated by Equation 11 [8].

$$\eta_t = \frac{\Delta G}{\Delta H} \tag{11}$$

where η_t is the thermodynamic efficiency, ΔG is the maximum energy produced by the fuel cell (Gibb's free energy in kJ/mol) and ΔH is the energy generated by the global reaction (or the enthalpy of formation in kJ/mol). However, in order to calculate the real efficiency of a fuel cell Equation 12 is necessary [8].

$$\eta_R = \eta_t \frac{E_R}{E_I} = \frac{\Delta G}{\Delta H} \frac{E_R}{E_I} \tag{12}$$

where η_R is the real efficiency, E_R is the real electric voltage produced by the fuel cell (V) and E_I is the ideal electric voltage of the chemical reaction (V).

In this case study, the real efficiency will be considered as the measurand, using Equation 12 as its model. The values and sources of uncertainty of inputs for a fuel cell operating with pure oxygen and hydrogen at standard conditions have been estimated from data cited in the literature [8, 9]. They are as follows:

Gibbs free energy (ΔG). The maximum free energy available for useful work is of 237.1 kJ/mol. In this example, one can suppose an uncertainty of 0.1 kJ/mol as a poor source of information, i.e. no probability information is available within the interval ranging from 237.0 kJ/mol to 237.2 kJ/mol. Thus, a uniform PDF can be associated with this input source using these values as minimum and maximum limits, respectively.

Enthalpy of formation (ΔH). The chemical energy, or enthalpy of formation, for the oxygen/hydrogen reaction at standard conditions is given as 285.8 kJ/mol. Again, considering an uncertainty of 0.1 kJ/mol, a uniform PDF can be associated with this input source using 285.7 kJ/mol and 285.9 kJ/mol as minimum and maximum limits, respectively.

Ideal voltage (E_I). The ideal voltage of a fuel cell operating reversibly with pure hydrogen and oxygen in standard conditions is 1.229 V (Nernst equation). It is possible to suppose an uncertainty of ± 0.001 V as a poor source of information, and have a uniform PDF associated with that input source in this interval.

Real voltage (E_R). The real voltage was measured as 0.732 V with a voltmeter that has a digital resolution of ± 0.001 V. The GUM recommends that half the digital resolution can be used as limits of a uniform distribution. Then, a uniform PDF can be associated with this input source in the interval of 0.7315 V to 0.7325 V.

Figure 2 shows the cause-effect diagram for the evaluation of the real efficiency and Table 1 summarizes the input sources and values. All input sources are considered to be type B sources of uncertainty since they do not come from statistical analysis. In addition, they are supposed to be non-correlated.

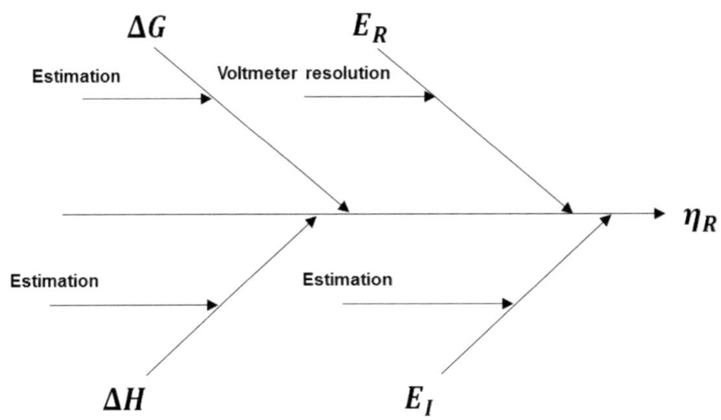

Figure 2. Cause-effect diagram for the fuel cell thermodynamic efficiency uncertainty estimation

Input source	Type	PDF	PDF parameters
Gibbs free energy (ΔG)	B	Uniform	Min: 237.0 kJ/mol; Max: 237.2 kJ/mol
Enthalpy of formation (ΔH)	B	Uniform	Min: 285.7 kJ/mol; Max: 285.9 kJ/mol
Ideal voltage (E_I)	B	Uniform	Min: 1.228 V; Max: 1.230 V
Real voltage (E_R)	B	Uniform	Min: 0.7315 V; Max: 0.7325 V

Table 1. Input sources and associated PDFs with their respective parameters for the estimation of uncertainty of the real efficiency of a fuel cell (Min stands for minimum value and Max stands for maximum value)

Monte Carlo simulation was set to run $M = 2\times 10^5$ trials of the proposed model, using the described input sources. The final histogram representing the possible values for the real efficiency of the cell is shown on Figure 3. Table 2 shows the statistical parameters obtained

http://dx.doi.org/10.5772/53014

for the final PDF corresponding to the histogram. The low and high endpoints represent the 95% coverage interval for the final efficiency result of 0.49412.

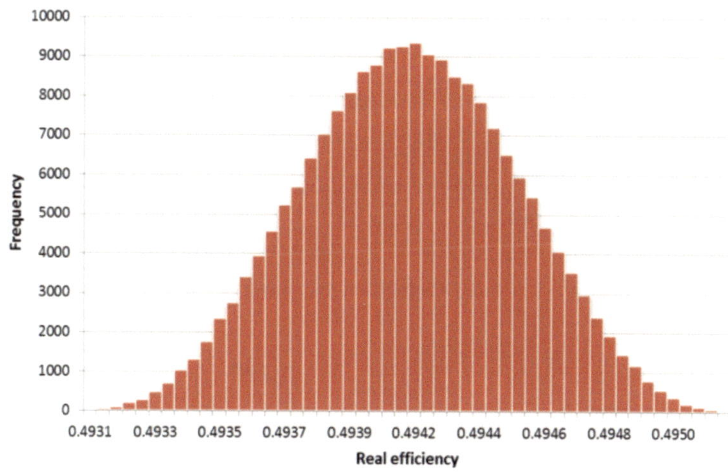

Figure 3. Histogram representing the resulting PDF for the real efficiency of a fuel cell estimated by Monte Carlo simulation

Parameter	Value
Mean	0.49412
Standard deviation	0.00034
Low endpoint for 95%	0.49346
High endpoint for 95%	0.49477

Table 2. Statistical parameters obtained for the Monte Carlo simulation of the real efficiency estimation model

In order to have a comparison with the traditional GUM methodology, Table 3 is shown with the results obtained by using the LPU. The number of effective degrees of freedom is infinite because all the input sources are uncertainties of type B. Consequently, for a coverage probability of 95%, the coverage factor obtained from a t-distribution is 1.96. It can be noted that the values obtained for the standard deviation of the resulting PDF (from the Monte Carlo simulation) and for the standard uncertainty (from the LPU methodology) are practically the same.

Parameter	Value
Combined standard uncertainty	0.00034
Effective degrees of freedom	∞
Coverage factor (k)	1.96
Expanded uncertainty	0.00067

Table 3. Results obtained for the real efficiency of a fuel cell uncertainty estimation using the GUM uncertainty approach, with a coverage probability of 95%

Even though results from both methodologies are practically the same, the GUM Supplement 1 provides a practical way to validate the GUM methodology with the Monte Carlo simulation results. This will be shown in detail in the next case studies.

7. Case studies: Measurement of torque

Torque is by definition a quantity that represents the tendency of a force to rotate an object about an axis. It can be mathematically expressed as the product of a force and the lever-arm distance. In metrology, a practical way to measure it is by loading the end of a horizontal arm with a known mass while keeping the other end fixed (Figure 4).

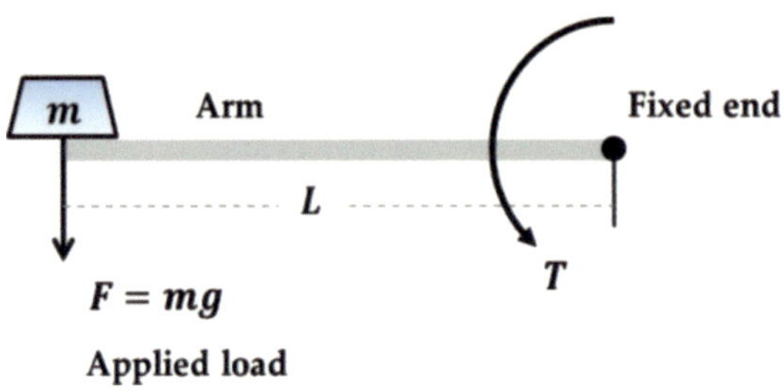

Figure 4. Conceptual illustration of the experimental setup for a measurement of torque (T), where F is the applied force, m is the mass of the load, g is the local gravity acceleration, L is the length of the arm

The model to describe the experiment can be expressed as follows:

$$T = mgL \tag{13}$$

where T is the torque, m is the mass of the applied load (kg), g is the local gravity acceleration (m/s^2) and L is the total length of the arm (m). In practice, one can imagine several more sources of uncertainty for the experiment, like for example the thermal dilatation of the arm as the room temperature changes. However, the objective here is not to exhaust all the possibilities, but instead, to provide basic notions of how to use the Monte Carlo methodology for uncertainty estimation based on a simple model. In this way, only the following sources will be considered:

Mass (m). In the example, the mass m was repeatedly measured for ten times in a calibrated balance, with a capacity of 60 kg. The average mass was 35.7653 kg, with a standard deviation of 0.3 g. This source of uncertainty is purely statistical and is classified as being of type A according to the GUM. The PDF that best represents this case is a Gaussian distribution, with mean of 35.7653 kg and standard deviation equal to the standard deviation of the mean, i.e. $0.3\ \text{g}/\sqrt{10} = 9.49 \times 10^{-5}$ kg.

In addition, the balance used for the measurement has a certificate stating an expanded uncertainty for this range of mass of 0.1 g, with a coverage factor $k = 2$ and a level of confidence of 95%. The uncertainty of the mass due to the calibration of the balance constitutes another source of uncertainty involving the same input quantity (mass). In this case, a Gaussian distribution can also be used as PDF to represent the input uncertainty, with mean of zero and standard deviation of $U / k = 0.1\ \text{g} / 2 = 0.00005$ kg, i.e. the expanded uncertainty divided by the coverage factor, resulting in the standard uncertainty. The use of zero as the mean value is a mathematical artifice to take into account the variability due to this source of uncertainty without changing the value of the quantity (mass) used in the model. More on this will be discussed later.

Local gravity acceleration (g). The value for the local gravity acceleration is stated in a certificate of measurement as 9.7874867 m/s², as well as its expanded uncertainty of 0.0000004 m/s², for $k = 2$ and 95% of confidence. Again, a Gaussian distribution is used as the PDF representing this input source, with mean of 9.7874867 m/s² and standard deviation of $U / k = (0.0000004\ \text{m/s}^2) / 2 = 0.0000002\ \text{m/s}^2$.

Length of the arm (L). The arm used in the experiment has a certified value for its total length of 1999.9955 mm, and its calibration certificate states an expanded uncertainty of 0.0080 mm, for $k = 2$ and 95% of confidence. The best PDF in this case is a Gaussian distribution with mean 1999.9955 mm and standard deviation of $U / k = 0.0080\ \text{mm} / 2 = 0.000004$ m.

Figure 5 illustrates the cause-effect diagram for the model of torque measurement. Note that there are three input quantities in the model, but four input sources of uncertainty, being one of the input quantities, the mass, split in two sources: one due to the certificate of the balance and other due to the measurement repeatability.

Table 4 summarizes all the input sources and their respective associated PDFs.

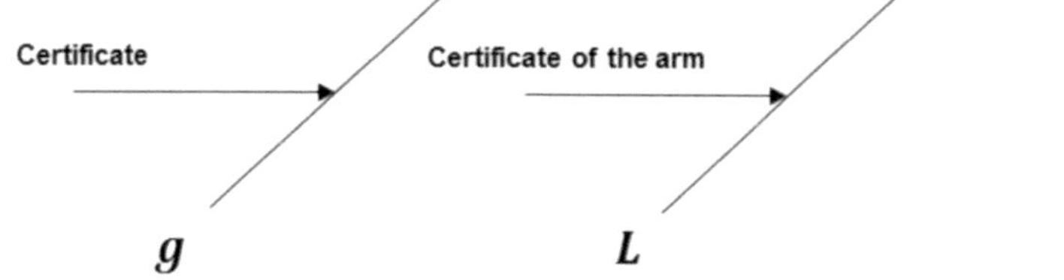

Figure 5. Cause-effect diagram illustrating the proposed model for the measurement of torque

Input source	Type	PDF	PDF parameters
Mass (m)			
– due to repeatability	A	Gaussian	Mean: 35.7653 kg; SD: 9.49 × 10^{-5} kg
– due to certificate	B	Gaussian	Mean: 0 kg; SD: 0.00005 kg
Local gravity acceleration (g)	B	Gaussian	Mean: 9.7874867 m/s^2; SD: 0.0000002 m/s^2
Length of the arm (L)	B	Gaussian	Mean: 1999.9955 m; SD: 0.000004 m

Table 4. Input sources and associated PDFs with their respective parameters for the estimation of uncertainty of torque measurement (SD stands for standard deviation)

Running the Monte Carlo simulation using $M = 2\times 10^5$ trials leads to results shown on Figure 6 and Table 5. It is important to note that the two input sources due to the mass are added together in the model, in order to account for the variability of both of them. Figure 6 shows the histogram constructed from the values of torque obtained by the trials. Table 5 contains the statistical parameters corresponding to the histogram. The low and high endpoints represent the 95% coverage interval for the final torque result of 700.1034 N.m.

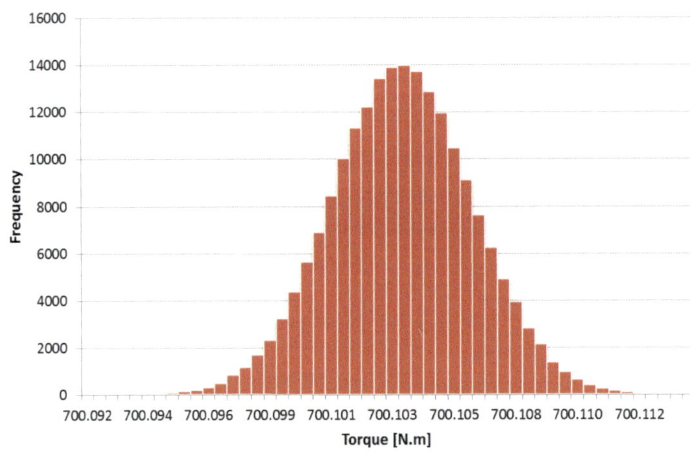

Figure 6. Histogram representing the resulting PDF for the torque measurement estimated by Monte Carlo simulation

Parameter	Value
Mean	700.1032 N.m
Standard deviation	0.0025 N.m
Low endpoint for 95%	700.0983 N.m
High endpoint for 95%	700.1082 N.m

Table 5. Statistical parameters obtained for the Monte Carlo simulation of the torque measurement model

Once more a comparison with the GUM approach is done and the results obtained by this methodology are shown on Table 6, for a coverage probability of 95%.

Parameter	Value
Combined standard uncertainty	0.0025 N.m
Effective degrees of freedom	30
Coverage factor (k)	1.96
Expanded uncertainty	0.0050 N.m

Table 6. Results obtained for the torque model using the GUM uncertainty approach, with a coverage probability of 95%

As commented before, the GUM Supplement 1 presents a procedure on how to validate the LPU approach addressed by de GUM with the results from Monte Carlo simulation. This is accomplished by comparing the low and high endpoints obtained from both methods. Thus, the absolute differences d_{low} and d_{high} of the respective endpoints of the two coverage intervals are calculated (Equations 14 and 15) and compared with the numerical tolerance δ of the standard uncertainty defined by Equation 10. If both d_{low} and d_{high} are lesser than δ, the GUM approach can be validated in this instance.

$$d_{low} = | y - U(y) - y_{low} | \quad (14)$$

$$d_{high} = | y + U(y) - y_{high} | \quad (15)$$

where y is the measurand estimate, $U(y)$ is the expanded uncertainty obtained by the GUM approach and y_{low} and y_{high} are the low and high endpoints of the PDF obtained by the Monte Carlo simulation for a given coverage probability, respectively.

In the case of the torque example, d_{low} and d_{high} are respectively calculated as 9.93×10^{-6} N.m and 4.12×10^{-6} N.m. Also, to obtain δ, the standard uncertainty 0.0025 N.m can be written as 25×10^{-4} N.m, considering two significant digits, then $\delta = 1/2 \times 10^{-4}$ N.m $= 5 \times 10^{-5}$ N.m. As both d_{low} and d_{high} are lesser than δ, the GUM approach is validated in this case.

When working with cases where the GUM approach is valid, like the example given for the measurement of torque, the laboratory can easily continue to use it for its daily uncertainty estimations. The advantages of the GUM traditional approach is that it is a popular widespread and recognized method, that does not necessarily require a computer or a specific software to be used. In addition, several small laboratories have been using this method since its publication as an ISO guide. It would be recommended however that at least one Monte Carlo run could be made to verify its validity, according to the criteria established (numerical tolerance). On the other hand, Monte Carlo simulations can provide reliable results on a wider range of cases, including those where the GUM approach fails. Thus, if their use for the laboratory would not increase the overall efforts or costs, then it would be recommended.

Now, extending the torque measurement case further, one can suppose that the arm used in the experiment has no certificate of calibration, indicating its length value and uncertainty, and that the only measuring method available for the arm's length is by the use of a ruler with a minimum division of 1 mm. The use of the ruler leads then to a measurement value of 2000.0 mm for the length of the arm. Though, in this new situation very poor information about the measurement uncertainty of the arm's length is available. As the minimum division of the ruler is 1 mm, one can assume that the reading can be done with a maximum accuracy of up to 0.5 mm, which can be thought as an interval of ± 0.5 mm as limits for the measurement. However, no information of probabilities within this interval is available, and therefore the only PDF that can be assumed in this case is a uniform distribution, on which there is equal probability for the values within the whole interval. The uniform PDF then has 1999.5 mm as lower limit and 2000.5 mm as higher limit.

After running the Monte Carlo simulation with $M = 2\times 10^5$ trials in this new situation, new results are obtained, as shown in Figure 7 (histogram) and Table 7 (statistical parameters).

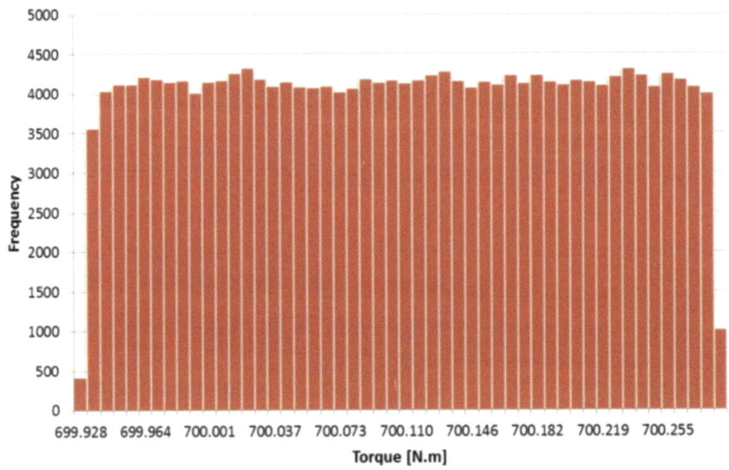

Figure 7. Histogram representing the resulting PDF for the torque measurement estimated by Monte Carlo simulation (measuring the non-certified arm with a ruler)

As can be noted, the resulting PDF changed completely, from a Gaussian-like shape (Figure 6) to an almost uniform shape (Figure 7). This is a consequence of the relatively higher uncertainty associated with the arm length in the new situation, as well as the fact that the PDF used for it was a uniform distribution. Thus, the strong influence of this uniform source was predominant in the final PDF. It is important to note that in the GUM methodology this new PDF would be approximated to a t-distribution, which has a very different shape.

Also as a result, the new standard uncertainty, represented by the standard deviation on Table 7 (0.1011 N.m), is higher than the one found in the former simulation, as shown in Table 5 (0.0025 N.m).

Estimating the uncertainty in this new situation by the traditional GUM approach, i.e. using the LPU and the Welch-Satterthwaite formula, one can obtain the results shown on Table 8.

http://dx.doi.org/10.5772/53014

Parameter	Value
Mean	700.1035 N.m
Standard deviation	0.1011 N.m
Low endpoint for 95%	699.9370 N.m
High endpoint for 95%	700.2695 N.m

Table 7. Statistical parameters obtained for the Monte Carlo simulation of the torque measurement model (measuring the non-certified arm with a ruler)

Parameter	Value
Combined standard uncertainty	0.1011 N.m
Effective degrees of freedom	∞
Coverage factor (*k*)	1.96
Expanded uncertainty	0.1981 N.m

Table 8. Results obtained for the torque model by using the GUM uncertainty approach and measuring the non-certified arm with a ruler, with a coverage probability of 95%

In this new situation, $d_{low}=3.18\times10^{-2}$ N.m and $d_{high}=3.18\times10^{-2}$ N.m, and the standard uncertainty 0.1011 N.m can be written as 10×10^{-2} N.m, considering two significant digits, then $\delta=1/2\times10^{-2}$ N.m $=5\times10^{-3}$ N.m. Thus, as both d_{low} and d_{high} are higher than δ, the GUM approach is not validated in this case. Note that considering only one significant digit, i.e. using a less rigid criterion, $\delta=1/2\times10^{-1}$ N.m $=5\times10^{-2}$ N.m and the GUM approach is validated.

8. Case studies: Preparation of a standard cadmium solution

This example is quoted from the EURACHEM/CITAC Guide [10] (Example A1) and refers to the preparation of a calibration solution of cadmium. In this problem, a high purity metal (Cd) is weighted and dissolved in a certain volume of liquid solvent. The proposed model for this case is shown on Equation 16.

$$c_{Cd}=\frac{1000mP}{V} \tag{16}$$

where c_{Cd} is the cadmium concentration (mg/L), m is the mass of the high purity metal (mg), P is its purity and V is the volume of the final solution (mL). The factor 1000 is used to convert milliliter to liter.

The sources of uncertainty in this case are identified as follows:

Purity (P). The purity of cadmium is quoted in the supplier's certificate as being 99.99% ± 0.01%. Thus, the value of P is 0.9999 and its uncertainty can be only be assumed to be in a uniform PDF as there is no extra information from the manufacturer concerning the probabilities within the interval. In this case the uniform PDF would have maximum and minimum limits of ± 0.0001, i.e. P would range from 0.9998 to 1.0000.

Mass (m). The mass of metal is obtained from its weighting in a certified balance. The value of mass for Cd is obtained as m = 0.10028 g. The uncertainty associated with the mass of the cadmium is estimated, using the data from the calibration certificate and the manufacturer's recommendations on uncertainty estimation, as 0.05 mg. As this is provided as a standard uncertainty in this example, a Gaussian PDF can be assumed with mean 0.10028 g and standard deviation of 0.05 g.

Volume (V). The total volume of solution is measured by filling a flask of 100 mL and has three major influences: calibration of the flask, repeatability and room temperature.

The first input source is due to filling of the flask, which is quoted by the manufacturer to have a volume of 100 ml ± 0.1 mL measured at a temperature of 20 °C. Again, poor information about this interval is available. In this particular case, the EURACHEM guide considers that it would be more realistic to expect that values near the bounds are less likely than those near the midpoint, and thus assumes a triangular PDF for this input source, ranging from 99.9 mL to 100.1 mL, with an expected value of 100.0 mL.

The uncertainty due to repeatability can be estimated as a result of variations in filling the flask. This experiment has been done and a standard uncertainty has been obtained as 0.02 mL. A Gaussian PDF is then assumed to represent this input source, with mean equal to zero and standard deviation of 0.02 mL.

The last input source for the volume is due to the room temperature. The manufacturer of the flask stated that it is calibrated for a room temperature of 20 °C. However the temperature of the laboratory in which the solution was prepared varies between the limits of ± 4 °C. The volume expansion of the liquid due to temperature is considerably larger than that for the flask, thus only the former is considered. The coefficient of volume expansion of the solvent is 2.1×10^{-4} °C^{-1}, which leads to a volume variation of ± (100 mL × 4 °C × 2.1×10^{-4} °C^{-1}) = ± 0.084 mL. So, as this is also a source with poor information, a uniform PDF is assumed in this interval, ranging from -0.084 mL to 0.084 mL.

A simple cause-effect diagram for this case study is presented in Figure 8 and the input sources are summarized in Table 9.

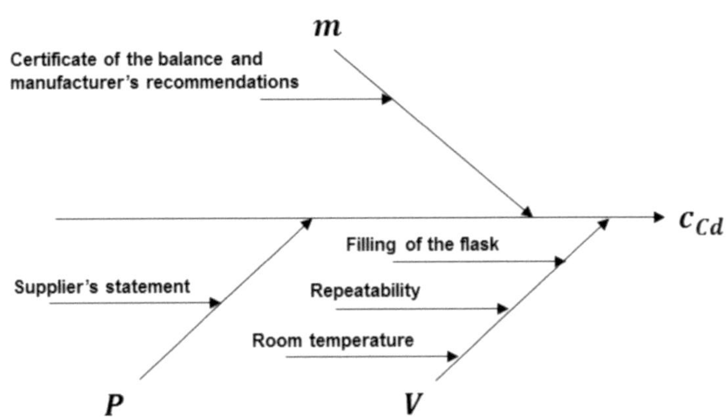

Figure 8. Cause-effect diagram for the preparation of a standard cadmium solution

Input source	Type	PDF	PDF parameters
Purity (*P*)	B	Uniform	Min: 0.9998; Max: 1.0000
Mass (*m*)	B	Gaussian	Mean: 100.28 mg; SD: 0.05 mg
Volume (*V*)			
– due to filling	B	Triangular	Mean: 100 mL; Min: 99.9 mL; Max: 100.1 mL
– due to repeatability	A	Gaussian	Mean: 0 mL; SD: 0.02 mL
– due to temperature	B	Uniform	Min: -0.084 mL; Max: 0.084 mL

Table 9. Input sources and associated PDFs with their respective parameters for the estimation of uncertainty of the concentration of a Cd standard solution (SD means standard deviation, Min stands for minimum value and Max stands for maximum value)

Monte Carlo simulation was done using $M = 2\times 10^5$ trials and the results are shown in Figure 9 (histogram) and Table 10 (statistical parameters).

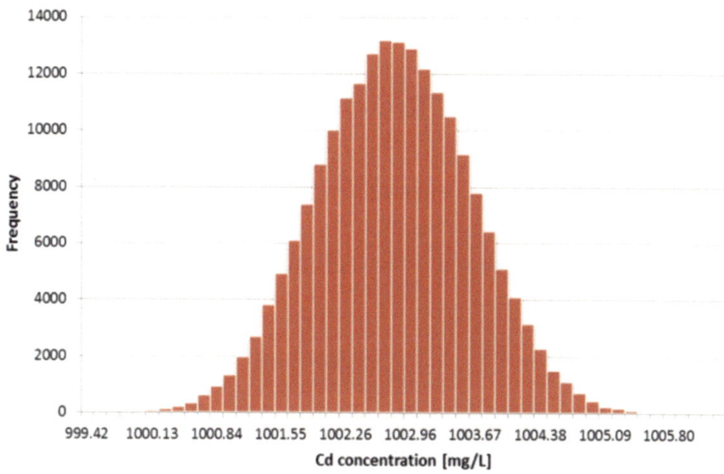

Figure 9. Histogram representing the resulting PDF for the concentration of a Cd standard solution estimated by Monte Carlo simulation

Parameter	Value
Mean	1002.705 mg/L
Standard deviation	0.835 mg/L
Low endpoint for 95%	1001.092 mg/L
High endpoint for 95%	1004.330 mg/L

Table 10. Statistical parameters obtained for the Monte Carlo simulation of the concentration of a Cd standard solution

Again, a comparison is made to the results found when using the GUM approach for a coverage probability of 95% (Table 11). Combined standard uncertainty (GUM approach) and standard deviation (Monte Carlo simulation) have practically the same value.

Parameter	Value
Combined standard uncertainty	0.835 mg/L
Effective degrees of freedom	1203
Coverage factor (k)	1.96
Expanded uncertainty	1.639 mg/L

Table 11. Results obtained for the concentration of a Cd standard solution model by using the GUM uncertainty approach, with a coverage probability of 95%

The endpoints obtained from both methods were compared using the numerical tolerance method proposed in the GUM Supplement 1. In this case, $d_{low} = 3.13 \times 10^{-2}$ mg/L and $d_{high} = 7.90 \times 10^{-3}$ mg/L, and writing the standard uncertainty as 84×10^{-2} mg/L (using two significant digits), $\delta = {}^{1}/_{2} \times 10^{-2}\text{mg/L} = 5 \times 10^{-3}$ mg/L, which is lower than both d_{low} and d_{high}, and then the GUM approach is not validated.

9. Case studies: Measurement of Brinell hardness

The last example to be presented in this chapter will show a simple model for the measurement of Brinell hardness. This test is executed by applying a load on a sphere made of a hard material over the surface of the test sample (Figure 10).

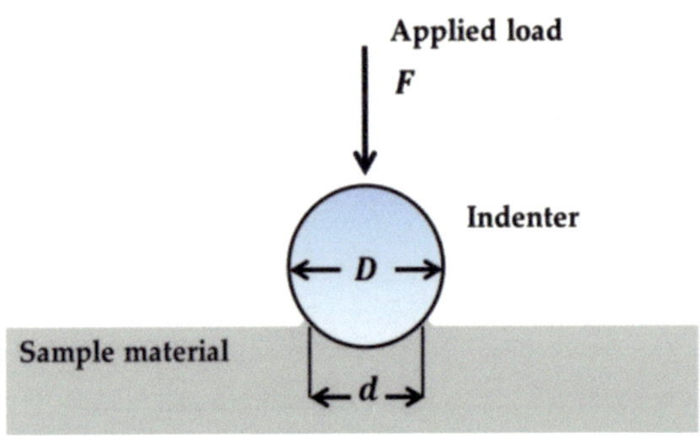

Figure 10. Schematic representation of a Brinell hardness test

During the test the sphere will penetrate through the sample leaving an indented mark upon unloading. The diameter of this mark is inversely proportional to the hardness of the material of the sample.

The model used here for the Brinell hardness (HB) is represented in Equation 17:

$$HB = \frac{0.204F}{\pi D\left(D - \sqrt{D^2 - d^2}\right)} \tag{17}$$

http://dx.doi.org/10.5772/53014

where F is the applied load (N), D is the indenter diameter (mm) and d is the diameter of the indentation mark (mm).

The input sources of uncertainty for this case study are:

Load (F). A fixed load is applied by the hardness test machine and is indicated as being 29400 N. The certificate of the machine indicates an expanded uncertainty of 2%, with $k = 2$ and a coverage probability of 95%. The best distribution to use in this case is a Gaussian PDF with mean 29400 N and standard deviation of $U / k = (0.02 \times 29400 \text{ N}) / 2 = 294$ N.

Indenter diameter (D). The sphere used as indenter has a certificate of measurement for its diameter with the value of 10 mm. Its expanded uncertainty, as indicated in the certificate, is 0.01 mm, for $k = 2$ and a coverage probability of 95%. Again, a Gaussian PDF should be used, with a mean of 10 mm and standard deviation of $U / k = 0.01 \text{ mm} / 2 = 0.005$ mm.

Diameter of the mark (d). The diameter of the indented mark was measured 5 times with the help of an optical microscope and a stage micrometer. The mean value was 3 mm, with a standard deviation of 0.079 mm. Besides the contribution due to repeatability, one could also consider the influence from the calibrated stage micrometer, but for the sake of simplicity, this source will be neglected. Thus, in this case a Gaussian PDF with mean 3 mm and standard deviation of $0.079 \text{ mm} / \sqrt{10} = 0.035$ mm would best represent the diameter of the mark.

Figure 11 shows the cause-effect diagram for this case study and Table 12 summarizes all the input sources of uncertainty.

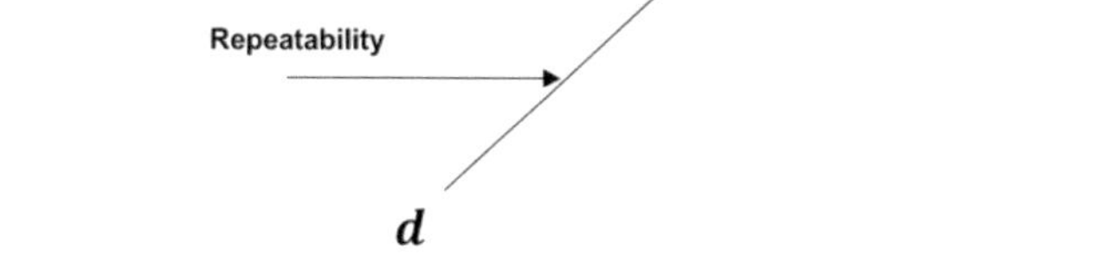

Figure 11. Cause-effect diagram for the measurement of Brinell hardness

Input source	Type	PDF	PDF parameters
Load (F)	B	Gaussian	Mean 29400 N; SD: 294 N
Indenter diameter (D)	B	Gaussian	Mean: 10 mm; SD: 0.005 mm
Diameter of the mark (d)	A	Gaussian	Mean: 3 mm; SD: 0.035 mm

Table 12. Input sources and associated PDFs with their respective parameters for the estimation of uncertainty of a Brinell hardness test (SD means standard deviation)

Monte Carlo simulation results for $M = 2\times 10^5$ trials are shown in Table 13, as well as the resulting PDF for the Brinell hardness values in Figure 12.

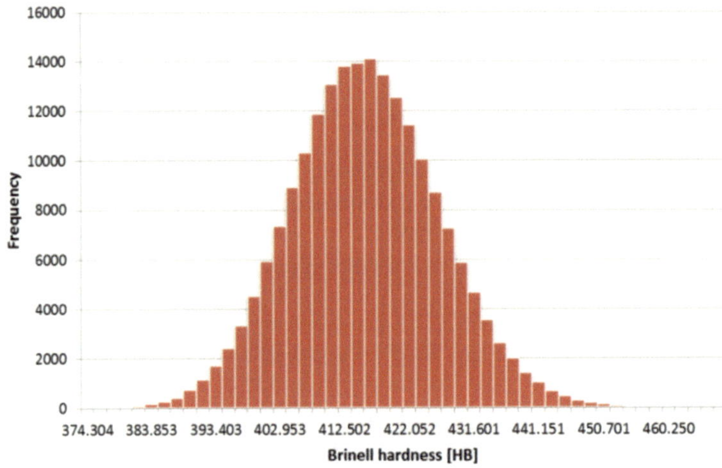

Figure 12. Histogram representing the resulting PDF for the Brinell hardness estimated by Monte Carlo simulation

Parameter	Value
Mean	415 HB
Standard deviation	11 HB
Low endpoint for 95%	394 HB
High endpoint for 95%	436 HB

Table 13. Statistical parameters obtained for the Monte Carlo simulation of the Brinell hardness measurement model

Results obtained by using the GUM approach in this case are show on Table 14.

Parameter	Value
Combined standard uncertainty	11 HB
Effective degrees of freedom	5
Coverage factor (k)	2.57
Expanded uncertainty	28 HB

Table 14. Results obtained for the Brinell hardness model by using the GUM uncertainty approach, with a coverage probability of 95%

Although the values of combined standard uncertainty (from the GUM approach) and standard deviation (from Monte Carlo simulation) are practically the same, the GUM approach is not validated using the numerical tolerance methodology. In this case, $\delta = 0.5$ HB, and the differences $d_{low} = 7.3$ HB and $d_{high} = 5.9$ HB, which are higher than δ.

The main difference of this case study to the others presented in this chapter is due to the non-linear character of the Brinell hardness model, which can lead to strong deviations from the GUM traditional approach of propagation of uncertainties. In fact, Monte Carlo simulation methodology is able to mimic reality better in such cases, providing richer information about the measurand than the GUM traditional approach and its approximations. In order to demonstrate this effect, one can suppose that the standard deviation found for the values of diameter of the indenter mark were 10 times higher, i.e. 0.35 mm instead of 0.035 mm. Then, Monte Carlo simulation would have given the results shown on the histogram of Figure 13, with statistical parameters shown on Table 15, for $M = 2 \times 10^5$ trials.

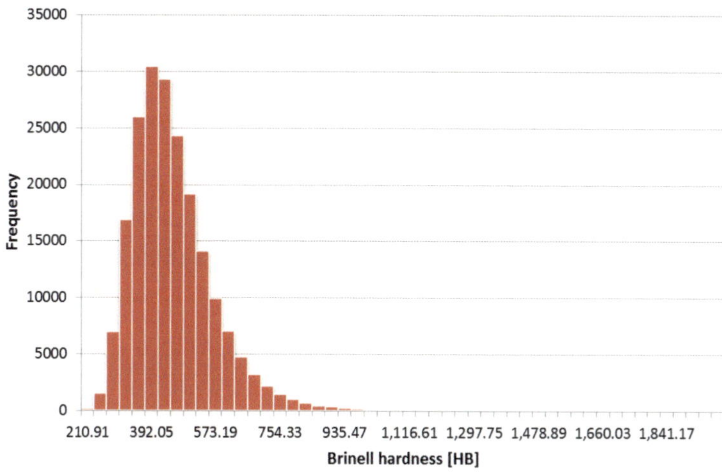

Figure 13. Histogram representing the resulting PDF for the Brinell hardness estimated by Monte Carlo simulation (with 0.35 mm instead of 0.035 mm as standard deviation of *d*)

Parameter	Value
Mean	433 HB
Median	414 HB
Standard deviation	114 HB
Low endpoint for 95%	270 HB
High endpoint for 95%	708 HB

Table 15. Statistical parameters obtained for the Monte Carlo simulation of the Brinell hardness measurement model (with 0.35 mm instead of 0.035 mm as standard deviation of *d*)

As can be observed, the resulting PDF for the Brinell hardness is strongly skewed to the left (lower values of *HB*). This behavior is a consequence of having a predominant uncertainty component (or input source) in a model that has non-linear characteristics. The unusual shape of this PDF gives an idea of how much the GUM approach can misestimate the coverage interval of the measurand when supposing a t-distribution as its final distribution.

It also can be noted that the expected mean calculated for the PDF (433 HB) is shifted to higher values in this case if compared with the expected value of 415 HB found in the former simulation (or by direct calculation of *HB*). Table 15 also shows the value of the median (the value that equally divides the sample values in two halves) as 414 HB, which is much closer to the expected value of 415 HB. In fact, for skewed distributions the median is generally considered to be the best representative of the central location of the data.

Table 16 shows the results obtained for this new situation by using the GUM approach.

Parameter	Value
Combined standard uncertainty	100 HB
Effective degrees of freedom	4
Coverage factor (*k*)	2.78
Expanded uncertainty	278 HB

Table 16. Results obtained for the Brinell hardness model by using the GUM uncertainty approach (with 0.35 mm instead of 0.035 mm as standard deviation of *d*), for a coverage probability of 95%

Calculating the differences of the endpoints between the two methods yields d_{low} = 133 HB and d_{high} =16 HB, which are much higher than δ = 0.5 HB, invalidating the GUM approach, as expected.

10. Conclusions

The GUM uncertainty framework is currently still the most extensive method used on estimation of measurement uncertainty in metrology. Despite its approximations, it suits very well on a wide range of measurement systems and models.

However, the use of numerical methods like Monte Carlo simulations has been increasingly encouraged by the Joint Committee for Guide in Metrology (JCGM) of the Bureau International des Poids et Mesures (BIPM) as a valuable alternative to the GUM approach. The simulations rely on the propagation of distributions, instead of propagation of uncertainties like the GUM, and thus are not subjected to its approximations. Consequently, Monte Carlo simulations provide results for a wider range of models, including situations in which the GUM approximations may not be adequate (see section 4 for GUM limitations), like for example when the models contain non-linear terms or when there is a large non-Gaussian input source that predominates over the others.

The practical use of Monte Carlo simulations on the estimation of uncertainties is still gaining ground on the metrology area, being limited to National Institutes of Metrology and some research groups, as it still needs more dissemination to third party laboratories and institutes. Nevertheless, it has proven to be a fundamental tool in this area, being able to address more complex measurement problems that were limited by the GUM approximations.

http://dx.doi.org/10.5772/53014

Author details

Paulo Roberto Guimarães Couto[1], Jailton Carreteiro Damasceno[2] and Sérgio Pinheiro de Oliveira[1]

*Address all correspondence to: prcouto@inmetro.gov.br

1 Mechanical Metrology Division, Inmetro, Duque de Caxias, Brazil

2 Materials Metrology Division, Inmetro, Duque de Caxias, Brazil

References

[1] ISO IEC 17025:2005 – General requirements for the competence of testing and calibration laboratories. International Organization for Standardization, Geneva; 2005.

[2] JCGM 200:2012 – International Vocabulary of Metrology – Basic and General Concepts and Associated Terms (VIM). Joint Committee for Guides in Metrology; 2012.

[3] JCGM 100:2008 – Evaluation of measurement data – Guide to the expression of uncertainty in measurement. Joint Committee for Guides in Metrology; 2008.

[4] JCGM 101:2008 – Evaluation of measurement data - Supplement 1 to the "Guide to the expression of uncertainty in measurement" – Propagation of distributions using a Monte Carlo method. Joint Committee for Guides in Metrology; 2008.

[5] Lepek A. A computer program for a general case evaluation of the expanded uncertainty. Accreditation and Quality Assurance 2003; 8(6) 296-299.

[6] Wichmann BA, Hill ID. Generating good pseudo-random numbers. Computational Statistics & Data Analysis 2006; 51(3) 1614–1622.

[7] U.S. Department of Energy. Energy Efficiency & Renewable Energy. http://www.eere.energy.gov/hydrogenandfuelcells/fuelcells/index.html (accessed 1 August 2012).

[8] Pilatowsky I, Romero RJ, Isaza CA, Gamboa SA, Sebastian PJ, Rivera W. Cogeneration Fuel Cell-Sorption Air Conditioning Systems. Springer; 2011.

[9] Oliveira SP, Rocha AC, Filho JT, Couto PRG. Uncertainty of Measurement by Monte-Carlo Simulation and Metrological Reliability in the Evaluation of Electric Variables of PEMFC and SOFC Fuel Cells. Measurement 2009, 42(10) 1497-1501.

[10] EURACHEM/CITAC Guide CG4. Quantifying Uncertainty in Analytical Measurement. EURACHEM/CITAC; 2012.

Chapter 3

Fractional Brownian Motions in Financial Models and Their Monte Carlo Simulation

Masaaki Kijima and Chun Ming Tam

Additional information is available at the end of the chapter

http://dx.doi.org/10.5772/53568

1. Introduction

Fractional Brownian motion (fBm) was first introduced within a Hilbert space framework by Kolmogorov [1], and further studied and coined the name 'fractional Brownian motion' in the 1968 paper by Mandelbrot and Van Ness [2]. It has been widely used in various scientific fields, most notability in hydrology as first suggested in [3]. It also plays an important role in communication technology by enriching the queuing theory in terms of simulating real network traffic.

In recent years, it has been steadily gaining attention in the area of finance, as it appears that the traditional stochastic volatility model driven by ordinary Brownian motion implies geometric time-decay of the volatility smile, which is much faster than in what we see in real market data (which has a hyperbolic decay). Such stylized feature is called the *volatility persistence*, see [4] for detail discussion about the statistical test for the existence of long-range memory (author has also proposed a robust extension of the R/S statistics for that particular purpose). Several modeling approaches have been suggested capturing this persistence in conditional variance either via a unit-root or long memory process. In order to keep the pricing-framework largely intact, it is more interesting to study the long memory process, and fBm has a particular good match due to its similarity to the ordinary Brownian motion and its Gaussian properties.

In this chapter, we will outline several approaches to simulate fractional Brownian motion with $H>1/2$, including the exact methods and approximate methods, where the Hurst Index H is a parameter used in literature to generalize Brownian motion into fractional Brownian motion, first made popular by Benoit Mandelbrot, which we will give a detail definition in Definition 1.1. We also provide a brief introduction of the truncated fractional Brownian motion (long-memory model in continuous time) as proposed in [5,6].

INTECH
open science | open minds

© 2013 The Author(s). Licensee InTech. This chapter is distributed under the terms of the Creative Commons Attribution License http://creativecommons.org/licenses/by/3.0), which permits unrestricted use, distribution, and reproduction in any medium, provided the original work is properly cited.

1.1. Financial motivation and backgrounds

Numerous empirical studies have pointed out that, in options markets, the implied volatility back-out from the Black-Scholes equation displays volatility skews or smiles; the smile effect, which is well known to practitioners, refers to the U-shape price distortion on the implied volatility surface.

In Hull and White [7] and Scott [8], they have proposed this feature of volatility to be captured by stochastic regime, known as the *stochastic volatility model:*

$$\begin{cases} \frac{dS(t)}{S(t)} = \mu(t,S_t)dt + \sigma(t)dB^1(t) \\ d(\ln\sigma(t)) = k(\theta - \ln(\sigma(t))dt + \nu dB^2(t)) \end{cases} \tag{1}$$

Here, S(t) is the asset price and σ(t) is the instantaneous volatility at time t, and $\{B^1(t),\ B^2(t)\}$ are ordinary standard Brownian motions. Hull and White [7] have shown that, the price of European option at time t of exercise date T is the conditional expectation of the Black Scholes option pricing formula where the constant volatility from the original formula is replaced by the quadratic average over the period $[t, T]$:

$$\sigma_{t,T}^2 = \frac{1}{T-t}\int_t^T \sigma^2(u)d(u) \tag{2}$$

Such models are successful at capturing the symmetric smile and skewness of the implied volatility by imposing relations between the driving Brownian motions in (1) (symmetric smile is explained by independence while skewness can be explained by linear correlation).

Due to the temporal aggregation effect evident in (2), however, the smile effect deteriorates along with time-to-maturity since the temporal aggregation gradually erases the conditional heteroskedasticity; in the standard stochastic volatility setup, this particular decay is much faster than what is observed in market data. The phenomenon of slow decaying volatility smile is known as the *volatility persistence* (long-range dependence of volatility process). This phenomenon is particularly poignant for high frequency data, for which the conditional variance process displays near unit-root behavior.

Furthermore, we emphasize the existence of such phenomenon collaborated by large quantities of researches, pointing out that the conditional volatility of asset returns also displays long range dependence: [9-12] have discussed extensively the evidence of such phenomenon in empirical data. Bayesian estimation in [13] of stochastic volatility models shows similar patterns of persistence.

Motivated by this inadequacy, long-memory process was deemed more appropriate enrichment for this purpose. Hence, fractional Brownian motion is a prime candidate among all long-memory process given its tractability and similarity with the ordinary Brownian motion: both the fractional Brownian motion and ordinary Brownian motion are self-similar with similar Gaussian structure. For discussions of estimation and evidence of the long-range dependence in conditional variance of asset returns, the reader is referred to [10] and section 3.1 of [14].

Now, we provide a formal definition of fractional Brownian motion (fBm). We adopt the definition as given in [15].

Definition 1.1 Let $H \in (0,1)$ be a constant. A fractional Brownian motion $\{B^H(t)\}_{t\geq 0}$ with Hurst index H is a continuous and centered Gaussian process with covariance function

$$\mathbb{E}[B^H(t)B^H(s)] = \frac{1}{2}(t^{2H} + s^{2H} - |t-s|^{2H}) \tag{3}$$

In particular, for $H = \frac{1}{2}$, it reduces to the ordinary Brownian motion with $\mathbb{E}[B^H(t)B^H(s)] = \min(t, s)$.

From equation (3) we have the following properties:

1. $B^H(0)=0$ and $E[B^H(t)]=0$, $\forall t \geq 0$.
2. $B^H(\cdot)$ has stationary increment: $B^H(t+s) - B^H(s)$ has the same distribution as $B^H(t)$ for any $s, t \geq 0$.
3. $B^H(\cdot)$ is self-similar, meaning that $B^H(Tt)$ has the same distribution law as $(T)^H B^H(t)$.
4. $B^H(\cdot)$ is a Gaussian process with the variance $E[B^H(t)^2] = t^{2H}$, $\forall t \geq 0$.
5. $B^H(\cdot)$ has continuous trajectories.

Fractional Brownian motions are divided into three very different categories: $H < \frac{1}{2}$, $H = \frac{1}{2}$, $H > \frac{1}{2}$. This is of particular importance because there is a deterministic difference between the case of $H < \frac{1}{2}$ and $H > \frac{1}{2}$, as we introduce the mathematical notion of long-range dependence.

Definition 1.2 (Long-range dependence) A stationary sequence $\{X_n\}_{n \in \mathrm{N}}$ exhibits long-range dependence if the autocovariance function $\gamma(n) := cov(X_k, X_{k+n})$ satisfies

$$\lim_{n \to \infty} \frac{\gamma(n)}{cn^{-\alpha}} = 1 \tag{4}$$

This can be written as $(n) \sim |n|^{-\alpha}$,

In this case, for some constants c and $\alpha \in (0,1)$, the dependence between X_k and X_{k+n} decays slowly as $n \to \infty$ and

$\sum_{n=1}^{\infty} \gamma(n) = \infty$

If we set $X_k = B^H(k) - B^H(k-1)$ and $X_{k+n} = B^H(k+n) - B^H(k+n-1)$ and apply equation (3), we have

$$\gamma_H(n) = \frac{1}{2}\left[(n+1)^{2H} + (n-1)^{2H} - 2n^{2H}\right]$$

where $\gamma_H(n) = cov\left(B^H(k) - B^H(k-1),\ B^H(k+n) - B^H(k+n-1)\right)$. In particular,

$$\lim_{n\to\infty} \frac{\gamma_H(n)}{H(2H-1)n^{2H-2}} = 1$$

Therefore, we conclude that: for $H > 1/2$, $\sum_{n=1}^{\infty} \gamma_H(n) = \infty$, and for $H < 1/2$, $\sum_{n=1}^{\infty} |\gamma_H(n)| < \infty$. Hence, only in the case of $H > 1/2$, fractional Brownian motions display long-memory dependence.

As pointed out in [16], large lags difference between $\gamma(\cdot)$ may be difficult to estimate in practice, so that models with long-range dependence are often formulated in terms of self-similarity. Self-similarity allows us to extrapolate across time scales and deduce long time behavior from short time behavior, which is more readily observed.

Because we are interested in capturing the long-memory phenomenon observed in financial markets, the rest of this chapter will only concern the case of $H > 1/2$.

1.2. Stochastic integral representation

In the original paper [2], Mandelbrot and van Ness represent the fBm in stochastic integral with respect to the ordinary Brownian motion:

$$B^H(t) = \frac{1}{\Gamma\left(H + \frac{1}{2}\right)}\left(\int_{-\infty}^{0}\left[(t-s)^{H-\frac{1}{2}} - (-s)^{H-\frac{1}{2}}\right]dB(s) + \int_0^t (t-s)^{H-\frac{1}{2}}\, dB(s)\right) \tag{5}$$

where $\Gamma(\cdot)$ is the gamma function.

They have also included an alternative representation of the fBm which is the basis of the model in [5,6]:

$$\hat{B}^H(t) = \int_0^t \frac{(t-s)^{H-\frac{1}{2}}}{\Gamma\left(H + \frac{1}{2}\right)} dB(s) \tag{6}$$

This version of fBm is 'truncated' in the sense that the integration from negative infinity to zero in equation (5) is truncated. We will refer to the model (6) as the 'truncated fractional Brownian motion' in the rest of this chapter. As pointed out in [2], the representation (6) was first proposed by Paul Lévy to define the fBm by the Riemann-Liouville fractional integral, while the original integral in equation (5) is the Weyl fractional integral.

The definition (6) of fBm is in general not asymptotically covariance-stationary, even though it retains self-similarity. For further technical discussion and rigorous definition of the truncated fractional Brownian motion, we refer the reader to [5].

Given the difference, if one employs analytical tools such as Malliavin calculus should be applied with care and note the differences between the two versions of fBM. [17] offers an in-depth discussion of the theoretical differences.

2. Fractional brownian motions in financial models

We first look at several examples that utilize the fractional Brownian motions in the realm of financial modeling.

2.1. Asset price model

In the previous section, we mention that the motivation of fBms in finance models is to capture the long-range dependence in the volatility process. However, it is worth discussing the possibility of applying it to the asset process itself.

In practice, it is considered that an asset process driven by fBm will result in arbitrage. The idea is that, since for $H \neq 1/2$, $B^H(t)$ is not a semimartingale in continuous time, the asset process described by $B^H(t)$ violates the NFLVR (no free lunch with vanishing risk), a weaker version of arbitrage, and thus doesn't admit an equivalent martingale measure according to Theorem 7.2 of [18]. Such findings and construction of arbitrage can be found in Rogers [19].

In contrast, Cheridito [20] has given multiple classes of trading strategies that allow various level of arbitrages (NFLVR, arbitrage in the classical sense and strong arbitrage) under fBm driven assets, and shown that the arbitrages are all eliminated if the inter-transaction time is not zero, i.e., the classes of strategies become arbitrage-free. Such assumption is reasonable in practice, given the physical limit and non-zero transaction cost. For more information on arbitrage theory and its generalization, the reader is referred to [18-20].

2.2. Stochastic volatility model

As we have mentioned in the introductory section, the main motivation for fBm is to capture the volatility persistence, the stylized feature observed in empirical data. There are several prominent models involving a volatility process with fBm. Here, we just outline several of them.

2.2.1. Long-memory continuous model

In [5, 6], Comte and Renault consider the following stochastic volatility model driven by fBm:

$$\begin{cases} \dfrac{dS(t)}{S(t)} = rdt + \sigma(t)dB(t) \\ \sigma(t) = \sigma_0 e^{x(t)} \\ dx(t) = -kx(t)dt + \nu d\hat{B}^H(t) \end{cases} \tag{7}$$

where the log-volatility term follows a fractional-OU process driven by the truncated fBm (6). The asset price process follows a geometric Brownian motion with volatility persistence.

Although Mandelbrot [2] deemed it as signifying the origin too heavily, the model (7) is easier and more robust than the ordinary fBms from the perspective of simulation. A simulation example is explored in Section 5.

2.2.2. *Affine fractional stochastic volatility model*

In [21], Comte et al. assume that the squared-volatility process follows

$$\sigma^2(t) = \theta + X^{(\alpha)}(t) \tag{8}$$

where $X^{(\alpha)}(t)$ is defined by the fractional integral:

$$X^{(\alpha)}(t) = \int_{-\infty}^{t} \frac{(t-s)^{H-1/2}}{\Gamma(H+1/2)} x(s)ds \tag{9}$$

Similar treatment of the fractional integration is outlined in [5]. The affine structure in (8) is similar to the one originally studied by Duffie et al. [22].

The affine structure is adopted for the extra tractability, and thus better suited for practical option pricing and hedging than the original idea (7). In fact, Comte et al. [21] have shown that this model can better depict the difference between the short and long memory properties in the resulting option prices.

2.2.3. *Martingale expansion*

Fukasawa [23] adopts and expands the asymptotic expansion technique first proposed by Yoshida [24] of European option prices around the Black-Scholes equation by means of perturbation technique and partial Malliavin calculus. It is shown that the logarithm of the asset process can be expressed as

$$\ln S_t = Z_t = rt - \frac{1}{2}\int_0^t g(Y_s^n)^2 ds + \int_0^t g(Y_s^n)\left[\theta dW_s' + \sqrt{1-\theta^2}dW_s\right]$$

with

$$Y_s^n = y + \epsilon_n W_s^H, \quad W_t^H = \int_0^t K_H(t,s)dW_s'$$

Here, r is the riskless rate, $\theta \in (-1,1)$, $y \in \mathbb{R}$ is a constant, (W, W') is a 2-dimensional standard (independent) Brownian motion, $\epsilon_n \to 0$ is a deterministic sequence for $n \to \infty$, and $g(\cdot)$ is the stochastic volatility process which is an adapted process for the minimal filtration.

Note that W_t^H is a fractional Brownian motion with Hurst index H, where $K_H^t(t, s)$ is the kernel of the stochastic integral representation over a finite interval of Brownian motion. According to [15], pertaining to our interest, for the case of $H > 1/2$, the kernel has the following expression:

$$K_H(t, s) = c_H s^{1/2-H} \int_s^t (u-s)^{H-3/2} u^{H-1/2} du$$

where

$$c_H = \left\{ \frac{H(2H-1)}{\beta(2-2H, H-1/2)} \right\}^{1/2}$$

Then, according to Corollary (2.6) of Fukasawa [23], the implied volatility can be expressed as

$$\sigma\left\{1 - \frac{\epsilon_n}{2} \rho_{13} d_2\right\} + o(\epsilon_n) = aT^{H-1/2}\log(K/S) + \sigma + bT^{H+1/2} + o(\epsilon_n) \tag{10}$$

where d_2 is the typical argument in the $N(d_2)$ of the Black-Scholes formula, and

$$\rho_{13} = \frac{2\theta g'(y) c_H' T^H}{g(y)}, \quad \sigma = g(y), \quad a = \frac{\theta g'(y) c_H'}{\sigma} \epsilon_n, \quad b = -a\left(r - \frac{\sigma^2}{2}\right) \tag{11}$$

Equation (10) can be seen as an approximation ϵ_n is the model parameter calibrated from market data. This shape of this approximation remains largely stationary, to check the accuracy of the approximation, we have no means but performing Monte Carlo simulation of fBm.

3. Simulation with exact methods

First, we look at methods that completely capture the covariance structure and true realization of the fractional Brownian motion (fBm) or fractional Gaussian noise (fGn). Any method described in this section has their starting point at the covariance matrix. The approximate scheme we see later is merely numerically close to the value of fBm (or fGn) or asymptotically coincides with it. The collection of algorithm in this section is not meant to be exhaustive. For more algorithm and discussion, see [25].

3.1. Hosking method

The Hosking method utilizes the well-known conditional distribution of the multivariate Gaussian distribution on a recursive scheme to generate samples based on the explicit covariance structure. This method generates a general stationary Gaussian process with given covariance structure, not limited to generating fBms.

More specifically, this algorithm generates an fGn sequence $\{Z_k\}$ and fBm is recovered by accumulative sum. That is, the distribution of Z_{n+1} conditioned on the previous realization $Z_n, \ldots Z_1, Z_0$ can be explicitly computed.

Denote $\gamma(k)$ as the autocovariance function of the zero-mean process:

$\gamma(k) := \mathbb{E}(X_n X_{n+k})$

where we assume for convenience that $\gamma(0)=1$. For $n, k=0,1,2\ldots$, we have the following recursive relationship for the $(n+1)\times(n+1)$ autocovariance matrix $\Gamma(n)=\{\gamma(i-j)\}_{i,j=0,\ldots,n}$:

$$\Gamma(n+1)=\begin{pmatrix} 1 & c(n)' \\ c(n) & \Gamma(n) \end{pmatrix} \tag{12}$$

$$=\begin{pmatrix} \Gamma(n) & F(n)c(n) \\ c(n)'F(n) & 1 \end{pmatrix} \tag{13}$$

where $c(n)$ is the $(n+1)$ -column vector with elements $c(n)_k=\gamma(k+1),\ k=0,\ \ldots,\ n$ and $F(n)=(1(i=n-j))_{i,j=0,\ldots,n}$ is the $(n+1)\times(n+1)$ 'mirrored' identity matrix

$$F(n)=\begin{pmatrix} 0 & \cdots & 0 & 1 \\ 0 & \cdots & 1 & 0 \\ \vdots & ⋰ & \vdots & \vdots \\ 1 & 0 & 0 & 0 \end{pmatrix}$$

Theorem 3.1 (Multivariate Gaussian distribution) Any multivariate Gaussian random vector z can be partitioned into z_1 and z_2 with the mean vector and covariance matrix with the corresponding partition:

$$\mu=\begin{bmatrix} \mu_1 \\ \mu_2 \end{bmatrix} \quad \mathbf{\Sigma}=\begin{bmatrix} \mathbf{\Sigma}_{11} & \mathbf{\Sigma}_{12} \\ \mathbf{\Sigma}_{21} & \mathbf{\Sigma}_{22} \end{bmatrix} \tag{14}$$

The distribution of z_1 conditioned on $z_2=a$ is a multivariate normal $(z_1 \mid z_2=a) \sim N(\bar{\mu}, \bar{\mathbf{\Sigma}})$ with

$$\bar{\mu}=\mu_1+\mathbf{\Sigma}_{12}\mathbf{\Sigma}_{22}^{-1}(a-\mu_2) \tag{15}$$

$$\bar{\mathbf{\Sigma}}=\mathbf{\Sigma}_{11}-\mathbf{\Sigma}_{12}\mathbf{\Sigma}_{22}^{-1}\mathbf{\Sigma}_{21} \tag{16}$$

If we substitute equation (12) into the partition in (14) with $\mathbf{\Sigma}_{11}=1,\ \mu=0$, we have the following expression for the conditional distribution:

$$\mu_{n+1} = \mathbb{E}(Z_{n+1} | Z_n, \ldots, Z_0) = c(n)'\Gamma(n)^{-1} \begin{pmatrix} Z_n \\ \vdots \\ Z_1 \\ Z_0 \end{pmatrix} \tag{17}$$

$$\sigma_{n+1}^2 = Var(Z_{n+1} \mid Z_n, \ldots, Z_0) = 1 - c(n)'\Gamma(n)^{-1}c(n) \tag{18}$$

With $Z_0 \sim N(0,1)$, subsequently X_{n+1} for $n = 0, 1, \ldots$ can be generated.

Taking the inverse of $\Gamma(\cdot)$ at every step is computational expensive; the algorithm proposed by Hosking [26] computes the inverse $\Gamma(n+1)^{-1}$ recursively. The next result is due to Dieker [25].

Proposition 3.1 (Hosking algorithm for simulating fGn) Define $d(n) = \Gamma(n)^{-1}c(n)$, and applying the blockwise method of inversion on equation (13):

$$\Gamma(n+1) = \frac{1}{\sigma_n^2} \begin{pmatrix} \sigma_n^2\Gamma(n)^{-1} + F(n)d(n)d(n)'F(n) & -F(n)d(n) \\ -d(n)'F(n) & 1 \end{pmatrix} \tag{19}$$

where σ_{n+1}^2 satisfies the recursion

$$\sigma_{n+1}^2 = \sigma_n^2 - \frac{(\gamma(n+1) - \tau_{n-1})^2}{\sigma_n^2} \tag{20}$$

with $\tau_n := d(n)'F(n)c(n) = c(n)'F(n)d(n)$. Also, the recursion for $d(n+1) = \Gamma(n+1)^{-1}c(n+1)$ is obtained as

$$d(n+1) = \begin{pmatrix} d(n) - \phi_n F(n)d(n) \\ \phi_n \end{pmatrix}$$

where

$$\phi_n = \frac{\gamma(n+2) - \tau_n}{\sigma_n^2}$$

With $\mu_1 = \gamma(1)Z_0$, $\sigma_1^2 = 1 - \gamma(1)^2$, $\tau_0 = \gamma(1)^2$, μ_{n+1}, σ_{n+1}^2, τ_{n+1} can be readily computed, and fractional Brownian motion is recovered by the cumulative summation.

This algorithm is also applicable to non-stationary processes (see [27] for details). Even though this algorithm is very simple and easy to understand and sample paths can be generated on-the-fly, the complexity of this algorithm is of $O(N^2)$ and computational (as well as memory) expense of this algorithm grows at a prohibitive speed.

3.2. Cholesky method

Given that we are dealing with the covariance structure in matrix form, it is natural to go with the Cholesky decomposition: decomposing the covariance matrix into the product of a lower triangular matrix and its conjugate-transpose $\Gamma(n)=L(n)L(n)^*$. If the covariance matrix is proven to be positive-definite (the situation will be addressed in the next subsection), $L(n)$ will have real entries and $\Gamma(n)=L(n)L(n)'$.

Suppose that in matrix form the $(n+1)\times(n+1)$ product is given by

$$\begin{pmatrix} \gamma(0) & \gamma(1) & \gamma(2) & \cdots & \gamma(n) \\ \gamma(1) & \gamma(0) & \gamma(1) & \cdots & \gamma(n-1) \\ \gamma(2) & \gamma(1) & \gamma(0) & \cdots & \gamma(n-2) \\ \vdots & \vdots & \vdots & \ddots & \vdots \\ \gamma(n) & \gamma(n-1) & \gamma(n-2) & \cdots & \gamma(0) \end{pmatrix} = \begin{pmatrix} l_{00} & 0 & 0 & \cdots & 0 \\ l_{10} & l_{11} & 0 & \cdots & 0 \\ l_{20} & l_{21} & l_{22} & \ddots & \vdots \\ \vdots & \vdots & \vdots & \ddots & 0 \\ l_{n0} & l_{n1} & l_{n2} & \cdots & l_{nn} \end{pmatrix} \times \begin{pmatrix} l_{00} & l_{10} & l_{20} & \cdots & l_{n0} \\ 0 & l_{11} & l_{21} & \cdots & l_{n1} \\ 0 & 0 & l_{22} & \cdots & l_{n2} \\ \vdots & \vdots & \vdots & \ddots & \vdots \\ 0 & 0 & 0 & 0 & l_{nn} \end{pmatrix}$$

It is easy to see that $l_{00}^2=\gamma(0)$ and that $l_{10}l_{00}=\gamma(1)$ and $l_{10}^2+l_{11}^2=\gamma(0)$ on $i=1$ (2nd row). For $i\geq 1$, the entries of the lower triangular matrix can be determined by

$$l_{i,0}=\frac{\gamma(i)}{l_{0,0}}$$

$$l_{i,j}=\frac{1}{l_{j,j}}\left(\gamma(i-j)-\sum_{k=0}^{j-1} l_{i,k}l_{j,k}\right),\quad 0<j\leq n$$

$$l_{i,i}^2=\gamma(0)-\sum_{k=0}^{i-1} l_{i,k}^2$$

Given independent, identically distributed (i.i.d.) standard normal random variables $(V_i)_{i=0,\ldots,n+1}$, the fGn sequence is generated by

$$Z_{n+1}=\sum_{k=0}^{n+1} l_{n+1,k}V_k$$

Or in matrix form, we have $Z(n)=L(n)V(n)$. If $\Gamma(n)$ is assumed to be positive-definite, the non-negativity of $l_{i,i}^2$ is guaranteed and $L(n)$ is guaranteed to be real. The covariance structure of the process is captured, since

$$Cov(Z(n))=Cov(L(n)V(n))=L(n)Cov(V(n))L(n)'=L(n)L(n)'=\Gamma(n) \tag{21}$$

Even though the Cholesky method is easy to understand and implement, the computation time is $O(N^3)$, which renders this scheme extremely uneconomical in practice. To resolve this problem, we will proceed to another exact method. The idea is similar to retain the same relation as equation (21), but with a different decomposition.

3.3. Fast fourier transform method

As we have seen from the last section, using the Cholesky decomposition seems to be the most straightforward idea to simulate Gaussian process with a given covariance structure;

but, it also is the most rudimentary and thus slow. In order to improve upon the speed, the idea of utilizing the fast Fourier transform (FFT) was proposed by Davies and Harte [28] and further generalized by Dietrich and Newsam [29].

Similar to the idea before, this method tries to find a decomposition of the covariance matrix as $\Gamma = GG'$ and the sample is generated by $y = Gx$ for given standard normal random variable x. Then, on the given covariance structure, we have

$$Cov(y) = Cov(Gx) = G\,Cov(x)G' = GG' = \Gamma$$

The idea is to 'embed' the original covariance matrix a circulant matrix in order to carry out the FFT. Before we outline the idea, we shall give out some detail of the linkage between Fourier transform and the circulant matrix.

Definition 3.1 (Circulant matrix) Circulant matrix is a special case of the Toeplitz matrix where each row vector is shifted to the right (the last element is shifted back to the beginning of the row). In matrix form, an n-by-n circulant matrix can be written as

$$C = \begin{pmatrix} c_0 & c_{n-1} & c_{n-2} & \cdots & c_1 \\ c_1 & c_0 & c_{n-1} & \cdots & c_2 \\ c_2 & c_1 & c_0 & \cdots & c_3 \\ \vdots & \vdots & \vdots & \ddots & \vdots \\ c_{n-1} & c_{n-2} & \cdots & c_1 & c_0 \end{pmatrix}$$

Remark: As one can see, the first row/column completely describes the whole matrix, and it can be put more succinctly in the following form:

$$c_{j,k} = c_{j-k\,(mod\;n)}, \quad \text{where } 0 \le j,\ k \le n-1$$

Note that the indices range from 0 to n-1 instead of the usual convention that ranges from 1 to n.

Definition 3.2 (Generating circulant matrix) We define an n-by-n *generating circulant matrix* by

$$G = \begin{pmatrix} 0 & 0 & 0 & \cdots & 0 & 1 \\ 1 & 0 & 0 & \cdots & 0 & 0 \\ 0 & 1 & 0 & \cdots & 0 & 0 \\ 0 & 0 & 1 & \cdots & 0 & 0 \\ \vdots & \vdots & \vdots & \ddots & \vdots & \vdots \\ 0 & 0 & 0 & 0 & 1 & 0 \end{pmatrix}$$

By a simple calculation, we can see that the 'square' of the generating circulant matrix is given by

$$G^2=\begin{pmatrix} 0 & 0 & 0 & \cdots & 1 & 0 \\ 0 & 0 & 0 & \cdots & 0 & 1 \\ 1 & 0 & 0 & \cdots & 0 & 0 \\ 0 & 1 & 0 & \cdots & 0 & 0 \\ \vdots & \vdots & \vdots & \ddots & \vdots & \vdots \\ 0 & 0 & 0 & 1 & 0 & 0 \end{pmatrix}$$

From the point of view of row and column operation of the matrix, this can be seen as each row of the matrix being shifted one element forward, where the bumped element is replaced to the end of the row (it can also be thought of as the whole row is shifted down and the bumped row is placed back on top, but this is irrelevant to our interest). Arbitrary power can be deduced accordingly; this operation has a cycle of n iterations.

The generating circulant matrix is served as our building block. Looking back at our original circulant matrix, we have a corresponding polynomial

$$p(x)=c_0+c_1x+c_2x^2+\cdots+c_{n-1}x^{n-1} \tag{22}$$

Then, the original circulant matrix C can be expressed as

$$C=\begin{pmatrix} c_0 & c_{n-1} & c_{n-2} & \cdots & c_2 & c_1 \\ c_1 & c_0 & c_{n-1} & \cdots & c_3 & c_2 \\ c_2 & c_1 & c_0 & \cdots & \vdots & c_3 \\ c_3 & c_2 & c_1 & \cdots & \vdots & \vdots \\ \vdots & \vdots & \vdots & \ddots & \vdots & c_{n-1} \\ c_{n-1} & c_{n-2} & c_{n-3} & \cdots & c_1 & c_0 \end{pmatrix}$$

$$C=p(G)=c_0 1+c_1G+c_2G^2+\cdots+c_{n-1}G^{n-1} \tag{23}$$

This can be verified by doing the row-operation of arbitrary power on G as shown above. It can be shown that each operation is one-element sub-diagonal compared to the previous power.

Definition 3.3 (Fourier matrix) The Fourier matrix is introduced as

$$F=\begin{pmatrix} 1 & 1 & 1 & \cdots & 1 & 1 \\ 1 & \xi & \xi^2 & \cdots & \xi^{n-2} & \xi^{n-1} \\ 1 & \xi^2 & \xi^{2\times 2} & \cdots & \vdots & \xi^{n-2} \\ 1 & \xi^3 & \xi^{3\times 2} & \cdots & \vdots & \vdots \\ \vdots & \vdots & \vdots & \ddots & \vdots & \xi^2 \\ 1 & \xi^{n-1} & \xi^{n-2} & \cdots & \xi^2 & \xi \end{pmatrix}$$

Here, we define the n-th unity root as $\omega = e^{2\pi i \frac{1}{n}}$, and $\xi = \bar{\omega} = e^{-2\pi i \frac{1}{n}}$ is the conjugate of the unity root.

The Fourier matrix can be defined using the positive argument ω instead of ξ. Also, as we will see later, some definition includes the normalizing scalar $\frac{1}{\sqrt{n}}$ (or $\frac{1}{n}$). This is analogous to the continuous counterpart of the Fourier integral definition $F(f) = \int_{-\infty}^{\infty} x(t) e^{-2\pi i f t} dt$ or $\int_{-\infty}^{\infty} x(t) e^{2\pi i f t} dt$, as long as the duality is uphold by the opposite sign in the exponential power in the inverse Fourier transform. This duality will be restated in the diagonalization representation of the circulant matrix later.

Proposition 3.2 If $\frac{1}{\sqrt{n}}$ normalizes the Fourier matrix, then $\frac{1}{\sqrt{n}} F$ is a unitary matrix. It is symmetric (i.e., $F^T = F$), and the inverse of the Fourier matrix is given by

$$F^{-1} = \left(\frac{\sqrt{n}}{\sqrt{n}} F^{-1} \right) = \frac{1}{\sqrt{n}} \left(\frac{1}{\sqrt{n}} F \right)^{-1} = \frac{1}{\sqrt{n}} \left(\frac{1}{\sqrt{n}} \bar{F}^T \right) = \frac{1}{n} \bar{F} = \frac{1}{n} \begin{pmatrix} 1 & 1 & 1 & \cdots & 1 & 1 \\ 1 & \omega & \omega^2 & \cdots & \omega^{n-2} & \omega^{n-1} \\ 1 & \omega^2 & \omega^{2\times 2} & \cdots & \vdots & \omega^{n-2} \\ 1 & \omega^3 & \omega^{3\times 2} & \cdots & \vdots & \vdots \\ \vdots & \vdots & \vdots & \ddots & \vdots & \omega^2 \\ 1 & \omega^{n-1} & \omega^{n-2} & \cdots & \omega^2 & \omega \end{pmatrix}$$

Proposition 3.3 If we multiply the Fourier matrix with the generating circulant matrix, we have

$$FG = \begin{pmatrix} 1 & 1 & 1 & \cdots & 1 & 1 \\ 1 & \xi & \xi^2 & \cdots & \xi^{n-2} & \xi^{n-1} \\ 1 & \xi^2 & \xi^{2\times 2} & \cdots & \vdots & \xi^{n-2} \\ 1 & \xi^3 & \xi^{3\times 2} & \ddots & \vdots & \vdots \\ \vdots & \vdots & \vdots & \ddots & \vdots & \xi^2 \\ 1 & \xi^{n-1} & \xi^{n-2} & \cdots & \xi^2 & \xi \end{pmatrix} \begin{pmatrix} 0 & 0 & 0 & \cdots & 0 & 1 \\ 1 & 0 & 0 & \cdots & 0 & 0 \\ 0 & 1 & 0 & \cdots & \vdots & 0 \\ 0 & 0 & 1 & \ddots & \vdots & \vdots \\ \vdots & \vdots & \vdots & \ddots & \vdots & 0 \\ 0 & 0 & 0 & \cdots & 1 & 0 \end{pmatrix} = \begin{pmatrix} 1 & 1 & \cdots & 1 & 1 & 1 \\ \xi & \xi^2 & \cdots & \xi^{n-2} & \xi^{n-1} & 1 \\ \xi^2 & \xi^{2\times 2} & \cdots & \vdots & \xi^{n-2} & 1 \\ \xi^3 & \xi^{3\times 2} & \ddots & \vdots & \vdots & 1 \\ \vdots & \vdots & \ddots & \vdots & \xi^2 & 1 \\ \xi^{n-1} & \xi^{n-2} & \cdots & \xi^2 & \xi & 1 \end{pmatrix}$$

This is the same as shifting (rotating) the first column to the back of the matrix, and is also equivalent to multiplying the first row with ξ^0, the 2nd row with ξ^1 , etc. In matrix operation, it can be seen as

$$FG = \begin{pmatrix} \xi^0 & 0 & 0 & \cdots & 0 & 0 \\ 0 & \xi^1 & 0 & \cdots & 0 & 0 \\ 0 & 0 & \xi^2 & \cdots & \vdots & 0 \\ 0 & 0 & 0 & \ddots & \vdots & \vdots \\ \vdots & \vdots & \vdots & \ddots & \ddots & 0 \\ 0 & 0 & 0 & \cdots & 0 & \xi^{n-1} \end{pmatrix} \begin{pmatrix} 1 & 1 & 1 & \cdots & 1 & 1 \\ 1 & \xi & \xi^2 & \cdots & \xi^{n-2} & \xi^{n-1} \\ 1 & \xi^2 & \xi^{2\times 2} & \cdots & \vdots & \xi^{n-2} \\ 1 & \xi^3 & \xi^{3\times 2} & \ddots & \vdots & \vdots \\ \vdots & \vdots & \vdots & \ddots & \vdots & \xi^2 \\ 1 & \xi^{n-1} & \xi^{n-2} & \cdots & \xi^2 & \xi \end{pmatrix} = \Lambda F$$

where Λ is the diagonal matrix with the k-th diagonal $\Lambda_k = \xi^k, \; for \; 0 \le k \le n-1$. It follows that

$$FGF^{-1}=\Lambda \tag{24}$$

That is, the Fourier matrix diagonalizes the generating circulant matrix with eigenvalues $\{\xi^k\}_{0\le k\le n-1}$.

Theorem 3.2 The circulant matrix is decomposable by the Fourier matrix, i.e. $C=F^{-1}\Lambda F$ with eigenvalue matrix $\Lambda=\{p(\xi^k)\}_{k=0\ldots n-1}$. Also, with equation (23), the diagonalization of C can be written as

$$FCF^{(-1)}=F(c_0 1+c_1 G+c_2 G^2+\cdots+c_{(n-1)}G^{n-1})F^{-1}$$

$$=c_0 1+c_1(FGF^{-1})+c_2(FGF^{-1})^2+\cdots+c_{n-1}(FGF^{-1})^{n-1}$$

$$=\begin{pmatrix} p(1) & 0 & 0 & \cdots & 0 & 0 \\ 0 & p(\xi) & 0 & \cdots & 0 & 0 \\ 0 & 0 & p(\xi^2) & \cdots & \vdots & 0 \\ 0 & 0 & 0 & \ddots & \vdots & \vdots \\ \vdots & \vdots & \vdots & \ddots & \vdots & 0 \\ 0 & 0 & 0 & \cdots & 0 & p(\xi^{n-1}) \end{pmatrix}$$

Note that $(FGF^{-1})^2=FGF^{-1}FGF^{-1}=FGGF^{-1}=FG^2F^{-1}$. The other powers can be deduced iteratively.

This theorem gives us the fundamental theoretical framework to build up the FFT exact simulation of fBms. The basic idea of the simulation is to embed the covariance matrix into a bigger circulant matrix to carry out the discrete Fourier transform as outlined above (with technique of FFT). Such technique is called Circulant Embedding Method (CEM), and is outlined in Dietrich and Newsam [29] and Perrin et al. [30].

Suppose that we need sample size of N (N should be a power of 2, i.e. $N=2^g$ for some $g\in\mathbb{N}$ for the sake of convenience when facilitating FFT). Generate the N-by-N covariance matrix Γ with entries $\Gamma_{j,k}=\gamma(|j-k|)$, where γ is the covariance function given in the definition of fractional Gaussian noise (fGn), by

$$\Gamma=\begin{pmatrix} \gamma(0) & \gamma(1) & \cdots & \gamma(N-1) \\ \gamma(1) & \gamma(0) & \cdots & \gamma(N-2) \\ \vdots & \vdots & \ddots & \vdots \\ \gamma(N-1) & \gamma(N-2) & \cdots & \gamma(0) \end{pmatrix}$$

The technique to simulate fGn with FFT is called the Circulant Embedding Method (CEM), generalized by Davies and Harte [28], and consists of embedding this covariance matrix into a bigger M-by-M (with $M = 2N$) circulant covariance matrix C such as

$$C=\begin{pmatrix} \gamma(0) & \gamma(1) & \cdots & \gamma(N-1) & 0 & \gamma(N-1) & \gamma(N-2) & \cdots & \gamma(2) & \gamma(1) \\ \gamma(1) & \gamma(0) & \cdots & \gamma(N-2) & \gamma(N-1) & 0 & \gamma(N-1) & \cdots & \gamma(3) & \gamma(2) \\ \vdots & \vdots & \ddots & \vdots & \vdots & \vdots & \vdots & \ddots & \vdots & \vdots \\ \gamma(N-1) & \gamma(N-2) & \cdots & \gamma(0) & \gamma(1) & \gamma(2) & \gamma(3) & \cdots & \gamma(N-1) & 0 \\ 0 & \gamma(N-1) & \cdots & \gamma(1) & \gamma(0) & \gamma(1) & \gamma(2) & \cdots & \gamma(N-2) & \gamma(N-1) \\ \gamma(N-1) & 0 & \cdots & \gamma(2) & \gamma(1) & \gamma(0) & \gamma(1) & \cdots & \gamma(N-3) & \gamma(N-2) \\ \vdots & \vdots & \ddots & \vdots & \vdots & \vdots & \vdots & \ddots & \vdots & \vdots \\ \gamma(1) & \gamma(2) & \cdots & 0 & \gamma(N-1) & \gamma(N-2) & \gamma(N-3) & \cdots & \gamma(1) & \gamma(0) \end{pmatrix}$$

where the covariance matrix is embedded on the top left hand corner. It is sufficient to point out that

$$C_{0,k}=\begin{cases}\gamma(k), & k=0,\ \ldots,\ N-1\\ \gamma(2N-k), & k=N+2,\ \ldots,\ 2N-1\end{cases}$$

Remark: As Perrin et al. [30] have pointed out, the size M can be $M\geq 2(N-1)$, and the case $M=2(N-1)$ is minimal embedding. For any other choice of M, the choice of $C_{0,N},\ \ldots,\ C_{0,M-N+1}$ is arbitrary and can be conveniently chosen as long as the symmetry of the matrix is upheld; more zeros can be padded if M is bigger to make C circulant. For the rest of the chapter, we will concern ourselves with the case $M = 2N$.

From Theorem 3.2, we know that, given any circulant matrix, it can be decomposed as $C=Q\Lambda Q^*$, where

$$(Q)_{j,k}=\frac{1}{\sqrt{2N}}\exp\left(-2\pi i\frac{jk}{2N}\right),\ \ for\ j,\ k=0,\ \ldots,\ 2N-1 \tag{25}$$

The matrix Λ is the diagonal matrix with eigenvalues

$$\lambda_k=\sum_{j=0}^{2N-1}c_{0,j}\exp\left(2\pi i\frac{jk}{2N}\right),\ \ for\ j,\ k=0,\ \ldots,\ 2N-1 \tag{26}$$

This differs slightly from the previous definition, but similar to the continuous counterpart; the sign of the exponential power in the Fourier transform is just conventional difference. The approach is identical as long as the duality is maintained. That is, if written in the form of $C=Q\Lambda Q^*$, the sign of the exponential power of the component in Q and Λ should be opposite. In the case of the previous theorem where $C=F^{-1}\Lambda F$, it is easy to check that F^{-1} and $\Lambda(\xi)$ indeed have the opposite sign in the exponential power.

It should be noted that C is not guaranteed to be positive-definite. Davies and Harte [28] suggest setting zero every negative value that may appear in Λ. In Perrin et al. [30], they prove that the circulant covariance matrix for fGn is always non-negative definite, so the approach is feasible without any modification. The reader is referred to Dietrich and Newsam [29] and Wood and Chan [31] for more detail on dealing with this issue.

Assuming that C is positive definite and symmetric, the eigenvalues are positive and real. The 'square root' of C is readily formed, $S = Q\Lambda^{1/2}Q^{*}$, where $\Lambda^{1/2}$ is the diagonal matrix with eigenvalues 1, $\sqrt{\lambda_1}$, …, $\sqrt{\lambda_{2N-1}}$. It is easy to check that $SS^{*} = SS' = C$. So, S has the desired properties we look for.

Theorem 3.3 (Simulation of fGn with FFT) The simulation of the sample path of fGn, we are going to simulate $y = SV$, consists of the following steps:

1. Compute the eigenvalues $\{\lambda_k\}_{k=0,\ldots,2N-1}$ from equation (26) by means of FFT. This will reduce the computational time from $O(N^2)$ to $O(NlogN)$.
2. Calculate $W = Q^{*}V$.
3. Generate two standard normal random variables $W_0 = V_0^{(1)}$ and $W_N = V_N^{(1)}$
4. For $1 \le j < N$, generate two standard normal random variables $V_j^{(1)}$ and $V_j^{(2)}$ and let

$$W_j = \frac{1}{\sqrt{2}}\left(V_j^{(1)} + i\, V_j^{(2)} \right)$$

$$W_{2N-j} = \frac{1}{\sqrt{2}}\left(V_j^{(1)} - i\, V_j^{(2)} \right)$$

1. Compute $Z = Q\Lambda^{1/2}W$. This can be seen as another Fourier transform of the vector $\Lambda^{1/2}W$:
2. $Z_k = \frac{1}{\sqrt{2N}} \sum_{j=0}^{2N-1} \sqrt{\lambda_j} W_j \exp\left(-2\pi i \frac{jk}{2N} \right)$
3. It is identical to carry out FFT on the following sequence:

$$w_j = \begin{cases} \sqrt{\frac{\lambda_0}{2N}} V_0^{(1)} & j = 0; \\ \sqrt{\frac{\lambda_j}{4N}} \left(V_j^{(1)} + iV_j^{(2)} \right) & j = 1, \ldots, N-1; \\ \sqrt{\frac{\lambda_N}{2N}} V_N^{(1)} & j = N; \\ \sqrt{\frac{\lambda_j}{4N}} \left(V_{2N-j}^{(1)} - iV_{2N-j}^{(2)} \right) & j = N+1, \ldots, 2N-1; \end{cases}$$

Due to the symmetric nature of the sequence, the Fourier sum of $\{w_j\} = \{Z_k\}_{k=0}^{2N-1}$ is real. The first N samples have the desired covariance structure. But, since the 2nd half of samples (N… $2N$-1) are not independent of the first N samples, this sample cannot be used.

1. Recover fBm from the recursive relationship:
2. $B^H(0) = 0;\ B^H(i) = B^H(i-1) + Z_{i-1}$ *for* $1 \le i \le N$

4. Approximate methods

As we have seen in the previous section, the exact methods all take on the covariance structure matrix as starting point and try to reproduce the covariance structure by different decomposition. That can be time and resource consuming, so rather it is preferable to have approximation of the fractional Brownian motion that permits robust simulation.

In this section, we will start with the Mandelbrot representation due to historical reason and move onto several other methods that provide us with better understanding of the process and increasing robustness.

4.1. Mandelbrot representation

Recalling from Section 2.3, fractional Brownian motion permits a stochastic integral representation. To approximate equation (5), it is natural to truncate the lower limit from negative infinity to some point, say at $-b$:

$$\widetilde{B}^H(n)=C_H\left(\sum_{k=-b}^{0}\left[(n-k)^{H-\frac{1}{2}}-(-k)^{H-\frac{1}{2}}\right]B_1(k)+\sum_{k=0}^{n}(n-k)^{H-\frac{1}{2}}B_2(k)\right) \tag{27}$$

Note that the C_H is not the same constant term as in equation (5), because one has to re-calculate the normalizing factor due to the truncation. As pointed out in [25], the recommended choice of b is $N^{3/2}$. Even though this is a straightforward way to generate fractional Brownian motion, it is rather inefficient. It is included in this section for the sake of completeness.

4.2. Euler hypergeometric integral

fBm permits the stochastic integral form involving the Euler hypergeometric integral:

$$B^H(t)=\int_0^t K_H(t,s)dB(s) \tag{28}$$

where $B(s)$ is the standard Brownian motion and

$$K_H(t,s)=\frac{(t-s)^{H-\frac{1}{2}}}{\Gamma\left(H+\frac{1}{2}\right)}F_{2,1}\left(H-\frac{1}{2};\frac{1}{2}-H;H+\frac{1}{2};1-\frac{t}{s}\right) \tag{29}$$

is the hypergeometric function, which can be readily computed by most mathematical packages. By discretizing (28), at each time index t_j, we have

$$B^H(t_j)=\frac{n}{T}\sum_{i=0}^{j-1}\left(\int_{t_i}^{t_{i+1}}K_H(t_j,s)ds\right)\delta B_i \tag{30}$$

where $\delta B_i = \sqrt{\frac{T}{n}}\Delta B_i$ and ΔB_i is drawn according to the standard normal distribution. This means that $\{\delta B_i\}_{i=1\ldots n}$ is the increments of a scaled Brownian motion on $[0, T]$ with quadratic variation T. The inner integral can be computed by the Gaussian quadrature efficiently.

4.3. Construction by correlated random walk

This particular algorithm proposed in [32] of constructing fBm relies on the process of correlated random walks and summation over generated paths. This is similar to the generation of ordinary Brownian method through summation of the sample paths of normal random walk, which is related to the central limit theorem.

Definition 4.1 (Correlated Random Walk) For any $p \in [0,1]$, denote X_n^p as the correlated random walk with persistence index p. It consists of a jump on each time-step with jump size of either +1 or -1 such that:

- $X_0^p = 0,\ P(X_1^p = -1) = \frac{1}{2},\ P(X_1^p = +1) = \frac{1}{2}$
- $\forall n \geq 1,\ \epsilon_n^p \equiv X_n^p - X_{n-1}^p$ which equals either +1 or -1
- $\forall n \geq 1,\ P(\epsilon_{n+1}^p = \epsilon_n^p \mid \sigma(X_k^p,\ 0 \leq k \leq n)) = p$

Theorem 4.1 For any $m \geq 1,\ n \geq 0$, we have

$$\mathbb{E}[\epsilon_m^p \epsilon_{m+n}^p] = (2p-1)^n \tag{31}$$

In order to add additional randomness into the correlated random walks, we replace the constant persistence index p with a random variable μ, and we denote the resulting correlated random walk as X_n^μ. Or, to put it more formally, denote by P^p the law of X^p for a given persistence index p. Now, consider a probability measure μ on $[0,1]$, which we call the corresponding probability law P^μ, the annealed law of the correlated walk associated to μ. Note that $P^\mu := \int_0^1 P^p d\mu(p)$.

Proposition 4.1 For all $m \geq 1,\ \ n \geq 0$, we have

$$\mathbb{E}[\epsilon_m^\mu \epsilon_{m+m}^\mu] = \int_0^1 (2p-1)^n d\mu(p) \tag{32}$$

The next result is due to Enriquez [32]. The proof is based on Lemma 5.1 of Taqqu [33].

Theorem 4.2 For $\frac{1}{2}<H<1$, denote by μ^H the probability on $\left[\frac{1}{2}, 1\right]$ with density $(1-H)2^{3-2H}(1-p)^{1-2H}$. Let $(X^{\mu^H,i})_{i\geq 1}$ be a sequence of independent processes with probability law P^{μ^H}. Then,

$$\mathsf{L}^D \lim_{N\to\infty} \mathsf{L}\lim_{N\to\infty} c_H \frac{X^{\mu^H,1}_{[Nt]} + \cdots + X^{\mu^H,M}_{[Nt]}}{N^H\sqrt{M}} = B_H(t) \tag{33}$$

where $c_H = \sqrt{\frac{H(2H-1)}{\Gamma(3-2H)}}$, L stands for the convergence in law, and L^D means the convergence in the sense of weak convergence in the Skorohod topology on $D[0,1]$, the space of cadlag functions on $[0,1]$. Here, $[\cdot]$ is the floor function and rounds the argument to the closest integer, M is the number of trajectories of correlated random walks and N is number of time steps.

Remark: For H=1/2, there is a similar expression (see [32]). The order of limit in equation (33) is important, because if reversed, the sum would result in 0. Theorem 4.2 is mostly for theoretical construction.

In [32], the above theorem is further simplified from double summations into a single summation by applying Berry-Essen bound: As long as $M(N)$ is of order $O(N^{2-2H})$,

$$\mathsf{L}^D \lim_{N\to\infty} c_H \frac{X^{\mu^H,1}_{[Nt]} + \cdots + X^{\mu^H,M(N)}_{[Nt]}}{N^H\sqrt{M(N)}} = B_H(t) \tag{34}$$

In practice, any probability measure with moment equivalent to $\frac{1}{n^{2-2H}L(n)}$, where L is a slowly varying function, will be used. This could be shown by Karamata's theorem, for which further elaboration is found in [33]. In [32], three families of equivalent measures are provided, and specifically the 2nd family of the measures $(\mu'_{H,k})_{k>0}$ is most appropriate for simulation purpose: For $H>\frac{1}{2}$, $\mu'_{H,k}$ has the density of $1-\frac{\left(1-U^{\frac{1}{k}}\right)^{\frac{1}{2-2H}}}{2}$ with the corresponding normalizing factor $c'_{H,k}=\frac{c_H}{\sqrt{k}}$. U is a standard uniform random variable. The error given by the Berry-Essen bound for $H>\frac{1}{2}$ is given by

$$0.65 \times D_H N^{1-H} / \sqrt{kM} \tag{35}$$

where $D_H = \sqrt{\frac{6(2H-1)}{(H+1)(2H+1)}}$. Here, k serves as a control variable of order $k(N)=o(N)$, and the error term contains $\frac{1}{\sqrt{k}}$ which can be seen as a way to restrict error with the price of distortion of the covariance relation in X_N, though it is advisable to keep $k \le 1$. For more discussion on the choice of *k*, we refer to Section 4 of [32].

Theorem 4.3 (Simulation of fBm with correlated random walk) Simulating fBm with correlated random walk for the case of $H > \frac{1}{2}$ consists of the following steps:

1. Calculate *M*(*N*) by the tolerable error level from equation (35). Calculate $\lfloor NT \rfloor$, where $\lfloor\,\rfloor$ is the floor function, and create time-index $\{t_i\} : \{1, 2, \ldots, \lfloor NT \rfloor\}$.

2. Simulate M independent copies of $\left\{\mu_{H,k}^j\right\}_{j=1\cdots M} = 1 - \frac{\left(1 - U^{\frac{1}{k}}\right)^{\frac{1}{2-2H}}}{2}$ for M trajectories.

3. Simulate *M* copies of correlated random walks:

   - If $t_i = 1$, $\epsilon_1^j = 2 * Bernoulli\left(\frac{1}{2}\right) - 1$, $X_1^j = \epsilon_1^j$
   - If $t_i > 1$, $\epsilon_{t_j}^j = \epsilon_{t_{j-1}}^j * \left(2 * Bernoulli\left(\mu_{H,k}^j\right) - 1\right)$, $X_{t_j}^j = X_{t_{j-1}}^j + \epsilon_{t_j}^j$

4. At each t_j, calculate

   - $$B^H(t_j) = c_H' \frac{X_{\lfloor Nt_j \rfloor}^{\mu^{H,1}} + \cdots + X_{\lfloor Nt_j \rfloor}^{\mu^{H,M}}}{N^H \sqrt{M}}$$

Remark: For any given time-horizon *T*, it is easier to simulate the path of $B^H(1)$ with given resolution *N* and scale it to arrive at $B^H(T) = T^H B^H(1)$.

This algorithm is interesting from a theoretical point of view, since it gives us a construction of fractional Brownian motion reflecting its ordinary Brownian motion counterpart with the help of central limit theorem. But, in practice, it might not be fast enough for simulation purpose that requires large number of simulated paths.

4.4. Conditional random midpoint displacement

This algorithm is put forth by Norros et al. [34] and uses the similar approach to compute the conditional distribution of the fractional Gaussian noises as we have seen in the Hosking algorithm in Section 3.1. The difference is that this algorithm does not completely capture the covariance of all the sample points, instead it chooses certain number of points of the generated samples and uses a different ordering to do conditioning on (recall that, in the Hosking method, the conditioning is done by chronological order).

Again we are interested in the stationary fractional Gaussian noises and will back out the fractional Brownian motion on the time interval $[0,1]$, which can be scaled back according to self-similarity relationship. We will first outline the idea of bisection method, which will be expanded into the conditional mid-point replacement scheme later on.

4.4.1. Bisection scheme and basic algorithm

In this section we adopt the notation in Norros et al. [34]: $Z(t)$ is the fractional Brownian motion, and $X_{i,j}$ is the fractional Gaussian noise of a certain interval j in a given level i.

The idea is to simulate $Z(t)$ on the interval $[0,1]$. First, given $Z(0)=0$ and $Z(1)$ with the standard normal distribution of $N(0,1)$, we compute the conditional distribution of $\{Z(\frac{1}{2}) \mid Z(0), Z(1)\} \sim N(\frac{1}{2}Z(1), 2^{-2H} - \frac{1}{4})$. The bisection involves the indices i and j, where i indicates the 'level' and j for the 'position. Let

$X_{i,j} = Z(j \cdot 2^{-i}) - Z((j-1) \cdot 2^{-i})$, for $i=0,1,2, \ldots, \; j=1, \ldots 2^i$

It is easy to see that, at any given level i, the interval [0,1] is divided into 2^i sub-intervals.

If we denote $(i-1)$ th level as the 'mother-level', it will be divided twice finer in the next level. So given any interval on the mother level, it is easy to observe the relationship

$$X_{i,2j-1} + X_{i,2j} = X_{i-1,j} \tag{36}$$

Because of equation (36), it is enough to just generate $X_{i,j}$ for odd number j. So, let us proceed from left to right, assuming that the sample points $X_{i,1}, \ldots X_{i,2k}$ have already been generated $(k \in \{0,1, \ldots, 2^{i-1}-1\})$. For the point $X_{i,2k+1}$, we have

$$X_{i,2k+1} = e(i,k)\left[X_{i,\max(2k-m+1,1)}, \ldots, X_{i,2k}, X_{i-1,k+1}, \ldots, X_{i-1,\min(k+n,2^{i-1})}\right]' + \sqrt{v(i,k)}U_{i,k} \tag{37}$$

where $U_{i,k}$ are i.i.d. standard Gaussian random variables $i=0,1, \ldots; k=0,1, \ldots, 2^{(i-1)}-1$. Equation (37) can be rewritten as

$$\begin{aligned} X_{i,2k+1} &= e(i,k)\left[X_{i,\max(2k-m+1,1)}, \ldots, X_{i,2k}, X_{i-1,k+1}, \ldots, X_{i-1,\min(k+n,2^{i-1})}\right]' + \sqrt{v(i,k)}U_{i,k} = \\ &\mathbb{E}\left[X_{i,2k+1} \mid X_{i,\max(2k-m+1,1)}, \ldots, X_{i,2k}, X_{i-1,k+1}, \ldots, X_{i-1,\min(k+n,2^{i-1})}\right] \end{aligned} \tag{38}$$

$$v(i,k) = Var\left[X_{i,2k+1} \mid X_{i,\max(2k-m+1,1)}, \ldots, X_{i,2k}, X_{i-1,k+1}, \ldots, X_{i-1,\min(k+n,2^{i-1})}\right] \tag{39}$$

As mentioned before, this scheme conditions on a fixed number of past samples instead of the whole past, where the two integers $(m \geq 0, \; n \geq 1)$ indicate the number of the intervals the expectation and variance are conditioned on, and is called RMD(m,n). Looking at (38) and (39) " $X_{i,\max(2k-m+1,1)}, \ldots, X_{i,2k}$ " indicates that there are at most m neighboring increments to the left of the interval in question ($X_{i,2k+1}$), and " $X_{i-1,k+1}, \ldots, X_{i-1,\min(k+n,2^{i-1})}$ " indicates that there are at most n neighboring increments to the right of the interval.

Denote by Γ_{ik} the covariance matrix with $X_{i,2k+1}$ as the first entry, and $X_{i,\max(2k-m+1,1)}, \ldots, X_{i,2k}, X_{i-1,k+1}, \ldots, X_{i-1,\min(k+n,2^{i-1})}$ as the rest of the entries. Then, we have

$$\Gamma_{ik} = Cov\left(\left[X_{i,2k+1}, X_{i,\max(2k-m+1,1)}, \dots, X_{i,2k}, X_{i-1,k+1}, \dots, X_{i-1,\min(k+n,2^{i-1})}\right]\right)$$

where

$$Cov([x_1, x_2, \dots, x_n]) = \begin{pmatrix} Cov(x_1, x_1) & Cov(x_1, x_2) & \cdots & Cov(x_1, x_n) \\ Cov(x_2, x_1) & Cov(x_2, x_2) & \cdots & Cov(x_2, x_n) \\ \vdots & \vdots & \ddots & \vdots \\ Cov(x_n, x_1) & Cov(x_n, x_2) & \cdots & Cov(x_n, x_n) \end{pmatrix}$$

Similar to (14)-(16), we can partition Γ_{ik} as

$$\Gamma_{ik} = \begin{pmatrix} Var(X_{i,2k+1}) & \Gamma_{ik}^{(1,2)} \\ \Gamma_{ik}^{(2,1)} & \Gamma_{ik}^{(2,2)} \end{pmatrix}$$

Note that $\Gamma_{ik}^{(1,2)} = (\Gamma_{ik}^{(2,1)})'$. Hence, we have

$$e(i, k) = \Gamma_{ik}^{(1,2)} (\Gamma_{ik}^{(2,2)})^{-1} \tag{40}$$

$$v(i, k) = \frac{|\Gamma_{ik}|}{|\Gamma_{ik}^{(2,2)}|} \tag{41}$$

By the stationarity of the increment of Z and by self-similarity, $e(i, k)$ is independent of i and k when $2k \geq m$ and $k \leq 2^{i-1} - n$ (meaning that the sequence is not truncated by $\max(\cdot)$ and $\min(\cdot)$), and it only depends on i only when $2^i < m + 2n$.

4.4.2. *On-the-fly RMD(m,n) generation*

Norros et al. [34] further propose that, instead of having the previous level (i-1) completely generated first, partition and conditioning can be done 'on-the-fly', meaning that we can have multiple unfinished levels going at the same time. Unlike the previous RMD(m,n) scheme, the level here is defined differently.

First define the 'resolution' by δ, as the smallest interval that we will be dealing with in this scheme. Note that this is different from the previous sub-section where at the i-th level $\delta = 2^{-i}$, which can be bisected finer indefinitely. In the on-the-fly RMD scheme, the minimum interval length is defined as δ.

At each level i, the interval $[0, 2^i \delta]$ is split finely into interval with length of δ and $X_{i,k}$ samples are generated on each point until all points within the interval are filled. Then, the trace is expanded to the next level $i+1$, the interval $[0, 2^{i+1}]$, and this procedure can be considered as 'enlargement'. So, instead of having a pre-determined time-horizon and zooming in with twice-finer resolution in the original RMD scheme, the new RMD scheme has a pre-determined resolution and expand twice-fold the horizon at each level.

Within the same interval $[0, 2^i]$, the following rules are applied for the inner intervals:

1. Must have n-1 (or all) right-neighboring intervals (of which, have the same length as the mother-interval).
2. Also, there should be m (or all) left-neighboring intervals (of which, have the same length as the interval being considered).
3. If there are intervals that satisfy both the conditions above, choose the one as left as possible.
4. When all intervals are filled out, expand to the next level by 'enlargement'.

Here we use

$$Y_{i,j} = Z\left(j \cdot 2^i \delta\right) - Z\left((j-1) \cdot 2^i \delta\right), \; i = 0,1, \; \ldots, \; j = 1,2, \; \ldots \tag{42}$$

instead of $X_{i,j}$ to avoid confusion with the original RMD scheme notation.

Similar to the ordinary RMD, we have the following equations from the conditional distribution of multivariate Gaussian processes: The enlargement stage is defined by

$$Y_{i,1} = \mathbb{E}[Y_{i,1} \mid Y_{i-1,1}] + \sqrt{Var[Y_{i,1} \mid Y_{i-1,1}]} U_{i,1} = e(i, 1) Y_{i-1,1} + \sqrt{v(i, 1)} U_{i,1} \tag{43}$$

Inner interval points are constructed similar to the ordinary RMD scheme (the right-neighboring intervals are of level i+1 instead of i-1) as

$$Y_{i,2k+1} = e(i, k)\left[Y_{i,\max(2k-m+1,1)}, \; \ldots, \; Y_{i,2k}, \; Y_{i+1,k+1}, \; \ldots, \; Y_{i+1,\min(k+n,N_{i+1})}\right]' + \sqrt{v(i, k)} U_{i,k} \tag{44}$$

where N_{i+1} is the last generated increment on the (i+1)-th level. The order of splitting for the on-the-fly scheme is given in Figure 1, where its ordinary RMD counterpart's splitting order is also given.

Norros et al. [34] have done an extensive comparison between on-the-fly RMD schemes in terms of accuracy and robustness compared to the FFT and aggregate methods. On-the-fly RMD and FFT are significantly faster than the aggregate method, and on-the-fly RMD can generate samples with no fixed time-horizon, while for FFT the whole trace has to be generated before it can be used. So, RMD seems superior in terms of flexibility.

4.5. Spectral method

In this subsection, we will look into the spectral method of approximating the fractional Gaussian noises, which has the origin from spectral analysis in physics: A time-domain can be transformed into a frequency-domain without loss of information through Fourier transform. With the typical Fourier-time series, the original input is deterministic and transformed into the spectral density that represents the magnitude of different frequencies in the frequency domain. It is possible to extend this approach to analyzing stochastic processes.

Though it is impossible to study all realization, it is possible to analyze in a probabilistic/distribution sense by observing the expected frequency information contained in the autocovariance function.

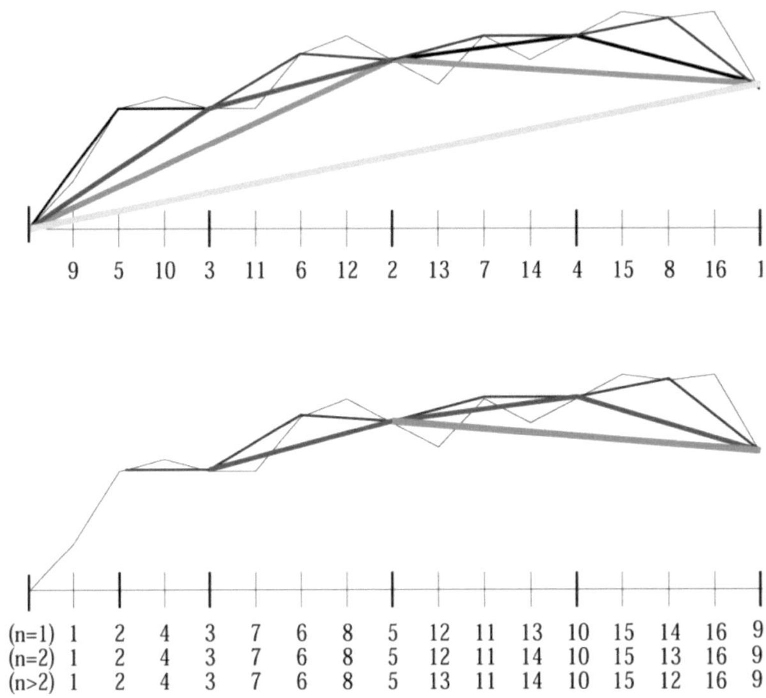

Figure 1. The order of splits by the ordinary RMD(m,n) scheme (top) and the on-the-fly RMD(m,n) scheme (bottom). Note that, for the on-the-fly scheme, the order changes according to the choice of n.

Spectral density is computed for frequencies, $-\pi \leq \lambda \leq \pi$, as

$$f(\lambda)=\sum_{j=-\infty}^{\infty} \gamma(j)\exp(ij\lambda) \tag{45}$$

The $\gamma(\cdot)$ here is the autocovariance function, which can be recovered by the inverse formula

$$\gamma(j)=\frac{1}{2\pi}\int_{-\pi}^{\pi} f(\lambda)\exp(-ij\lambda) \tag{46}$$

The spectral density of the fGn can be approximated according to [25] and [35] as

$$f(\lambda)=2\sin(\pi H)\Gamma(2H+1)(1-\cos\lambda)[|\lambda|^{-2H-1}+B(\lambda, H)] \tag{47}$$

where

$$B(\lambda, H)=\sum_{j=1}^{\infty}\{(2\pi j+\lambda)^{-2H-1}+(2\pi j-\lambda)^{-2H-1}\}$$

Note that the domain is only $-\pi \leq \lambda \leq \pi$, since any frequency higher would only correspond to amplitude between our desired sample points.

The problem with the above expression is that there is no known form for $B(\lambda, H)$, Paxson [35] proposes the following scheme for $B(\lambda, H)$:

$$B(\lambda, H)\cong \widetilde{B}_3(\lambda, H)=a_1^d+b_1^d+a_2^d+b_2^d+a_3^d+b_3^d+\frac{a_3^{d'}+b_3^{d'}+a_4^{d'}+b_4^{d'}}{8H\pi}$$

where

$$d=-2H-1, d'=-2H, a_k=2k\pi+\lambda, b_k=2k\pi-\lambda$$

Moreover, with the help of the Whittle estimator, Paxson [35] shows that

$$\widetilde{B}_3(\lambda, H)''=[1.0002-0.000134\lambda](\widetilde{B}_3(\lambda, H)-2^{-7.65H-7.4})$$

gives a very robust and unbiased approximation for the $B(\lambda, H)$. See Appendix A of [35] for a detailed comparison and justification of this approximation.

With the approximation scheme for the spectral density at hand, we can now look at the spectral analysis of a stationary discrete-time Gaussian process (fractional Gaussian noise; fGn) $X=\{X_n : n=0, \ldots, N-1\}$, which can be represented in terms of the spectral density $f(\lambda)$ as

$$X_n=\int_0^{\pi}\sqrt{\frac{f(\lambda)}{\pi}}\cos(n\lambda)dB_1(\lambda)-\int_0^{\pi}\sqrt{\frac{f(\lambda)}{\pi}}\sin(n\lambda)dB_2(\lambda)$$

where B_1 and B_2 are independent standard Brownian motions and the equality is understood in terms of distribution. Define $\xi_n(\lambda)=\sqrt{\frac{f(\lambda)}{\pi}}\cos(n\lambda)$ and fix some integer l . After setting $t_k=\frac{\pi k}{l}$ for $k=0, \ldots, l-1$, we can approximate it by a simple function $\xi_n^{(l)}$ defined on $[0, \pi]$ for $0\leq n\leq N-1$ by

$$\xi_n^{(l)}(\lambda)=\sqrt{\frac{f(t_1)}{\pi}}\cos(nt_1)1_{\{0\}}(\lambda)+\sum_{k=0}^{l-1}\sqrt{\frac{f(t_{k+1})}{\pi}}\cos(nt_{k+1})1_{(t_k, t_{k+1}]}(\lambda) \tag{48}$$

which is similar to the typical construction of stochastic integral.

Define the sine counterpart as $\theta_n^{(l)}(\lambda)$, and then integrate both $\xi_n^{(l)}(\lambda)$ and $\theta_n^{(l)}(\lambda)$ with respect to $dB_1(\lambda)$ and $dB_2(\lambda)$ on $[0, \pi]$ to approximate X_n . Then, we have

$$\hat{X}_n^{(l)}=\sum_{k=0}^{l-1}\sqrt{\frac{f(t_{k+1})}{l}}[\cos(nt_{k+1})U_k^{(0)}-\sin(nt_{k+1})U_k^{(1)}] \tag{49}$$

where $U_k^{(\cdot)}$ are i.i.d. standard normal random variables. $U_k^{(0)}$ and $U_k^{(1)}$ are independent, as they are resulted from integration from the two aforementioned independent Brownian motions.

Similar to the Fourier transform approach, the fGns can be recovered by applying the FFT to the sequence of $\hat{X}_n^{(l)}$ efficiently to the following coefficient:

$$a_k = \begin{cases} 0, k=0 \\ \frac{1}{2}\left(U_{k-1}^{(0)} + iU_{k-1}^{(1)}\right), \ k=1,\dots,l-1 \\ U_{k-1}^{(0)}\sqrt{\frac{f(t_k)}{l}}, \ k=l \\ \frac{1}{2}\left(U_{2l-k-1}^{(0)} + iU_{2l-k-1}^{(1)}\right), \ k=l+1,\dots,2l-1 \end{cases} \tag{50}$$

It is easy to check that the covariance structure of fGns can be recovered, with the help of product-to-sum trigonometric identity, as

$$Cov\left(\hat{X}_m^{(l)}, \hat{X}_n^{(l)}\right) = \sum_{k=0}^{l-1} \frac{f(t_{k+1})}{l}\cos((m-n)t_{k+1})$$

$$\cong 2\int_0^{\pi} \frac{f(\lambda)}{2\pi}\cos(n\lambda)d\lambda$$

$$= \frac{1}{2\pi}\int_{-\pi}^{\pi} f(\lambda)\exp(-in\lambda)d\lambda = \gamma(n)$$

Paxson [35] has also proposed another method for simulating fGns, where in [25] it was proven to be related to (50) with the case $l = N/2$:

$$b_k = \begin{cases} 0, k=0 \\ \sqrt{\frac{R_k f(t_k)}{N}}\exp(i\Phi_k), \ k=1,\dots,N/2-1 \\ \sqrt{\frac{f(t_{N/2})}{2N}}U_{N/2}^{(0)}, \ k=N/2 \\ b_k^*, \ k=N/2+1,\dots,N-1 \end{cases} \tag{51}$$

Here, R_k is a vector of exponentially distributed random variables with mean 1, and Φ_k are uniformly distributed random variables on $[0,2\pi]$ independent of R_k. This method is of order $Nlog(N)$, and only one FFT is required instead of 2 times compared to the Davis-Harte FFT method. Hence, it is about 4 times faster.

Remark: The Paxson algorithm in (54) is improved by Dieker [25] to retain the normality of the sequence and its relationship with the original spectral representation.

5. A numerical example: fBm volatility model

Finally, this section provides a numerical example of Monte Carlo simulation of fBm volatility model. In Section 2.3, we have briefly mentioned the truncated fractional Brownian motion. This section outlines the stochastic volatility model explored by Comte and Renault [6]. We follow the example given in [6], with the following setup to simulate the volatility process:

$$\begin{cases} \sigma(t)=\sigma_0 e^{x(t)} \\ dx(t)= - kx(t)dt + \nu d\hat{B}^H(t) \end{cases} \tag{52}$$

where ν is the volatility factor of the log-volatility process $x(t)$. The volatility process is the exponential of an OU-process driven by the truncated fBm. Also, we assume that $x(0)=0,\ k>0,\ \frac{1}{2}<H<1$.

Solving the OU-process with integrating factor, we have

$$x(t)=\int_0^t \nu e^{-k(t-s)} d\hat{B}^H(s) \tag{53}$$

By applying the fractional calculus or using the formulas provided in [5], we can formulate $x(t)$ in another way as

$$x(t)=\int_0^t a(t - s)dB(s) \tag{54}$$

where $B(t)$ is an ordinary standard Brownian motion and

$$a(\theta)=\frac{\nu}{\Gamma\left(H + \frac{1}{2}\right)}\frac{d}{dx}\int_0^\theta e^{-ku}(\theta - u)^{H-\frac{1}{2}}du=\frac{\nu}{\Gamma\left(H + \frac{1}{2}\right)}\left(\theta^{\alpha} - ke^{-\theta}\int_0^\theta e^{ku}u^{\alpha}\,du\right) \tag{55}$$

By applying the ordinary discretization scheme to (54), we have

$$\tilde{x}(t)=\sum_{j=1}^{t_N=t} a\left(t_N - \frac{t_j - 1}{n}\right)\left(B(t_j) - B(t_{j-1})\right) \tag{56}$$

Here, the coefficient $a(\cdot\,)$ can be calculated by symbolic packages such as matlab and mathematics. In our case of OU-process, it is a summation of constant with incomplete gamma function and gamma function.

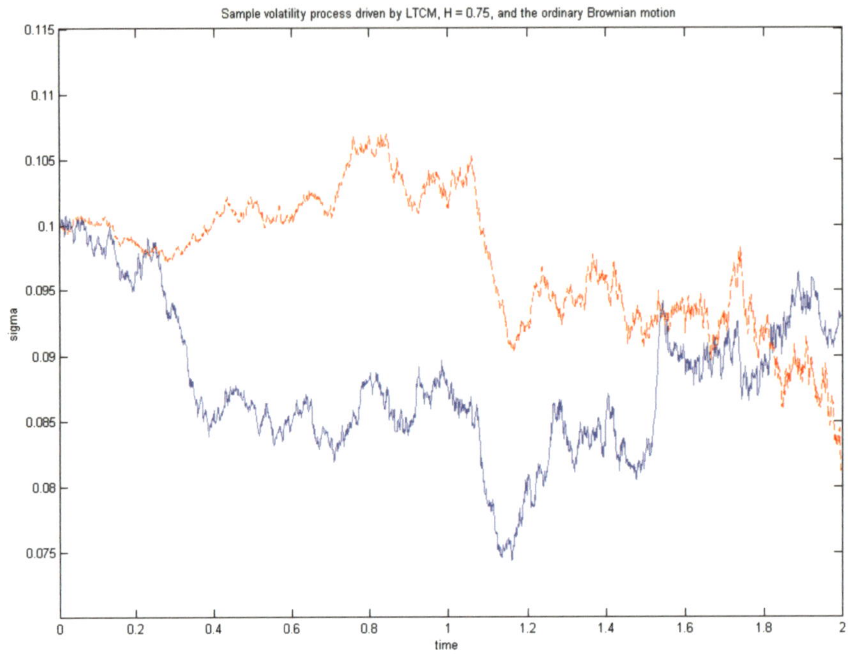

Figure 2. shows a sample path of $\sigma(t)=\exp(\tilde{x}(t))$ for $k=1$, $\sigma_0=0.1$, $v=0.3$, $H=0.75$, $T=2$. For the purpose of comparison, a sample path of the volatility process driven by an ordinary OU-process (the dotted line): $\sigma(t)=\exp(y(t))$, where $y(t)=\int_0^t ve^{-k(t-s)}dB(s)$, is shown alongside, which has the same parameters except the Hurst index.

The sample path of the fractional-OU driven volatility process has shown more of a persistent trend, i.e. more prominent trend (more smooth and less reversal) compared to the ordinary-OU driven volatility process, which is what to be expected according [5]. This approach only imitate fractional Brownian motion if the time-step in discretization scheme is very small, renders it not robust enough for practical purpose. But for analytical purpose, it can be shown it is equivalent to the S-transform approach outlined in [36].For more discussion of its statistical property and justification of its stability as compared to the original stationary version, we direct the reader to [5] and [6]. We provided this approach for the sake of completeness and readers' interest.

We have also included fractional Brownian motion simulatedsimulated by the circulant-embeddingmethod, with the same parameters as above in Figure 3. This approach is more robust since the covariance structure does not depends on the step-size. Figure 3 shows a sample path of $(t)=\exp(x(t))$, where $x(t)$ is the fBM generated by the circulant-embedding FFT with the same parameters as Figure 2: $k=1$, $\sigma_0=0.1$, $v=0.3$, $H=0.75$, $T=2$ .In these two examples, the fractional Brownian motions are scaled, so that the variance of $B^H(T)$ equals to the ordinary Brownian motion $B^{1/2}(T)$.

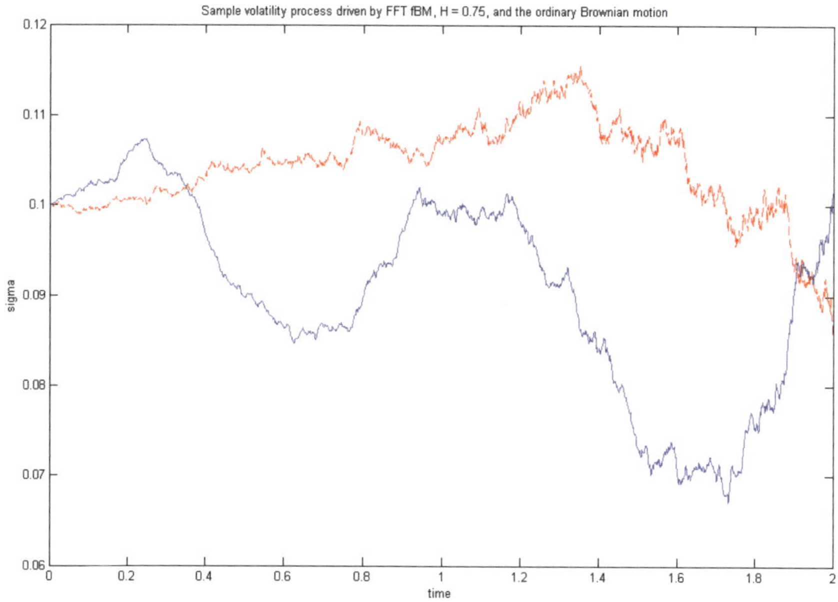

Figure 3.

6. Conclusion

Motivated by the inadequacy in capturing long-dependence feature in volatility process of the traditional stochastic volatility framework, we explore the possibility of fractional Brownian motion (fBm) in financial modeling and various schemes of the Monte Carlo simulation. Starting from the general definition, fBm can be considered as an extension of the ordinary Brownian motion with an autocovariance function that depends on both time indices instead of just the minimum between the two.

With different values of Hurst index, we can distinguish fractional Brownian motion into three different cases: $H < \frac{1}{2}$, $H = \frac{1}{2}$ and $H > \frac{1}{2}$. Since only the case of $H > \frac{1}{2}$ displays a long-dependence behavior, that is the case we are interested in. Several prominent examples of fBm in financial modeling are given.

Simulation schemes are divided into the exact schemes and approximate schemes. While the former will capture the complete structure for the whole length of sample size, the latter either approximates the value of the real realization or truncates the covariance structure for robustness.

We start with the exact scheme of Hosking algorithm that utilizes the multivariate Gaussian distribution of fractional Gaussian noises and simulates the sample points conditioned on the previous samples. Alternatively, instead of simulating each conditioned on the past sample points, we can first construct the covariance matrix of the size of the sample we want, and proceed to find the 'square root' of the covariance matrix and multiply with a standard normal variable vector, for which the product vector will be the fractional Gaussian noise (fGn) with exact covariance structure as the covariance matrix. To find the 'square root', we first investigate the Cholesky decomposition, but the computational and memory expense is too large to be feasible in practice. In contrast, fast Fourier transform (FFT) simulation embeds the original covariance matrix in a larger circulant matrix and simulates by diagonalizing the circulant matrix into the product of eigenvalue matrix and unitary matrix. The FFT method is significantly more robust than the previous schemes.

We then look into the approximate schemes; namely the construction of fBm with correlated random walks, which can be viewed as an extension of construction of Brownian motion with ordinary random walk. This method gives us interesting insight into the true working of fBm, especially the idea of long-range dependence. This approach is not only interesting and easy to implement, but also the error can be calculated explicitly. The drawback of this approach is that the speed slows down significantly with large sample points, and the trade-off is made based on the error function. The last simulation approach we look at is the conditional random midpoint displacement (RMD) scheme, which is mathematically similar to the Hosking scheme, but with fixed number of past sample points it conditions on. The on-the-fly version of RMD scheme can indefinitely generate sample points with given resolution. Finally, we include the spectral method for approximating fBm.

Comparing all the schemes and also referring the studies done in [34], we conclude that if the time-horizon is known beforehand, the FFT/spectral schemes would be the best scheme due to the high speed and accuracy. Alternately, if samples should be generated indefinitely, the on-the-fly conditioned RMD scheme seems to offer similar level of accuracy and speed as the FFT scheme.

At last, we provided numerical examples for the truncated version of fBM proposed in [5, 6], as well as the fBM generated by FFT for comparison in robustness.

Acknowledgements

We wish to express our gratitude to Professor Alex Novikov for sharing relevant research materials with us, and Professor Bernt Øksendal and Professor Enriquez Nathanaël for interesting discussions and remarks.

Author details

Masaaki Kijima and Chun Ming Tam

Graduate School of Social Sciences, Tokyo Metropolitan University, Japan

References

[1] Kolmogorov, A.N. (1940), `Wienersche Spiralen und einige andere interessante Kurvenim Hilbertschen Raum', *C.R. (Doklady) Acad. URSS (N.S)*, 26, 115-118.

[2] Mandelbrot, B.B. and Van Ness, J.W. (1968), `Fractional Brownian Motions, Fractional Noises and Applications', *SIAM Review*, 10, 422–437.

[3] Mandelbrot, B.B. (1965), `Une classe de processus homothgtiques a soi; Application a la loi climatologique de H. E. Hurst', *C.R. Acad. Sci. Paris*, 260, 3274-3277.

[4] Lo A.W. (1991), `Long-Term Memory in Stock Market Price', *Econometrca*, 59, 1279-1313.

[5] Comte, F. and Renault, E. (1996), `Long Memory Continuous Time Models', *J. Econometrics*, 73, 101-149.

[6] Comte, F. and Renault, E. (1998), `Long Memory in Continuous-Time Stochastic Volatility Models', *Mathematical Finance*, 8, 291-323.

[7] Hull, J. and White, A. (1987), `The Pricing of Options on Assets with Stochastic Volatilities', *Rev. Finan. Studies*, 3, 281-300.

[8] Scott, L. (1987), `Option Pricing when the Variance Changes Randomly: Estimation and an Application', *J. Financial and Quant. Anal.*, 22, 419-438.

[9] Ding, Z., Granger, C.W.J. and Engle, R.F. (1993), `A Long Memory Property of Stock Market Returns and a New Model', *J. Empirical Finance*, 1, 83-106.

[10] Crato, N. and de Lima, P. (1994), `Long-Range Dependence in the Conditional Variance of Stock Returns,' *Economics Letters*, 45, 281-285.

[11] Baillie, R.T., Bollerslev, T. and Mikkelsen, H.O. (1996), `Fractionally Integrated Generalized Autoregressive Conditional Heteroskedasticity', *J. Econometrics*, 74, 3-30.

[12] Bollerslev, T. and Mikkelsen, H.O. (1996), `Modeling and Pricing Long Memory in Stock Market Volatility', *J. Econometrics*, 73, 151-184.

[13] Jacquier, E., Polson, N.G. and Rossi, P.E. (1994), `Bayesian Analysis of Stochastic Volatility Models', *J. Bus. and Econ. Statistics*, 12, 371-417.

[14] Breidt, F.J., Crato, N. and de Lima, P. (1998), `The Detection and Estimation of Long Memory in Stochastic Volatility', *J. Econometrics*, 83, 325-348.

[15] Biagini, F., Hu, Y., Øksendal, B. and Zhang T. (2008), *Stochastic Calculus for Fractional Brownian Motion and Applications*, Springer.

[16] [16] Cont, R. (2007), `Volatility Clustering in Financial Markets: Empirical Facts and Agent-Based Models', In: Kirman, A. and Teyssiere, G. (ed.), *Long Memory in Economics*, Springer, 289-310.

[17] Marinucci, D. and Robinson, P.M. (1999), `Alternative Forms of Fractional Brownian Motion', *J. Statistical Planning and Inference*, 80, 111-122.

[18] Delbaen, F. and Schachermayer, W. (1994), `A General Version of the Fundamental Theorem of Asset Pricing', *Math. Ann.*, 300, 463-520.

[19] Rogers, L.C.G. (1997), `Arbitrage with Fractional Brownian Motion', *Mathematical Finance*, 7, 95-105.

[20] Cheridito, P. (2003), `Arbitrage in Fractional Brownian Motion Models', *Finance and Stochastics*, 7, 533-553.

[21] Comte, F., Coutin, L. and Renault, E. (2012), `Affine Fractional Stochastic Volatility Models', *Annals of Finance*, 8, 337-378.

[22] Duffie, D., Pan, R. and Singleton, K. (2000), `Transform Analysis and Asset Pricing for Affine Jump-Diffusion', *Econometrica*, 68, 1343-1376.

[23] Fukasawa, M. (2011), `Asymptotic Analysis for Stochastic Volatility: Martingale Expansion', *Finance and Stochastics*, 15, 635-654.

[24] Yoshida, N. (2001), `Malliavin Calculus and Martingale Expansion', *Bull. Sci. Math.*, 125, 431-456.

[25] Dieker, T. (2002), *Simulation of Fractional Brownian Motion*, Master Thesis, Vrije Universiteit, Amsterdam.

[26] Hosking, J.R.M. (1984), `Modeling Persistence in Hydrological Time Series Using Fractional Differencing', *Water Resources Research*, 20, 1898-1908.

[27] Brockwell, P.J. and Davis, R.A. (1987), *Time Series: Theory and Methods*, Springer, New York.

[28] Davies, R.B. and Harte, D.S. (1987), `Tests for Hurst Effect', *Biometrika*, 74, 95-102.

[29] Dietrich, C.R. and Newsam, G.N. (1997), `Fast and Exact Simulation of Stationary Gaussian Processes through Circulant Embedding of the Covariance Matrix', *SIAM J. Sci. Computing*, 18, 1088-1107.

[30] Perrin, E., Harba, R., Jennane, R. and Iribarren, I. (2002), `Fast and Exact Synthesis for 1-D Fractional Brownian Motion and Fractional Gaussian Noises', *IEEE Signal Processing Letters*, 9, 382-384.

[31] Wood, A.T.A. and Chan, G. (1994), `Simulation of Stationary Gaussian Processes in 0,1d ', *J. Computational and Graphical Statistics*, 3, 409-432.

[32] Enriquez, N. (2004), `A Simple Construction of the Fractional Brownian Motion', *Stochastic Processes and Their Applications*, 109, 203-223.

[33] Taqqu, M. (1975), `Weak Convergence to Fractional Brownian Motion and to the Rosenblatt Process', *Z. Wahr. Verw. Gebiete*, 31, 287-302.

[34] Norros, I., Mannersalo, P. and Wang, J.L. (1999), `Simulation of Fractional Brownian Motion with Conditionalized Random Midpoint Displacement', *Advances in Performance Analysis*, 2, 77-101.

[35] Paxson, V. (1997), `Fast, Approximate Synthesis of Fractional Gaussian Noise for Generating Self-Similar Network Traffic', *Computer Communication Review*, 27, 5-18.

[36] Bender, C. (2003), 'An S-Transform approach to integration with respect to a fractional Brownian motion', Bernoulli, 9(6), p. 955–983.

Chapter 4

Monte-Carlo-Based Robust Procedure for Dynamic Line Layout Problems

Wai Kin (Victor) Chan and Charles J. Malmborg

Additional information is available at the end of the chapter

http://dx.doi.org/10.5772/53195

1. Introduction

Most material flow based layout techniques assume that the designer has access to data describing the rate of movement of unit loads in a facility. This data is typically in the form of process routings and forecasted production volumes that can be reformulated as material flow rates between workcenters. Using product and facility data in this form, alternative layouts are evaluated using measures of material handling volume distance, i.e., the total unit load travel distance needed to execute a production schedule. Most line layout methods are aimed at finding the volume distance minimizing assignment of workcenters to locations in a facility for specific production and process data. In many practical situations, product and process information is not known with certainty or may be subject to future changes resulting from model changeovers, seasonal variations, etc. Uncertainty and/or dynamic variation in production data motivates the proactive management of risk in applying line layout algorithms. A designer seeking to avert inflexibility with dynamically changing production data and/or under-performance with stochastic production data is more apt to favor solutions exhibiting robustness as opposed to those which minimize a single measure of expected performance. In this study, volume distance robustness corresponds to meeting minimum acceptable performance standards for most or all operating scenarios. This objective is contrary to the logic of line layout algorithms that focus on the computationally difficult problem of finding the best performing solution for a fixed operating scenario. Achieving robustness requires techniques that can identify reliable measures of solution performance for each operating scenario to efficiently terminate the search for layout alternatives.

This study investigates line layout strategies focused on volume distance robustness. Uncertainty in layout information is represented through discrete probability distributions of material flow rates and workcenter space requirements. Recent research suggesting that Monte

INTECH
open science | open minds

© 2013 The Author(s). Licensee InTech. This chapter is distributed under the terms of the Creative Commons Attribution License http://creativecommons.org/licenses/by/3.0), which permits unrestricted use, distribution, and reproduction in any medium, provided the original work is properly cited.

Carlo simulation techniques can be applied to map the distribution of volume distance values in the solution space corresponding to deterministic line layout problems is exploited to define stopping criteria for robust procedures. A line layout algorithm is proposed which uses these sampling procedures to first construct a mapping of the volume distance solution space for each parameter set, and then identify layouts meeting minimum performance standards for all potential operating scenarios.

The next section describes uncertainty in the information base associated with line layout problems and describes previous work associated with solving stochastic problems and the empirical mapping of volume distance distributions. The third section describes a robust algorithm for solving the stochastic and/or dynamic line layout problem. In the fourth section, two test problems are introduced and computational experience with the procedure is described. The fifth section extends the study by allowing nonlinear material handling costs. The final section offers a summary and conclusions.

2. Background information

Most layout techniques assume a deterministic, static production environment with many of these methods based on a variation of the quadratic assignment problem (Koopmans and Beckman 1957) which usually, although not always, assumes equal workcenter areas. Numerous linear-integer models for layout problems based on the quadratic assignment problem (QAP) have been proposed including Kaufman and Broeckx (1978), Ritzman et al. (1979), Bazaraa and Sherali (1980), Burkard and Bonninger (1983), and Frieze and Yadegar (1983), Heragu and Kusiak (1991), and others. Given the NP completeness of the QAP (Sahni and Gonzalez 1976), many heuristic methods have also been proposed which have increasingly focused on optimization tools such as simulated annealing, genetic algorithms and tabu search to improve the performance of local search procedures, (see Burkard and Rendl 1984, Wilhelm and Ward 1987, Goldberg 1988). Heragu and Alfa (1992) present a detailed performance comparison of several of these heuristics. Skorin-Kapov (1990, 1994) adapted tabu search to the QAP using the two phase "tabu-navigation procedure". Kelly et al. (1994) developed diversification strategies and applied them to the QAP independently of search procedures such as tabu search, simulated annealing, and genetic algorithms.

The assumption of static production data contrasts with many applications where there is known to be time variation in the parameters driving layout design. Increasingly, researchers are addressing such dynamic variations of the problem. Rosenblatt (1986) presented a dynamic programming strategy for the stochastic layout problem that could be applied in either an optimal or heuristic mode. Lacksonen and Enscore (1993) modified the QAP to prototype the dynamic layout problem to minimize flow costs and rearrangement costs over discrete time periods and compared five alternative solution methods. Conway and Venkataraman (1994) used a genetic search algorithm to solve the constrained dynamic layout problem (CDLP) and found it to be effective in solving the sample problems presented in Rosenblatt (1986). Lacksonen (1994) extended the analysis of dynamic layout problems by developing heuristic procedures for the QAP applicable to problems where workcenters have varying areas.

http://dx.doi.org/10.5772/53195

Other studies have modeled parameter uncertainty that is associated with stochastic variation in product mix, production volume and process routings. Previous studies addressing stochasticity in layout problems include Rosenblatt and Lee (1986) which assumes that demands for individual products are characterized by three alternative levels; low, medium and high. Their method for resolving uncertainty involved the enumeration of all possible demand scenarios and evaluation of layout alternatives for each scenario with respect to expected volume distance and maximum regret criteria. The method then identified robust solutions as those within a given percentage of the optimal for each scenario and both criteria. The study assumed equal workcenter space requirements and feasibility to enumerate all potential layout alternatives for each scenario. Other studies have attempted to address stochasticity by proposing measures of flexibility as a basis for solving the layout problem. Gupta (1986) proposed a simulation strategy for generating material flow rates and then used a CRAFT-like procedure to solve for a layout associated with each scenario. A flexibility measure based on a penalty measure associated with workcenter travel distances, not material flow rates, was used to find a solution. Webster and Tyberghein (1980) proposed a performance measure for individual layouts based on volume distance performance across the set of potential material flow scenarios.

Rosenblatt and Kropp (1992) have presented a formulation of the single period stochastic layout problem. A variation of the formulation presented in that study can be based on the following parameters:

- n : the number of workcenters and workcenter locations, (and load transfer points), in a facility,
- S : the number of potential material flow scenarios that could occur in the application problem,
- m_{ijs} : the expected volume of material flow between workcenters i and j within material flow scenario s, in unit handling loads per unit time, for $i, j = 1,...,n$ and $s = 1,...,S$,
- p_s : the probability that material flow scenario s is realized for $s = 1,...,S$, $0 \le p_s \le 1$, $p_s > 0$.
- d_{yz} : the travel distance between workcenter locations y and z,
- $d(i,j)^k$: the travel distance between workcenters i and j associated with layout alternative k for $k = 1,...,n!$, where $d(i,j)^k = d_{yz}$ when workcenters i and j are assigned to locations y and z, respectively.

The expected volume distance can then be formulated as:

$$\min_k v_k = p_s \Sigma\Sigma \sum_{i=1}^{n}\sum_{j=1}^{n} m_{ij} d(i,j)^k \text{ for } k = 1,...,n!. \quad (1)$$

In contrast to their use in Rosenblatt and Kropp (1992), the p_s probability terms could also represent the proportion of time that a system operates under scenario s. If layout rearrangement were not feasible, this interpretation of p_s could be applied in the same formulation of v_k for dynamic layout problems. Assuming workcenters of equal area, Rosenblatt and Kropp (1992) computed a weighted average flow matrix and solved the problem as a quadratic assignment problem (QAP). They related the results from this procedure to a flexible facilities design measure proposed by Shore and Tompkins (1980) known as the total expected facility penalty. This measure is based on the regret value of using a layout designed for one scenario under the changing conditions of the other states.

The motivation to focus on a single set of expected parameter values in most of the studies described above is related to the computational difficulty of solving the QAP. Simultaneous consideration of multiple production scenarios requires interpretation of the performance of candidate layout alternatives relative to the set of all possible layout alternatives. In effect, this requires knowledge about the optimal solution, (possibly by solving the QAP), for the parameter sets associated with each production scenario. To address this problem, one study was focused on analyzing the form of the distribution of volume distance values associated with the solution space for 6,400 line layout problems representing a diverse range of material flow parameters (Malmborg and Bukhari 1997). For each of the 6,400 randomly generated line layout problems, the corresponding volume distance distributions were enumerated and analyzed. Fit parameters for volume distance distributions were formulated to represent several well-known distributions including the uniform, gamma, normal and exponential. For every case examined, the fit of the volume distance values to a normal distribution was several orders of magnitude better than any of the other distributions studied. This suggested that the population of $n!$ volume distance values tended toward normality for any set of material flow parameters used in these line layouts. The implication of the findings was that for static line layout problems, designers can usually assume that the corresponding volume distance distribution is normally distributed and its parameters can be estimated through a reasonably low volume of random sampling. In a follow-up study, Bukhari et.al. (1998) analyzed the volume distance distributions for 231,200 line layout problems representing a carefully constructed cross section of material flow and travel distance parameters. Order of magnitude differences observed in fit statistics from that study also supported the extension of the normality result to more general cases of line layout problems.

To assess whether analogous inferences could be made for line layout problems with varying workcenter space requirements, another study investigated the feasibility of mapping the form of volume distance functions associated with more general forms of line layout problems (Malmborg 1999). This investigation considered a range of material flow and space requirements distributions. Using random samples representing between 0.25% and 2.5% of the solution space for problems with $n = 8$, and 0.014% to 0.28% of the solution space for problems with $n = 10$, it was shown that reasonably accurate estimates of the form of the volume distance distribution could be generated. Accuracy in this case was measured by the proportion of the true volume distance distribution replicated by the estimated distribution for a given sample size and resolution of the histogram describing the volume distance distribution. Although the results of the latter investigation suggested that volume distance distributions for line layout problems with dynamic distance functions do not generally follow a normal distribution, the ease and accuracy with which the form of the volume distance distribution could be empirically estimated was insensitive to both the distribution of space requirements and material flow parameters.

The significance of the three studies investigating the feasibility of mapping volume distance distributions is that simulation techniques may provide a viable means for generating "context" for the evaluation of line layout solutions. This could provide a basis for quickly identifying "good" quality solutions for line layout problems associated with individual production scenarios and therefore yield a method to support risk averting line layout strategies aimed at finding robust solutions. This possibility is explored in more detail in the following section.

3. A robust line layout procedure

Building on the studies described in the previous section, a robustness based line layout procedure is described below:

Step 1. Identify the production scenarios associated with a problem including; n, S, m_{ijs} and p_s for $i, j = 1,...,n$ and $s = 1,...,S$.

Step 2. For each production scenario, select a sample size m, and use simulation to map the form of the corresponding volume distance distribution. Do this by randomly generating m line layouts and computing:

$$v_{xs} = \sum_{i=1}^{n} \sum_{j=1}^{n} m_{ijs} d_x(i,\ j) \qquad for\ x = 1,\ ...,\ m,$$

where $d_x(i,j)$ denotes the distance between workcenters i and j in randomly generated line layout x. This step yields the values h_{ys} for $y = 1,...,r$ and $s = 1,...,S$ where r denotes the number of cells of equal width used to characterize the histogram of all possible volume distance values, and h_{ys} denotes the proportion of observations in cell y of the estimated volume distance distribution for $y = 1,...,r$ and $s = 1,...,S$. For each scenario, cell y is characterized by an upper bound UB_{ys}, and a lower bound LB_{ys}, which correspond to the maximum and minimum volume distance values defining the range for cell y. Compute the expected volume distance distribution characterized by the objective function:

$$v_x = p_s \sum_{i=1}^{n} \sum_{j=1}^{n} m_{ijs} d(i,\ j)^k \quad fork = 1,\ ...,\ n!\ \ and\ \ x = 1,\ ...,\ m.$$

and compute h_y for $y = 1,...,r$.

Step 3. Define the minimum performance criterion for each scenario, β_s for $s = 1,...,S$ and $0 \leq \beta_s \leq 1$, and the minimum overall performance criterion for the expected value, β, $0 \leq \beta \leq 1$. To satisfy the minimum performance criterion for scenario s, the volume distance value of a candidate solution, v_s, must place it in the lower $(1-\beta_s)\times 100$ percentile of estimated volume distance values for all possible line layouts.

Step 4. Using any appropriate procedure, generate candidate solutions. One example naïve procedure can be the following. First, randomly select one workcenter from n workcenters and assign it to location 1. Second, randomly select one workcenter from the remaining $n - 1$ workcenters and assign it to location 2. Repeat the above step until only one workcenter remains, which will be assigned to location n. This is a simple unbiased procedure to generate one candidate solution. It can be repeated as many times as needed to obtain more candidate solutions. However, we should note that identical solutions are possible when this procedure is repeated.

For each candidate, compute v_s and c_s where $c_s = y$ if $LB_{ys} \leq v_s < UB_{ys}$ and $1 \leq c_s \leq r$ for $s = 1,...,S$. Compute analogous measures for the expected volume distance case, v and c. Terminate the search when a solution satisfies:

$$\sum_{y=c_s}^{r} h_{ys} \geq \beta_s \quad for \quad s=1, \ldots, S \qquad and \qquad \sum_{y=c}^{r} h_s \geq \beta \ .$$

The procedure described above defines a robust solution as one where the percentile volume distance value falls within a pre-specified range for each production scenario. It could be applied whether or not the p_s probability values are known. If these values are known, they can be used, along with other considerations, to guide the determination of the β_s aspiration values for $s = 1,...,S$. The expected value case is equivalent to the weighted flow matrix approach as described in Rosenblatt and Kropp (1992). In that study, it is argued that solving this problem directly tends, in itself, to yield a surprisingly robust solution. This possibility is investigated in further detail in the section below.

4. Applications of the robust line layout procedure

To study the procedure described in the preceding section, variations of two sample problems introduced in Malmborg (1999) are utilized. The paragraphs below illustrate the implementation of the four step procedure for the two sample problems.

4.1. Sample problem 1

Step 1. The first sample problem is based on the uniformly distributed, ten workcenter problem presented in Malmborg (1999). To generate a stochastic variation of this problem, nine additional material flow scenarios were randomly generated using the uniform distribution with $n = 10$ workcenters. Thus, Problem 1 consists of $S = 10$ production scenarios where it is assumed that $p_s = 1/n = 0.10$ for $s = 1,...,10$. Workcenter areas, (denoted as a^i for $i = 1,...,n$), are generated using the "ABC curve" concept as described in Graves, et.al., (1977). For all sample problems, a total facility area of 1000 square yards and a workcenter space requirements rank ordering of $a_1 \geq a_2 \geq ... \geq a_{10}$ is assumed. For randomly generated Problem 1, a 25%/75% distribution of space requirements holds, i.e., 25% of the workcenters require 75% of the total area in the facility. Thus, a fit parameter of $w = 0.2075$ results from solving, $0.25^w = 0.75$, and space requirements for individual workcenters are given by:

$$a_i = 1000[\ (i/10)^w - ((i-1)/10)^w\ ]\ for\ i = 1,\ ...,\ 10,\ \text{yielding:}$$

$$\{a_1,\ a_2,\ ...,\ a_{10}\} = \{620,\ 96,\ 63,\ 48,\ 39,\ 33,\ 29,\ 26,\ 24,\ 22\}.$$

(To facilitate performance validation of the procedure, each workcenter in the two sample problems is assumed to have a width of exactly one unit with unit load travel originating and terminating at centroids. This assumption reduces the sample problem for each scenario to a line layout with exactly 10! = 3,628,800 decision alternatives where the global optimal solution can be ascertained.)

Step 2. For the first sample problem, a sample size of $m = 10,000$ representing 0.275% of the size of the solution space for each scenario was selected based on recommendations reported in Malmborg (1999). A total of $r = 100$ cells were defined for the histogram associated with each scenario. The sampling procedure involved random generation of 10,000 sequences of size 10, i.e., line layouts, and then constructing a corresponding frequency histogram of volume distance values for each scenario. Sampling was done with replacement. A sample size of $m = 10,000$ provides reasonably accurate estimates of the volume distance histogram as measured by the fit performance measure:

$$F_s = \sum_{y=1}^{r} min\{f_{ys},\ h_{ys}\},$$

where f_{ys} denotes the proportion of observations in cell y of the actual volume distance distribution for scenario s. The results from using $m = 10,000$ and $r = 100$ with sample Problem 1 are:

$$F_1=0.966,\ \ F_2=0.966,\ \ F_3=0.964,\ \ F_4=0.969,\ \ F_5=0.963$$

$$F_6=0.972,\ \ F_7=0.962,\ \ F_8=0.956,\ \ F_9=0.960,\ \ F_{10}=0.966,$$

with $F = 0.964$ for the overall expected value of volume distance function. The F_s fit statistics summarized above are normalized for the actual distributions. That is, they represent the proportion of observations in the estimated distribution for each scenario which fall within the correct cells of the actual distributions for that scenario. For the estimated volume distance distributions, cell widths were obtained using $(UB_{ms} - LB_{1s})/m$ with:

$$LB_{ys} = LB_{1s} + (y - 1)\,(UB_{ms} - LB_{1s})\,/\,m \;\; and \;\; UB_{ys} = LB_{ys} + (UB_{ms} - LB_{1s})\,/\,m.$$

For the first sample problem, the values of LB_{1s} and UB_{ms} for the estimated and actual volume distance distributions are summarized in Figure 1. The "actual" values of LB_{1s} in Figure 1 correspond to the volume distance values for the global optimal solutions for the line layout problem associated with each operating scenario.

Step 3. The minimum performance criteria for sample Problem 1 were fixed to be $\beta_s = 0.98$ for $s = 1,\ldots,10$ with $\beta = 0.995$.

Step 4. The equivalent of a simple random sampling procedure was used to generate alternative line layouts. This was based on using the same 10,000 random sequences of size 10 used to generate the mapping of the volume distance distributions for each scenario. By programming the procedure to retain solutions meeting the above criteria, 11 line layout solutions were generated. The ranked percentile values (i.e., c values), for these of these 11 solutions are summarized in Figure 2. For all of these solutions, volume distance values associated with individual scenarios are in the lowest percentile of the estimated population of all possible solutions while the expected volume distance value lies within the lowest one half percentile of the estimated population of all possible solutions.

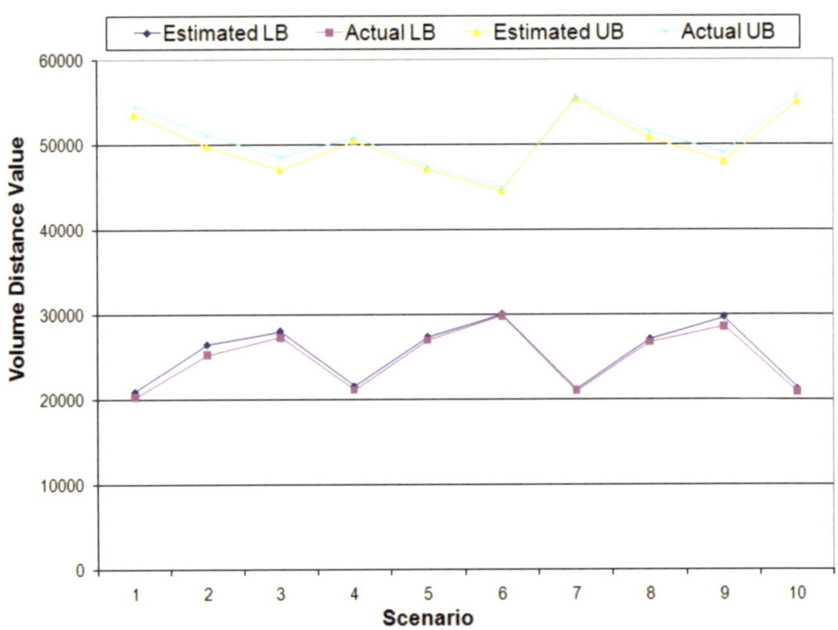

Figure 1. Comparison of Estimated and Actual Bounds for Each Scenario: Problem 1

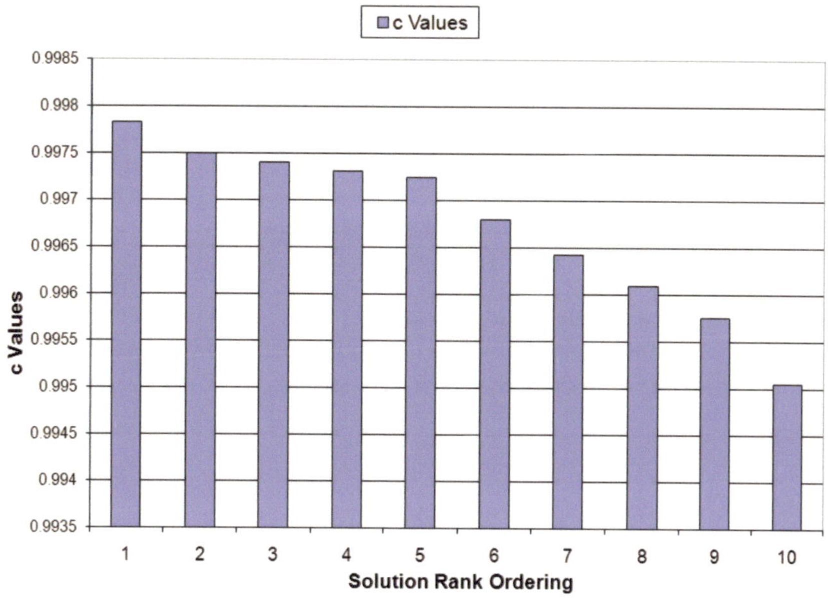

Figure 2. Ranked percentile Values for Problem 1 Solutions Meeting the Volume Distance Criteria

4.2. Sample problem 2

Step 1. The second sample problem was designed to illustrate a situation where both material flow parameters and workcenter area requirements are uncertain. In this ten workcenter problem, a total of twelve operating scenarios are based on the four sets of material flow parameters based on the uniform, normal, exponential and gamma distributions, and the three values of w illustrated below:

$$w=0.75: \{a_1, a_2, ..., a_{10}\} = \{178, 121, 106, 98, 92, 87, 84, 81, 78, 76\}$$

$$w=0.50: \{a_1, a_2, ..., a_{10}\} = \{316, 131, 101, 85, 75, 67, 62, 58, 54, 51\}$$

$$w=0.25: \{a_1, a_2, ..., a_{10}\} = \{562, 106, 71, 55, 46, 39, 35, 31, 28, 26\}$$

The four material flow matrices used in Problem 2 are taken directly from Malmborg (1999). Equal probability scenarios are assumed with $p_s = 1/12 = 0.0833$ for $s = 1,...,12$.

Step 2. Once again, a sample size of $m = 10,000$ representing 0.275% of the size of the solution space for each scenario was selected where $r = 100$ and sampling was done with replacement. Relative to the accuracy of estimates of the volume distance histogram as measured by the F_s fit performance measure, the results from sample Problem 2 are:

$$F_1=0.962, \ F_2=0.967, \ F_3=0.965, \ F_4=0.966, \ F_5=0.967, \ F_6=0.961$$

$$F_7=0.968, \ F_8=0.936, \ F_9=0.947, \ F_{10}=0.967, \ F_{11}=0.971, \ F_{12}=0.966,$$

with $F = 0.962$ for the overall expected value of volume distance function. As with sample Problem 1, the F_s fit statistics summarized above are normalized for the actual distributions. For each of the twelve scenarios associated with sample Problem 2, Figure 3 summarizes the cell boundaries associated with the estimated and actual volume distance distributions. In the figure, "actual" values of LB_{1s} correspond to the volume distance values for the global optimal solutions for the line layout problem associated with each operating scenario.

Step 3. The minimum performance criteria for sample Problem 2 were fixed to be $\beta_s = 0.99$ for $s = 1,\ldots,12$ with $\beta = 0.998$.

Step 4. Once again using a simple random sampling procedure to generate 10,000 alternative line layouts, line layout solutions meeting the minimum performance were identified. A total of nine solutions were found meeting these criteria with their ranked c values summarized in Figure 4.

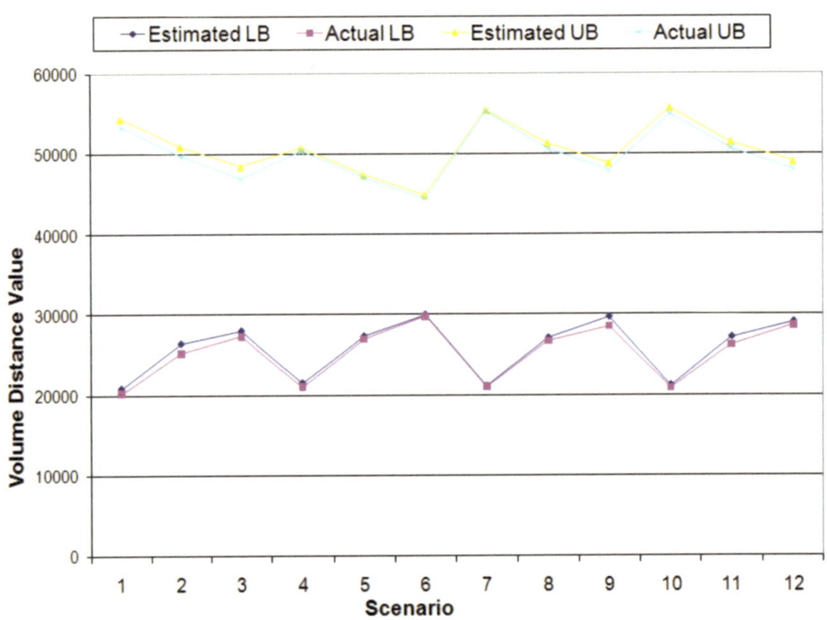

Figure 3. Comparison of Estimated and Actual Bounds for Each Scenario: Problem 2

http://dx.doi.org/10.5772/53195

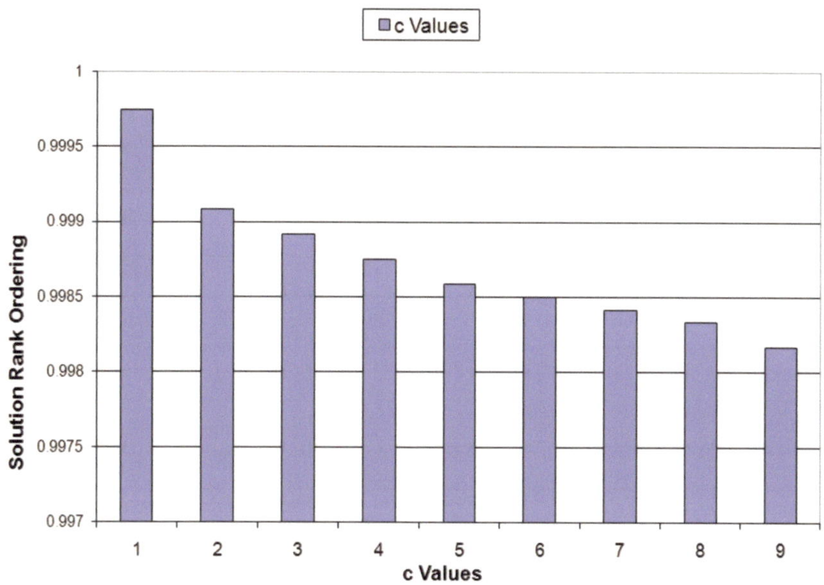

Figure 4. Ranked Percentile Values for Problem 2 Solutions Meeting the Volume Distance Criteria

Table 1 summarizes how each of the best solutions obtained from the method for Problems 1 and 2 compares to the global optimal solution for each scenario. For all scenarios, the best solution is within 10% of the global optimal solution. Clearly, the significance of these results depends on the extent to which the underlying volume distance distributions have been accurately estimated. However, based on the results in Figures 1 and 3, the empirical estimation of volume distance functions appears to be within reasonable accuracy for most practical problems where secondary criteria normally result in some tradeoffs of volume distance anyway. In addition, the results generally support the assertion of Rosenblatt and Kropp (1992) that solving dynamic line layout problems using the weighted average flow matrix tends to yield robust solutions.

Sample Problem 1:

Global		**Best**	**Percent**
Scenario:	Optimal Solution	Discovered Solution	Deviation
1	19012	20573	8.21%
2	18382	19404	5.56%
3	18284	19003	3.93%
4	19429	21060	8.39%
5	17850	19026	6.59%
6	20028	20784	3.77%
7	19869	20347	2.41%
8	20722	22186	7.06%
9	20626	21262	3.08%
10	18901	19752	4.50%

Sample Problem 2:

Global		**Best**	**Percent**
Scenario:	Optimal Solution	Discovered Solution	Deviation
1	20276	21498	6.03%
2	25291	27322	8.03%
3	27344	30023	9.80%
4	21103	21483	1.80%
5	27025	27559	1.98%
6	29862	30434	1.92%
7	21065	21335	1.28%
8	26754	27415	2.47%
9	28608	30170	5.46%
10	20901	21529	3.00%
11	26239	27195	3.64%
12	28644	29793	4.01%

Table 1. Comparison of Global Optimal and Best Observed Volume Distance Objective Functions By Individual Problem Scenarios for Sample Problems 1 and 2.

http://dx.doi.org/10.5772/53195

5. Nonlinear materials handling costs

When materials handling costs are nonlinear, the dynamic line layout problem cannot be reduced to the single QAP described in equation (1). This section assumes that four conventional materials handling devices are used in a facility, (i.e., four non-automated but possibly mechanized types of equipment) [Chan and Malmborg, 2010b]. Adapting a variation of the ergonomics-based device selection criteria similar to that presented in, [Al-Araidah et al., 2006], we use the following volume and distance based rules to drive device selection in the current study and arbitrarily assume the unit movement costs as shown below:

	$d(i,j)^k$ Range (ft.)	Maximum m_{ij} (units moved)	Cost/ft.
Hand Pallet Truck	$d(i,j)^k \leq 25$	4	\$0.18
Electric Pallet Truck	$25< d(i,j)^k \leq 63$	6	\$0.25
Stand Up Rider Truck	$63< d(i,j)^k \leq 125$	∞	\$0.28
Cushion Tire Lift Truck	$d(i,j)^k >125$	∞	\$0.30

Based on these distance ranges and capacity limits, the version of the dynamic line layout problem addressed in the current study can be summarized as:

$$\underset{k}{\text{Min}}\ v_k = \sum_{s=1}^{S}\sum_{i=1}^{n}\sum_{j=1}^{n} f(i,j,s)^k p_s \text{ , for } k = 1,...,n! \text{ where}$$

$$f(i,j,s)^k = \begin{cases} 0.18d(i,j)^k \text{ for } d(i,j)^k \leq 25 \text{ and } m_{ijs} \leq 4, \\ 0.25d(i,j)^k \text{ for } d(i,j)^k \leq 25 \text{ and } 4 \leq m_{ijs} \leq 6, \\ 0.25d(i,j)^k \text{ for } 25<d(i,j)^k \leq 63 \text{ and } m_{ijs} \leq 6, \\ 0.28d(i,j)^k \text{ for } 25<d(i,j)^k \leq 63 \text{ and } m_{ijs} > 6, \\ 0.28d(i,j)^k \text{ for } 63<d(i,j)^k \leq 125, \\ 0.30d(i,j)^k \text{ for } d(i,j)^k > 125 \end{cases} \tag{2}$$

Apart from nonlinear materials handling costs precluding the reduction of the line layout problem to a single QAP, variation in work center space requirements limits the use of optimization procedures that exploit a static parameter set describing the distances between the candidate locations in a facility. As described in, [Malmborg, 1999], the n(n – 1)/2 parameters representing distances between pair wise combinations of work center locations in a facility remains fixed in a line layout problem when work centers have equal areas. When work centers have unequal areas, the set of $d(i,j)^k$ parameter values change with each change in the assignment of work centers to locations in a facility. To illustrate, consider a simple line layout with three work centers A, B, C having areas, $a_1 = 20$, $a_2 = 10$, $a_3 = 30$ and arranged along a line with bidirectional travel, work center widths equal to one, and movement between work center centroids. The work center line layout sequences, {A-B-C} and {A-C-B} would respectively yield the distances between work centers given by:

$$Sequence:\{A-B-C\}\rightarrow\begin{bmatrix} d(A,A)^k=0, & d(A,B)^k=15, & d(A,C)^k=35 \\ d(B,A)^k=15, & d(B,B)^k=0, & d(B,C)^k=20 \\ d(C,A)^k=35, & d(C,B)^k=20, & d(B,C)^k=0 \end{bmatrix}$$

$$Sequence:\{A-C-B\}\rightarrow\begin{bmatrix} d(A,A)^k=0, & d(A,B)^k=45, & d(A,C)^k=25 \\ d(B,A)^k=45, & d(B,B)^k=0, & d(B,C)^k=20 \\ d(C,A)^k=25, & d(C,B)^k=20, & d(B,C)^k=0 \end{bmatrix}$$

This dynamic shifting in the $d(i,j)^k$ parameter set prevents the use of solution procedures that exploit static distance between location parameters, [Heragu and Kusiak, 1991, Bukhari et al., 1998].

The robust procedure described in Section 3 is used to solve this dynamic line layout problem with nonlinear materials handling costs and unequal work centers areas. The effectiveness of this simple procedure lies in the degree to which small vs. large random samples can identify a significant number of candidate solutions satisfying the candidacy conditions for acceptable values of β. The extent to which small sample sizes can accurately represent the distribution of cost values in a layout problem relative to large samples can be illustrated using a histogram fitting approach described in, [Malmborg, 1999]. To assess the extent to which small samples can be used to accurately estimate the distribution of materials handling cost values, the sample problem summarized in Table 2 is examined where n=9 and S=8. Table 2 presents the eight material flow matrices, scenario probabilities, and work center space requirements for this sample problem. The space requirements for the problem are generated based on an approximate total of 400 unit areas for the facility, i.e., $a_1 + a_2 + \ldots + a_n = A = 400$. Space requirements for individual areas are generated using the fit parameter, w, $0 \leq w \leq 1$, where:

$$a_i = A[(i/n)^w - ((i-1)/n)^w], \ \text{for}\ i = 1, \ \ldots, n \ \text{and}\ w = 0.25.$$

The w fit parameter imposes alternative distributions of space requirements in a facility and can be used to control the disparity between the largest and smallest work centers. For example, to approximate a space distribution where 20% of work centers consume 80% of total space in a facility, the fit parameter is obtained by solving, $i^w = 0.2^w = 0.8$ ▪ $w = \ln(0.8)/\ln(0.2) \approx 0.139$. The above equation is then used to estimate points along the curve resulting in the work center area values shown in the example of Table 2 where a fit parameter of $w = 0.25$ is used, (application of this definition yields a total of 404 unit areas after rounding off). The advantage of this representation is that it enables variation in the distribution of space requirements in computational studies using a single parameter.

s=1	s=2	s=3	s=4
0,5,4,8,1,2,6,2,8	0,3,2,3,7,4,8,9,3	0,2,4,8,1,6,6,4,4	0,4,6,8,1,1,8,7,6
4,0,6,4,7,3,4,5,4	4,0,6,2,1,6,4,9,8	2,0,2,7,6,6,8,2,4	9,0,7,2,2,1,7,6,7
6,7,0,9,1,7,6,4,9	6,1,0,9,3,9,4,6,3	3,5,0,5,6,6,9,7,4	3,1,0,6,9,5,5,9,5
9,2,5,0,9,4,4,6,8	1,7,6,0,8,8,8,4,3	5,1,8,0,5,6,9,1,5	5,3,3,0,4,7,9,1,6
4,7,8,3,0,4,3,5,8	7,1,8,8,0,1,8,1,3	8,7,5,4,0,1,3,2,3	7,7,4,9,0,1,9,2,8
3,5,1,7,9,0,1,5,6	2,4,2,9,3,0,7,2,3	6,4,2,1,5,0,8,4,7	7,7,7,2,2,0,7,2,2
4,3,4,7,2,7,0,6,9	4,9,1,3,8,2,0,7,3	3,5,5,8,9,4,0,1,3	8,5,4,1,4,1,0,4,4
4,6,2,2,1,1,4,0,7	6,6,9,7,4,7,3,0,8	6,4,9,5,7,5,2,0,5	3,9,7,1,3,2,4,0,9
5,3,5,7,6,6,8,4,0	1,8,7,4,2,3,7,3,0	8,9,3,9,2,5,4,3,0	4,4,4,5,7,8,6,8,0

s=5	s=6	s=7	s=8
0,3,2,7,3,3,5,2,5	0,6,4,8,1,9,4,9,5	0,9,2,9,2,4,5,6,2	0,2,5,6,8,6,3,5,5
2,0,4,4,4,3,7,7,3	5,0,4,7,9,8,2,8,6	4,0,9,5,2,2,2,7,3	7,0,6,9,5,7,2,9,6
2,6,0,6,7,2,6,4,8	1,7,0,4,8,4,8,9,6	1,3,0,7,5,7,3,8,2	5,2,0,8,1,9,3,7,9
7,3,8,0,4,6,7,7,1	2,4,2,0,2,9,5,7,2	2,2,2,0,8,1,9,5,3	4,3,4,0,9,5,1,5,2
3,5,6,4,0,1,6,2,4	5,9,5,4,0,6,1,7,2	4,4,3,7,0,6,1,4,2	9,5,9,1,0,1,2,3,8
5,1,9,2,8,0,6,5,2	8,8,9,2,3,0,9,7,5	1,6,4,1,6,0,8,3,7	6,2,7,6,9,0,5,9,2
8,2,6,9,1,9,0,7,9	9,5,7,1,1,1,0,2,5	4,1,5,5,7,4,0,3,5	3,9,1,6,3,1,0,9,2
7,6,3,8,6,6,3,0,2	4,4,2,5,2,3,7,0,9	1,7,6,9,6,6,9,0,3	1,3,9,2,8,1,6,0,5
6,8,1,4,1,5,8,2,0	1,6,3,8,3,2,3,1,0	1,3,3,1,6,1,5,3,0	7,5,5,9,6,8,1,6,0

with

$p_1=0.0436,\ p_2=0.1515,\ p_3=0.0759,\ p_4=0.1366,\ p_5=0.1732,\ p_6=0.1867,\ p_7=0.0748,\ p_8=0.1586$

$a_1=232,\ a_2=44,\ a_3=28,\ a_4=24,\ a_5=20,\ a_6=16,\ a_7=16,\ a_8=12,\ a_9=12$

Table 2. Sample Dynamic Line Layout Problem with n=9, S=8.

Assuming that the nine work centers each have a width of exactly one unit area, work centers are arranged along a line where bidirectional travel is used, and load transfer points correspond to work center centroids, the histograms of the materials handling cost values for the sample problem are obtained for the eight material flow scenarios using a resolution of r = 50 cells. Table 3 presents the b^{sj} values for s = 1,..., S and j = 1,..., r. A line plot of these values is presented in Figure 5 which clearly illustrates the discontinuous nature of the materials handling cost distribution resulting from the materials handling device selection rule. Using the alternative sample sizes of q=1000, 2500, 5000, 7500 and 10000, 20000, 50000 and 90000, (respectively representing 0.275%, 0.689%, 1.378%, 2.067%, 2.75%, 5.5%, 13.75%, and 24.75% of the sample space for n=9), sequences are randomly generated and the h_{sj} estimates are obtained. Table 4 presents the F_s values resulting from each of the eight random samples. The results in Table 4 suggest that larger samples do little to improve the fit of estimated cost distributions relative to smaller samples. This finding is consistent with that reported in, [Malmberg, 1999], where a similar phenomenon is observed with volume distance distributions. A similar observation has also been made in other studies [Chan and Malmborg, 2010a, 2011]

Material Flow Scenarios:
12345678
0.0050.0040.0040.0040.0040.0040.0040.004
0.0180.0170.0170.0170.0160.0170.0170.017
0.0180.0190.0200.0190.0190.0190.0190.019
0.0230.0220.0220.0220.0230.0210.0220.023
0.0370.0370.0390.0370.0370.0360.0370.039
0.0450.0450.0460.0460.0460.0450.0450.046
0.0420.0430.0420.0430.0430.0430.0440.043
0.0270.0280.0260.0270.0280.0290.0280.026
0.0070.0080.0060.0070.0070.0080.0070.006
0.0000.0000.0000.0000.0000.0000.0000.000
0.0000.0000.0000.0000.0000.0000.0000.000
0.0000.0000.0000.0000.0000.0000.0000.000
0.0000.0000.0000.0000.0000.0000.0000.000
0.0000.0000.0000.0000.0000.0000.0000.000
0.0000.0000.0000.0000.0000.0000.0000.000
0.0000.0000.0000.0000.0000.0000.0000.000
0.0000.0000.0000.0000.0000.0000.0000.000
0.0040.0040.0040.0040.0040.0050.0030.004
0.0120.0120.0130.0120.0120.0120.0120.012
0.0200.0200.0210.0210.0200.0200.0210.021
0.0240.0240.0250.0240.0240.0240.0240.024
0.0210.0210.0220.0200.0220.0200.0200.021
0.0310.0310.0330.0320.0320.0310.0320.033
0.0410.0410.0430.0420.0420.0410.0410.042
0.0370.0370.0360.0370.0370.0370.0380.037
0.0240.0240.0220.0230.0230.0240.0240.022
0.0080.0070.0060.0060.0060.0070.0070.006
0.0000.0000.0000.0000.0000.0000.0000.000
0.0000.0000.0000.0000.0000.0000.0000.000
0.0000.0000.0000.0000.0000.0000.0000.000
0.0050.0050.0060.0060.0050.0060.0050.006
0.0130.0140.0150.0140.0140.0150.0130.014

http://dx.doi.org/10.5772/53195

0.0230.0230.0240.0240.0240.0240.0230.024
0.0280.0280.0290.0290.0290.0280.0280.029
0.0260.0260.0260.0250.0260.0250.0260.026
0.0320.0330.0340.0340.0340.0340.0330.034
0.0380.0380.0390.0390.0390.0380.0390.038
0.0310.0320.0300.0310.0310.0310.0320.031
0.0260.0250.0250.0250.0250.0260.0250.025
0.0210.0210.0210.0210.0210.0210.0200.021
0.0260.0270.0280.0270.0270.0280.0270.027
0.0340.0360.0370.0360.0360.0360.0350.036
0.0400.0400.0420.0410.0410.0410.0400.042
0.0520.0520.0540.0540.0540.0530.0530.053
0.0520.0520.0500.0510.0510.0510.0520.051
0.0430.0430.0420.0420.0430.0420.0430.042
0.0330.0320.0300.0310.0310.0310.0320.030
0.0190.0170.0160.0160.0160.0160.0170.016
0.0100.0090.0080.0080.0090.0080.0090.008
0.0020.0020.0010.0010.0020.0010.0020.001

Table 3. Parameter Values, b_{sj} for $s=1,\ldots,S$ and $j=1,\ldots,r$ for the Nine Work Center Sample Problem with $n=9$, $S=8$, $r=50$.

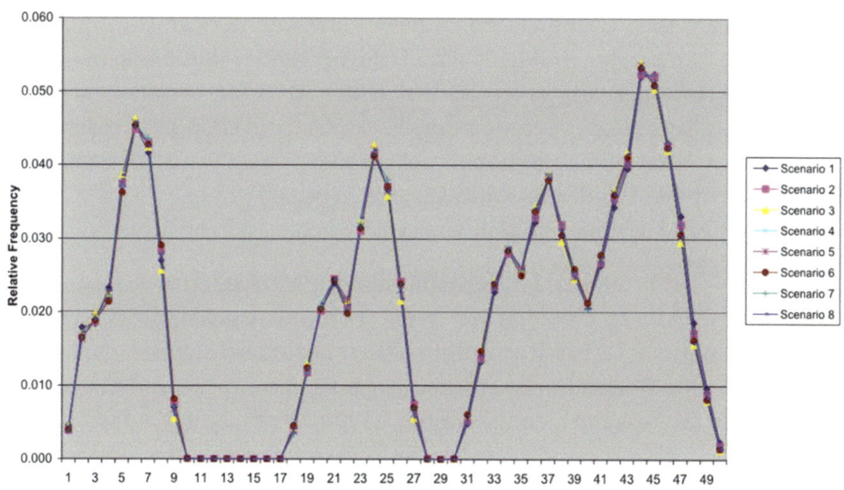

Figure 5. Materials Handling Cost Histograms for the Eight Material Flow Scenarios: $n=9$, $S=8$, $r=50$.

	q=1000	q=2500	q=5000	q=7500	q=10K	q=20K	q=50K	q=90K
1	0.839	0.819	0.806	0.808	0.823	0.826	0.826	0.823
2	0.833	0.823	0.809	0.808	0.822	0.825	0.817	0.816
3	0.837	0.821	0.806	0.807	0.820	0.824	0.820	0.818
4	0.834	0.822	0.804	0.805	0.819	0.822	0.814	0.813
5	0.834	0.819	0.802	0.804	0.817	0.820	0.817	0.816
6	0.835	0.816	0.804	0.806	0.819	0.823	0.821	0.814
7	0.835	0.818	0.801	0.803	0.819	0.821	0.817	0.817
8	0.836	0.824	0.810	0.810	0.823	0.826	0.816	0.816
9	0.836	0.824	0.807	0.809	0.823	0.827	0.822	0.822

Table 4. F_s Values for Various q and s Parameters With $r = 50$ for the Nine Work Center Problem.

6. Summary and conclusions

A procedure has been proposed for finding robust solutions to dynamic line layout problems. It is based on finding line layout solutions that meet minimum aspiration criteria for each operating scenario associated with a line layout problem. Following the simulation based strategy reported in Malmborg (1999), the procedure is to estimate the form of the volume distance distribution corresponding to each parameter set associated with a line layout problem. These estimates provide context for evaluating the performance of line layout solutions associated with the different operating scenarios that describe a line layout problem. Candidate layouts are then identified which meet minimum performance standards for all possible scenarios. Two sample problems with ten workcenters and one same problem with nonlinear material handling costs were studied which involved variation in material flow parameters and the distribution of space among workcenters. In each case, reasonably accurate estimates of volume distance distributions were obtained using just 10,000 random samples of line layout alternatives. Candidate solutions with expected volume distance values within roughly 5% of the global optimal solution were easily obtained in both cases.

The results from this study suggest a reasonable strategy for dealing with some dynamic line layout problems. Since these problems are generally unmanageable from a computational perspective, solution strategies based on optimization of volume distance for a static parameter set do not generally provide an attractive course of action. More importantly, such an approach may not adequately address the risks associated with inflexibility in the face of dynamically changing production conditions and/or under-performance resulting from stochastic variation in the production environment. Solutions exhibiting robustness provide a more effective alternative for dealing with the variation found in the majority of practical situations. The results from this study strongly suggest that finding such solutions, in many instances, should not prove particularly difficult.

http://dx.doi.org/10.5772/53195

Acknowledgements

The author expresses thanks for thoughtful reviewer comments that have improved this paper.

Author details

Wai Kin (Victor) Chan* and Charles J. Malmborg

*Address all correspondence to: chanw@rpi.edu

Department of Industrial and Systems Engineering, Rensselaer Polytechnic Institute, Troy, New York, USA

References

[1] Al-araidah, O, Krishnamurthy, A, & Malmborg, C. J. Simulated Annealing Algorithm for Block Layout Problems", International Journal of Production Research, 44(20), 4417-4429.

[2] Bazaraa, M. S, & Sherali, M. D. (1980). Benders' Partitioning Scheme Applied to a New Formulation of the Quadratic Assignment Problem", Naval Research Logistics Quarterly, , 27(1), 29-41.

[3] Bukhari, F, Malmborg, C. J, & Mcdermott, C. (1998). Predicting Volume Distance Performance for Line layout Problems With Static Distance Functions", International Journal of Production Research, , 36(9), 2339-2354.

[4] Burkard, R. E, & Bonninger, T. (1983). A Heuristic for Quadratic Boolean Programming with Applications to Quadratic Assignment Problems", European Journal of Operational Research, , 13, 274-386.

[5] Burkard, R. E, & Rendl, F. (1984). A Thermodynamically Motivated Simulation Procedure for Combinatorial Optimization Problems", European Journal of Operational Research, , 17, 169-174.

[6] Chan, W. K. V, & Malmborg, C. A Monte Carlo Simulation Based Heuristic Procedure for Solving Dynamic Line Layout Problems for Facilities Using Conventional Material Handling Devices." International Journal of Production Research, (2010a). , 48(1), 2937-2956.

[7] Chan, W. K. V, & Malmborg, C. Monte Carlo Simulation Methods for Dynamic Line Layout Problems with Nonlinear Movement Costs." European Journal of Industrial Engineering, (2010b). , 4(1), 40-58.

[8] Chan, W. K. V, & Malmborg, C. Monte Carlo Simulation Based Procedures for Solving Block Layout Problems." European Journal of Industrial Engineering, 5(1), (2011).

[9] Conway, D. G, & Venkataramanan, M. A. (1994). Genetic Search and the Dynamic Facility Line layout Problem", Computers and Operations Research, , 21(8), 955-960.

[10] Frieze, A. M, & Yadegar, J. (1983). On the Quadratic Assignment Problem", Discrete Applied Mathematics, , 5(5), 89-98.

[11] Goldberg, D. E. (1988). Genetic Algorithms in Search, Optimization and Machine Learning, Addison-Wesley Publishing Co., New York.

[12] Graves, S. C, Hausman, W. H, & Schwarz, L. B. (1977). Storage- Retrieval Interleaving in Automatic Warehousing Systems", Management Science, , 23(9), 935-945.

[13] Gupta, R. M. (1986). Flexibility in Line layouts: A Simulation Approach", Material Flow, , 3, 243-250.

[14] Heragu, S. S, & Alfa, A. S. (1992). Experimental Analysis of Simulated Annealing Based Algorithms for the Line layout Problem", European Journal of Operational Research, , 57, 190-202.

[15] Heragu, S. S, & Kusiak, A. (1991). Efficient Models for the Facility Line layout Problem", European Journal of Operational Research, , 53, 1-13.

[16] Kaufman, L, & Broeckx, F. (1978). An Algorithm for the Quadratic Assignment Problem using Benders' Decomposition", European Journal of Operational Research, , 2, 204-211.

[17] Kelly, J. P, Laguna, M, & Glover, F. (1994). A Study of Diversification Strategies for the Quadratic Assignment Problem", Computers and Operations Research, , 21(8), 885-893.

[18] Koopmans, T. C, & Beckman, M. (1957). Assignment Problems and the Location of Economic Activities", Econometrica, , 25, 53-76.

[19] Lacksonen, T. A. (1994). Static and Dynamic Line layout Problems With Varying Areas", Journal of the Operational Research Society, , 45(1), 59-69.

[20] Lacksonen, T. A, & Enscore, E. E. (1993). Quadratic Assignment Algorithms for the Dynamic Line layout Problem", International Journal of Production Research, , 31(3), 503-517.

[21] Malmborg, C. J. (1999). Estimating Volume Distance Characteristics for Line Line layout Problems With Dynamic Distance Distributions", International Journal of Production Research, , 37(2), 375-392.

[22] Malmborg, C. J, & Bukhari, F. (1997). Material Flow Analysis and Volume Distance Sampling in Heuristic Line layout Procedures", International Journal of Production Research, , 35(7), 2045-2063.

[23] Ritzman, L. P, Bradford, J, & Jacobs, R. (1979). A Multiple Objective Approach to Space Planning for Academic Facilities", Management Science, , 25(9), 895-906.

[24] Rosenblatt, M. J. (1986). The Dynamics of Plant Line layout", Management Science, , 32(1), 76-86.

[25] Rosenblatt, M. J, & Kropp, D. (1992). The Single Period Stochastic Plant Line layout Problem", IIE Transactions, , 24(2), 169-176.

[26] Rosenblatt, M. J, & Lee, H. L. (1986). A Robustness Approach to Facilities Design", International Journal of Production Research, , 25(4), 479-486.

[27] Sahni, S, & Gonzalez, T. (1976). P-Complete Approximation Problem", Journal of Associated Computing Machinery, , 23(3), 555-565.

[28] Shore, R. H, & Tompkins, J. A. (1980). Flexible Facilities Design", AIIE Transactions, , 12(2), 200-205.

[29] Skorin-kapov, J. (1990). Tabu Search Applied to the Quadratic Assignment Problem", ORSA Journal on Computing, , 2(1), 33-45.

[30] Skorin-kapov, J. (1994). Extensions of a Tabu Search Adaptation to the Quadratic Assignment Problem", Computers and Operations Research, , 21(8), 855-965.

[31] Webster, D. B, & Tyberghein, M. B. (1980). Measuring Flexibility in Job Shop Line layouts", International Journal of Production Research, , 18(1), 21-29.

[32] Wilhelm, M. R, & Ward, T. L. (1987). Solving Quadratic Assignment Problems by Simulated Annealing", IIE Transactions, , 19(3), 107-119.

Chapter 5

Comparative Study of Various Self-Consistent Event Biasing Schemes for Monte Carlo Simulations of Nanoscale MOSFETs

Shaikh Ahmed, Mihail Nedjalkov and
Dragica Vasileska

Additional information is available at the end of the chapter

http://dx.doi.org/10.5772/53113

1. Introduction

1.1. Semiclassical electron transport

Semiclassical Boltzmann transport has been the principal theory in the field of modeling and simulation of semiconductor technology since its early development. To date, most commercial device simulations including the full-band Monte Carlo (FBMC) method are based on the solution of the Boltzmann transport equation (BTE) and its simplified derivatives such as the hydrodynamic (HD) equations and the drift-diffusion (DD) model. The Boltzmann transport equation expresses the global variation of the non-equilibrium distribution function, $f(\boldsymbol{r}, \boldsymbol{k}, t)$, under the influence of various applied and built-in forces. In its most general form and for non-parabolic bands the BTE reads:

$$\frac{\partial f}{\partial t} + \mathbf{v} \cdot \nabla_r f + \frac{\mathbf{F}}{\hbar} \cdot \nabla_{\mathbf{k}} f = \left. \frac{\partial f}{\partial t} \right|_{coll}, \tag{1}$$

where v is the carrier group velocity. The terms on the left-hand side describe the change in the distribution function with respect to time, spatial gradients, and applied fields. The right-hand side represents the dissipation terms in the system, which account for the change of the distribution function due to various scattering mechanisms that balance the driving terms on the left. The Boltzmann equation is valid under the assumptions of semiclassical transport as follows [1]: (1) *effective mass* approximation; (2) First *Born approximation* for the

INTECH
open science | open minds

© 2013 The Author(s). Licensee InTech. This chapter is distributed under the terms of the Creative Commons Attribution License http://creativecommons.org/licenses/by/3.0), which permits unrestricted use, distribution, and reproduction in any medium, provided the original work is properly cited.

collisions in the limit of small perturbation for the electron-phonon interaction and instantaneous collisions; (3) Scattering probability is independent of external forces; (4) Particle interactions are uncorrelated and forces are constant over distances comparable to the electron wave function; and (4) The *phonons* are usually treated as being in equilibrium, although the condition of non-equilibrium phonons may be included through an additional phonon transport equation.

Full analytical solutions of the BTE are possible only under very restrictive assumptions. The two classes of computational/numerical techniques that are used to solve the BTE are as follow [2][3][4][5]: (1) First, in *deterministic methods*, the BTE is discretized using a variety of methods (such as discrete ordinates, spherical harmonics, collision probabilities, nodal methods) and then solved numerically. However, direct numerical methods are limited by the complexity of the equation, which in the complete three-dimensional (3D) time-dependent form requires seven independent variables for time, space and momentum; (2) The second class of techniques, named *Monte Carlo* methods, construct a *stochastic model* in which the expected value of a certain random variable is equivalent to the value of a physical quantity to be determined [6][7][8][9]. The expected value is estimated by the average of many independent samples representing the random variable. Random numbers, following the distributions of the variable to be estimated, are used to construct these independent samples. There are two different ways to construct a stochastic model for Monte Carlo calculations. In the first case, the physical process is stochastic and the Monte Carlo calculation involves a computational simulation of the *real* physical process. This is achieved by tracing the trajectories of individual carriers as they are accelerated by the electric field and experience random scattering events. The particle movements between scattering events are usually described by the laws of classical mechanics, while the probabilities of the various scattering processes and the associated transition rates are derived from quantum mechanical calculations. The randomness of the events is treated in terms of computer generated random numbers, distributed in such a way as to reflect these probabilities. In the other case, a stochastic model is constructed *artificially*, such as the solution of deterministic equations by Monte Carlo [10]. Both the deterministic and the Monte Carlo stochastic methods have computational errors. Deterministic methods are computationally fast but less accurate; whereas Monte Carlo methods are computationally slow yet arbitrarily accurate. *A great advantage of particle-based Monte Carlo methods is that it provides a unique and thorough insight into the underlying device physics and carrier transport phenomena* [11]. This insight originates from the very nature of the method employed that relies on a detailed simulation of a large ensemble of discrete charge carriers in the device active region. Therefore, the full *time-dependent* distribution function and related macroscopic quantities of interest can be extracted directly from the simulation.

In the last decade, with the continued downsizing of device dimensions into the nanoscale regime, many new and challenging questions have emerged concerning the physics and characterization of these small devices. However, contrary to the technological advances, present state-of-the-art in device simulation is lacking in the ability to treat the new challenges pertaining to device scaling [12]. First, for devices where *gradual channel approximation* (analytical modeling) cannot be used due to the two-dimensional nature of the electrostatic potential and the electric fields driving the carriers from source to drain, *drift-diffusion* models have been exploited. These models are valid, in general, for large devices in which the fields are not that high so that there is no degradation of the mobility due to the electric field. The validity of the drift-diffusion models can be extended to take into account the velocity saturation effect with the introduction of field-dependent mobility and diffusion coefficients. When velocity overshoot becomes important, drift diffusion model is no longer valid and *hydrodynamic model* may be considered. The hydrodynamic model has been the workhorse for technology development and several high-end commercial device simulators have appeared including Silvaco, Synopsys, Crosslight, etc. The advantage of the hydrodynamic model is that it allows quick simulation runs. However, standard hydrodynamic models do not provide a sufficiently accurate description since they neglect significant contributions from the tail of the phase space distribution function in the active region of the device. Also, the velocity overshoot in hydrodynamic models depends upon the choice of the energy relaxation time. The smaller is the device, the larger is the deviation when using the same set of energy relaxation times. In addition, the energy relaxation times are material, device geometry and doping dependent parameters, so their determination ahead of time is not possible. To avoid the problem of the proper choice of the energy relaxation times, a direct solution of the Boltzmann Transport Equation using the *Monte Carlo method* is the best method of choice. To-date, most semiclassical device simulations have been based on stochastic Monte Carlo solution methods, which involve the simulation of particle trajectories rather than the direct solution of partial differential equations. An additional problem arises in small structures, where one must begin to worry about the effective size of the carriers themselves. In the nanoscale regime, the charge transport is expected to be dominated by *quantum effects* throughout the active region. Quantum effects in the surface potential will have a profound impact on both the amount of charge, which can be induced by the gate electrode through the gate oxide, and the profile of the channel charge in the direction perpendicular to the surface (the transverse direction). Also, because of the two-dimensional confinement of carriers in the channel region, the mobility (or microscopically speaking, the carrier scattering) will be different from the three-dimensional (bulk) case. A well-known approach to study the impact of spatial confinement on mobility behavior is based on the self-consistent solution of the 3D Poisson–1D Schrödinger–3D Monte Carlo, which demands enormous computational resources as it requires storage of position dependent scattering tables that describe carrier transition between various subbands. In the smallest size devices, for a full quantum mechanical description, various quantum formalisms based on density matrices [13], Wigner functions [14], Feynman path integrals [15], and non-equilibrium Green's functions (NEGF) [16] have been developed and proposed with varying success to address these issues. The Green's functions approach is the most exact, but at the same time appears, from the historical literature perspective, as the most difficult of all. In contrast to, for example, the Wigner function approach (which is Markovian in time), the Green's functions method allows one to consider simultaneously correlations in space and time or space and energy, both of which are expected to be important in nanoscale devices. However, today, although the NEGF transport formalism has been well-established, accurate and full three-dimensional modeling of scattering-dominated transport in realistically-sized semiconductor devices using the NEGF approach is prohibitively expensive and the computational burden needed for its actual implementation are perceived as a great challenge. A successful utilization of the Green's function approach available commercially is the NEMO (Nano-Electronics Modeling) simulator [17], which is effectively 1-D and is primarily applicable to resonant tunneling diodes. On the other hand, within the semiclassical Boltzmann transport formalism, for modeling quantum effects in nanostructures, recently, different forms of *quantum effective potentials* have been proposed [18][19][20][21][22], and when used in conjunction with the BTE, provide satisfactory level of accuracy. The idea of quantum potentials is quite old and originates from the hydrodynamic formulation of quantum mechanics, first introduced by de Broglie and Madelung [23][24], and later developed by Bohm [25]. The work presented here focuses mainly on the modeling and simulations of nanoscale MOSFET structures within a *quantum-corrected* Monte Carlo transport framework.

2. The Monte Carlo method

Monte Carlo (MC) method was originally used and devised by Fermi, Von Neumann and Stanislaw Ulam to solve the BTE for transport of neutrons in the fissile material of the atomic bomb during the Manhattan Project of World War II [26]. Since these pioneering times in the mid 1940's, the popularity and use of the MC method has grown with the increasing availability of faster and cheaper digital computers. Its application to the specific problems of high-field electron transport in semiconductors is first due to Kurosawa [27] in 1966. Shortly afterwards the Malvern, UK, group [28] provided the first wide application of the method to the problem of the *Gunn effect* in GaAs. Applications to Si and Ge flourished in the 1970s, with an extensive work performed at the University of Modena, Italy. In the mid-1970s, a physical model of silicon was developed, capable of explaining major macroscopic transport characteristics. The band structure models were represented by simple analytic expressions accounting for nonparabolicity and anisotropy. The review articles by C. Jacoboni and L. Reggiani [29] and by Peter J. Price [30] provide a comprehensive and deep historical and technical perspective.

The Monte Carlo method is the most popular method used to solve the Boltzmann transport equation without any approximation made to the distribution function. In the Monte Carlo method, particles are used to represent electrons (holes) within the device. For *bulk* simulations, the momentum and energy of the particles (electrons and/or holes) are continuously updated. For actual *device* simulations, the real space position of the particle is updated as well. As time evolves, the updated momentum (and corresponding energy) is calculated from the various forces applied on the particle for that time step. The general concept of a Monte Carlo simulation is that the electrons (holes) are accelerated by an electric field until they cover a predetermined free-flight time. At the end of this, a scattering mechanism (due to impurities, lattice vibrations, etc.) is randomly chosen based on its relative frequency of occurrence, which randomize the momentum and energy of charge particles in time. The basic steps in a typical Monte-Carlo *device* simulation scheme include (see Refs. [31][32][33]):

http://dx.doi.org/10.5772/53113

1. Initialization.
2. Solution of the field (Poisson) equation: determine forces on electrons.
3. Simulate the electron dynamics (free-flight and scattering):
   a. Accelerate the electrons.
   b. Determine whether the electron experiences a scattering/collision.
   c. If electron scatters, select the scattering mechanism.
   d. Update the electron position, energy and wavevector.
4. Charge assignment to the numerical nodes/grids.
5. Compute measurable quantities such as average energy, average velocity, and mobility of the particle ensemble.
6. Repeat steps 2-5 for each iteration.

The *initialization* includes the calculation/setting of various material parameters such as the electronic band structure, scattering rates and (particularly for *device* simulation) the definition of the computational domain and initial electron distributions. In order to determine device characteristics, such as drain current in a MOSFET, it is necessary to solve the carrier transport equations using the device parameters (including doping concentration and type, channel length, channel width, and oxide thickness) and boundary conditions (such as terminal voltages) for the particular device being simulated. The device is divided into grids/cells by a numerical discretization technique (usually finite difference method). In the actual implementation, for each dimension, maximum number of node points is set as a program parameter and the relevant array sizes are optimally (often dynamically) allocated. Provision may be kept for using nonuniform mesh spacing along different axial dimensions of the device. The source and drain contact charges are then calculated by multiplying the doping density with the volume of a single cell. Then, the Poisson equation is solved for the applied gate bias only (keeping source/drain/substrate bias equal to zero) and the resulting potential distribution is used to populate/generate carriers in each of the cells in the active region through the use of appropriate equilibrium distribution function (usually Fermi-Dirac). It is always convenient to begin the simulation in thermodynamic equilibrium where the solution is known. When an electron is introduced in the device active region, the real space coordinates of the electron are determined based upon the position of the node where it is being added. Under the assumption of charge-neutrality, the total number of free carriers within the device must equal the total number of ionized dopants. In the non-equilibrium simulation, the remaining boundary biases are applied at different contacts/terminals (source/drain/substrate). The program control is then transferred to the Monte Carlo iterative transport/dynamics kernel. Here, for each pre-selected time step (typically fractions of femtosecond) the carriers undergo the free-flight-scatter sequence. During a time interval, Δt, each electron is accelerated according to Newton's second law of motion. For a semiconductor with *ellipsoidal* constant energy surfaces, such as silicon, the effective mass is a tensor quantity. Using Hering-Vogt transformation [31]

$$k_i^* = \sqrt{\frac{m^*}{m_i}} k_i \quad i = x, y, z \tag{2}$$

where m_i is the effective mass of the particle in the ith (x, y, or z) direction, one can make a transformation from k-space to k^*-space in which the constant energy surfaces are *spherical*. In the original k-space, due to the mass anisotropy, the constant energy surfaces are ellipsoidal. To determine the time between scattering events (free-flight time), the electron energy at the time of scattering must be known, since the scattering rate is a function of the electron energy. The rates for various scattering mechanisms included into the Monte Carlo model are pre-tabulated (in number of collisions per second) as a function of energy, which are usually calculated quantum mechanically using perturbation theory. Once the type of scattering terminating the free flight is selected, the final energy and momentum (as well as band or subband) of the particle due to this type of scattering must be selected. For elastic scattering processes such as ionized impurity scattering, the energy before and after scattering is the same. In contrast, for the interaction between electrons and the vibrational modes of the lattice described as quasi-particles known as phonons, electrons exchange finite amounts of energy with the lattice in terms of emission and absorption of phonons. The final k-vector is then chosen randomly. After a new k-vector is chosen, a new free-flight time is determined. The electron is then accelerated for the remainder of the time interval or until it encounters another scattering event.

To simulate an actual *device* such as a MOSFET, the device boundaries must be treated properly. The Ohmic contacts are often assumed to be perfect absorbers, so carriers that reach them simply exit the device. At the end of each time step, thermal electrons are injected from the contacts to maintain space-charge neutrality therein. The noncontacted free surfaces are treated as reflecting boundaries. For field-effect transistors, roughness at the surface of the channel can cause scattering. A simple approach is to treat some fraction of the encounters with the surface as specular scattering events and the remainder as diffusive scattering events. The specific fraction is usually selected to match transport measurements, such as the low-field mobility as a function of the transverse electric field. A carrier deletion scheme is also implemented at this stage. When completed, randomly distributed charges from the Monte Carlo simulations are assigned to the nearest node points using an appropriate charge-assignment method. A proper charge assignment scheme must ensure proper coupling (match) between the charged particles and the actual Coulomb forces acting on the particles, and thereby maintain zero self-force and a good spatial accuracy of the forces. Once the updated grid charge distribution is known, Poisson equation is then solved to determine the resulting potential distribution within the device. It is important to note that the electron concentration (in an n-MOSFET simulation) is *not* updated based upon the potential at the node point. In contrary, the hole concentration at each node point is calculated using the updated node potential with the assumption that the hole quasi-Fermi level is equal to that of the electrons (quasi-static approximation). The error introduced with the assumption that the quasi-Fermi levels for electrons and holes are equal is small since the hole concentration is negligible in the active region of the (n-MOSFET) device. The force on each elec-

http://dx.doi.org/10.5772/53113

tron is then interpolated from the nearest node points. The resultant electric field is then used to drive the carriers during the free-flight in the next time step. The whole process is repeated for several thousand iterations until the steady state is achieved. In summary, the Monte Carlo algorithm consists of generating random free-flight times for each particle, choosing the type of scattering occurring at the end of the free-flight, changing the final energy and momentum of the particle after scattering, and then repeating the procedure for the next free flight. At any time, sampling the particle motion throughout the simulation allows for the statistical estimation (by averaging over the particles within each slab of the active region) of physically interesting and key device quantities such as the single particle distribution function, average carrier density, velocity, mobility, and energy versus position. Lundstrom [32], Tomizawa [33], and Kunikiyo *et al.* [34] discuss the application of this approach to the simulation of two-dimensional transistors. A detailed description of a 3D Monte Carlo device simulator can be found in Refs. [31] and [35].

3. Description of the Monte Carlo device simulator

The major computational components of the 3-D Monte Carlo device simulator (MCDS 3-D) used in this work are shown in Figure 1. Regarding the Monte Carlo transport kernel, intravalley scattering is limited to acoustic phonons. For the intervalley scattering, both *g*- and *f*-phonon processes have been included. It is important to note that, by group symmetry considerations, the zeroth-order low-energy *f*- and *g*-phonon processes are forbidden. Nevertheless, three zeroth-order *f*-phonons and three zeroth-order *g*-phonons with various energies are usually assumed [28]. This selection rule has been taken into account and two high-energy *f*- and *g*-phonons and two low-energy *f*- and *g*-phonons have been considered. The high-energy phonon scattering processes are included via the usual zeroth-order interaction term, and the two low-energy phonons are treated via a first-order process [36]. The first-order process is not really important for low-energy electrons but has a significant contribution for high-energy electrons. The low-energy phonons are important in achieving a smooth velocity saturation curve, especially at low temperatures. The phonon energies and coupling constants in this model are determined so that the experimental temperature-dependent mobility and velocity-field characteristics are consistently recovered [37].

Figure 2 shows the rates for various scattering mechanisms as a function of electron energy used in the MCDS 3-D simulator. At present, impact ionization and surface-roughness scattering are not included in the model. Impact ionization is neglected, as, for the drain biases used in the simulation, electron energy is typically insufficient to create electron-hole pairs. Also, since it is not quite clear how surface roughness scattering can be modeled when carriers are displaced from the interface due to the quantum confinement effects, it is believed that its inclusion is most likely to obscure the quantum confinement effects. Also, band-to-band tunneling and generation and recombination mechanisms have not been included in the simulations.

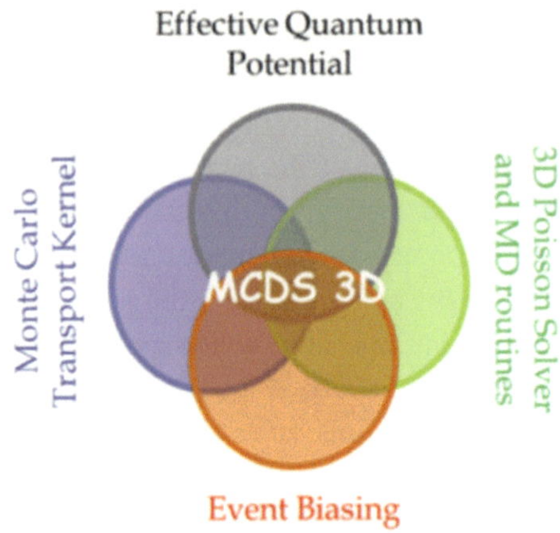

Figure 1. Three-dimensional Monte Carlo device simulator (MCDS 3-D) and the associated models/kernels used in this work.

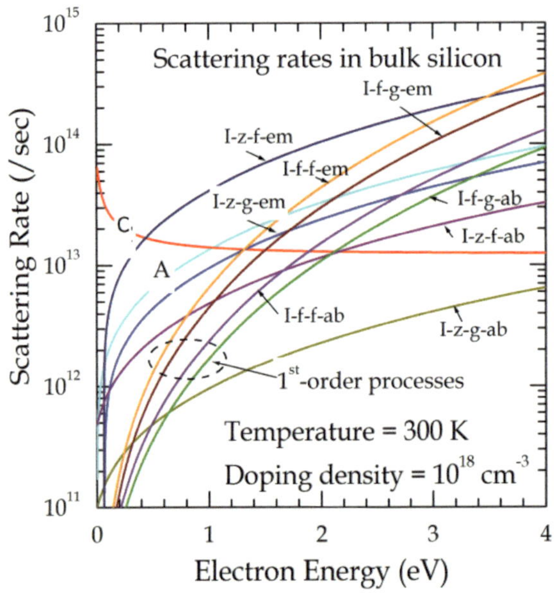

Figure 2. Rates for various scattering mechanisms as a function of electron energy used in the MCDS 3-D simulator.

The Incomplete Lower-Upper (ILU) decomposition method has been employed for the solution of the 3D Poisson equation. To treat full Coulomb (electron-ion and electron-electron) interactions properly, the simulator implements two real-space molecular dynamics (MD) schemes: the particle-particle-particle-mesh (P^3M) method and the corrected Coulomb approach. The effective force on an electron is computed as a combination of the short-range molecular dynamics force and the long-range Poisson force. The implementation details of these models and methodologies have been discussed in Ref. [35].

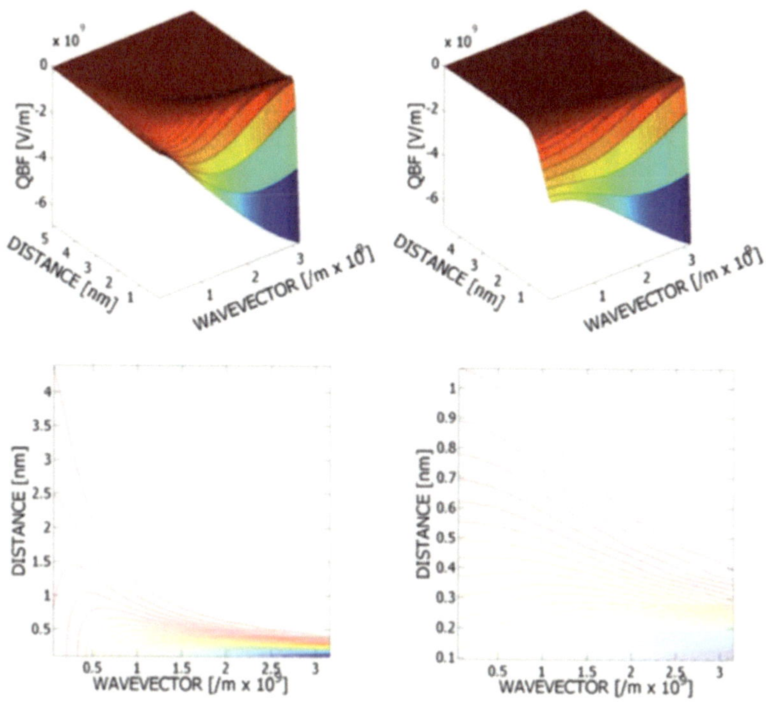

Figure 3. Variation of the quantum barrier field (QBF) as a function of distance from the Si/SiO_2 interface and wavevector k_y along the depth (left panel: low energy electrons, right panel: high energy electrons).

Quantum mechanical size-quantization effects have been accounted for via a parameter-free effective potential scheme [38]. The approach is based on a perturbation theory around thermodynamic equilibrium and derived from the idea that the semiclassical Boltzmann equation with the quantum corrected potential and the Wigner equation should possess the same steady state. It leads to an effective potential/field, which takes into account the discontinuity at the Si/SiO_2 barrier interface due to the difference in the semiconductor and the oxide affinities. It possesses no fitting parameters, as the size of the electron (wavepacket) is determined from its energy. The resultant quantum potential is, in general, two-degrees smoother than the original Coulomb and barrier potentials of the device, i.e. possesses two more classical derivatives, which essentially eliminates the problem of the statistical noise. The calculated quantum barrier field (QBF) for low-energy (left column) and high-energy (right column) electrons are shown in Figure 3 having the following salient features: (1) QBF decays almost exponentially with distance from the Si/SiO_2 interface proper; (2) QBF increases with increasing the wavevector of the carriers along the normal direction; (3) The contour plots clearly reveal the fact that the electrons with lower momentum feel the quantum field far from the interface proper, and (4) A similar trend is also observed with the variation in electron energy—electrons with higher energy can reach the vicinity on the interface, thus, behaving as classical point-like particles.

The *device output current* is determined using two different yet consistent methods [31]: (1) In the first approach, the charges (electrons) entering and exiting each terminal/contact are tracked with time. The *net* number of charges over a period of the simulation experiment is then used to calculate the *terminal* current. The net charge crossing a terminal boundary is determined by

$$Q(t) = q\left(n_{absorbed}(t) - n_{injected}(t)\right) + \varepsilon \int E_y(x,t)\,dy, \tag{3}$$

where q is the electronic charge, $n_{absorbed}$ is the number of particles that are absorbed by the contact, $n_{injected}$ is the number of particles that have been injected at the contact, E_y is the vertical field at the contact. The second term in (3) on the right-hand-side accounts for the displacement current due to the changing field at the contact. Eq. (3) assumes that the contact is at the top of the device and that the fields in the x and z direction are negligible. The net charge calculations are made for both the source and the drain contacts. Figure 4 shows a typical plot of net terminal charges for a 2 ps simulation run. The terminal current is measured from the slope of $Q(t)$versus time plot. In steady state, the current can be calculated by

$$I = \frac{dQ(t)}{dt} = \frac{q(n_{net})}{\Delta t}, \tag{4}$$

where n_{net} is the net number of particles (electrons) exiting the contact over a fixed period of time, Δt. It is important to note that in steady state the source current must be equal to the drain current. Therefore, for proper current measurements only those portions of the curves where the two slopes are equal, is considered. Note that the method is quite noisy, due to the discrete nature of the electrons; (2) In the *second* method, the *channel* current is calculated from the sum of the electron velocities in a portion of the channel region of the device. The electron (channel) current density through a cross-section of the device is given by

$$J = qnv_d, \tag{5}$$

where v_d is the average electron drift velocity and n is the carrier concentration. If there are a total of N particles in a differential volume, $dV = dL \cdot dA$, the current found by integrating (5) over the cross-sectional area, dA, is

$$I = \frac{qNv_d}{dL}, \tag{6}$$

or,

http://dx.doi.org/10.5772/53113

$$I = \frac{q}{dL} \sum_{n=1}^{N} v_x(n), \tag{7}$$

where $v_x(n)$ is the velocity along the channel of the nth electron. The device is divided into several sections along the x-axis, and the number of electrons and their corresponding velocity is added for each section after each free-flight. The total x-velocity in each section is then averaged over several time-steps to determine the current for that section. Total device current can be determined from the average of several sections, which gives a much smoother and noise-free result compared to counting terminal charges. By breaking the device into sections, individual section currents can be compared to verify that there is conservation of particles (constant current) throughout the device. Note that the sections in the vicinity of the source and drain regions may have a large y-component in their velocity and should be excluded from the current calculations. Finally, by using several sections in the channel, the average energy and velocity of electrons along the channel can be observed to ensure proper physical characteristics.

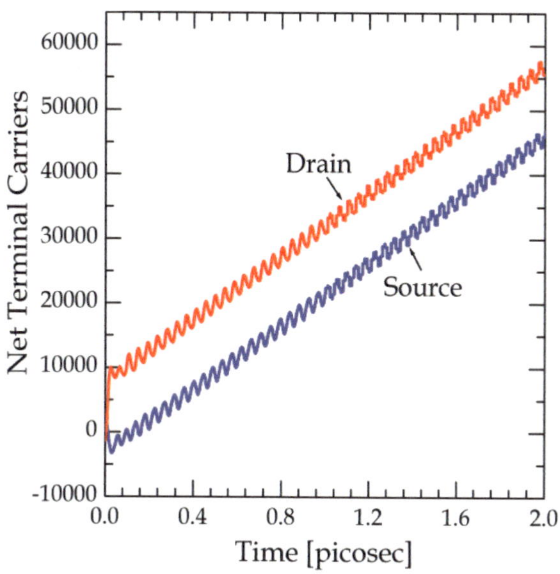

Figure 4. Typical plot of cumulative net charge at the source and the drain contacts.

4. Statistical enhancement: The self-consistent event biasing scheme

Statistical enhancement in Monte Carlo simulations aims at reduction of the time necessary for computation of the desired device characteristics. Enhancement algorithms are especially useful when the device behavior is governed by rare events in the transport process. Such events are inherent for sub-threshold regime of device operation, simulations of effects due to discrete dopant distribution as well as tunneling phenomena. Virtually all Monte Carlo device simulators with statistical enhancement use *population control* techniques [39]. They are based on the heuristic idea for splitting of the particles entering a given phase space region Ω of interest. The alternative idea—to enrich the statistics in Ω by biasing the probabilities associated with the transport of classical carriers—gives rise to the *event-biasing* approach. The approach, first proposed for the Ensemble Monte Carlo technique (time-dependent problem) [40], has been recently extended for the Single Particle Monte Carlo technique (stationary problem) [41]. In the next section, the basic steps of derivation of the approach in presence of both initial and boundary conditions has been discussed. Utilized is the linearity of the transport problem, where Coulomb forces between the carriers are initially neglected. The generalization of the approach for *Hartree carriers* has been established in the iterative procedure of coupling with the Poisson equation. Self-consistent simulation results are presented and discussed in the last section.

4.1. Theory of Event Biasing

The Ensemble Monte Carlo (EMC) technique is designed to evaluate averaged values $\langle A \rangle$ of generic physical quantities a such as carrier density and velocity given by

$$\langle A \rangle(\tau) = \int dQ A(Q) f(Q) = \int dQ f_0(Q) g(Q). \tag{8}$$

Where $Q=(k, r, t)$and Equation (8) denotes the integration over the phase space and time $t \in (0, \infty)$, and $A=a\theta_\Omega \delta(t-\tau)$ introduces the indicator θ_Ω of the phase space domain, where the mean value is evaluated at time τ. Equation (8) is the usual expression for a statistical mean value, augmented by a time integral with the purpose to conveniently approach the formal theory of integral equations. It has been shown that the Boltzmann equation can be formulated as a Fredholm integral equation of a second kind with a free term f_0. The latter is determined by the initial condition in evolution problems [38][42] or, in the case of stationary transport, by the boundary conditions [42]. The second equality in (8) follows from the relationship between an integral equation and its adjoint equation. It shows that the mean value $\langle A \rangle$ is determined by f_0 and by the solution of the adjoint Boltzmann equation

$$g(Q') = \int dQ K(Q', Q) g(Q) + A(Q') \tag{9}$$

$$K = S(\mathbf{k}, \mathbf{k}', \mathbf{r}) e^{-\int_{t'}^{t} \lambda(\mathrm{K}(y), \mathrm{R}(y)) dy} \theta_D(\mathrm{r}) \delta(\mathrm{r}' - \mathrm{r}) \theta(t - t') \tag{10}$$

where S is the usual scattering rate from lattice imperfections, λ is the total out-scattering rate, θ_D is the device domain indicator, which is discussed later, θ is the Heaviside function and the trajectories, initialized by (k, r, t'), are formulated with the help of the electrical force F and the velocity v as

$$\mathrm{K}(t) = k + \int_{t'}^{t} \mathrm{F}(\mathrm{R}(y))dy, \tag{11}$$

and

$$\mathrm{R}(t) = \mathrm{r} + \int_{t'}^{t} \mathrm{v}(\mathrm{K}(y))dy. \tag{12}$$

If both, initial f_i and boundary f_b conditions are taken into account, it can be shown that f_0 becomes

$$f_0(Q) = f_i(\mathrm{k},\mathrm{r})e^{-\int_0^t \lambda(\mathrm{K}(y),\mathrm{R}(y))dy} + \int_0^t \mathrm{v}_\perp(\mathrm{k}) f_b(\mathrm{k},\mathrm{r},t_b) e^{-\int_{t_b}^t \lambda(\mathrm{K}(y),\mathrm{R}(y))dy} dt_b. \tag{13}$$

While f_i is defined only at the initial time $t=0$, the function f_b is defined only at the device boundary Γ and for values of k such that the corresponding velocity inwards the domain, D. $\mathrm{v}_\perp$ is the velocity component normal to Γ so that a velocity-weighted distribution drives the particle flux, injected into the device at times $t_b \le t$. f_0 in (13) governs both the transient and the stationary behavior of a device. The latter is established in the long time limit, provided that f_b is time independent. Usually f_b is assumed to be the equilibrium distribution function.

A recursive replacement of equation (9) into itself gives rise to the von-Neumann expansion, where the solution g is presented as a sum of the consecutive iterations of the kernel on A. If replaced in (8), the expansion gives rise to the following series for $\langle A \rangle$:

$$\langle A \rangle(\tau) = \sum_i \langle A \rangle_i(\tau) \tag{14}$$

Consider the second term in (14) augmented with the help of two probabilities P_0 and P to become expectation [41] value of a random variable (r.v.):

$$\langle A \rangle_2 = \int dQ' dQ_1 dQ_2 P_0(Q') P(Q',Q_1) P(Q_1,Q_2) \frac{f_0(Q')}{P_0(Q')} \frac{K(Q',Q_1)}{P(Q',Q_1)} \frac{K(Q_1,Q_2)}{P(Q_1,Q_2)} A(Q_2). \tag{15}$$

It takes values determined by the second half with a probability given by the product in the first half in equation (15). $\langle A\rangle_2$ is evaluated according to the numerical Monte Carlo theory as follows. P_0 and P are used to construct numerical trajectories: (i) $P_0(Q')$ selects the initial point Q' of the trajectory. (ii) $P(Q', Q)$ selects the next trajectory point Q provided that Q' is given. The fraction W_2 in front of A, called *weight*, is a product of weight factors $\frac{f_0}{P_0}$, and $\frac{K}{P}$ evaluated at the corresponding points $Q_0 \to Q_1 \to Q_2$, selected by application of $P_0 \to P \to P$. The sample mean of N realizations of the r.v., calculated over N trajectories $(Q' \to Q_1 \to Q_2)_n$, $n = 1 \ldots N$, estimates the mean value $\langle A\rangle_2$:

$$\begin{aligned} \langle A\rangle_2 &= \frac{1}{N}\sum_{n=1}^{N}(W_2 A)_n \\ \langle A\rangle &= \frac{1}{N}\sum_{n=1}^{N}(WA)_n \end{aligned} \tag{16}$$

The iterative character of the multiple integral (15) has been used to introduce a consecutive procedure for construction of the trajectories. It can be shown that a single trajectory, obtained by successive applications of P, contributes to the estimators of all terms in (14) simultaneously i.e. the procedure is generalized in (16) for a direct evaluation of $\langle A\rangle$. Next, one establishes the link between (16) and the EMC technique, which is due to particular choice of the initial, P_0^B, and transition, P^B, densities. P^B, which can be deduced from (10), is a product of the conditional probabilities for free-flight and scattering, associated with the evolution of the real carriers. The ratio K / P^B is then the domain indicator θ_D which takes values 1 (one) if the trajectory belongs to D and 0 (zero) otherwise. The choice of P_0^B is complicated by the presence of both initial and boundary terms in (13). They decompose (16) into two terms which are evaluated separately as

$$\langle A\rangle = \frac{1}{N_1}\sum_{n=1}^{N_1}(WA)_n + \frac{1}{N_2}\sum_{n=1}^{N_2}(WA)_n. \tag{17}$$

The initial probability P_0^B for each estimator is obtained from f_i and $v_\perp f_b$ respectively, with the help of two normalization factors: the number of initial carriers N_i and the total number N_J of the injected particles into the device. The ratio f_0 / P_0^B for each of the estimators becomes N_i and N_J respectively, and can be eliminated by the choice $N_1 = N_i$ and $N_2 = N_J$. The two sums can be merged back to give

$$\langle A\rangle = \sum_{n=1}^{N_i+N_J}(WA)_n = \sum_{n=1}^{N_\tau}\theta_\Omega(n)a_n. \tag{18}$$

Equation (18) accounts that only trajectories which belong to D give contributions. As only the endpoint of such trajectories matters for the estimator, we speak about particles inside the device. N_τ is the number of such particles at time τ, and $\theta_\Omega(n)$ is 1 or 0 if the n-th particle is inside or outside Ω. All particles have weight unity and evolve as real Boltzmann carriers and the EMC technique for transport problems posed by initial and boundary conditions is recovered. A choice of alternative probabilities is called *event biasing*. Biased can be the probabilities for initial and/or boundary distributions, free-flight duration, type of scattering and the selection of the after-scattering state direction. It can be shown that (18) is generalized to $\langle A\rangle=\sum_{n=1}^{N_\tau^b} W_n\theta_\Omega(n)a_n$ where the position of the N_τ^b biased particles is accounted in θ_Ω.

The Boltzmann equation for Coulomb carriers becomes nonlinear via the interaction component $\mathrm{F}(f)(\mathrm{r}, t)$ of the electric force. As the results of the previous section are based on the linearity of the integral equations involved, it is no more possible to apply the steps used to derive the event biasing. The solution is sought in the iterative procedure of coupling of the EMC technique with the Poisson equation. The latter is discretized, as stated earlier, by a decomposition of the device region into mesh cells, ψ_l. The particle system is evolved in time intervals $\Delta t \simeq 0.1$ fs. At the end of each time step, at say time τ, the charge density $eC(\mathrm{r}_l, \tau)$ is calculated and assigned to the corresponding grid points. One uses the relation between C_l and the distribution function $f_{l,m}=f(\mathrm{r}_l, \mathrm{k}_m, \tau)$, which is estimated with the help of (18) by introducing a mesh ϕ_m in the wavevector space, $(\Omega_{l,m}=\psi_l\phi_m)$, as

$$f_{l,m}=\frac{\sum_n \theta_{\Omega_{l,m}}(n)}{V_{\Omega_l}V_{\phi_m}}C_l=\sum_m f_{l,m}V_{\phi_m}N_\tau=\sum_l C_l V_{\psi_l} \tag{19}$$

The charge density C_l is used to find the solution of the Poisson equation, which provides an update for the electric force $\mathrm{F}(\mathrm{r}, t)$. The latter governs the trajectories evolving the particles in the next time interval $(\tau, \tau+\Delta t)$. Between the steps of solving the Poisson equation the electric field is *frozen* so that event biasing can be applied. Assume that at time τ the particles emerge with weights W_n. Due to the event biasing the behavior of the biased particles differs from that of the EMC particles. The distribution function of the biased particles $f_{l.m}^{num}$ obtained from the above formula is entirely different from $f_{l,m}$. Nevertheless, as seen from (15), any biasing does not change the values of the physical averages. The Boltzmann distribution function is recovered by using the weights W_n as

$$f_{l,m}=\frac{\sum_n W_n\theta_{\Omega_l,m}(n)}{V_{\Omega_l}V_{\phi_m}}. \tag{20}$$

Accordingly, the correct F is provided by the Poisson equation. As the evolution is Markovian, $f_{l,m}$ presents the initial condition for the next time step. Numerical particles, having distribution $f_{l.m}^{num}$ and weights W_n present a biased initial condition for this step. The initial weight will be updated in the time interval $(\tau, \tau + \Delta t)$ by the weight factors according to the chosen biased evolution. It follows that the particle weights *survive* between the successive iteration steps, which completes the proof of the self-consistent biasing scheme.

4.2. Event biasing methods employed

Three different event-biasing techniques have been employed in this work. The chosen biasing techniques aim at increasing the number of *numerical* particles in the channel, but keep the total particle number in the device constant (for example, equal to 10^5). Particles, which enrich the high energy domain of the distribution on the expense of obtaining weights less than unity readily overcome the source potential barrier. Particle number in the low energy domain is less than the conventional ones, with higher weights and remain longer in the S/D regions. The methods are discussed in the following.

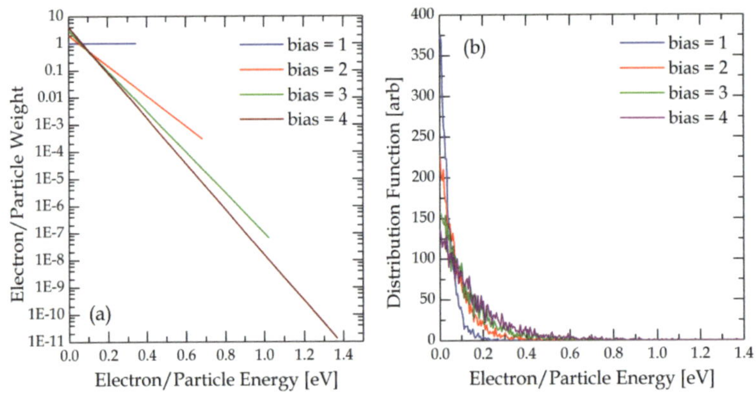

Figure 5. Weighting scheme used in the temperature-biasing method.

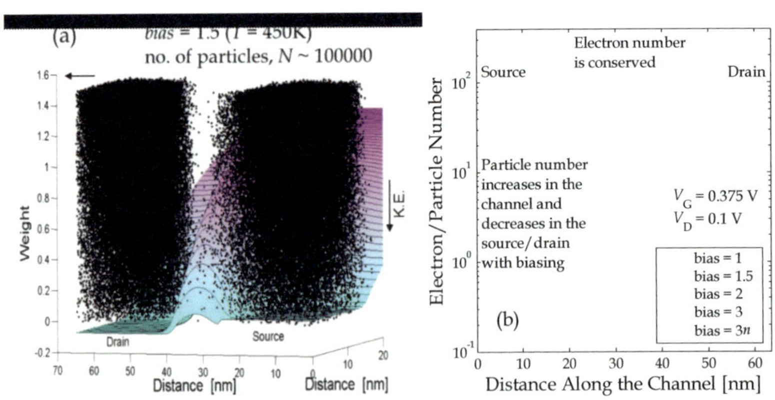

Figure 6. a) Weight distribution for $T = 450$K, and (b) Biasing decreases numerical particle number in the source/drain regions while increases the number in the channel region. Here 3*n* stands for *numerical* particles under *bias* = 3.

4.2.1. Biasing the initial/boundary temperature

Denoting the equilibrium distribution,

$$f_{eq}(\varepsilon,T)=\frac{1}{\bar{\varepsilon}}e^{-\frac{\varepsilon}{\bar{\varepsilon}}}, \tag{21}$$

where, ε is the individual carrier energy and $\bar{\varepsilon}=1.5k_BT$, one chooses a biased distribution

$$f_0^{\,b}(\varepsilon,T_b)=\frac{1}{\bar{\varepsilon}_b}e^{-\frac{\varepsilon}{\bar{\varepsilon}_b}}, \tag{22}$$

which corresponds to higher temperature $T_b = bias \times T$ ($bias > 1$). Having higher kinetic energy, the numerical particles readily overcome the source potential barrier and enrich the statistics in the channel. The weight distribution is governed by the formula

$$weight = bias\cdot\frac{\exp\left(-\varepsilon/\bar{\varepsilon}\right)}{\exp\left(-\varepsilon/\bar{\varepsilon}_{bias}\right)}. \tag{23}$$

The biasing scheme is illustrated in Figure 5. Increasing T_b increases the spread of the weight (and hence the distribution function) further away from unity which may lead to an increased variance of the physical averages, obtained by the mean of heavy and light particles. Thus finding the appropriate bias is a matter of compromise between the need for more particles in the channel (high temperature) and keeping the spread of the weight low (low temperature). The particle weight distribution for a particular choice of $bias$ = 1.5 (corresponding to a temperature of 450K) is shown in Figure 6(a). That biasing increases the numerical particle number in the channel region by decreasing the same in the S/D regions in illustrated in Figure 6(b) with $bias=3$. Also noticeable is the fact that different values of $bias$ do not change the actual number of physical electrons throughout the device region.

4.2.2. Particle Split

Particle weight is controlled by choosing a desired weight $w1$ of the numerical particles with kinetic energy below given level $\varepsilon1$ and weight $w2$ with kinetic energy above $\varepsilon1$. f^b is obtained from f_{eq} as follows:

$$\begin{aligned} f_0^{\,b}(\varepsilon)&=\frac{f_{eq}(\varepsilon)}{w1}, \quad \varepsilon\le\varepsilon_1 \\ f_0^{\,b}(\varepsilon)&=\frac{f_{eq}(\varepsilon)}{w2}, \quad \varepsilon>\varepsilon_1 \end{aligned} \tag{24}$$

$w2$ is obtained as a function of $w1$ and $\varepsilon 1$ from the condition for normalization of f^b:

$$w2 = \frac{w1 \cdot e^{-\frac{\varepsilon}{\bar{\varepsilon}}}}{w1 - 1 + e^{-\frac{\varepsilon}{\bar{\varepsilon}}}}. \tag{25}$$

A choice of $w1 > 1$ effectively reduces the number of particles below $\varepsilon 1$ as compared to the unbiased case. In both the above cases of biasing heavy particles which enter the channel perturb the statistics accumulated by a set of light weight particles (Figure 7). It is thus desirable to apply the technique of particle splitting in parallel to the temperature biasing in order to minimize the spread of the weight.

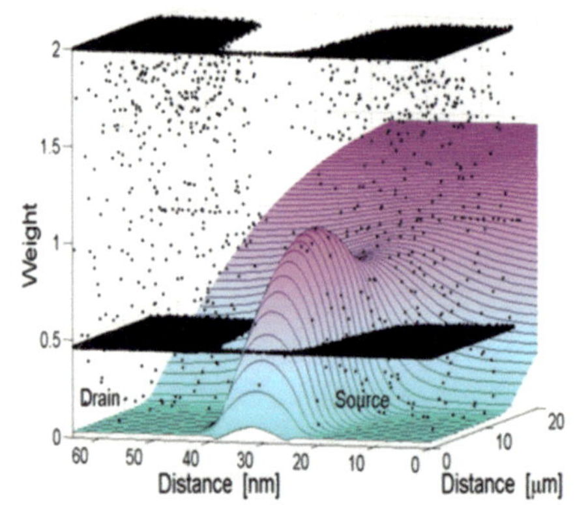

Figure 7. Particle split method and the distribution of particles in the device active region.

4.2.3. Biasing Phonon Scattering (e-a)

Artificial carrier heating can be achieved by biasing the phonon scattering rates. For a given scattering mechanism, the probability for phonon absorption is increased at the expense of phonon emission, controlled by a parameter $w1$,

$$\begin{aligned} \lambda_{em}^{b} &= \frac{\lambda_{em}}{w}, \quad w > 1 \\ \lambda_{abs}^{b} &= \lambda_{abs} + \left(\lambda_{em} - \frac{\lambda_{em}}{w} \right). \end{aligned} \tag{26}$$

If in the course of the simulation, a phonon absorption is selected, the particle weight is updated by a multiplication with $\lambda_{abs} / \lambda_{abs}^{b}$, otherwise with $\lambda_{em} / \lambda_{em}^{b}$. The distribution of the flight time is not affected, because the sum of emission and absorption rate is not changed.

http://dx.doi.org/10.5772/53113

4.3. Results from biasing experiments

The MOSFET chosen for the simulation experiments has gate length of 15 nm, channel doping of 2×10^{19}cm^{-3}, and oxide thickness of 0.8 nm. Similar device has already been fabricated by Intel [43]. The applied potential V_G = 0.375V, V_D = 0.1V correspond to a subthreshold regime at lattice temperature T = 300 K.

Figure 8 shows the standard deviation in electron number as a function of evolution time in a certain cell within the channel region. One can clearly see the improvement achieved from the use of event biasing techniques in the simulation. The standard deviation is least for method (a) where the initial/boundary temperature of the electrons is biased (at T = 450 K).

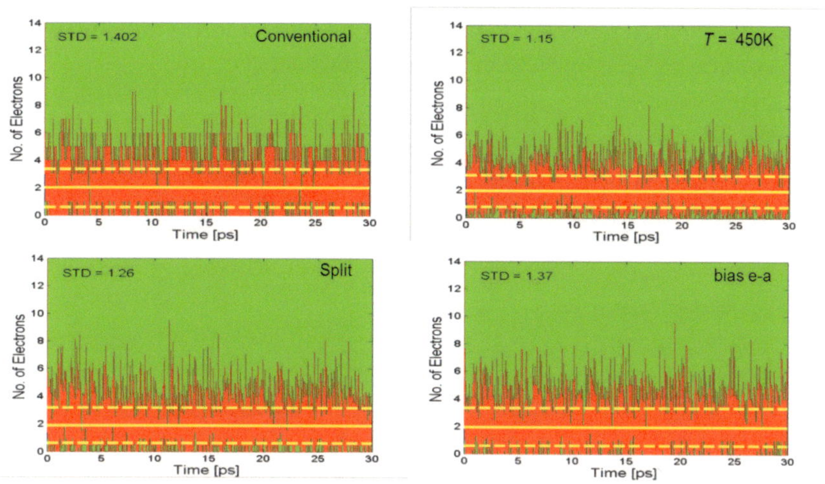

Figure 8. Enhancement of channel statistics: reduction of standard deviation in number of electrons in a particular cell in the channel region.

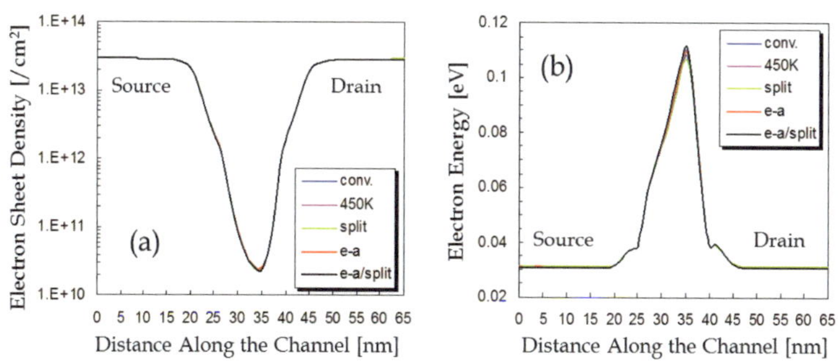

Figure 9. Biasing recovers precisely the self-consistent (a) average sheet density and (b) average kinetic energy of the electrons.

Regarding the validation of the biasing techniques, *first*, the consistency of the biasing techniques in the thermodynamic limit of a very large number (10^5) of simulated particles is investigated. Both Boltzmann (conventional) and biased stochastic processes must give the same evolution of the physical averages. Figure 9 shows that the biased experiments recover precisely the physical averages of electron sheet density and electron energy along the channel of the device.

Secondly, the convergence of the cumulative averages for the *channel* and *terminal* currents obtained from the velocity and particle counting, respectively, is investigated. Biasing the phonon scattering rates (e-a) is applied in the half of the source region near the barrier in a 4 nm depth. Figure 10 (top panel) shows the biased *channel current* as compared to the EMC (conventional) result for 30 ps evolution time. The 5% error region (straight lines) around the mean value is entered 2.5 ps earlier and the convergence is better. The *channel current* from the boundary temperature biasing (T = 450K) is shown in the bottom panel of Figure 10. The temperature-biased curve shows a superior behavior.

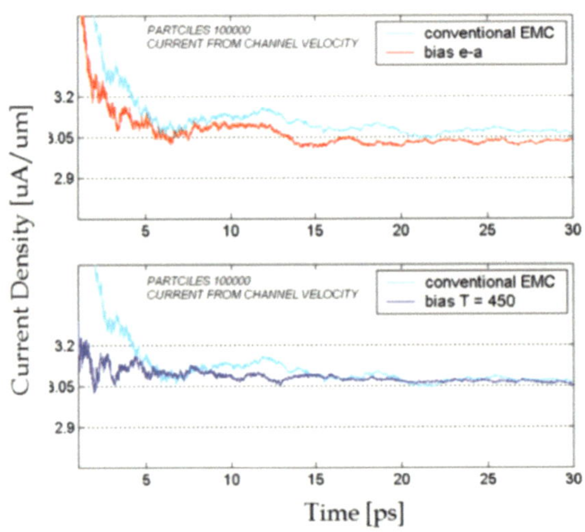

Figure 10. Comparison of *channel currents* obtained from (1) biased e-a rates (top panel), and (2) biased boundary distribution (bottom panel) methods from velocity consideration.

The corresponding *terminal currents* (shown in Figure 11) are much noisier and show long-time correlations due to the inter-particle interactions. The e-a biased curve is very unstable and enters the 5% error region in Figure 11 (top panel), after 15 ps evolution. One can associate this behavior with numerical error. The poor statistics is due to the appearance of very heavy (W >2) particles in the source as can be seen in Figure 12(a). To check this, it is sufficient to apply the conventional particle *splitting* coupled with the e-a biasing. The result is presented by the dotted curve in Figure 11. The behavior is significantly improved with the expense of a 30% increase of the simulated particles (the corresponding weight distribution is shown in Figure 12(b)). The terminal current corresponding to the biasing of the temperature of the injected particles again shows a superior behavior. This is due to an improved weight control. The weight, determined during the injection remains constant in the evolution. Its maximal value for T = 450 K is exactly 1.5 as depicted in Figure 6(a). Furthermore the probability for interaction with the impurities, which dominates the source/drain regions, drops for the majority of the particles due to their high energies. The conventional splitting technique cannot achieve such superiority. The terminal current from *particle split* technique is shown by the dotted curve on Figure 11 (bottom panel). The behavior of the curve resembles the EMC counterpart. An improvement is expected if the $w2$ particles are additionally split, which recovers the *conventional* split technique.

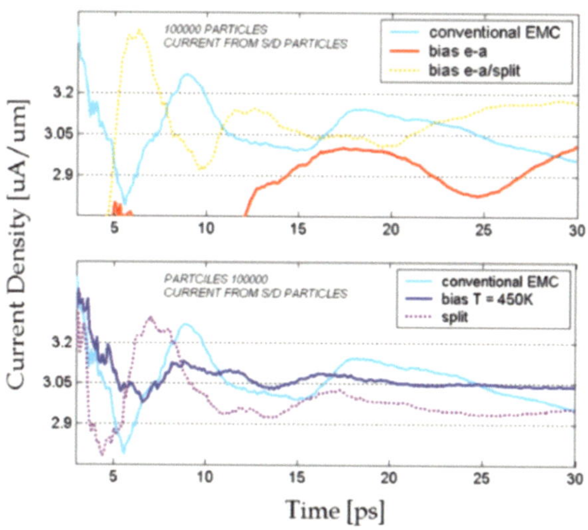

Figure 11. *Terminal currents* obtained from various methods by particle counting.

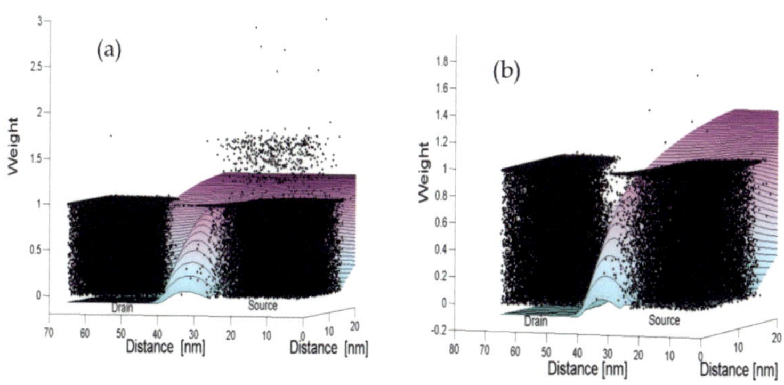

Figure 12. Numerical particle weight distribution in (a) e-a biasing, and (b) e-a/split biasing.

5. Conclusion

In conclusion, three event biasing techniques for particle-based Monte Carlo simulations of semiconductor devices have been derived in presence of both initial and boundary conditions and generalized for self-consistent simulations. All these approaches are confirmed and validated by simulations of a MOSFET with a channel length of 15 nm in the subthreshold regime of operation. A bias technique, particularly useful for small devices, is obtained by injection of hot carriers from the boundaries. The coupling with the Poisson equation requires a precise statistics in the source/drain regions. It is shown that a combination of event biasing and population control approaches is advantageous for this purpose.

Acknowledgements

Shaikh Ahmed would like to thank Sharnali Islam for her assistance in editing the text. This work was partially supported by the National Science Foundation (Grant No. ECCS-1102192). Computational resource/time supported by the ORAU/ORNL High-Performance Computing Grant 2009 is acknowledged. Mihail Nedjalkov would like to acknowledge the Austrian Science Fund (FWF) P21685-N22 and the Bulgarian Science Fund DTK 02/44.

Author details

Shaikh Ahmed[1], Mihail Nedjalkov[2] and Dragica Vasileska[1*]

*Address all correspondence to: vasileska@asu.edu

1 Department of Electrical and Computer Engineering, Southern Illinois University at Carbondale, Carbondale, USA

2 Institute for Microelectronics, Technical University of Wien, Austria

3 School of Electrical, Computer and Energy Engineering, Arizona State University, Tempe, USA

References

[1] Iafrate G. Introduction. In: Ferry DK., Jacoboni C. (ed.) Quantum Transport in Semiconductors. Plenum Press: New York and London; 1992. pxv-xxi.

[2] Ferry DK. Semiconductor Transport. Taylor & Francis: London, UK; 2000.

[3] Lewis EE., Miller, WF. Computational Methods of Neutron Transport, American Nuclear Society, Inc.: La Grange Park, Illinois; 1993.

[4] Majumdar A. Development of a Multiple Perturbation Monte Carlo Method for Eigenvalue Problems and Implementation on Parallel Processors. Ph.D. dissertation: The University of Michigan; 1996.

[5] Duderstadt JJ., Martin WR. Transport Theory. John Wiley & Sons: New York; 1979.

[6] Hammersley JM. et al. Monte Carlo Methods. John Wiley & Sons: New York; 1964.

[7] Lux I., Koblinger L. Monte Carlo Particle Transport Methods: Neutron and Photon Calculations. CRC Press: Florida; 1991.

[8] Rubinstein RY. Simulation and the Monte Carlo Method. John Wiley & Sons: New York; 1981.

[9] Spanier J., Gelbard EM. Monte Carlo Principles and Neutron Transport Problems. Addison-Wesley: Reading, Massachusetts; 1969.

[10] Kosina H., Nedjalkov M., Selberherr S. Theory of the Monte Carlo method for semiconductor device simulation. IEEE Transactions on Electron Devices 2000; 47 1898–1908.

[11] Fjeldly TA., Shur MS. Simulation and Modeling of Compound Semiconductor Devices. In: Shur MS. (ed.) Compound Semiconductor Electronics: The Age of Maturity. World Scientific; 1996. 317–364.

[12] Vasileska D., Mamaluy D., Khan H. R., Raleva K., Goodnick SM. Semiconductor Device Modeling. Journal of Computational and Theoretical Nanoscience 2008; 5 1–32.

[13] Ferry DK., Goodnick SM. Transport in Nanostructures. Cambridge University Press; 1997.

[14] Wigner E. On the quantum correction for thermodynamic equilibrium. Phys. Rev 1932; 40 749–759.

[15] Feynman R., Kleinert H. Effective classical partition functions. Phys. Rev. A 1986; 34 5080–5084.

[16] Datta S. Quantum Transport: Atom to Transistor. Cambridge University Press; 2005.

[17] Lake R., Klimeck G., Bowen RC., Jovanovic D. Single and multiband modeling of quantum electron transport through layered semiconductor devices J. Appl. Phys. 1997; 81 7845.

[18] Iafrate GJ., Grubin HL., Ferry DK. Utilization of quantum distribution functions for ultra-submicron device transport. Journal de Physique 1981; 42 (Colloq. 7) 307–312.

[19] Ferry DK., Zhou JR. Form of the quantum potential for use in hydrodynamic equations for semiconductor device modeling. Phys. Rev. B 1993; 48 7944–7950.

[20] Ferry DK. Effective potential and the onset of quantization in ultrasmall MOSFETs. Superlattices and Microstructures 2000; 28 419–423.

[21] Ringhofer C., Gardner CL. Smooth QHD model simulation of the resonant tunneling diodes. VLSI Design 1998; 8 143–146.

[22] Vasileska D., Khan H., Ahmed SS. Modeling Coulomb effects in nanoscale devices. Journal of Computational and Theoretical Nanoscience 2008; 5(9) 1793–1827.

[23] Broglie L. De. Sur la possibilité de relier les phénomènes d'interference et de diffraction á la théorie des quanta de luminère. C. R. Acad. Sci. Paris 1926; 183 447–448.

[24] Madelung E. Quantatheorie in hydrodynamischer form. Z. Phys. 1926; 40 322–326.

[25] Bohm D. A suggested interpretation of the quantum theory in terms of hidden variables I and II. Phys. Rev. 1952; 85 166–193.

[26] Fischetti M., Laux S. Monte Carlo study of electron transport in silicon inversion layers. Physical Review B 1993; 48 2244–22743.

[27] Kurosawa. J. Phys. Soc. Jpn. 1966; 21 424.

[28] Fawcett W., Boardman DA., Swain S. J. Phys. Chem. Solids 1970; 31 1963.

[29] Jacoboni C., Reggiani L. The Monte Carlo Method for the Solution of Charge Transport in Semiconductors with Applications to Covalent Materials. Rev. Modern Phys 1983; 55 645–705.

[30] Price PJ. Semiconductors and Semimetals 1979; 14 249–308.

[31] Gross WJ. Three-dimensional particle-based simulations of deep sub-micron MOSFET devices. Ph. D. dissertation: Arizona State University; 1999.

[32] Lundstrom M. Fundamentals of Carrier Transport. Cambridge University Press; 2000.

[33] Tomizawa K. Numerical Simulation of Submicron Semiconductor Devices. Artech House: Boston; 1993.

[34] Kunikuyo T., Takenaka M., Kamakura Y., Yamaji M., Mizuno H., Morifuji M. A Monte Carlo simulation of anisotropic electron transport in silicon using full band structure and anisotropic impact-ionization model. Journal of Applied Physics 1994; 75 297–312.

[35] Ahmed SS. Quantum and Coulomb Effects in Nanoscale Devices. Ph.D. dissertation: Arizona State University; 2005.

[36] Ferry DK. First-Order Optical and Intervalley Scattering in Semiconductors. Phys. Rev. B 1976; 14 1605–1609.

[37] Gross WJ., Vasileska D., Ferry DK. 3D Simulations of Ultra-Small MOSFETs with Real-Space Treatment of the Electron-Electron and Electron-Ion Interactions. VLSI Design 2000; 10 437–452.

http://dx.doi.org/10.5772/53113

[38] Ahmed SS., Ringhofer C., Vasileska D. Parameter-Free Effective Potential Method for Use in Particle-Based Device Simulations. IEEE Transactions on Nanotechnology 2005; 4 465–471.

[39] Wordelman C., Kwan T., Snell C. Comparison of statistical enhancement methods for Monte Carlo semiconductor simulations. IEEE Transactions on Computer-Aided Design 1998; 17(12) 1230–1235.

[40] Rota L., Jacoboni C., Poli P. Weighted Ensemble Monte-Carlo. Solid-State Electronics 1989; 32(12) 1417–1421.

[41] Kosina H., Nedjalkov M., Selberherr S. The stationary Monte-Carlo method for device simulaton–Part I and Part II. Journal of Applied Physics 2003; 93(6) 3553–3571.

[42] Jacoboni C. Principles of Quantum Transport. In: Ferry D., Jacoboni C. (ed.) Quantum Transport in Semiconductors. Plenum Press: New York and London; 1992. p1–15.

[43] Jacoboni C. A New Approach to Monte Carlo Simulation. PRIEDM, IEEE Electron Devices Society 1989; 469–472.

[44] Chau R., Boyanov B., Doyle B., Doczy M., Datta S., Hareland S., Jin B., Kavalieros J., Metz M. Silicon nano-transistors for logic applications. Proceedings of the 4th Int. Symp. on Nanostructures and Mesoscopic Systems, 17-21 February 2003, Tempe Mission Palms Hotel, Temepe, Arizona, USA.

Chapter 6

Atomistic Monte Carlo Simulations on the Formation of Carbonaceous Mesophase in Large Ensembles of Polyaromatic Hydrocarbons

R. Khanna, A. M. Waters and V. Sahajwalla

Additional information is available at the end of the chapter

http://dx.doi.org/10.5772/53370

1. Introduction

Nano-carbons comprise a class of advanced materials generally associated with high strength and light weight with applications as composites, heat-sinks and battery electrodes, and in the aerospace, automotive and sports-equipment industries [1]. On the molecular scale, carbon materials are composed largely of graphene layers – planar layers of carbon atoms which are covalently bonded into hexagonal aromatic rings [2]. These graphene layers pack together and fold over one another to form a variety of different microscopic textures. The amount of order present in this texture greatly influences the macroscopic mechanical properties of the material, and so is an important consideration for the materials engineer. A well-ordered texture, for example, can be readily converted into an anisotropic, graphitic structure (in a process known as graphitisation), whereas a highly disordered texture tends to simply fuse into an isotropic, glassy structure [3]. The clear distinction between these two types of carbons (graphitising and non-graphitising respectively) was originally made by Frankin in 1951 [4] based on the X-ray diffraction of several carbon materials.

Carbon materials are often derived from the poly aromatic hydrocarbons, a major component of pitch materials. 80% of industrial carbon is produced from pitch precursors, particularly from petroleum-derived pitches [5]. Pitch is a cheap material, and its low cost gives it a wide range of potential applications. When a pitch is converted into a carbon material, the degree of textural ordering of the graphene layers depends strongly on the formation of a mesophase at high temperatures. A range of carbonaceous materials are formed from pitch precursors, the nanostructures of which are dependent upon the formation of this mesophase. Examples of these include carbon fibres, nanofibres, nanotubes, and foams.

INTECH
open science | open minds

© 2013 The Author(s). Licensee InTech. This chapter is distributed under the terms of the Creative Commons Attribution License http://creativecommons.org/licenses/by/3.0), which permits unrestricted use, distribution, and reproduction in any medium, provided the original work is properly cited.

One of the key issues during the processing of carbon materials is the formation carbonaceous mesophase, a liquid crystalline phase that can form during the heat treatment of a variety of pitch materials [6, 7]. As the anisotropy of the final product is determined to some extent by this phase, the formation or otherwise of this phase is a key step in the production of long-range ordered carbon structures. It therefore becomes important to understand the role played by factors such as molecular size, shape, the presence of aliphatic rings etc. driving this phase transformation [8].

Despite the importance of this phase, little is known about its fundamental atomistic behaviour. It is currently very difficult to obtain polycyclic aromatic hydrocarbons in sufficient purity for experimental studies of the phase behaviour [9]. Pitches generally contain a large distribution of molecule sizes/shapes and the isolation of a specific molecule is very difficult unless these molecules are artificially grown under controlled conditions [10]. Another key difficulty is that the polymerisation of the molecules is unavoidable at the temperatures required to experimentally observe the mesophase, thereby destroying the original molecule being studied [11]. To the best of our knowledge, a direct fundamental experimental investigation on carbonaceous meso-phase is currently not possible on a molecular level.

Polycyclic aromatic hydrocarbons (PAH) of high molecular weight (> 400 Daltons) are the primary constituents of pitches [12]. These are formed *in situ* by cyclization, dehydrogenation, and polymerization during carbonization of diverse organic materials [13]. Although carbonaceous meso-phase has been experimentally observed in a number of systems, these are generally complex mixtures of thousands of molecules. The fundamental information regarding specific molecular constituents is difficult to come by from experimental data. Molecular weights of about 600 or more are believed to be required for the formation of carbonaceous mesophase, the discotic nematic liquid crystalline intermediate that provides an effective route to long-range (> 1 μm) crystalline order in carbonaceous materials [14].

Molecular modelling and computer simulation can play an especially important role in such a study. There have been a number of molecular modelling studies focused on non-covalent PAH interactions [15-17], but the size and complexity of the molecules involved have restricted most studies to energy calculations on polyaromatic clusters (dimers, trimers, and tetramers) and simulations of large disk ensembles using molecular pseudo-potentials [18,19]. These large PAH molecules assemble by non-covalent interactions into supra-molecular structures. There have been a few interesting studies of Gay-Berne discotic phase behaviour [20], but there is no obvious way to relate detailed molecular structure (aliphatic groups, non-planar heterocylic rings, irregular polyaromatic cores) to the empirical potential parameters.

Our group has developed an isobaric-isothermal Monte Carlo technique for simulating large ensembles of discotic molecules based on massive summation of atomic pair potentials [21]. This technique explicitly uses description of atom locations with no adjustable potential parameters. A parametric study of molecular structural features such as non-planar aliphatic rings, irregularly-shaped polyaromatic cores was carried out. The formation of carbonaceous meso-phase was reported in an irregular pitch molecule containing 58C and 28H atoms. The phase behaviour was found to be sensitive to minor perturbations in the molecular structure.

A study was also carried out on a large regular molecule that also showed the formation of meso-phase [22].

In this paper, we report computer simulations results on the phase behaviour of five organic molecules in a range of sizes and shapes. The aim is to determine the effect of molecular size and shape on the formation of carbonaceous meso-phase towards developing an understanding of basic mechanisms and factors affecting this transition. The article is organised as follows. In section 2, we present details of molecules under investigation and their specific features. Simulation algorithms, macromolecular interaction potentials and results on ordered ground state structures are presented in Section 3. Computer simulations at elevated temperatures for determining the phase behaviour will be presented in Section 4. A brief discussion on the mechanisms of phase transition and conclusions will be presented in Section 5.

2. Molecular structures

A number of criteria were used in the choice of model molecules.

1. **Shape:** Each molecule was to have a shape which resembled a disc. Hexagonal rotational symmetry was enforced, keeping the molecules as close to a circular shape as possible. This shape contrasts with the irregular shapes of pitch mesogens studied previously with this technique allowing a quantitative comparison to be made based on molecular regularity. On the other hand, it closely resembles with parametric discotic mesogens studied in non-atomistic simulations.

2. **Molecular weight:** The molecules were selected to represent a variety of molecular weights covering the range 400-1000 Da, the range typical for mesophase-forming pitches [23]. Several molecular weights lying close to and yet outside of this range were also selected to study critical limits of molecular weights.

3. **Planarity:** It has been shown [21] that changes in molecular planarity can have a significant impact on mesophase formation. Aliphatic rings are not entirely planar, and necessarily introduce additional hydrogen atoms that are out of plane from the rest of the molecule. A fully aromatic structure, on the other hand, enforces planarity. One study was also carried out on an irregular shaped non-planar molecule containing an aliphatic ring.

Five molecules were investigated in this study. Their specific details are given below:

a. **Coronene:** This regular shaped molecule contains seven aromatic rings containing 24C and 12H atoms on the edges of outer rings. Its molecular weight is 300 Daltons. It is one of the largest molecules that have been isolated and investigated experimentally.

b. **Hexa-benzo coronene:** This regular shaped molecule contains thirteen aromatic rings containing 42C and 18H atoms on the edges of outer rings. Its molecular weight is 523 Daltons. It can be constructed by adding six benzene rings on the outer edges of a coronene molecule.

c. **Circum-coronene:** This regular shaped molecule contains nineteen aromatic rings containing 54C and 18H atoms on the edges of outer rings. Its molecular weight is 667 Daltons. It can be constructed by adding 12 benzene rings on the outer circumference of a coronene molecule.

d. **Dodeca-benzo-circumcoronene:** This regular shaped molecule contains thirty one aromatic rings containing 84 C and 24H atoms on the edges of outer rings. Its molecular weight is 1033 Daltons. It can be constructed by adding 12 benzene rings on the outer circumference of a circum coronene molecule.

e. **Representative pitch molecule:** This irregular shaped molecule contains one aliphatic ring and seventeen aromatic rings. It contains 58C and 24H atoms. Its molecular weight is 720 Daltons. Some studies on this molecule were performed treating aliphatic ring as an aromatic ring to make the molecule planar in order to compare its behaviour with other four molecules under investigation.

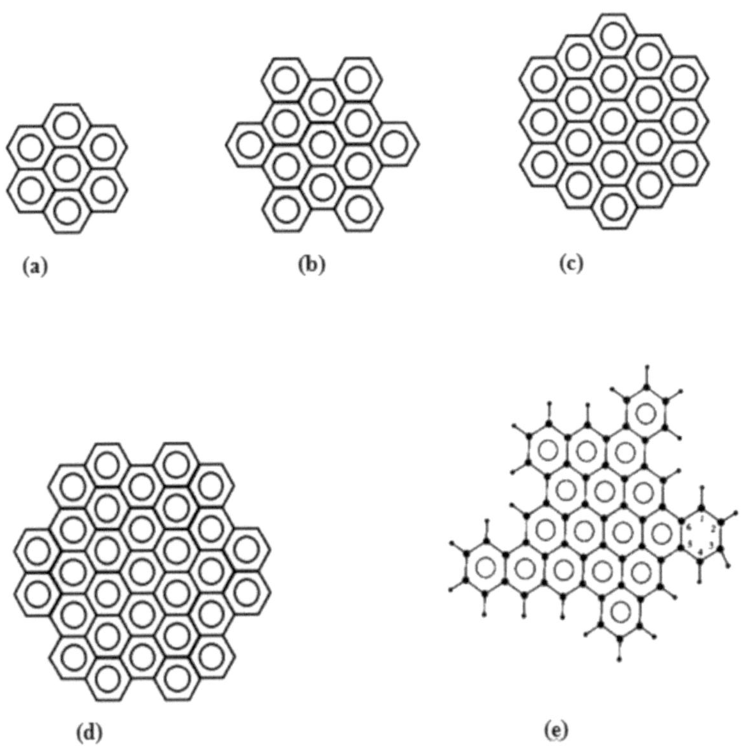

Figure 1. Molecular structures under investigation (a) Coronene, (b) Hexa-benzo coronene, (c) Circum-coronene, (d) Dodeca-benzo-circumcoronene, (e) Representative pitch molecule; the location of hydrogen atoms on the outer edges of the molecule has been shown explicitly.

3. Ground state ordered structures

3.1. Interaction potentials

A first step in investigating the high temperature phase behaviour of these molecules was to determine their ground state ordered structures as it is generally much easier to study order-disorder transitions from the ordered state than creating order from disorder, especially in the absence of experimental data. These simulations were carried out in two steps. Assuming the molecule to be rigid in nature, the energetics of molecular packing into one and two-dimensional aggregates was described by non-bonded atom-atom potentials (E^{nb}) and an electrostatic contribution (E^{el}) from the partial charges on various atoms.

$$U_{ij} = E_{ij}^{nb} + E_{ij}^{el} \tag{1}$$

We have used the MM2 force field of Allinger [24] for these computations and atomistic modelling of macromolecules. A more recent version of these force fields, MM3, incorporating a slightly larger size of atoms and somewhat softer potentials as compared to MM2, was found to be too soft, with rather weak repulsion at small distances and not very suitable in these simulations. [25] The non-bonded potential for the interaction of two molecules labelled as 1 and 2 is given by

$$E_{12}^{nb} = \sum_{i,j} A_{ij} \left[2.90x10\exp\left(\frac{-12.5r_{ij}}{B_{ij}} \right) - 2.25\left(\frac{B_{ij}}{r_{ij}} \right)^6 \right] \tag{2}$$

where r_{ij} is the distance between the atom i in the molecule 1 and the atom j in the molecule 2. A_{ij} and B_{ij} respectively represent non-bonded van der Waals energy and distance parameters. An average C-C bond length of 1.41Å and an average C-H bond length of 1.09 Å was used in these simulations. For the C-H bond, the bond length r_{ij} has to be shrunk by 8.5% before energy computations to account for the anisotropy of non-bonded interactions which depend on the relative orientations of interacting bond orbitals [26]. Because of π electron interactions, aromatic and saturated carbons need to be treated differently and have slightly different intermolecular potentials. The van der Waals interaction parameters for C and H atoms, based on MM2 semi-empirical potentials are listed in Table 1.

Interaction	Saturated hydrocarbon	
	A (Kcal/mol)	B(Å)
C-C	3.80	0.0440
C-H	3.34	0.0460
H-H	3.00	0.0470

Interaction	Saturated hydrocarbon	
	A (Kcal/mol)	B(Å)
H offset	0.915	0.915

Table 1. van der Waals parameters from MM2 force fields for saturated hydrocarbons [20]

The contributions from the electrostatic term, E^{el}, to the total packing energy of molecules were neglected for these hydrocarbons that lack dipoles. The neglect of electrostatic terms here is not believed to be a major limitation in the technique, and indeed they could be added within this framework if necessary, such as for systems involving hetero-atoms.

3.2. 2D Simulation of ordered structures

The ability of organic molecules to form an ordered crystalline array is one of the most remarkable occurrences in nature. While the crystal structure of a large number of organic solids has been measured experimentally, there is a great interest in predicting the structure of crystalline solids from first principles. This assumes a great significance for high-MW PAH, where a crystallographic investigation is not feasible for a number of reasons. Using the methodology developed by Perlstein [27], we have computed in two steps, a 2D structural arrangement for all molecules under investigation. In the first step, a lowest energy 1D aggregate structure was generated using Monte Carlo simulations. A 2D monolayer was then determined in the second step, consistent with lowest energy and closest packing. A Monte Carlo cooling technique was used for computing the global energy minimum and conformation of the molecule in different 1D aggregates [28].

One of the most remarkable features in organic crystallography is that only a very small number of 1D chains and 2D layers that actually occur in nature. Scaringe and Perez [29] have shown that only four types of 1D aggregates occured in 92% of all crystals: these include translation, screw (2_1 Screw), glide and inversion. Scaringe has shown that these can combine to form only seven types of layers. 1D aggregate containing five PAH molecules was constructed in four most probable symmetry arrangements. The binding energy of the aggregate corresponds to half the binding energy of the central molecule in the aggregate. In the initial configuration, the centre of mass of the molecule was placed at the origin of an orthogonal coordinate system and then all atoms in the molecule were put in place. This molecule, in an arbitrary orientation, was treated as the original. The z-axis was chosen as the axis of symmetry.

The energy of the aggregate was computed using equations (1) and (2). Using a random number generator, random changes to three orientation angles and translation/offset distances were generated within preset limits. The maximum range of these variables was determined by ± θ_{max}, $z_{min} - z_{max}$ and $x_{min} - x_{max}$. While θ_{max} was chosen as 10°, the changes in the x and z distances were kept to a maximum of 6Å. A new aggregate was constructed using modified dimensions and the energy change was computed. The change in dimensions was accepted for $\Delta E \leq 0$. For $\Delta E > 0$, the change could be accepted with a transition probability W, [30] defined as

$$W = \exp(-\Delta E/k_B T)/[1+\exp(-\Delta E/k_B T)] \qquad (3)$$

where k_B and T are respectively the Boltzmann constant and temperature. A dimensionless, reduced temperature parameter, T* ($= k_B T / A_{c\text{-}c}$), was used to represent the simulation cell temperature. $A_{c\text{-}c}$ (=3.8 kcal/mol) represents the nonbonding C-C interaction parameter A from MM2 force fields (Table 1). W was compared to a random number, chosen uniformly between 0 and 1. The change was accepted for and the Monte Carlo step was repeated with the new configuration. The following cooling schedule was used in the search for the global minimum.

Using large values of angular and positional changes, Monte Carlo simulations were started at high temperature, e.g., T* = 4 and 50 cycles were carried out. The system was cooled to 0.9T* with the dimensional changes also reduced by a factor of 0.9 after which another 50 cycles were carried out. System cooling was continued in small steps until the temperature reached 0.1T. Treating the final state thus obtained as the new initial state, the simulations were restarted from step (1). The energy changes and downhill energy movements were monitored throughout. The entire process was repeated at least twenty times. Simulations were continued till no further decrease in energy could be observed. These simulations typically required approximately 1 hour of CPU time.

With continuous thermal cycling and downward energy movement, the system was expected to reach the lowest energy configuration at the end of simulations. While the final configuration was expected to be the global minimum, it is quite probable that the system may pass through other very low energy states during these simulation cycles. Whenever the energy of an aggregate went below a certain preset energy level, its molecular configuration and energy were recorded. It was then possible to establish the lowest energy configuration unambiguously in all cases.

Molecule	1D Symmetry	X Dimension (Å)	Y Dimension (Å)	Angle (°)
Coronene	Screw	8.0	4.7	45
Hexa-benzo coronene	Screw	10.2	4.5	45
Circum-coronene	Screw	11.6	4.67	45
Dodeca-benzo-circumcoronene	Translation	16.5	3.35	6
Coal-tar pitch molecule	Translation	15.8	4.1	35

Table 2. Ground state crystal structures in 2 dimensions

It can be seen that for coronene, the simulated Herring Bone structure with screw 1D symmetry compared very well with the experimentally determined structure for this molecule. This structure was also favoured by hexa-benzo coronene as well as by circum-coronene. Other two molecules favoured translational symmetry. The lowest energy configuration in 2D needs to satisfy the close packing criterion as well, these vertical columns were tilted with respect to the horizontal in order to conserve space while avoiding an overlap between the atoms of neighbouring molecules.

4. High temperature phase behaviour

4.1. Simulation algorithm

An isothermal-isobaric Monte Carlo simulation approach was used to study the phases exhibited by the model PAH molecules as a function of temperature. The simulation lattice was a 16 x 16 monolayer, with the molecules occupying the ordered lattice in their ground state configuration. The outer ring of molecules in the simulation lattice was used as fixed walls, giving the cell a fixed volume. While the molecules in the outer ring were kept fixed and did not undergo any change in orientation or position during a simulation run, these participated in the energy computations of inner cell molecules. The application of pressure after a number of constant volume runs, allowed for the volume and shape changes to the simulation cell permitting the structure to attain its natural state. Pressure also contributed to system energy through a $P\Delta V$ term, where P is the pressure parameter and ΔV is the change in the simulation cell volume. The details of the Monte Carlo algorithm are as follows.

A molecule was chosen at random from the inner 14 x 14 simulation lattice. Keeping the molecule rigid, it was allowed one of the five possible moves: three changes to the molecular orientation and two positional movements. Maximum ranges of angular rotation were: $\Delta\theta_{max}$: ± 3°, and displacement: horizontal motion ΔX_{max}: ±1Å, and vertical motion ΔZ_{max}: ±0.5Å. A number set between 0 and 1 was divided into five equal subsets, which were then allocated to specific molecular movements. A random number η was chosen uniformly between 0 and 1 and directed to the appropriate subset. The deviation of η from the midpoint of the subset, determined the sign and the magnitude of the specific movement. Simulations were also carried out by simultaneously applying multiple movements to a given molecule. These however showed a poor convergence with most of the moves becoming energetically unfavourable and were rejected.

The energy of the system was computed before and after the molecular movement. The computation of energies was the most time consuming part of the simulation algorithm. The cut-off distance for atomic interactions was kept at 15Å. Energy computations were carried out on the selected molecule within a 5x5 neighbour cell around it. A further increase in the size of the interaction cell was found quite unnecessary at all temperatures. The energy change due to the molecular move was calculated. The molecular movement was accepted for $\Delta E \leq 0$. For $\Delta E > 0$, the move could be accepted with the Boltzmann transition probability.

The simulations were carried with the reduced temperature parameter T ranging from 0.1 to 1.5 and the pressure parameter P ranging from 1 to 10. Temperature and pressure were kept constant during a given run. Typically 100,000 to 500,000 Monte Carlo cycles were found sufficient ensuring the system had reached equilibrium. Each cycle consisted on ~2000 molecule trial moves at constant volume followed by a trial shape change, in which the dimensions of the simulation cell were randomly altered. Some of the simulations were also carried out where the final temperature was reached in two to three steps instead of a single jump from 0 to the final temperature. The final equilibrium configuration was analysed in terms of system energy, centre of mass/atomic positions and molecular orientations, and the orientational order parameter $S\,(=\frac{3}{2}<\cos^2(\theta)>-\frac{1}{2}$; where the brackets denote the average over all molecules). A number of pressure parameters were trialled, a parameter of 5.0 was found to be quite adequate for most simulations. These simulations can take up to 60 hours of CPU time. Most of the simulations used batch processing as these Monte Carlo algorithms cannot be efficiently transformed for parallel processing. Up to five alternatives were used near phase transformations and up to three alternatives were used for temperatures away from the transition. The phase transitions were approached from the high temperature and the low temperature sides and simulation time was much extended (up to 3 times) to account for the critical slowing down near a phase transition and an increased level of fluctuations.

4.2. Simulation results:

Simulation results from five model molecules are presented below.

4.2.1. Coronene

Carbonaceous mesophase was not observed in the case of coronene. This result was expected because of the small size of the molecule. It showed a complete transformation from the ordered phase to random orientational and positional disorder with increasing temperatures and simulation time. A typical energy plot of the system is shown in Figure 2.

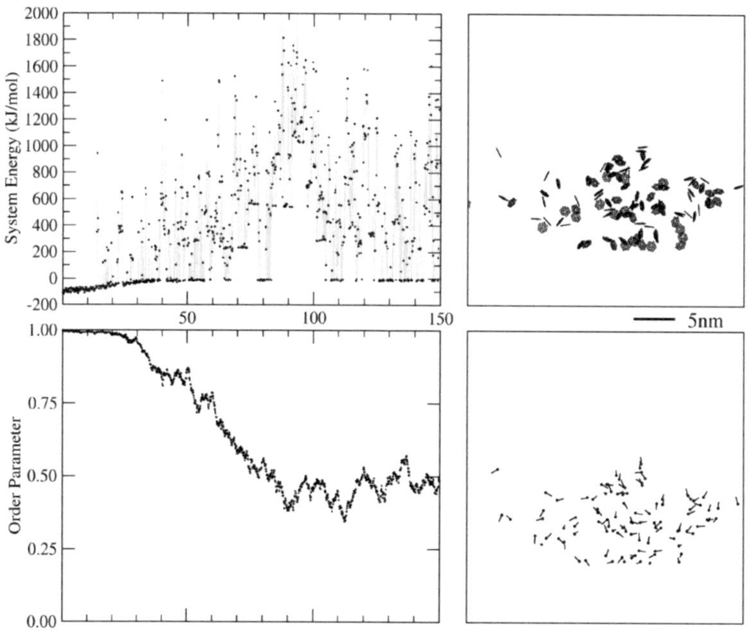

Time (x10^5 MCSS)

Figure 2. Energy vs time (Monte Carlo steps per site) for coronene. Very high energy spikes represent disorder as various molecules tend to come too close leading to high increases in the repulsive component in system energies.

4.2.2. Hexa-benzo Coronene

Hexa-benzo Coronene also showed a behaviour quite similar to that of coronene with the system going directly to complete disorder from the initially ordered state. The orientational order parameter also showed a continuous decrease from 1 to 0.1 with molecules oriented quite randomly after high temperature simulations on the system. There was no evidence of columnar or orientational ordering for this molecule.

4.2.3. Circum-coronene

The results for this molecule were quite different from those observed for the two smaller molecules. Plots of energy and order parameter are presented as a function of temperature in Figure 3. The energy was seen to increase with temperature; a very well defined phase transition could clearly be seen at T=0.2 that reached completion ~0.4. The system remained fairly stable at this energy and order parameter for T=2.0.

At $P = 5$, the structures obtained in simulations $T = 0.10$ to 0.18 were consistent with the ground state solid structure of the material, the only major difference being a few void spaces. From $T = 0.2$ to 0.28, an intermediate phase can be identified, followed by an isotropic liquid for $T \geq 0.30$. Between phase at $T = 0.18$ and $T = 0.2$ there was little change in system energy; however, temperatures above this point showed a marked increase in system energy proportional to temperature. This change in slope suggests that a phase transformation may have occurred at this point. Further evidence of a phase change is the sudden drop in order parameter (from $S_{eq} = 0.995$ to 0.967), as well as an increase in the order parameter's standard deviation by an order of magnitude (from $\sigma_S = 0.001$ to 0.013). A discontinuity in an order parameter, with continuous system energy, is another feature typical of second-order phase transitions.

As indicated by the order parameter, the transition was associated with a decrease in the order of the molecular packing, as some molecules break away from the columns and into the voids between (see Figure 4). This behaviour represents the onset of fluidity within the system, suggesting that this phase represents a columnar-type mesophase. A clear columnar phase can be seen in Figure 4b.

4.2.4. Dodeca-benzo-circumcoronene

This regular molecule has the shape of a disc, quite large in size and appears to satisfy basic criteria for the formation of a mesophase. The evolution of order parameter as a function of scaled temperature is shown in Figure 5. Four distinct regions with changing order parameter can clearly be identified. Energy plots also showed a similar trend indicating various phase changes in the system.

Figure 6 shows the centre of mass of molecule in the ground state and their initial relaxation as the temperature is increased slightly to 0.3 (7a). Although columns have tilted significantly, orientational order is being maintained to a great extent. As the temperature is increased further to T=1.1, columns are getting disturbed and molecular disorientation is setting in. The orientational order is still being maintained to a certain extent. At high temperature (T=2.0),

http://dx.doi.org/10.5772/53370

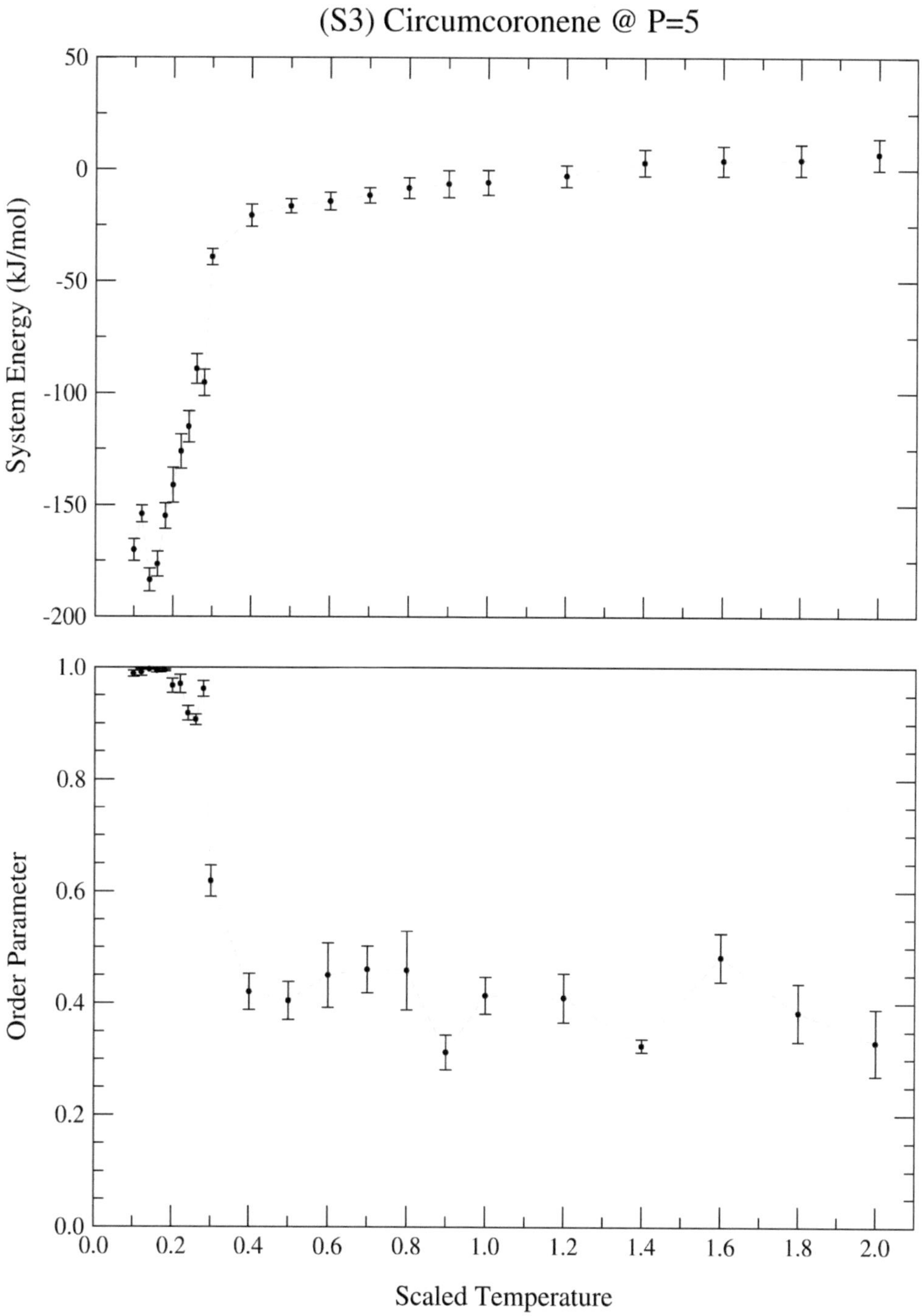

Figure 3. System energy and orientational order parameter as a function of temperature.

Figure 4. Molecular arrangements as a function of temperature (a) T= 0.18 (b) T= 0.2

system is completely disordered. Both centre of mass as well as molecular orientation is completely destroyed.

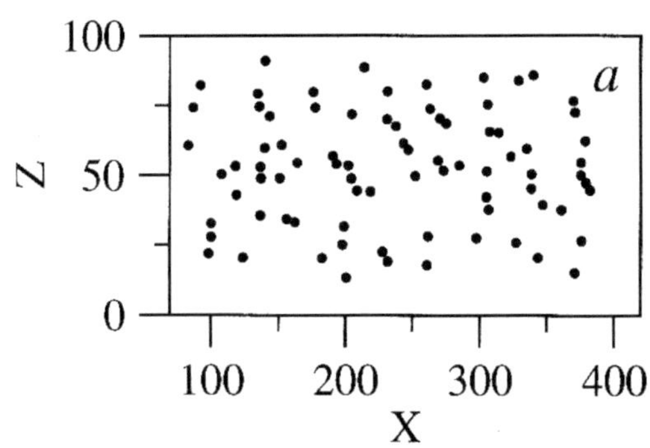

Figure 5. Simulation results for the molecule as a function of temperature

4.2.5. *Representative pitch molecule*

Two sets of studies were carried out on the representative pitch molecule. In one case, the aliphatic ring was treated as being distinct from the aromatic ring with additional hydrogen atoms being out of plane of the main molecule. Secondly, the aliphatic ring was treated as an aromatic ring resulting in a planar molecule. High temperature simulation results for both molecules are given in Figure 7. Three well-defined phases can be seen clearly for the non-planar molecule while using NPT ensemble. These transitions were however not very well defined for constant volume simulations. This is to be expected as some of these transitions were accompanied by a volume change and could be suppressed to an extent in a fixed volume simulation.

For the non-planar molecule, three distinct discontinuities, suggesting possible phase transitions can be seen. The discontinuities in the energy plot also resulted in corresponding breaks in the orientational order parameter. The planar molecule showed only two

http://dx.doi.org/10.5772/53370

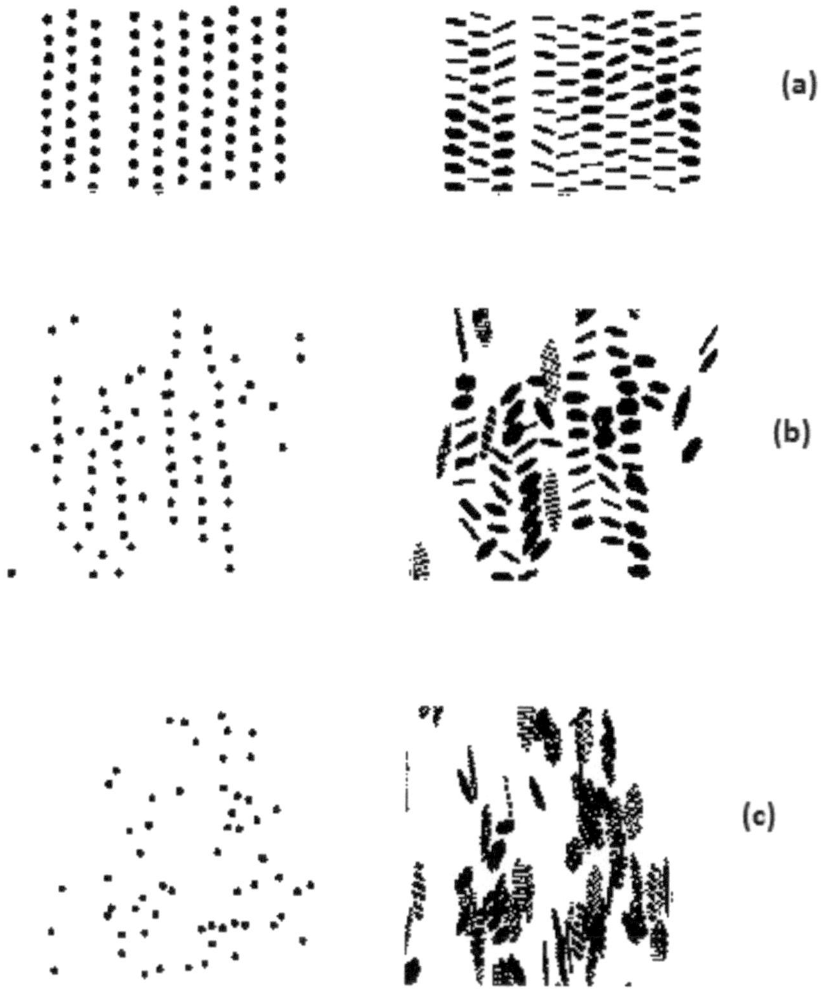

Figure 6. Centre of mass and molecular orientation for a range of temperatures (a) T=0.3, (b) T= 1.1 and (c) T=2.0.

structural transformations for the range of temperatures and pressures investigated. Regime I in (b) appears to be quite similar to the regime I observed for the non-planar molecule. But the transition temperature (~0.6) in this case is much higher than the corresponding temperature (~ 0.27) for the non-planar molecule. Similarly the transition to regime II has also shifted to a much higher temperature (~0.95) as compared to the ~ 0.55 for the non-planar molecule.

In Figure 8, we have plotted the positions of centres of mass, directors and atomic positions at T=1.15 for both molecules. These results point towards the important role played by the molecular structure wherein minor changes in structure can result in significant changes in stacking behaviour and structural transition points.

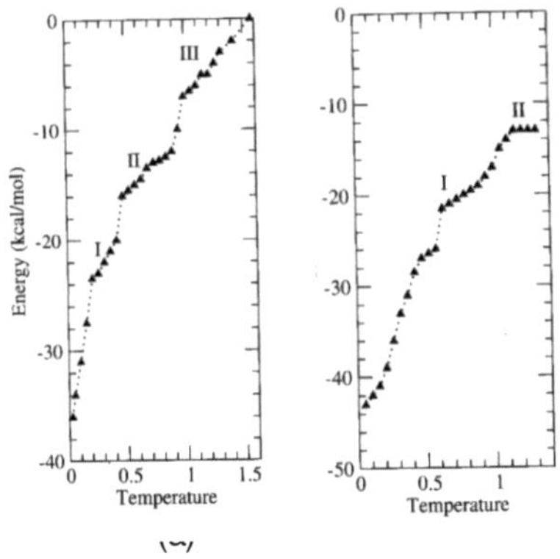

Figure 7. Energy vs. temperature phase diagram for the representative pitch molecule: (a) non-planar molecule and (b) planar molecule.

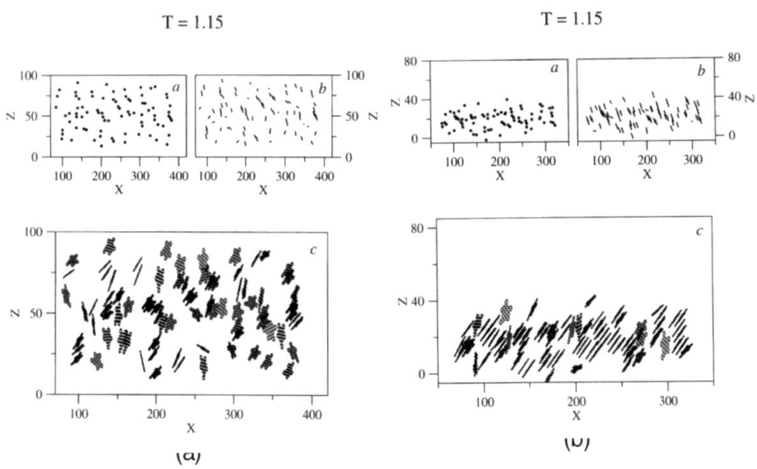

Figure 8. Simulation results at T=1.15 for representative pitch molecules: (a) non-planar molecule and (b) planar molecule. Plots *a*, *b* and *c* respectively represent centre of mass positions, molecular directors and atomic positions for the molecules.

5. Conclusions

An extensive investigation has been reported on a range of molecules to determine key factors that could affect the formation of carbonaceous mesophase. The effect of molecular weight is a critical factor controlling mesophase formation from pitch precursors. However, in practical systems, molecular weights are not constant; polymerisation processes during heat treatment can cause molecular structures to change. Usually, in thermo-tropic liquid crystals, the mesophase forms upon heating of a solid or cooling of a liquid [31]: solid → mesophase →

liquid. However, mesophase formation during the carbonisation of pitches usually occurs by a more complex route:

solid pitch → isotropic liquid → mesophase → solid semi-coke. The three transitions in this process chain can be described as (a) Melting (or softening) – this effectively represents a reversible reduction in viscosity, (b) Mesophase formation – this step is characterised by an irreversible increase in viscosity and the formation of an anisotropic liquid (mesophase), (c) Carbonisation – this transition signifies the fusing of the material into a brittle coke

The mesophase formation in carbon systems depends on more than simple thermo-tropic behaviour. At low temperature heat treatment, the pitch simply melts entering the isotropic liquid phase region. Once the temperature reaches a critical point, condensation and polymerisation begins, causing an increase in molecular weight which, in turn, makes the molecules more meso-genic. After sufficient polymerisation, the material enters the mesophase region. Further heat treatment increases the extent of polymerisation and cross-linking, fusing the material into a semi-coke.

Based on these experimental observations, it would be expected that the atomistic model as a representative of PAH systems, would show little or no mesophase formation for molecules of low molecular weight, representing the isotropic pitch melt at low temperatures (300-400 Da). Secondly, a strong tendency exists for mesophase formation for molecules of higher molecular weight, representing the partially polymerised pitch melt at higher temperatures (400-1000 Da)

The absence of mesophase formation in coronene and hexabenzocoronene in atomistic simulations is in good agreement with these results. However, there was no evidence of nematic mesophase behaviour and only limited evidence of columnar mesophase behaviour in circumcoronene. These molecules have molecular weights of 300, 523 and 667 Da respectively. Since coronene lies within the molecular weight range for non-polymerised isotropic pitches, its inability to form a mesophase was to be expected. Other two molecules lie well within the higher weight range, where mesophase formation is to be expected.

Dodeca-benzo-circumcoronene, on the other hand, clearly showed nematic mesophase behaviour over a large temperature range. This molecule has a molecular weight of 1033 Da, placing it at the upper end of the stated range for meso-genic pitches. Thus, the model is in agreement with the experimental observations of pitches. Significantly different results were obtained for irregular, high-MW PAH (720 Daltons) representative of those in pitch. The simulations show columnar phases at low temperatures and the gradual loss of long-range columnar order with heating.

It is important to note that typical mesophase-forming pitches are complex mixtures; interaction between molecules of different sizes is a complex phenomenon. It is difficult to separate the effects of average molecular weight from the effects of molecular weight distribution and molecular shape. Thus, the study of the effects of molecular weight presented here should be combined with similar studies of the effects of molecular weight distribution and molecular shape; once this is achieved, it may be possible to create testable, quantitative predictions.

Acknowledgements

We acknowledge National Computing Infrastructure (NCI) and Intersect Consortium, Australia for supercomputing resources, and Australian Research Council (ARC) for financial support.

Author details

R. Khanna[1], A. M. Waters[2] and V. Sahajwalla[1]

1 Centre for Sustainable Materials Research and Technology, School of Materials Science and Engineering, The University of New South Wales, NSW, Sydney, Australia

2 BlueScope Steel, Wollongong, NSW, Australia

References

[1] Minus, M. L, & Kumar, S. Carbon Fibers, in Kirk-Othmer Encyclopedia of Chemical Technology, John Wiley & Sons, Inc. (2007).

[2] Oberlin, A. High-resolution TEM studies of carbonization and graphitization, in Chemistry and Physics of Carbon, P.A. Thrower, Editor. (1989). Marcel Dekker, Inc.: New York. , 1-143.

[3] Marsh, H, Philip, J, & Walker, L. The formation of Graphitizable Carbons via Mesophase: Chemical and Kinetic Considerations, in Chemistry and Physics of Carbon, J. Philip L. Walker and P.A. Thrower, Editors. (1979). Marcel Dekker, Inc.: New York. , 229-286.

[4] Franklin, R. E. Crystallite Growth in Graphitizing and Non-Graphitizing Carbons. Proceedings of the Royal Society of London. Series A, Mathematical and Physical Sciences, (1951). , 209, 196-218.

[5] Manocha, L. M. Carbon Fibers, in Encyclopedia of Materials: Science and Technology. (2003). Elsevier Science Ltd. , 906-916.

[6] Brooks, J. D, & Taylor, G. H. The formation of graphitizing carbons from the liquid phase. Carbon (1965). , 3, 185-193.

[7] Brooks, J. D, & Taylor, G. H. Formation of graphitizing carbons from the liquid phase. Nature (1965). , 206, 697-699.

[8] Khanna, R, Waters, A. M, & Sahajwalla, V. Atomistic computer simulations on large ensembles of high-molecular-weight polyaromatic hydrocarbons. Comp. Mater Science (2010). SS113., 108.

[9] Goddard, R, Haenel, M. W, Herndon, W. C, Kruger, C, & Zander, M. Crystallization of large planar polycyclic aromatic hydrocarbons: The molecular and crystal structures of hexabenzo-coronene and benzo-dicoronene. J American Chemical Society (1995)., 117, 30-41.

[10] Schmitz-hübsch, T, Sellam, F, Staaub, R, Törker, M, Fritz, T, Kübel, C, Müllen, K, & Leo, L. Direct observation of organic-organic heteroepitaxy: perylene-tetracarboxylic-dianhydride on hexa-peri-benzocoronene on highly ordered pyrolytic graphite. Surface Science (2000)., 445, 358-367.

[11] Marsh, H, & Philip, J. Walker L in Chemistry and Physics of Carbon, Eds., Marcel Dekker, Inc.: New York (1979)., 1979, 229-286.

[12] Lewis, I. C. Thermotropic mesophase pitch. Carbon (1980)., 18, 191-196.

[13] Zander, M, & Collin, G. A Review of the significance of polycyclic aromatic chemistry for pitch science. Fuel (1993)., 72, 1281-1285.

[14] Marzec, A. Intermolecular interactions of aromatic hydrocarbons in carbonaceous materials: A molecular and quantum mechanics, Carbon (2000)., 38, 1863-1871.

[15] Miller, J. H, Smyth, K. C, & Mallard, W. G. Calculations of the dimerization of aromatic hydrocarbons: Implications for soot formation. Proc. Combustion Institute (1985)., 20, 1139-1147.

[16] Hunter, C. A, & Sandres, J. K M. The nature of π-π interactions, J. American Chemical Society (1990)., 112, 5525-5534.

[17] Murgish, J, Rodriguez, J. M, & Aray, Y. Molecular Recognition and Molecular Mechanics of Micelles of Some Model Asphaltenes and Resins. Energy and Fuels (1996)., 10, 68-76.

[18] Smith, G. D, & Jaffe, R. L. Comparative-Study of Force-Fields for Benzene. J. Physical Chemistry (1996)., 100, 9624-9630.

[19] Bates, M. A, & Luckhurst, G. R. Computer simulation studies of anisotropic system. XXVI. Monte Carlo investigations of a Gay-Berne discotic at constant pressure. J. Chemical Physics (1966)., 104, 6696-6709.

[20] Gay, J. G, & Berne, B. J. Modification of the overlap potential to mimic a linear site-site potential. J Chemical Physics (1981)., 74, 3316-3319.

[21] Khanna, R, Sahajwalla, V, & Hurt, R. H. An atomistic technique for simulating non-covalent interactions in large ensembles of high-molecular-weight polyaromatics. Carbon (2005)., 43, 67-77.

[22] Waters, A. M. Atomistic Computer Simulations on Nanostructured Carbon Materials, BTech Thesis ((2010). The University of New South wales, Sydney, Australia.

[23] Mochida, I, Yoon, S. H, & Korai, Y. Mesoscopic Structure and Properties of Liquid Crystalline Mesophase Pitch and Its Transformation into Carbon Fiber. The Chemical Record (2002)., 81-101.

[24] Allinger, N. L. MM2 A hydrocarbon force field utilizing and V2 torsional terms. Journal American Chemical Society (1989)., 1

[25] Allinger, N. L, Yuh, Y. H, Lii, J. H, & The, M. M. force field for hydrocarbons. Journal American Chemical Society (1989)., 111, 8551-8565.

[26] Williams, D. E. Nonbonded potential parameters derived from crystalline aromatic hydrocarbons. Journal Chemical Physics (1966)., 45, 3770-3778.

[27] Perlstein, J. Molecular self-assemblies: Monte Carlo predictions for the structure of the one-dimensional translation aggregate. Journal American Chemical Society (1992)., 114(1992), 1955-1963.

[28] Kitaigorodskii AI in Organic Chemical CrystallographyConsultants Bureau, New York, (1961).

[29] Scaringe, R. P, & Perez, S. A novel method for calculating the structure of small-molecule chains on polymeric templates. Journal Physical Chemistry (1987)., 91(1987), 2394-2403.

[30] Binder, K, Lebowitz, J. L, Phani, M. K, & Kalos, M. H. Monte Carlo Study of the Phase Diagrams of Binary Alloys with Face-Centered Cubic Lattice StructureActa Metallurgica (1981)., 29(1981), 1655-1665.

[31] Hurt, R. H, & Chen, Z. Y., Liquid Crystals and Carbon Materials, in Physics Today. (2000). American Institute of Physics., 39-41.

Chapter 7

Variance Reduction of Monte Carlo Simulation in Nuclear Engineering Field

Pooneh Saidi, Mahdi Sadeghi and Claudio Tenreiro

Additional information is available at the end of the chapter

http://dx.doi.org/10.5772/53384

1. Introduction

The Monte Carlo method is a numerical technique that using random numbers and probability to solve problems. It represents an attempt to model nature through direct simulation for any possible results, by substituting a range of values (a probability distribution) for any factor that has inherent uncertainty. The method is named after the city in the Monaco principality, because of roulette, a simple random number generator. The name and the systematic development of Monte Carlo method dates from about 1944.The name "Monte Carlo" refers to the Monte Carlo Casino in Monaco because of the similarity of statistical simulation to games of chance and was coined by Metropolis during the Manhattan Project of World War II, [1].

Monte Carlo is now used routinely in many fields, such as radiation transport in the Nuclear Engineering, Dosimetry in Medical Physics field, Risk Analysis, Economics… in all the applications the physical process of the solution is simulated directly based on the major components of a Monte Carlo algorithm that must be available during the simulations. The primary components of a Monte Carlo simulation are:

Probability density functions (pdf's) the physical system must be described by a set of pdf's;

Random number generator: a source of random numbers uniformly distributed on the unit interval must be available;

Sampling rule, a prescription for sampling from the specified pdf's;

Scoring: the outcomes must be accumulated into overall tallies or scores for the quantities of interest;

INTECH
open science | open minds

© 2013 The Author(s). Licensee InTech. This chapter is distributed under the terms of the Creative Commons Attribution License http://creativecommons.org/licenses/by/3.0), which permits unrestricted use, distribution, and reproduction in any medium, provided the original work is properly cited.

Error estimation: an estimate of the statistical error (variance) as a function of the number of trials and other quantities must be determined;

Variance reduction techniques: methods for reducing the variance in the estimated solution to reduce the computational time for Monte Carlo simulation;

Parallelization and vectorization algorithms to allow.

In the field of nuclear engineering, deterministic and stochastic (Monte Carlo) methods are used to solve radiation transport problems. Deterministic methods solve the transport equation for the average particle behavior and also contain uncertainties associated with the discretization of the independent variables such as space, energy and angle of the transport equation and can admit solutions that exhibit non-physical features. Although the physics of photon and electron interactions in matter is well understood, in general it is impossible to develop an analytic expression to describe particle transport in a medium. This is because the electrons can create both photons (e.g., as bremsstrahlung) and secondary or knock-on electrons (δ-rays) and conversely, photons can produce both electrons and positrons.[2] The Monte Carlo (MC) method obtains results by simulating individual particles and recording some aspects of their average behavior. The average behavior of particles in the physical system is then inferred from the average behavior of the simulated particles.[3] This method also enables detailed, explicit geometric, energy, and angular representations and hence is considered the most accurate method presently available for solving complex radiation transport problems. For example the most important role of Monte Carlo in radiotherapy is to obtain the dosimetric parameters with high spatial resolution.[4] As the cost of computing in the last decades continues to decrease, applications of Monte Carlo radiation transport techniques have proliferated dramatically. On the other hand, Monte Carlo techniques have become widely used because of the availability of powerful code such as BEAM, EGSnrc, PENELOPE and ETRAN/ITS/MCNP on personal computers. These codes able to accommodate complex 3-D geometries, inclusion of flexible physics models that provide coupled electron-photon and neutron-photon transport, and the availability of extensive continuous-energy cross section libraries derived from evaluated nuclear data files.[5]

It should be noted that these codes are general purpose, and are therefore not optimized for any particular application and are strongly depended on the solution subject. One of the difficulties associated with Monte Carlo calculations is the amount of computer time required to generate sufficient precision in the simulations. Despite substantial advancements in computational hardware performance and widespread availability of parallel computers, the computer time required for analog MC is still considered exorbitant and prohibitive for the design and analysis of many relevant real-world nuclear applications especially for the problems with complex and large geometry. But there are many ways (other than increasing simulation time) in the Monte Carlo method that users can improve the precision of the calculations. These ways known as Variance Reduction techniques and are required enabling the Monte Carlo calculation of the quantities of interest with the desired statistical uncertainty. Without the use of variance reduction techniques in complex problems, Monte Carlo code should run the problem continuously for weeks and still not obtain statistically significant reliable results. The goal of Variance Reduction techniques is to produce more accurate and precise estimate of the expected value than could be obtained in analog calculation with the same computational efforts. Variance reduction parameters are vary with problem types so iterative steps must be repeated to determine VR parameters for different problems.[6]

2. Conceptual role of the Monte Carlo simulation

The conceptual role of the Monte Carlo simulations is to create a model similar to the real system based on known probabilities of occurrence with random sampling of the PDFs.

This method is used to evaluate the average or expected behavior of a system by simulating a large number of events responsible for its behavior and observing the outcomes. Based on our experience concerning the distribution of events that occur in the system; almost any complex system can be modeled. Increasing the number of individual events (histories) improve the reported average behavior of the system.

In many applications of Monte Carlo the physical process is simulated directly and there is no need to even write down the differential equations that describe the behavior of the system. The only requirement is that the physical or mathematical system be described by probability density functions (PDF). Once the probability density functions are known the Monte Carlo simulation can proceed by random sampling from the probability density functions. Many simulations are then performed multiple trials or histories and the desired result is taken as an average over the number of observations. In many practical applications one can predict the statistical error the variance in this average result and hence an estimate of the number of Monte Carlo trials that are needed to achieve a given error

3. Accuracy, precision and relative error in Monte Carlo simulation

The first component of a Monte Carlo calculation is the numerical sampling of random variables with specified PDFs. Each random variable defines as a real number that is assigned to an event. It is random because the event is random and also is variable because the assignment of the value varies over the real values. In principle, a random number is simply a particular value taken on by a random variable.

When the random number generator is used on a computer, random number sequence is not totally random. Real random numbers are hard to obtain. A logarithm function made the random number and the function repeats itself over time. When the sequence walked through, it will start from the beginning. The typical production of random numbers is in the range between 0 and 1.

A sequence of real random numbers is unpredictable and therefore un-reproducible. A random physical process, for example radioactive decay, cosmic ray arrival times, nuclear interactions, and etc, can only generate these kinds of sequences. If such a physical process is used to generate the random numbers for a Monte Carlo calculation, there is no theoretical problem. The randomness of the sequence is therefore not totally random; this phenomenon is called pseudorandom. [7] Pseudo Random numbers look nearly random however when algorithm is not known and may be good enough for our purposes. Pesudo random numbers are generated according to a strict mathematical formula and therefore reproducible and not at all random in the mathematical sense but are supposed to be indistinguishable from a sequence generated truly randomly. That is, someone who does not know the formula is not supposed to be able to tell that a formula was used rather than a physical process. When using Monte Carlo simulation, it is desirable to have any variable depending on a uniform distributed variable, ϱ. The probability, *P*, that a random number is smaller for a certain value, *s*, should be equal for both distributions. [8]

$$P\ (x<\rho)=P\ (y<s) \tag{1}$$

The probability is in the range between 0 and 1, can be rewritten as a cumulative distribution:

$$\int_{-\infty}^{\rho} g(x)dx = \int_{-\infty}^{s} f(y)dy = \rho \tag{2}$$

The left side of equation (2) is the uniform distribution between 0 and 1 and *f(y)* is the distribution needed. In this way any distribution can be made with a uniform distribution.

Monte Carlo results are obtained by simulating particle histories and assigning a score x_i to each particle history. The particle histories typically produce a range of score depending on the selected tally. By considering the *f(x)* as the probability density function (pdf) for selecting a particle history that scores *x* to the estimated tally being, the true answer (or mean) is the expected value of *x*, where:[3]

$$E(X)=\int xf(x)dx=true\ mean \tag{3}$$

By assuming a scalar value for each Monte Carlo simulation output, the Monte Carlo sample mean of the first *n* simulation runs is defined as follow:

$$\bar{x}=\frac{1}{n}\sum_{i=1}^{n} x_i \tag{4}$$

Where x_i is the value of *x* selected from probability density function, *f(x)*, for the *ith* history and *n* is the total number of the histories which are calculated in the problem. The sample mean $\bar{x}$, is the average value of the x_i for all the histories used in the problem. But generally it does not give an accurate estimate, on the other hand there is no idea how much confidence can be considered in the estimate. So to evaluate the quantity of confidence in the estimation the sample variance can be used. Sample variance provides an estimate of how much the individual samples are spread around the mean value and is obtained as follow:

$$\delta^2=\int(x - E(X))^2 f(x)dx=E(x^2) - (E(x))^2 \tag{5}$$

Where δ^2 is the sample variance, *E(X)* is true mean and *f(x)* is the probability density function (pdf).

The standard deviation of scores has been obtained by the square root of the variance (δ^2), which is estimated via Monte Carlo method as *s*.

The standard deviation is obtained by the following equation:

$$s^2 = \frac{1}{n-1}\sum_{i=1}^{n}(x_i - \bar{x})^2 \sim \overline{x^2} - x_i^2 \tag{6}$$

Where

$$\overline{x^2} = \frac{1}{n}\sum_{i=1}^{n} x_i^2 \tag{7}$$

To define the confidence interval in Monte Carlo estimation two statistical theorems are used: the law of large number and the central limit theorem.

The law of large number provides an estimate of the uncertainty in the estimate without any idea concerning the quantity of *n* that must be consider in calculation in practice.

To define confidence interval for the precision of a Monte Carlo result, the Central Limit Theorem of probability is used as follow:[9]

$$\lim_{n\to\infty} \text{Prob}\left[E(x) + \alpha\frac{\delta}{\sqrt{n}} < \bar{x} < E(X) + \beta\frac{\delta}{\sqrt{n}}\right] = \frac{1}{\sqrt{2\pi}}\int_{\alpha}^{\beta} e^{\frac{-t^2}{2}} dt \tag{8}$$

Where α and β can be any arbitrary values and n is the number of histories in the simulation. According to Eq. (6), as the uncertainty is proportional to $\frac{1}{\sqrt{n}}$, by increasing the number of histories by quadrupled the uncertainty in the estimation will half, which is an inherent drawback of the Monte Carlo method. So for large *n*, in terms of the sample standard deviation, $s_{\bar{x}}$, the Eq. (6) can be rewritten as:

$$\text{Prob}\left[\alpha < \frac{\bar{x} - E(X)}{\sigma\sqrt{n}} < \beta\right] \sim \frac{1}{\sqrt{2\pi}}\int_{\alpha}^{\beta} e^{\frac{-t^2}{2}} dt \tag{9}$$

And for large *n* Eq.7 can be written as:

$$\text{Prob}\left[\frac{\bar{x} - \lambda s_{\bar{x}}}{\sqrt{n}} \le E(X) \le \frac{\bar{x} + \lambda s_{\bar{x}}}{\sqrt{n}}\right] \sim \frac{1}{\sqrt{2\pi}}\int_{-\lambda}^{\lambda} e^{-t^2/2} dt \tag{10}$$

λ is the number of standard deviation, from the mean, over which the unit normal is integrated to obtain the confidence coefficient. Results for various values of λ are shown in Table1. So to have confidence level the estimation for x is generally obtained as:

$$\bar{x} \pm \frac{\lambda s(x)}{\sqrt{n}} \tag{11}$$

For example for λ=1, the interval, $[\bar{x} - \frac{\lambda s(x)}{\sqrt{n}},\ \bar{x} + \frac{\lambda s(x)}{\sqrt{n}}]$ has a 68% chance of containing the true mean.

λ	0.25	0.50	1.00	1.5	2.00	3.00	4.00
Nominal Confidence Limit	20%	38%	68%	87%	95%	99%	99.99%

Table 1. Results for various values of λ

Eq. (8) shows that the deviation of the sample mean from the true mean approaches zero as $n \to \infty$, and the quantity of $\frac{\delta}{\sqrt{n}}$ present a measured of the deviation of the sample mean from the population mean by using n samples.

To construct a confidence interval for sample mean, $\overline{x}$, that has a specified probability of the containing the true unknown mean, the sample standard deviation $s(x)$,is used to approximate the population standard deviation, $\delta(x)$. But this required that $E(x)$ and δ^2 be finite and exist.

The sample variance of $\bar{x}$ is then given by:

$$s_{\bar{x}}^2 = \frac{s^2}{n} \tag{12}$$

It should be noted that the confidence intervals are valid only if the physical phase space is adequately sampled by the Monte Carlo calculation. The uncertainty of the Monte Carlo sampled physical phase space represents the precision of the simulation. There are several factors that can affect the precision such as tally type, variance reduction techniques and the number of histories simulated. Generally uncertainty or error caused by the statistical fluctuations of the x_i, refers to the precision of the results and not to the accuracy. Accuracy is a measure of how close the sample mean, $\bar{x}$, is to the true mean. (Figure 1)

On the other hand the difference between the true mean and the sample mean is called the systematic error. To estimate the relative error at the 1δ level which represents the statistical precision Eq. (10) is used. [10]

http://dx.doi.org/10.5772/53384

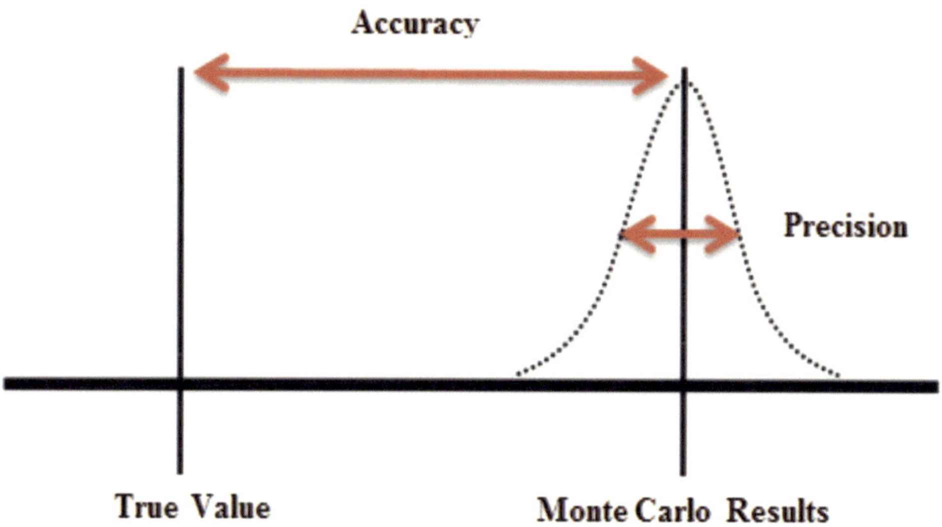

Figure 1. Schematic diagram of the definition for accuracy and precision

$$R = \frac{s_{\bar{x}}}{\bar{x}} \tag{13}$$

In terms of Central Limit Theorem, the estimated relative error squared R^2 should be proportional to $\frac{1}{n}$. So as each history will take on average, the same amount of computer time and the used computer time, T, in a Monte Carlo calculation should be directly proportional to n (the number of histories); therefore R^2T should be approximately constant. Thus, the metric of efficiency for a given tally, called the figure-of-merit (FOM), includes computer time as well and define as:[11]

$$FOM = \frac{1}{R^2 T} \tag{14}$$

Where R is the relative error for the sample mean, and T is the total computer time taken to simulate n histories.[12], [13]

The FOM is also a tally reliability indicator in the sense that if the tally is well behaved, the FOM should be approximately constant (with the possible exception of statistical fluctuations early in the problem), and is thus an important and useful parameter to assess the quality (statistical behavior) of a tally bin. If the FOM is not approximately constant, the confidence intervals may not include the expected score value *E(x)* the expected fraction of the time.

Considering the following form of the previous relation can show the significant of the actual value of the FOM. [14]

The above expression shows a direct relationship between computer time and the value of the FOM. Increasing the FOM for a given tally will subsequently reduce the amount of computer time required to reach a desired level of precision. Thus the FOM can be used to measure the efficiency when the variance reduction techniques have been used. The ratio of FOMs before and after using the variance reduction techniques, gives the factor of improvement.

Another use of FOM is to investigate the improvement of the new version of a Monte Carlo code.

The ratio of the FOMs for identical sample problems gives the factor of improvement. When the FOM is not a constant as a function of *n*, means that the result is not statistically stable; that is, no matter how many histories have been run, the important particles are showing up infrequently and have not yet been sampled enough.[3,9]

Another additional use of the FOM is to estimate the required computer time to reach a desired precision by considering: $T \sim 1/(R^2 \times FOM)$.

4. Variance reduction

The uncertainty of Monte Carlo simulation can be decreased by implementing some accurate physical models but this leads to longer calculation times. On the other hand, the accuracy of Monte Carlo dose calculation [15] is mainly restricted by the statistical noise, because the influence of Monte Carlo method approximations should be much smaller. This statistical noise can be decreased by a larger number of histories leading to longer calculation times as well. However, there are a variety of techniques to decrease the statistical fluctuations of Monte Carlo calculations without increasing the number of particle histories. These techniques are known as variance reduction.[16] Variance Reduction techniques are often possible to substantially decrease the relative error, *R*, by either producing or destroying particles, or both.

Decreasing the standard deviation, δ, and increasing the number of particle histories, *n*, for a given amount of computer time conflict with each other. Because decreasing δ requires more computer time per history and increasing *n*, results in less time per history [17] In general not all techniques are appropriate for all applications, also in some case some techniques tend to interfere with each other so choosing the Variance Reduction technique strongly depend on the solution.

The main goal of all the variance reduction techniques is to increase precision and decrease the relative error. The precision of the calculation is increased by increasing the number of particle histories but needs a large amount of computer running time so to accelerate the Monte Carlo simulation and reduce the computing time these techniques are applied.[16-17]

Monte Carlo variance reduction techniques can be divided into four classes:

The truncation method like geometry truncation, time and energy cut off;

The population control method like Russian roulette, geometry splitting and weight windows;

http://dx.doi.org/10.5772/53384

The modified sampling method (source biasing); and

The partially deterministic method like point detectors.

5. Popular variance reduction techniques

Several of the more widely used variance reduction techniques are summarized as follow:

5.1. Splitting/Roulette

Geometric Splitting/Russian roulette is one of the oldest and most widely used variance reduction techniques, and when used properly, can significantly reduce the computational time of a Monte Carlo calculation.

Approximately 50% of CPU time is consumed to track secondary and higher-order photons and the electrons they set in motion. It is possible to remove a part of these photons by Russian roulette. [18]

Generally when particles move from a region of importance I_i to a more important region I_j, ($I_i < I_j$), the particle is split into $n = I_j = I_i$ identical particles of weight w=n (if n is not an integer, splitting is done in a probabilistic manner so that the expected number of splits is equal to the importance ratio) it means that the number of particles is increased to provide better sampling and the weight of the particle is halved. Figure 2 shows a schematic diagram of geometry splitting, when a particle moves from a lower importance region to a region with higher importance. Splitting increases the calculation time and decreases the variance whereas Russian roulette does the complete opposite.[19]

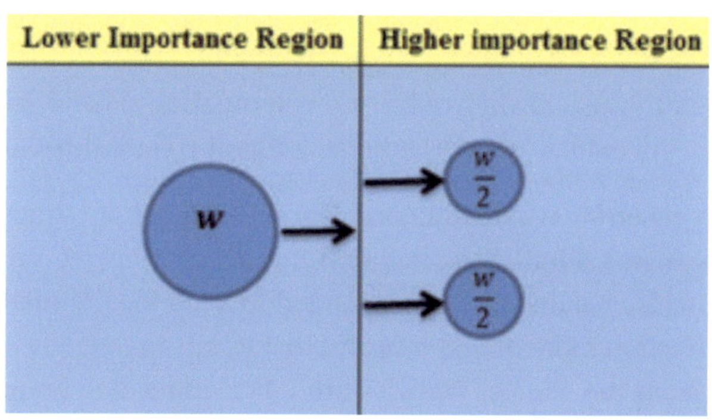

Figure 2. The splitting process

In case of moving to a less important region Russian roulette is played and the particle is killed with probability $1 - (I_j = I_i)$, or followed further with probability $I_j = I_i$ and weight $w \times I_i = I_j$.

It means that the particles are killed to prevent wasting time on them.(Figure 3)

The objective of these techniques is to spend more time sampling important spatial cells and less time sampling unimportant spatial cells. This is done by dividing the problem geometry into cells and assigning each cell *i,* an importance *Ii.*

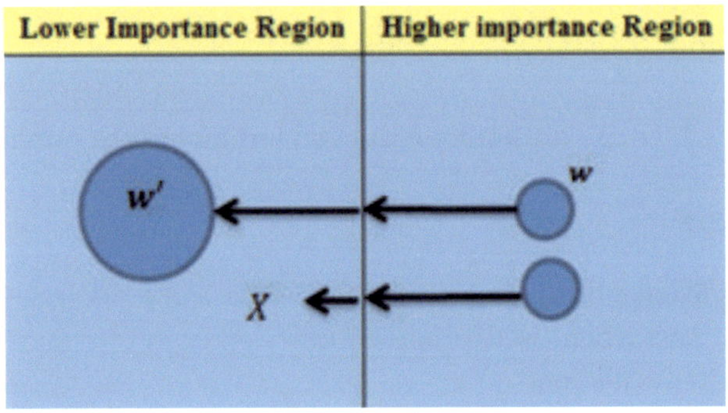

Figure 3. The Russian roulette process

Energy splitting/roulette are similar to geometric splitting/roulette except that energy splitting/roulette is performed on the energy domain rather that on the spatial domain.

Russian roulette can be shown that the weights of all particle tracks are the same in a cell no matter which geometrical path the tracks have taken to get to the cell, assuming that no other biasing techniques, e.g. implicit capture, are used. In the simulations if a track's energy drops through a prescribed energy level, the roulette game (based on the input value of the survival probability) is played. If the game is won, the track's history is continued, but its weight is increased by the reciprocal of the survival probability to conserve weight.[20] Russian roulette is frequently, if not always, used in radiation transport problems and can be applied at any time during the life of a particle, usually after an interaction has taken place. Russian roulette always increases variance since it cuts off histories that could still contribute to the detector, but it also always reduces the simulation time in compare with an implicit capture (which will explained later) scheme without weight thresholds.

Generally, in a deep penetration shielding problem the number of particles diminishes to almost nothing in an analog simulation, but splitting helps keep the numbers built up. To have accurate and precise results it is recommended to keep the population of tracks traveling in the desired direction more or less constant that is, approximately equal to the number of particles started from the source. Particles are killed immediately upon entering a zero importance cell, acting as a geometry cutoff. Geometry splitting/Russian roulette works well only in problems without any extreme angular dependence.[21] In the extreme case, if no particles ever enter an important cell where the particles can be split, the Splitting/Russian roulette is useless. Energy splitting and roulette typically are used together. Energy Splitting/roulette is independent of spatial cell. If the problem has space-energy dependence, the space-energy dependent weight window is normally a better choice.

Splitting and roulette are very common techniques in Monte Carlo simulation; not only because of their simplicity but also since they only deal with variance reduction via population control and do not modify pdfs, they can be used in addition to most other techniques to have more effect.

5.2. Energy cut off

A Monte Carlo simulation can be made much faster, by stopping a particle once its energy drops below certain threshold energy (cutoff energy). According to the particle energy and the material that the particle is travelling through, the travelling path length of the particle can estimate. If this path length is below the required spatial resolution, particles are terminated and assume their energy is absorbed locally. This can be done by energy cut off that terminate tracks and thus decrease the time per history. [22] Because low-energy particles can produce high energy particles, the energy cutoff can be used only when it is known that low-energy particles are either of zero or almost zero importance at the specific region (low energy particles have zero importance in some regions and high importance in others).[23] In the Monte Carlo simulations Ecut is the photon energy cut-off parameter. It means, if a scattered photon is created with energy less than Ecut the photon will not be transported and the energy deposited locally. According to the above explanation seems the smaller Ecut the more accurate are the results but there are two criteria that should be considered in the simulations for selecting Ecut: (a) the mean free path (MFP) of photons with energy equal or less than Ecut should be small in compared with the voxel sizes or (b) the energy fraction carried by photons with energy less than Ecut is negligible compared with the energy fraction deposited. In terms of efficiency selecting the higher Ecut results in decreasing the CPU time, but on the other hand, selecting a higher value for Ecut can makes it a source of additional statistical fluctuations if it becomes comparable or even bigger than the average energy deposited by electrons. In this case the answer will be biased (low) if the energy cutoff is killing particles that might otherwise have contributed in the process even if $N \rightarrow \infty$. [9]

5.3. Time cutoff

A time cutoff is like a Russian roulette, with zero survival probability. The time cutoff terminates tracks and thus decreases the computer time per history. Particles are terminated when their time exceeds the time cutoff. The time cutoff can only be used in time-dependent problems where the last time bin will be earlier than the cutoff. The energy cutoff and time cutoffs are similar; but more caution must be considered with the energy cutoff because low energy particles can produce high-energy particles, whereas a late time particle cannot produce an early time particle. [10]

6. Weight window technique/weight window generator

The weight window technique administers the splitting and rouletting of particles based on space and energy dependent importance. This technique is one of the most used and effective variance reduction methods that deals with both the direct decrease of variance via a large number of samples (through splitting) and the decrease of simulation time via Russian roulette, and is therefore a very effective variance reduction technique. On the other hand this technique combines Russian roulette and splitting.

To apply this variance reduction technique a lower weight bound and the width of the weight window for each energy interval of each spatial cell should be considered.

If a particle's weight is below the lower weight bound, Russian roulette is performed, and the particle's weight is either increased to be within the weight window or the particle is terminated. On the other hand, if the particle's weight is above the upper weight bound, the particle is split such that the split particles all have weights within the weight window. If the particle's weight falls within the weight window, no adjustment is performed.[24]

As shown in Figure 4, if a particle has a weight equal to w_{ini}, which is lower than w_L, Russian roulette will play with survival weight equal to w_s which is also provided by the user. It should be noted that the w_s has to be between the windows define by w_u and w_L. If w_{ini} is greater than w_u, the particle is split into a predefine number of particles until all the particles are within the defined window. If w_{ini} is within the window the particle continues with the same weight.

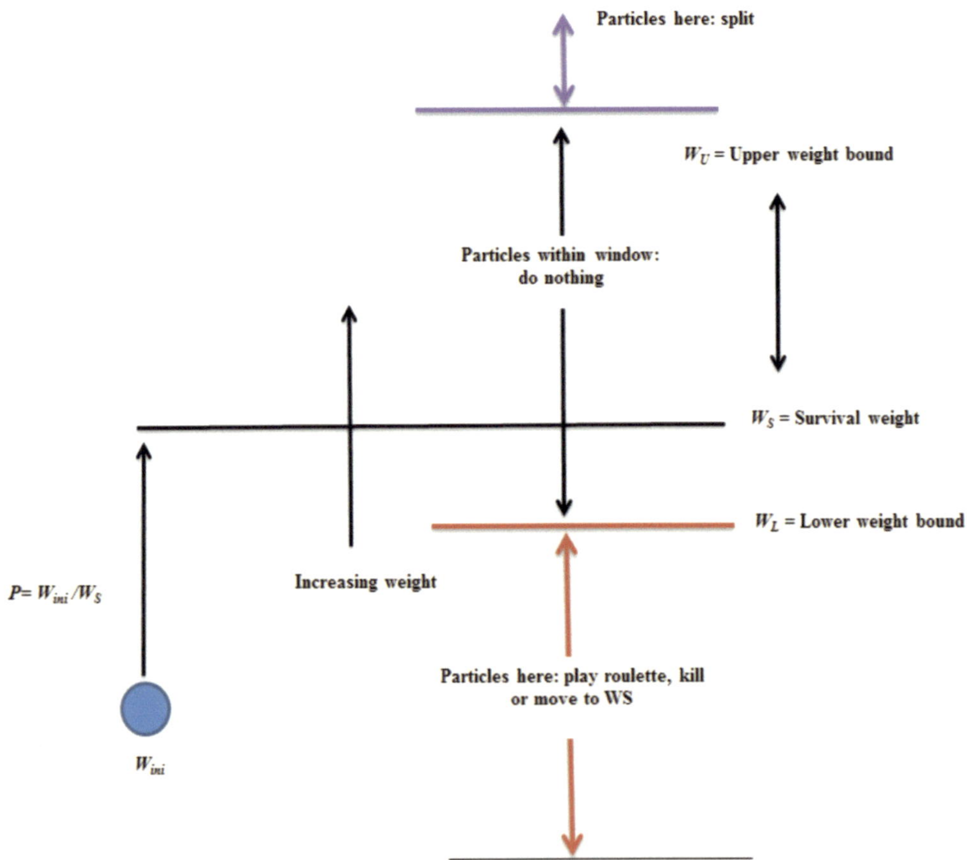

Figure 4. Schematic of the weight window technique [21]

One problem that may arise when using weight windows is that over-splitting might occur when a particle enters a region or it is generate in a region with higher weight than the upper limit of the weight window in that region. This can usually be solved by modifying some of the weight window parameters. [21]

The weight windows generator is used to determine weight windows for the simulations. When generating weight windows, it is easy to generate unwanted zeros. Zero weight windows in a region are either due to particles not entering that region or due to particles that did enter the region but did not add to the tally score. To increase the number of particles that enter or generate in a region of the system, a uniformly distributed volumetric photon source that covers the whole system is used.[25]

The weight window generator calculates the importance of each cell in the problem. This is done by noting that the importance of a particle at a point in phase space is equal to the expected score a unit weight particle would generate. Thus, the cell's importance can be estimated as follow:

$$\text{Importance} = \frac{\text{total score due to particles entering the cell}}{\textit{total weight entering the cell}} \tag{15}$$

As both the weight window and geometry splitting use the Russian roulette, there is a question concerning the difference between these two methods. The main differences are:

The weight windows are space–energy dependent whereas geometry splitting is only dependent on space;

The geometry splitting, splits the particles despite the weight of the particle but the weight window works completely in opposite way, it means before roulette is played and the particles split, the weight of the particle is checked against the weight window;

The geometry splitting is only applied at surfaces, but the weight window method is applied at surfaces and collision sites or both;

The geometry splitting method is based on the ration of importances across the surface but weight windows utilizes absolute weights;

As the geometry splitting is weight independent, will preserve any weight fluctuation but weight window can control weight fluctuation by other variance reduction techniques to force all particles in a cell to have a weight within a weight window.

The weight windows can be generated via the weight window generator but it requires considerable user understanding and intervention to work correctly and effectively.

7. Implicit capture

Implicit capture, survival biasing, and absorption by weight reduction are synonymous. Implicit capture is a very popular variance reduction technique in radiation transport MC simulations. The implicit capture technique involves launching and tracing packets of particles instead of one by one. At launch, each packet is assigned an initial weight W_0. The packet is traced with a step length distribution determined by the total attenuation coefficient, δ. Implicit capture is a variance reduction technique that ensures that a particle always survives a collision (i.e., the particle is never absorbed).

All of the variance reduction techniques vary the physical laws of radiation transport to sample more particles in regions of the phase-space that contribute to the objective.

To compensate for this departure from the physical laws of radiation transport, the concept of particle weight, w, is introduced, where the weight can be considered as the number of particles being transported. When a variance reduction technique is applied, the weight of the particle is adjusted using the following "conservation" formula: [20]

$$w\left(\textit{biased probability density function}\right) = w_0\left(\textit{unbiased probability density function}\right) \tag{16}$$

Where w_0 is the weight before the variance reduction technique is applied. In the implicit capture technique, a particle always survives a collision, but the particle emerges from the collision with a weight that has been reduced by a factor of δ_s / δ, which is the probability of scattering. Thus, the total particle weight is conserved.

If W_0 is the initial weight of the particle and the weight w that the particle will have after a collision, the relationship between them can be describe as follow:

$$w_0 \rightarrow \begin{cases} p = \frac{\delta_s}{\delta} & \text{if } W' = W \\ p^* = 1 - p & \text{if } W' = 0 \end{cases} \rightarrow \overline{W'} = pW_0 + p^* \times 0 = \frac{\delta_s}{\delta} W_0 \tag{17}$$

Where p is the probability of the particle being scattered after a collision, δ_s, is the scattering macroscopic cross-section, δ is the total macroscopic cross-section and $\overline{W'}$ is the expected outcome of the weight. For the implicit capture the particle always survives a collision with weight:

$$W' = \frac{\delta_s}{\delta} W_0 \tag{18}$$

When implicit capture is used rather than sampling for absorption with probability $\delta_s = \delta$, the particle always survives the collision and is followed with a new weight. Implicit capture can be assumed as a splitting process in which the particle is split into absorbed weight and surviving weight. [10] The main advantage of implicit capture is that a particle that has reached the vicinity of the tally region is not absorbed just before a score is made. In general Implicit capture always reduces the variance, but the total figure-of-merit may not improve, as the simulation time is increased because of the longer particle histories. It is, however, widely used because of its simplicity and ease of implementation.

8. Forced collisions

The forced collision method is a variance reduction scheme that increases sampling of collisions in specified regions.

If the number of mean-free paths (MFP) to the next photon interaction be larger than the simulated phantom thickness, the photon will leave the region of interest without any interacting or depositing energy. Prediction of this event is not possible and to have precision results the photon behaviour must be traced through the interest region until it escapes from the region. In this case the computing time spent on the transport of escaping photons is then wasted and if the fraction of escaping photons is very large, the simulation will be very inefficient. The forced collision technique improves the efficiency by considering only the fraction of photons that interact in the phantom.

As shown in Figure 5, when a specified particle enters a region defined as the forced collision region, the incident particle splits into un-collided and collided particles. The un-collided particle passes through the current cell without collision and is stored in the bank until later when its track is continued at the cell boundary. The collided particle is forced to collide within the specified cell.

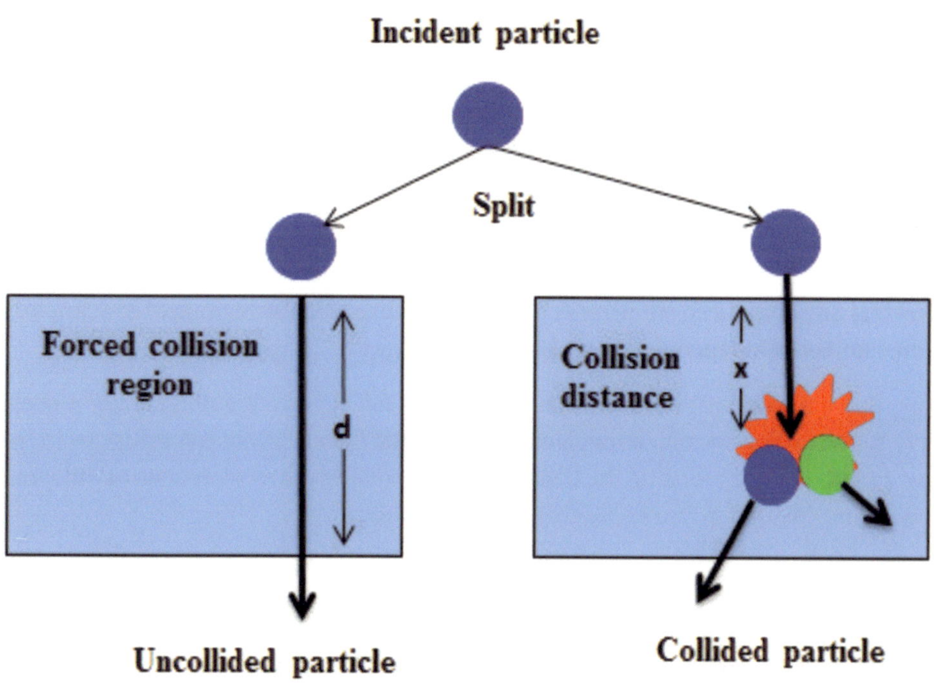

Figure 5. Schematic diagram of the forced collision. [26]

It means that the "passing-through case" and the "collision case" are analysed due to a single incident particle simulation. These split particles are weighted by the following Equation:

$$W_{uncoll} = W_0 e^{-\delta d}$$
$$W_{coll} = W_0 (1 - e^{-\delta d}) \tag{19}$$

Where W_0 is the initial weight of the particle, W_{uncoll} is the un-collided particle's weight and W_{coll} is the weight of collided particle. d is the distance to region surface in the particle's direction, and δ is the macroscopic total cross section of the region material. [26]

The probability of colliding within a distance x is given by:

$$Prob = 1 - e^{-\delta x} \tag{20}$$

The particle's weight is then reduced appropriately and Russian roulette is used to ensure that the calculation time is not increased significantly by the technique. [27]

9. Exponential transformation

The exponential transform also called path length stretching is a variance reduction technique designed to enhance efficiency for deep penetration problems (e.g. shielding calculations) or surface problems (e.g. build-up in photon beams). It is often used for neutron Monte Carlo simulation and is directly applicable to photons as well.

In applying the exponential transformation a stretching parameter is used to increase distances travelled in directions of interest, while in the use of Russian roulette and splitting other parameters are introduced to increase the death probabilities in regions of low importance and the number of independent particles found in regions of high importance. [7]

Exponential transformation samples the distance to collision from a non-analog probability density function. Specifically, it involves stretching the distance between collisions in the direction of interest and reducing the distance between collisions in directions of little interest by modifying the total macroscopic cross section as follow:

$$\delta^* = \delta(1 - p\mu) \tag{21}$$

Where δ^* is the modified total cross section, δ is the true total cross section, p is the exponential transform parameter used to vary the degree of biasing, $|p| < 1$, and μ is the cosine of the angle between the preferred direction and the particle's direction.

It should be mentioned that the exponential transformation technique can produce large weight fluctuations and subsequently produce unreliable mean and variance estimates. Exponential transformation generally decreases the variance but increases the time per history.[28]

Also it should be noted that due to the large weight fluctuations that can be produced by the exponential transform the exponential transform should be used accompanied by weight control.

10. Conclusion

In this chapter we discussed the accuracy, precision, relative error & figure of merit in the Monte Carlo simulation, the Monte Carlo method is considered to be the most accurate method presently available for solving radiation transport problems in nuclear engineering field but it is extremely expensive computationally, because this method should simulate individual particles and simulating the average behaviour of the particles in the system. Also for complex problems that the probability is small that a particle will contribute to the interest region, some form of variance reduction must be applied to reduce the required computer time to obtain the results with sufficient precision.

The disadvantage associated with Monte Carlo codes is that they require long calculation times to obtain well converged results, especially when dealing with complex systems. Computation time constitutes an important and a problematic parameter in Monte Carlo simulations, which is inversely proportional to the statistical errors so there comes the idea to use the variance reduction techniques.

In other word to shorten the calculation time and to decrease the error of the results obtained with Monte Carlo methods, i.e. to improve the efficiency of a Monte Carlo calculation, variance reduction techniques must be used so in this chapter we also discussed various variance reduction techniques. These techniques play an important role in reducing uncertainties and improving the statistical results. As already mentioned, it is possible to reduce the estimated variance of a sample for a given number of histories using techniques which increase the positive sampling efficiency and reduce the intrinsic dispersion of the contributions to the response, biasing the natural occurrence of more important paths and reducing the natural occurrence of less important, and especially 'nearly zero' importance paths.

In this chapter, several variance reduction strategies have been described with the aim of reducing CPU time.

In general assign the variance reduction techniques results in several factors that should be noted in the simulations:

Highly reliable systems

Financial engineering/quantitative finance

Simulation optimization

Lots of alternatives

Noisy gradient estimates

Metamodeling/mapping

Real-time control using simulation

The usage of variance reduction methods in Monte Carlo simulations is not straightforward. There is a problem that these methods may be used as a black box leading to results not being analysed correctly. Note, all of the variance reduction techniques have a certain amount of over-head associated with their use, and in many situations the cost of this over-head outweighs the advantages of the technique.

Author details

Pooneh Saidi[1], Mahdi Sadeghi[2] and Claudio Tenreiro[3,4]

1 Department of Medical Radiation Engineering, Science and Research Branch, Islamic Azad University, Tehran, Iran

2 Agricultural, Medical and Industrial Research School, Nuclear Science and Technology Research Institute, Karaj, Iran

3 Department of Energy Science, Sung Kyun Kwan University, Cheoncheon–Dong, Suwon, Korea

4 Universidad de Talca, Facultad de Ingeniería, Talca, Chile

References

[1] Anderson H.L. Metropolis, Monte Carlo and the MANIAC, Los Alamos Science 1986 14, 96–108.

[2] Rogers D.W.O. Monte Carlo Techniques in Radiotherapy, Ionizing Radiation Standards Institute for National Measurement Standards, Medical Physics 2002; 58(2) 63–70.

[3] Carter L.L., & Cashwell E.D. Particle transport simulation with the Monte Carlo method, ERDA Critical Review Series, 1975; TID-26607.

[4] Sadeghi M., Saidi P. & Tenreiro C. Dosimetric Characteristics of the Brachytherapy Sources Based on Monte Carlo Method. In Mode Ch.J. (ed) Applications of Monte Carlo Methods in Biology, Medicine and Other Fields of Science. InTech; 2011.p155-176.

[5] Rogers D.W.O. Fifty years of Monte Carlo simulations for medical physics. Phys. Med. Biol. 2006; 51(13) R287–R301.

[6] Osnes H. Variance reduction techniques for Monte Carlo simulation, ISSN 0808-2839. SINTEF and University of Oslo, 1997.

[7] Kahn H. Use of different Monte Carlo sampling techniques. In Symposium on Monte Carlo Methods, H.A. Meyered, John Wiley and Sons, New York 1956; 146- 190.

[8] Sjenitzer B. Variance reduction using the correction method on criticality calculations TU Delft, 2009.

[9] Kendall S.M. & Stuart A. The advanced theory of statistics, vol. 1, C. Griffin & Co., London, 4th edn., 1977.

[10] MCNP, A General Monte Carlo N-Particle Transport Code, Version 5, Volume I: Overview and Theory. X-5 Monte Carlo Team, Los Alamos national laboratory, April 24, 2003 (Revised 2/1/2008).

[11] Este G. & Cashwell E. MCNP1B Variance error estimator, TD-6-27-78. 1978; Los Los Alamos National Laboratory

[12] Wanger J.C., Peplow D.E. & Evans T.M. Automated variance reduction applied to nuclear well-logging problems. Nucl Tech 2009; 168(3) 799-809.

[13] OLSHER R.H. A practical look at Monte Carlo variance reduction methods in radiation shielding. Nucl Eng & Tech 2006; 38(3) 225-230.

[14] Briesmeister J.F. Editor, MCNP – A General Monte Carlo N-Particle Transport Code, Version 4A, LA-12625. 1993; Los Alamos National Laboratory.

[15] Nelson W.R., Hirayama H. & Rogers D.W.O. The EGS4 code system SLAC Report SLAC-265 Press W H, Teukolsky S A, Vetterling W.T and Flannery B.P. 1997, Numerical Recipes in Fortran 77, Cambridge: Cambridge University Press, 1985.

[16] Bielajew A.F. & Rogers D.W.O. the parameter reduced electron-step transport algorithm for electron Monte Carlo transport. Nucl. Instrum. Methods 1987 PRESTA; B 18 165–81.

[17] Haghighat A. & Wagner J.C. Monte Carlo Variance Reduction with Deterministic Importance Functions. Prog Nucl Energy 2003; 42(1) 25-53.

[18] Kawrakow I. & Fippel M. Investigation of variance reduction techniques for Monte Carlo photon dose calculation using XVMC. Phys. Med. Biol. 2000; 45(8) 2163–2183.

[19] Booth, T.E. & Hendricks J.S. Importance Estimation in Forward Monte Carlo Calculations, Nucl Tech & Fusion 1984; 5(1) 90-100.

[20] Wagner JC. & Haghighat A. Automated Variance Reduction of Monte Carlo Shielding Calculations Using the Discrete Ordinates Adjoint Function. Nucl Sci & Eng 1998, 128(2) 186–208.

[21] Kawrakow I & Fippel M. Investigation of variance reduction techniques for Monte Carlo photon dose calculation using XVMC. Phys. Med. Biol 2000; 45(8): 2163-2183.

[22] Noack K. Efficiency and reliability in deep-penetration Monte Carlo calculations, Ann. Nucl. Energy 1991, 18(6), 309-316.

[23] Booth T.E. A Sample problem in variance reduction in MCNP, LA-10363-MS, 1985; Los Alamos National Laboratory.

[24] Smith H.P. & Wagner J.C. A Case Study in Manual and Automated Monte Carlo Variance Reduction with a Deep Penetration Reactor Shielding Problem. Nucl Sci & Eng 2005; 149, 23–37.

[25] Rodriguez M., Sempau J. & Brualla L. A combined approach of variance-reduction techniques for the efficient Monte Carlo simulation of linacs. Phys Med Biol 2012; 57(10) 3013-24.

[26] Abe Sh. Watanabe Y. & Niita K. Sakamoto Y. Implementation of a forced collision method in the estimation of deposit energy distribution with the PHITS code. Prog Nucl Sci & Technology 2011; 2.477-480.

[27] Smith H.P. & Wanger J.C. A case study in manual and automated Monte Carlo variance reduction with a deep penetration reactor shielding problem. Nucl Mathematical & Computational Sci 2003; A Century in Review, A Century AnewGatlinburg, Tennessee, April 6-11, 2003, on CD-ROM, American Nuclear Society, LaGrange Park, IL (2003)

[28] Zhaohong B. & Xifan W. Studies on variance reduction technique of Monte Carlo simulation in composite system reliability evaluation. Elec Power Sys Res 2002; 63(1) 59-64

Chapter 8

Stochastic Models of Physicochemical Processes in Catalytic Reactions - Self-Oscillations and Chemical Waves in CO Oxidation Reaction

Vladimir I. Elokhin

Additional information is available at the end of the chapter

http://dx.doi.org/10.5772/53792

1. Introduction

It is well known that many processes of heterogeneous catalysis cannot be described correctly in terms of the Langmuir kinetics or, similarly, in terms of the law of surface action. As has been experimentally shown, not only phenomena related to the substantial spatial and energetic heterogeneity of the adsorbed layer [1] (restricted mobility of adsorbed species, phase transitions in the layer associated with the interaction of adsorbates on the surface, diffusion of adsorbed species into the subsurface layer resulting in the change of adsorption and catalytic properties of the surface, etc.) are very often observed in real catalytic systems, but also the rearrangement of the catalytic surface itself due to adsorption, desorption, reactions [2, 3], and the temperature factor (for example, the phase transition of surface roughening [4, 5]). In several cases, the effect of different surface defects appearing during the reaction or under high-temperature conditions (terraces, steps, kinks, point defects, etc.) on catalytic transformations is the determining factor. However, despite many experimental data, theoretical methods (both deterministic and statistical) used for the description and analysis of this type of nonideal catalytic systems are presently insufficiently developed.

In our opinion, the imitation (or statistical) simulation based on the Monte Carlo method [6] is one of the most efficient tool for describing the spatio-temporal dynamics of the behavior of adsorbates on the real catalytic surface, whose structure can change during the reaction. This method makes it possible to obtain qualitatively new results [7], which cannot be obtained by traditional phenomenological models (systems of differential equations). Several advantages of the Monte Carlo method that are especially important for the solution of the above-considered problem should be mentioned: (a) possibility of independent considera-

INTECH
open science | open minds

© 2013 The Author(s). Licensee InTech. This chapter is distributed under the terms of the Creative Commons Attribution License http://creativecommons.org/licenses/by/3.0), which permits unrestricted use, distribution, and reproduction in any medium, provided the original work is properly cited.

tion of the local environment of each adsorbed molecule or active center on the surface, (b) sufficiently simple algorithmic presentation of almost any concepts describing the processes occurring in terms of the generalized lattice gas model (including processes that cannot be described using analytical models), and (c) computer visualization of the simulated surface and adsorption layer (formation of structures, phase transitions, etc.). Possible spatio-temporal changes on the surface can be taken into account at the atomic-molecular level, which allows one to understand deeply and in detail mechanisms of heterogeneous catalytic reactions and facilitates substantially the interpretation of physicochemical experimental data.

There are some disadvantages of statistical models:

i. the dynamic behavior cannot be predicted on the basis of bifurcation analysis (this can be done by deterministic models with not too large dimensionality);

ii. it is difficult to take into account the real ratios between the rates of adsorption, reaction, and diffusion;

iii. small scales of systems under study. The two latter difficulties can be overcome by increasing of the effectiveness of simulations, or by implementation of parallel computation [8].

2. Self-oscillations and surface waves in CO oxidation reaction on platinum metals

Catalytic CO oxidation on platinum-group metals is a classical model reaction in heterogeneous catalysis. In addition to being of fundamental interest, this reaction is of great environmental significance as a means of removing carbon monoxide from exhaust gases. CO oxidation under far-from-equilibrium conditions can be accompanied by critical phenomena, such as multiple steady states, self-oscillations, traveling waves, and chaos [1, 9–18]. The successful attempts of searching for new catalytic reactions with this type of dynamic behavior resulted in the situation that presently we know more than fifty different oscillation systems [19] occurring under different experimental conditions on various types of catalysts. Various oscillation mechanisms have been discovered and investigated to date. They include surface structure transitions [1, 11], the formation of a "subsurface" oxygen layer [12-17], and the "explosive" interaction between adsorbed species [18]. A common feature in all these mechanisms is the spontaneous periodical transition of the metal surface from inactive to highly active catalytic state.

Use of physical methods with a high space resolution (<1 μm) made it possible to study *in situ* the formation of traveling chemical waves arising from the oscillatory dynamics of the reaction on Pt and Pd single-crystal surfaces [16, 17]. It was demonstrated that the conventional approaches using phenomenological kinetic equations (sets of differential equations) are inappropriate for describing the nature of spatiotemporal chemical waves on the metal surface [7]. So-called kinetic (dynamic) Monte Carlo models turned out to be the most suita-

http://dx.doi.org/10.5772/53792

ble. The most recent review of the application of these models to oscillatory reactions was given by Zhdanov [20]. Here, we present an overview of our Monte Carlo studies of the formation of self-oscillations and chemical waves in CO oxidation reaction over Pt(100) and Pd(110) single crystals, based on experimental data. The kinetic models for these surfaces differ in the detailed mechanism of the appearance of oscillations. Both models indicate oscillations of the CO_2 formation rate and adsorbed species concentrations. The oscillations are accompanied by wave phenomena on the model surface.

2.1. Pt(100): Simulation of self-oscillations and chemical waves

The detailed reaction mechanism used in the simulation of the self-oscillations [20-24] is based on experimental data, reported earlier [11-17]. It has been revealed that the self-oscillations of the CO oxidation rate are related with the reversible phase transition Pt(100)-(hex) ↔ (1 x 1). The platinum state in unreconstructed (1 x 1) phase is catalytically active because the sticking coefficient of oxygen, characterizing the probability of adsorption, is equal to $S^{1x1}(O_2) \approx 0.3 \div 0.4$ on (1 x 1) phase, in contrast with $S^{hex}(O_2) \approx 0.001$.

The mechanism of the reaction can be represented as (Scheme 1):

$$\text{(I)}\ CO + * \rightarrow CO_{ads};$$
$$\text{(II)}\ CO_{ads}^{hex} \rightarrow CO + *_{hex};$$
$$\text{(III)}\ CO_{ads}^{1\times1} \rightarrow CO + *_{1\times1}$$
$$\text{(IV)}\ (hex) \rightarrow (1 \times 1)\text{: } 4CO_{ads} \rightarrow 4CO_{ads}^{1\times1};$$
$$\text{(V)}\ (1 \times 1) \rightarrow (hex)\text{: } *_{1\times1} \rightarrow *_{hex};$$
$$\text{(VI)}\ O_2 + 2*_{1\times1} \rightarrow 2O_{ads}^{1\times1};$$
$$\text{(VII)}\ O_{ads}^{1\times1} + CO_{ads} \rightarrow CO_2 + *_{1\times1} + *;$$
$$\text{(VIII)}\ CO_{ads} + * \rightarrow * + CO_{ads}$$

Scheme 1.

Below, we present a brief description of the steps of this catalytic cycle. Step (I) is CO adsorption. The absence of indices at the active site $*$ means that CO, unlike oxygen, has the same sticking coefficient (S_{CO}) for $*_{hex}$ and $*_{1x1}$. Steps (II) and (III) are CO desorption. The rate constants of CO desorption from the surface phases (hex) and (1x1) differ by approximately 3÷4 orders of magnitude. Step (IV) is the (hex) → (1x1) phase transition. In accordance with [25], it is assumed that only CO molecules adsorbed simultaneously on the four nearest neighbor sites of the model grid can cause its transformation into the (1x1) structure (with some probability). Step (V) is the back structural transition (1x1) → (hex). Step (VI) is oxygen adsorption. The dissociative adsorption of O_2 takes place only on double nearest neighbor (1x1)-type sites. Step (VII) is CO_2 formation. The O_{ads}^{1x1} reacts with CO_{ads}^{1x1} and CO_{ads}^{hex} at equal rates, and the kinds of active sites remain unchanged. Step (VIII) is CO_{ads} diffusion. The adsorbed molecule CO_{ads} diffuses on the surface by hopping from its site to a random nearest neighbor empty site. As this takes place, the kinds of active sites remain unchanged. Along with steps (III) and (VII), diffusion (VIII) is a source of empty $*_{1x1}$ active sites, which are necessary for the dissociative adsorption of oxygen.

CO oxidation reaction on Pt(100) was simulated on an N×N grid of square cells with cyclic boundary conditions (usually, we took $N = 1000$). The state of a cell was set according to the rules determined by the detailed reaction mechanism. The time unit was a Monte Carlo (MC) step, which consisted of N×N choice and realization trials of the main elementary processes (steps (I)–(VII)). The probability of occurrence of each step for the adsorption, desorption, and chemical reaction processes was taken to be equal to the ratio of the rate constant of this step to the sum of the rate constants of all steps. The rate constants of steps (I)–(VII) at $T \sim 500$ K were taken from [26, Table 1].

After selecting one of the processes (steps (I)–(VII)) and performing a realization trial, we considered the internal cycle of diffusion, which consisted of M diffusion trials for CO_{ads} molecules (typically, M = 50–100). The CO oxidation rate and the reactant coverages of the surface were calculated after each MC step as the number of the resulting CO_2 molecules (or the number of cells in the corresponding state) divided by the total number of cells, N^2. The algorithm of the simulation of CO oxidation on Pt(100) is detailed elsewhere [21].

The Monte Carlo model of the reaction reveals oscillations of the reaction rate and the CO_{ads} and O_{ads} coverages of the surface and transformations between the surface phases (1x1) and (hex) under conditions similar to experimental results [21]. The oscillations, Figure 1, are accompanied by the propagation of concentration waves on the surface, Figure 2. The most noteworthy result of the simulation is the revealing of a narrow reaction zone before the front of the propagating oxygen wave, which suggests that the surface passes into a highly active catalytic state, Figure 3. It can be seen from Figures 2 and 3, that the local CO_2 formation rate is the lowest in the CO_{ads} layer, takes an intermediate value in the O_{ads} layer, and is the highest in the narrow reaction zone along the perimeter of the growing O_{ads} islands. Note that this narrow reaction zone is observed only when there is a propagating oxygen wave. A local increase in the CO_{ads} concentration on the surface causes the disappearance of the narrow reaction zone, as follows from the behavior of an oxygen island (A) in the upper left corner of Fig. 2. This island disappears as its oxygen reacts with CO_{ads}. Here, as O_{ads} is consumed, the vacated (1x1) phase turns into (hex). The observed difference between the local reaction rates can be explained in terms of competitive oxygen and carbon monoxide adsorption: the CO_{ads} layer inhibits the dissociative adsorption of oxygen, while the O_{ads} layer always has single vacant sites for monomolecular CO adsorption. The highest total reaction rate in an oscillation period is reached at the instant when the perimeter of the growing oxygen islands is the longest. At the final stage of the autooscillation cycle, the (1x1) phase turns into (hex) and the CO_{ads} coverage increases owing to CO adsorption on empty sites (both on (hex) and (1x1)). The appearance of a narrow reaction zone during oxygen wave propagation was observed experimentally in H_2 and CO oxidation on a Pt[100] oriented tip by atom-probe field ion microscopy with a resolution of ~5 Å [27] (the experimental setup is shown schematically in Fig. 3).

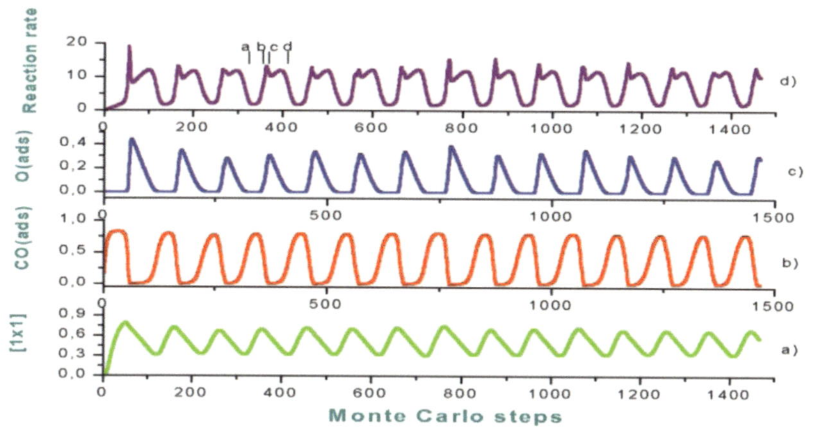

Figure 1. Self-oscillations of the model variables at M = 100 and *N* = 500. a) Coverage $*_{1x1} = *_{1x1} + CO_{ads}^{1x1} + O_{ads}^{1x1}$; b) $CO_{ads} = CO_{ads}^{1x1} + CO_{ads}^{hex}$; c) O_{ads}^{1x1}; d) specific reaction rate. Parameter values: $k_1 = 2.94\times 10^5$ ML/s Torr, $P_{CO} = 5\times 10^{-5}$ Torr, $k_2 = 4\ s^{-1}$, $k_3 = 0.03\ s^{-1}$, $k_4 = 3\ s^{-1}$, $k_5 = 2\ s^{-1}$, $k_6 = 5.6\times 10^5$ ML/s Torr, $P_{O2} = 10^{-4}$ Torr, [26, Table 1].

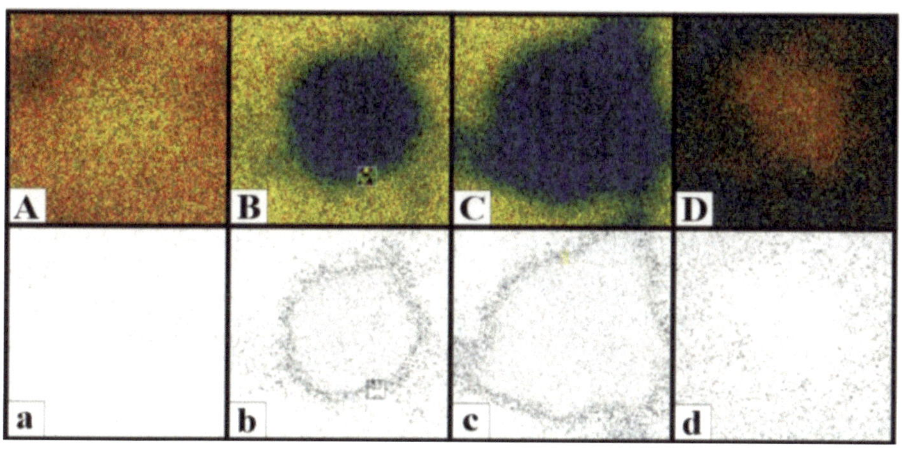

Figure 2. Snapshots reflecting the adsorbate distribution over the surface (capital letters) and the appropriate CO_2 formation rate intensity (small letters). On the A–D snapshots O_{ads} is painted blue, CO_{ads} on hex as red, CO_{ads} on (1×1) as yellow, empty $*_{1x1}$ as green. On the a–d snapshots a grey scale reflects the rate intensity. Snapshots A,a–D,d correspond to vertical bars (a, b, c, d) on the Fig.1d

Obviously, in order to synchronize the spatiotemporal changes in different areas of the surface, it is necessary to take into account the diffusion of the adsorbed species. However, the inclusion of diffusion into the set of randomly chosen main processes (in our case, steps (I)–(VII)) leads to an unreasonable increasing of the computational time because the diffusion rate constant is several orders of magnitude larger than the rate constants of the other processes. For this reason, most researchers employing kinetic Monte Carlo models in which diffusion must be taken into account consider an internal diffusion cycle, making M random transfer trials for the adsorbed substances (in our case, only CO_{ads}) after each of N×N realization trials of the main elementary processes. Since an increase in the diffusion cycle parameter M above 100 does not result in our case in quantitative or qualitative changes in the spatiotemporal dynamics of the reaction, we believe that the chosen value of the CO_{ads} diffusion rate parameter is sufficiently large for synchronization of the local processes. Likewise, decreasing the parameter M to 50 does not break the regularity of the oscillations, but somewhat reduces the oscillation period and amplitude. A further decrease in M to 30 randomizes the oscillation period and amplitude. In this case, adsorbed oxygen is always present on the surface (Fig. 4) as mobile patches of various shapes [21]. A similar turbulent spatiotemporal dynamics of substances adsorbed on the Pt(100) surface in CO oxidation was observed by photoelectron emission microscopy (PEEM) and by ellipsomicroscopy for surface imaging (EMSI).

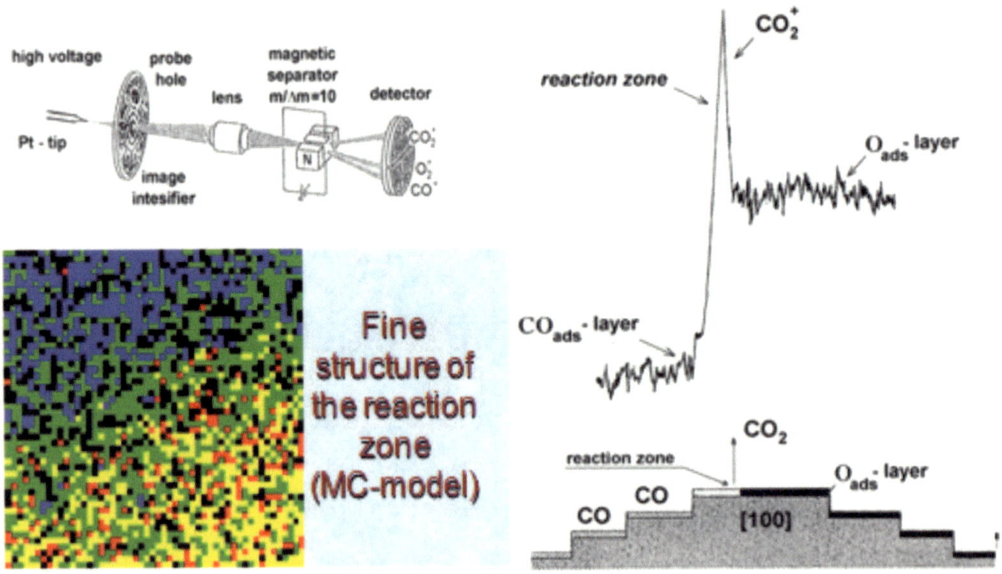

Figure 3. Experimental observation of the narrow reaction zone by means of atom-probe field ion microscopy with 5 Å resolution on a platinum tip [27]. The MC simulated fine structure corresponds to the enlarged inset on the Figure 2 B.

The kinetic Monte Carlo method provides a means to study the dependence of oscillation characteristics on reaction parameters. This can be done by varying some reaction parameter (e.g., CO partial pressure, P_{CO}) from one step to another and using the surface coverage configuration calculated in the previous step as the initial condition for the next step. In this way, we found that a reaction rate and surface coverage hysteresis takes place as P_{CO} is first raised and then decreased in the $10^{-5} \div 1.2 \times 10^{-4}$ Torr range at a fixed oxygen partial pressure of $P_{O2} = 2 \times 10^{-4}$ Torr [21]. At a higher P_{O2} /P_{CO} ratio, the Pt(100)-hex surface is almost free. As P_{CO} is raised, the CO_{ads}(1x1) phase appears. At $P_{CO} \sim 3 \times 10^{-5}$ Torr, oscillations set in, whose amplitude and period increase with increasing P_{CO}. At $P_{CO} \sim 10^{-4}$ Torr, the surface is completely covered by a CO_{ads}(1x1) layer. As P_{CO} is then decreased, the CO_{ads}(1x1) layer persists down to $P_{CO} \sim 5 \times 10^{-6}$ Torr because of the low probability of CO desorption. Therefore, it is the CO_{ads}(1x1) desorption constant that determined the lower limit of the hysteresis. The back transition (1x1) → (hex) occurs vary rapidly (clean-off reaction [23]) via steps (V)–(VII).

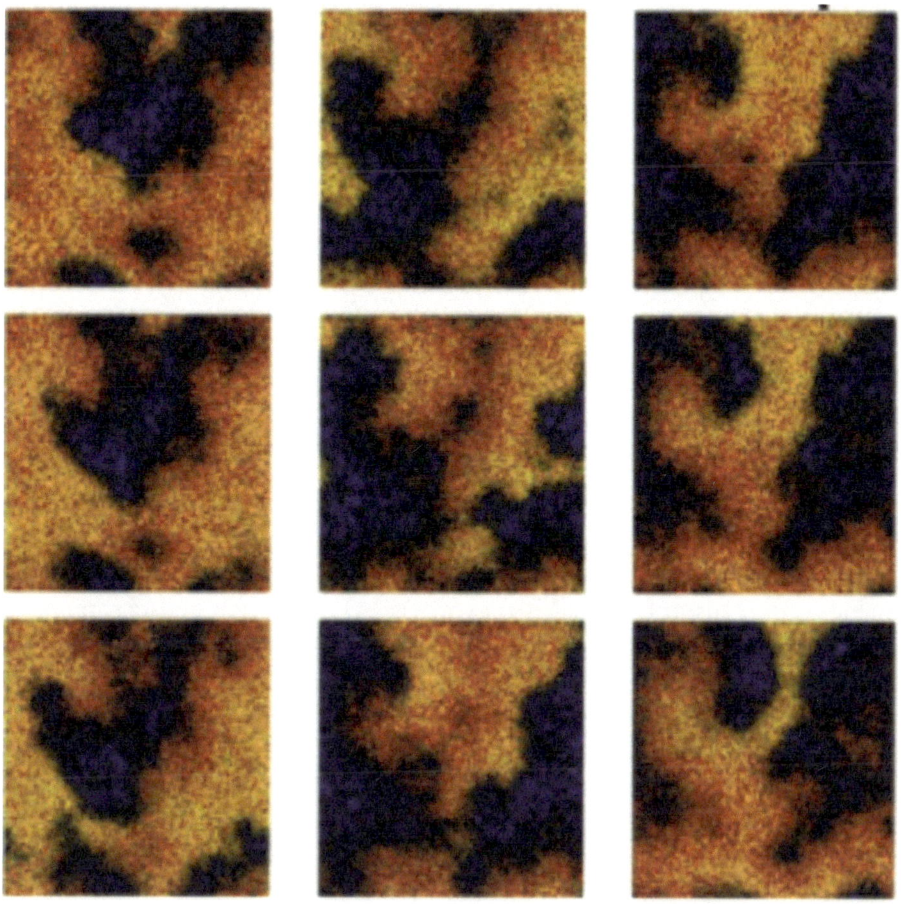

Figure 4. Snapshots reflecting the dynamics of adsorbate distribution over the surface in the case of low diffusion intensity, M = 30. The designations of adsorbates are the same as for Figure 2.

2.2. Pd(110): Simulation of oscillations and wave structures

As distinct from the oscillations on the Pt(100) surface, which are caused by surface phase transformation, the oscillations and wave phenomena on the Pd(110) surface are due to merely kinetic factors, specifically, changes in the catalytic and adsorption properties of the surface, including the oxygen sticking coefficient, due to the comparatively slow formation and consumption of subsurface oxygen, $O_{ads} \leftrightarrow O_{sub}$. The adsorption and catalytic properties of Pd(110) were studied by various kinetic and physical methods [see, e.g., 28]. A reaction mechanism taking into account the formation of subsurface oxygen O_{sub} [29] was suggested to explain the observed oscillations of the CO oxidation rate on Pt, Pd, and Ir. It is assumed in this mechanism that the resulting O_{sub} layer suppresses oxygen adsorption and favors the growth of a CO_{ads} layer (inactive surface) [29]. Nevertheless, the slow reaction between CO_{ads} and O_{sub} removes subsurface oxygen, thus making oxygen adsorption a more favorable process (active surface). This causes O_{sub} formation again, so the cycle is repeated.

Based on experimental data, the following detailed mechanism of CO oxidation on Pd(110) has been formulated, which was then used in the kinetic simulation of this reaction by the Monte Carlo method [30], Scheme 2:

Initial surface (∗):

(I) $O_{2(gas)} + 2* \rightarrow 2O_{ads}$

(II) $CO_{gas} + * \leftrightarrow CO_{ads}$

(III) $CO_{ads} + O_{ads} \rightarrow CO_2 + 2*$

Modified surface O_{sub}:

(IV) $O_{ads} + *_v \rightarrow *O_{sub}$

(V) $CO_{ads} + *O_{sub} \rightarrow CO_2 + 2* + *_v$

(VI) $CO_{gas} + *O_{sub} \leftrightarrow CO_{ads}O_{sub}$

(VII) $CO_{ads}O_{sub} \rightarrow CO_2 + * + *_v$

Scheme 2.

Here, ∗ and $*_v$ are active sites of the surface and of the subsurface layer. The first step is irreversible oxygen adsorption, and the second is CO adsorption and desorption. In the third step, CO_{ads} reacts with O_{ads} to yield the reaction product. Subsurface oxygen, O_{sub}, forms in the irreversible step (4). Step (5) is the slow reaction between O_{sub} and the nearest neighbor CO_{ads} molecules, which regenerates the initial active sites of the surface, ∗. The adsorbed species $CO_{ads}O_{sub}$ results both from CO adsorption from the gas phase (step (6)) and from CO_{ads} diffusion over active sites, both initial and modified (O_{sub}). The decomposition of the $O_{ads}O_{sub}$ complex yields CO_2 and vacates the ∗ and $*_v$ sites (step (7)). It is assumed that the heat of CO adsorption is lower on the modified sites O_{sub} than on the initial sites ∗; that is, the probability of $CO_{ads}O_{sub}$ desorption (step (6)) is higher than the probability of CO_{ads} desorption (step (2)). CO_{ads} can diffuse over the surface, obeying the following formal rules:

$$CO_{ads} + * \leftrightarrow * + CO_{ads}, \quad (1)$$

$$CO_{ads} + O_{sub} \leftrightarrow * + CO_{ads}O_{sub}, \quad (2)$$

$$CO_{ads}O_{sub} + O_{sub} \leftrightarrow O_{sub} + CO_{ads}O_{sub} \quad (3)$$

The shortened sequence of steps (I)-(V) [29] has frequently been used in the simulation of oscillations in catalytic oxidation reactions using either differential equations (see earlier reviews [13, 20]), or kinetic Monte Carlo methods [20], including our first study [31]. In our later studies [32-38], the conventional steps (1)-(5) in Scheme 2 were supplemented with the possible formation and consumption of the surface species $CO_{ads}O_{sub}$ (steps (6) and (7)). Note that steps (6) and (7) diminish the range of existence of oscillations in the (T, P_i) space.

The Pd(110) surface was modeled as an NxN square grid (in our simulations, N = 500-8000) with periodic (sometimes, zero, i.e., nonperiodic) boundary conditions. For Pd(110), a cell can assume one of five states (∗, CO_{ads}, O_{ads}, [O_{sub}], [$CO_{ads}O_{sub}$]) according to the rules given by the algorithm of the simulation of the detailed reaction mechanism (Scheme 2). Let us illustrate (Figure 5) the simulation algorithms, used in our simulation of CO oxidation dynamics on Pd(110) and Pt(100)] (with some excepts connected with the realization of the stage (*hex* → (1 x 1), when the four sites filled by CO_{ads} should be chosen for the success of the attempt) on the example of the simplified scheme, steps (I)-(V) [31].

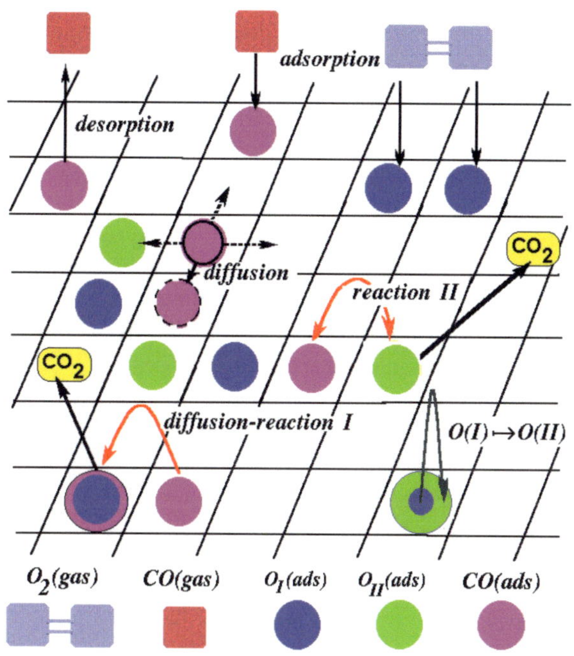

Figure 5. Schematic representation of the algorithm of the occurrence of the elementary processes on the example of shortened sequence of steps (I) - (V) [31] of the reaction mechanism (Scheme 2)

The rate coefficients k_i were recalculated as the probability of the realization of elementary processes w_i by the formula $w_i = k_i / \sum k_i$. Using a generator of random numbers uniformly distributed over the (0, 1) interval, we chose one of these processes according to the specified ratio of probabilities of their occurrence. Then, also using pairs of random numbers, the coordinates of one cell (or two adjacent cells, depending on chosen process) were determined from the N x N cells of the lattice.

The occurrence of the chosen process was imitated as follows (see Figure 5): (1) *Adsorption of CO.* The state of one arbitrarily chosen cell was checked. The free cell was occupied by adsorbed CO; when the cell was occupied, the attempt of adsorption was rejected. (2) *Desorption of CO.* When CO_{ads} was in the randomly chosen cell, it was removed from CO_{ads}, otherwise the attempt was rejected. (3) *Adsorption of oxygen.* The state of two adjacent randomly chosen cells was checked. When they were unoccupied, their state was changed to the state corresponding to the adsorbed oxygen. When at least one cell was occupied, the attempt of adsorption was rejected. (4) *Transformation of* O_{ads} *into* O_{sub}. When oxygen of the first type was in the randomly chosen cell, the cell was transformed into the state corresponding to oxygen of the second type O_{sub}, otherwise the attempt was rejected. The inverse transformation of O_{sub} into O_{ads} was not taken into account in this model. (5) *Reaction of* CO_{ads} *with* O_{sub}. When two randomly chosen adjacent cells contained the $\{CO_{ads}, O_{sub}\}$ pair, the pair was removed, and one more molecule of carbon dioxide formed was put into the reaction rate counter. The reaction rate was calculated after every Monte Carlo step (MC-step) (see below) as the number of the formed CO_2 molecules referred to the number of cells in the lattice. The surface coverage with the adsorbate was calculated similarly (the number of the cells occupied by the adsorbate was referred to the total number of the cells N^2). If the required pair was not observed, the attempt was rejected. This algorithm of occurrence of elementary stages (first, choice of the process and second, choice of the cell) makes it possible to take into account the dependence of the rate of the stage on the surface coverage with the adsorbates.

After every choice of one of the aforementioned processes and an attempt to perform this process, we consider the inner cycle of the CO_{ads}, diffusion, which included the M attempts of random choice of a pair of adjacent cells of the lattice. If the $\{CO_{ads}, *\}$ pair turned out to be this pair, CO_{ads} and $*$ in these cells interchanged their cells, i.e., diffusion took place.

The so-called MC-step consisting of NxN attempts of choice and occurrence of main elementary processes is used as the time unit in Monte Carlo models. During the step, each cell of the lattice is addressed, on average, once. Knowing the flows of reagents per surface unit (partial pressures and lattice sizes), one can go from MC-steps to the real time.

The oscillatory behavior of CO oxidation on Pd(110), which takes place via the detailed mechanism presented in Scheme 2, was revealed by computational experiments [30] using the following set of rate constants of the elementary steps (s^{-1}):

k_1	k_2	k_{-2}	k_3	k_4	k_5	k_6	k_{-6}	k_7
1	1	0.2	"infin"	0.03	0.01	1	0.5	0.02

Table 1.

The oscillations are accompanied by the wavelike propagation of adsorbed species over the surface. A dramatic increase in the reaction rate takes place at the minimum O_{sub} concentration value within one oscillation period simultaneously with the removal of the CO_{ads} layer and with the filling of the surface by adsorbed oxygen (Figure 6). Once the maximum reaction rate is achieved, a redistribution of adsorbed oxygen occurs: $O_{ads} \rightarrow O_{sub}$. The position of the $O_{sub}(t)$ peak determines the point at which the reaction rate begins to decrease. CO_{ads} accumulate on the surface, and this is accompanied by the removal of the O_{ads} layer. When the reaction rate is the lowest, the CO_{ads} molecules react slowly with O_{sub}. A decrease in the O_{sub} concentration to some critical values recreates the conditions necessary for subsequent O_{ads} adsorption, so the selfoscillation cycle is repeated. As the oxygen wave front propagates, there is a narrow reaction zone in the front of oxygen wave front enriched by empty active sites and with a local maximum of the CO_2 formation rate.

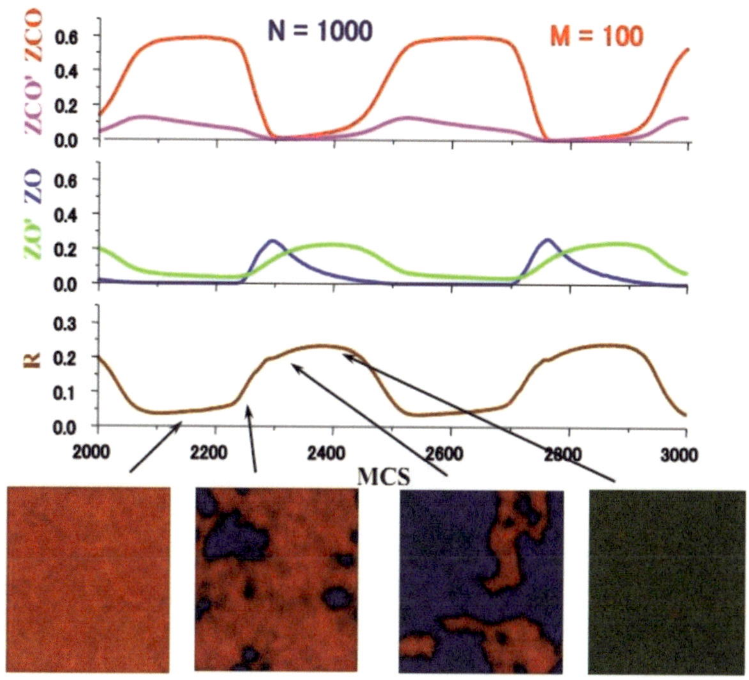

Figure 6. Reaction rate and coverages of surface species along with simulated snapshots displaying spatial distribution of different adsorbates over the surface at specific instants of time. O_{ads} is painted blue, O_{sub} as green, CO_{ads} as red, empty Pd sites as black.

Oxygen or CO adsorption on Pd(110) (Scheme 2, steps (1) and (2)) causes surface reconstruction into a so-called missing row structure, Pd(110)-(1x1) → (1x2) (Figure 7), and this is not accompanied by any change in the adsorption or catalytic properties of the surface. But the surface anisotropy is observed here: CO_{ads} molecules diffuse more rapidly along metal atom rows than in the transverse direction. We demonstrated [37] that, if this effect is taken into account in the Monte Carlo model of the reaction, then varying the M_x / M_y ratio (M_x is the number of CO_{ads} diffusion trials in the direction *x*, which coincides with the direction [1$\bar{1}$0] on the Pd(110)-(1x2) surface, and M_y is the number of CO_{ads} diffusion trials in the direction *y*, with the total diffusion rate in the internal cycle remaining invariable: $M_x + M_y = M$) will not change the dependences of the reaction rate and adsorbed species coverages on time (number of MC steps), Figure 8. But the propagation of surface oxygen waves on the Pd(110)-(1x2) surface is substantially anisotropic and the elliptic shape of oxygen waves depends on M_x/M_y. As the ratio M_x/M_y is increased, the propagating oxygen wave on the surface "elongates" in the $[1\bar{1}0]$ direction (allow me to remind that O_{ads} doesn't diffuse over the surface, only CO_{ads}!). The CO_{ads} diffusion anisotropy effect is especially pronounced in the simulation of spiral oxygen waves on the Pd(110) surface. The simulation of this kind of spatio-temporal structure is detailed in [34]. In our computational experiment, the isotropic diffusion regime ($M_x/M_y = 50/50$) was changed to an anisotropic diffusion regime with $M_x/M_y = 80/20$. This led to the "elongation" of the spiral oxygen wave along the $[1\bar{1}0]$ direction [37, 23], Figure 9. This asymmetric behavior is in good agreement with the experimental observation of spiral waves in this reaction by the PEEM method.

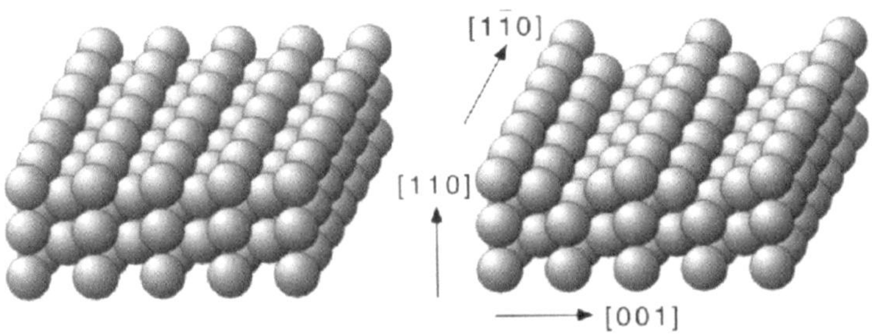

Figure 7. Reconstruction of the Pd(110)-(1x1) into the (1x2) "missing row" structure caused by oxygen or carbon monoxide adsorption.

Simulation of the CO oxidation dynamics on Pd(110) at a low CO_{ads} diffusion rate (M = 20) gave somewhat unexpected results [35, 36]. Decrease of M up to value M = 50 doesn't change significantly the oscillatory and wave dynamics, but decreasing to value M = 20 drastically change both the shape of oscillations and the spatiotemporal behavior of simulated surface waves. As in the case of Pt(100), period and amplitude of oscillations decrease considerably, the dynamic behavior of reaction rate and surface coverages demonstrate the intermittence (oscillatory regime I, Figure 10). During these oscillations oxygen (O_{ads}) is always present on the surface in the form of turbulent spatio-temporal structures (Figure 11a). It is seen from Figure 11a that the whole surface is divided in several islands oscillating with the same period but with a phase shift relative to each other, therefore the reaction rate and coverage's time dependencies demonstrate the intermittence peculiarities. Here one can observe on the surface the spatio-temporal pattern of complicated turbulent shape. The colliding oxygen islands form the spiral-like patterns. Step-by step decrease of oxygen partial pressure (remember, that the values for O_2 and CO adsorption coefficients, k_1, k_2, and k_6 (s^{-1}), can be treated as the product of the impingement rate ($k_i \times P_i$) and of the sticking coefficient (S)) leads to the gradual thinning of oxygen travelling waves, Figures 11b-e.

http://dx.doi.org/10.5772/53792

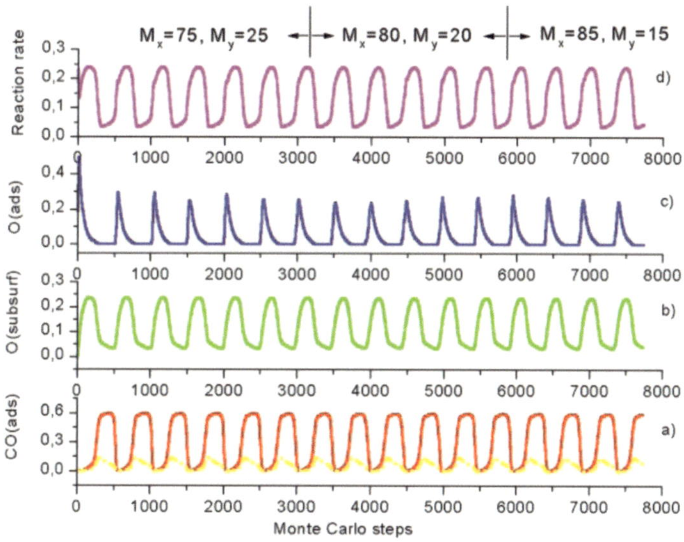

Figure 8. Dynamics of changes in surface coverages CO_{ads} (red lines) and $CO_{ads}O_{sub}$ (yellow lines), O_{sub} (green lines), O_{ads} (blue lines), and the specific reaction rate at different ratios M_x/M_y.

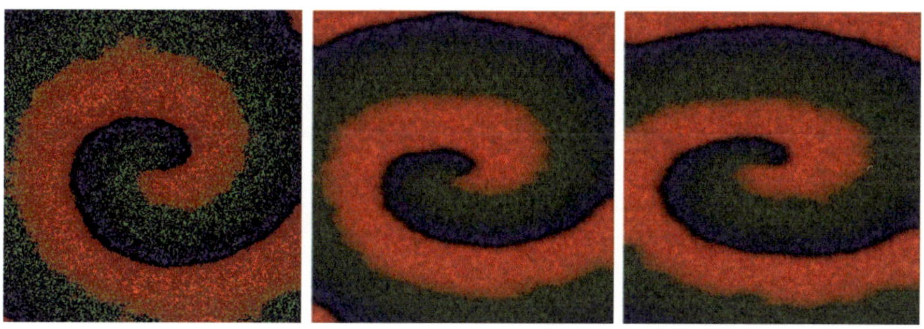

Figure 9. Evolution of the simulated spiral waves [34] in CO oxidation over Pd(110) after the switching the diffusion intensity M from isotropic regime (Mx/My = 50/50) to the anisotropic one (Mx/My = 80/20). The designations of adsorbates are the same as for Figure 6.

At low values of k_1 (Figure 11 d-f) the long and thin oxygen stripe (or "worm"-like) patterns are formed on the simulated surface, and the clear tendency of turbulent patterns to combine into spirals disappeared at $k_1 < 0.8$. The amplitude of oscillations diminished with decreasing of k_1. At last, at $k_1 = 0.71$ (Fig. 11 f), the oxygen stripe wave vanish slowly from the surface and the system transform to the low reactive state (the surface is predominantly covered by CO_{ads}).

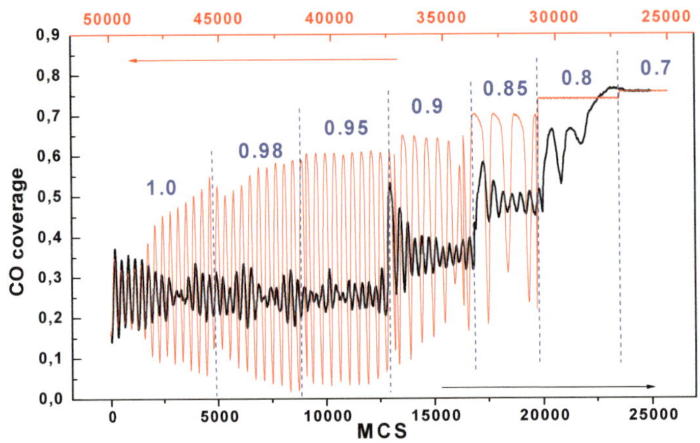

Figure 10. Hysteresis of oscillatory regimes in CO oxidation reaction over Pd(110) at decreasing (→) and increasing (←) of oxygen partial pressure (k_1). Intensity of CO_{ads} diffusion M = 20.

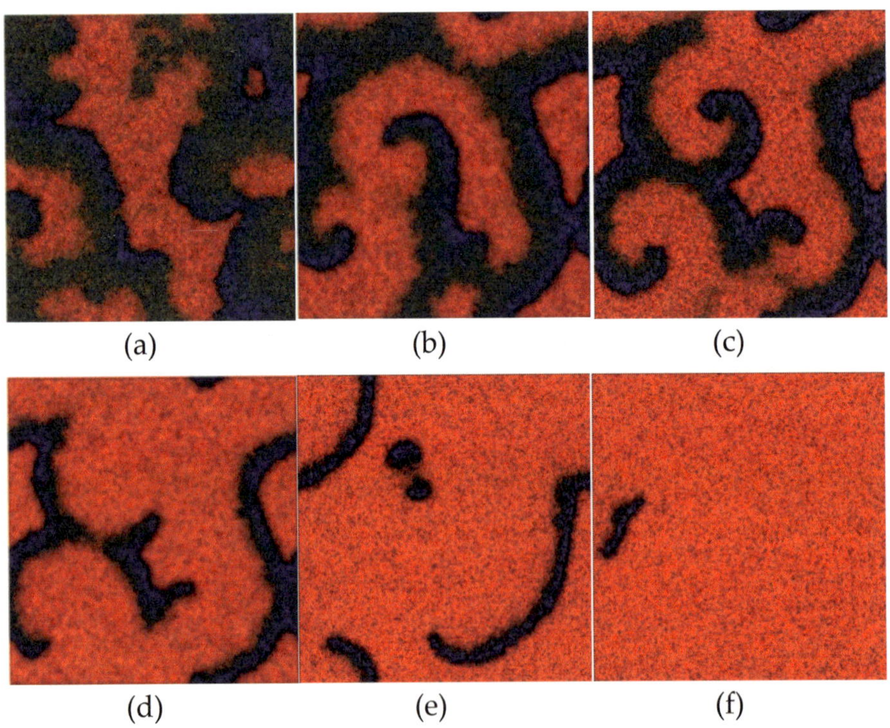

Figure 11. Typical snapshots reflecting the adsorbate distribution over the surface at step-by-step reducing of $P(O_2)$ (or k_1). a) $P(O_2)$ =1; b) $P(O_2)$ = 0.9; c) $P(O_2)$ = 0.85; d) $P(O_2)$ = 0.8; e) $P(O_2)$ = 0.73; f) $P(O_2)$ = 0.71. Intensity of CO_{ads} diffusion M = 20. The designations of adsorbates are the same as for Figure 6.

http://dx.doi.org/10.5772/53792

The reverse increasing of k_1 leads to hysteresis in oscillatory behavior. The oscillation appears only at $k_1 = 0.85$ via very fast "surface explosion" (Figure 12 a-h). It is surprising that the characteristics of oscillations differ drastically from those observed at gradual decreasing of k_1. Now the amplitude of oscillations in the regime II, Figure 10 (coverage's and reaction rate), is larger than in regime I, and instead of turbulent spiral-like pattern (Figure 11 a-c) we observe the alternately change of O_{ads} and CO_{ads} layers via growing cellular oxygen islands (Figure 12) similar to the case with large diffusion intensity (Figure 6). The interval of existence of these oscillations increased significantly. The simulations at higher lattice size N = 8000 in the lower boundary of the regime II ($k_1 = 0.83$) gave the "target"-like structures, which were observed experimentally [39], Figure 13.

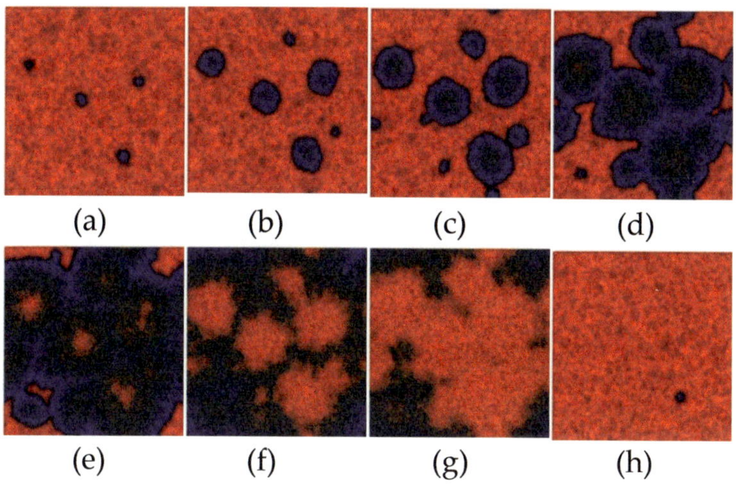

Figure 12. The snapshots illustrating the rise of oscillations (via surface explosion) at inverse step-by-step increasing of k_1 ($k_1 = 0.85$). The time interval between frames is 50 MC steps.

Only at $k_1 = 1$ occurs the transformation from the regime II to the regime I, Figure 10, – we observe again the turbulent patterns over the surface (Fig. 11 a). In the cases discussed above we perform the simulation experiments with constant P(CO), i.e., constant k_2 and k_6, changing over and back the O_2 partial pressure (k_1). When we performed the simulations with constant $k_1 = 1\ s^{-1}$, M = 20, and changing step-wise k_2 and k_6 (i.e., P(CO)) from 0.5 to 1.5 and back, we also obtained the hysteresis in oscillatory regime with similar spatiotemporal patterns on the surface.

It has been found in experiments that the different oscillatory windows could exist in the parameter space of the particular system, e.g., CO oxidation over Pt (100) [40], i.e., at different parameters (temperature and CO/O_2 ratio) two regions has been found at a constant total pressure where the rate oscillations and spatiotemporal formations have been observed. In our case two different oscillatory regimes with discriminate spatiotemporal dynamics have been revealed in simulations *in the same* variation interval of $P(O_2)$, Figure 10. That means, that at the same value of the key parameter (e.g., $k_1 = 0.85$) two different «cycles» could exist. The shape of «integral» oscillations and spatio-temporal patterns depends on the dynamic prehistory (shape-memory effect).

The interval of existence of oscillatory regime II is quite large: $0.98 > k_1 > 0.82$. Increasing k_1 in this interval leads to the increasing of the amplitude and decreasing of the period of oscillations. At low bound of this interval (i.e., at $k_1 = 0.83$) the target structures of growing oxygen islands has been observed (Figure 13) – during the oxygen island propagation CO have the possibility to adsorb into its centre. In this case the period of oscillations increased significantly (~ 2000 MCS).

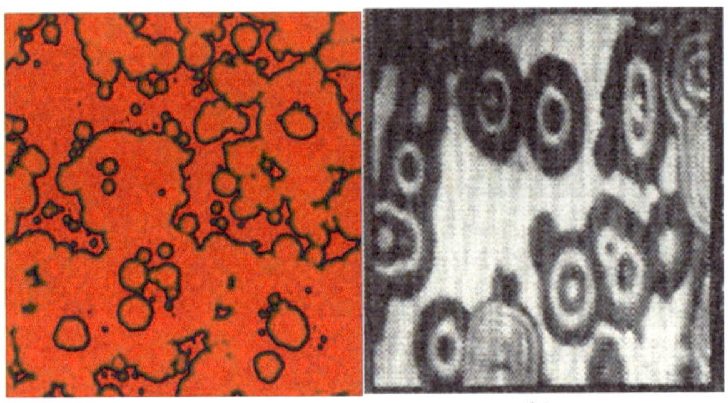

(a) (b)

Figure 13. a) Simulated "target" structures at the bottom of the oscillatory regime II ($k_1 = 0.83$), M = 20, N = 8000. b) adsorbed oxygen and carbon monoxide structures experimentally observed on the Pt(100) by Photo Emission Electron Microscopy (PEEM) [39]. Bright regions – CO_{ads}, dark regions – O_{ads}.

Figure 10 illustrates the whole scenario of k_1 change during our simulation experiments, exemplified by CO_{ads} dynamics.

3. Conclusion

As was stated in our review [41] published twenty years ago – "One may anticipate, that as early as the end of this decade, experimentally produced documentary movies "From the Life of Molecules" will be systematically compared with those obtained by means of computer experiments (e.g., by Monte Carlo method)". Now we can see, that these hopes began to justify (at least, partly):

It was revealed from the simulations that there exists a narrow reaction zone with maximal local rate of reaction when an oxygen wave propagates over the surface, and this was confirmed by APFIM data.

Accounting the anisotropy of the Pd(110) single crystal has no effect on the oscillation period and amplitude, but leads to elliptic oxygen patterns on the surface. The formation of these patterns is confirmed by surface space-resolved methods (e.g., PEEM).

A wide variety of chemical waves (cellular and turbulent patterns, spirals, rings, and strips) can be obtained by varying the parameters of the computational experiment. All of these patterns were actually observed in experimental studies of the oscillatory dynamics of catalytic reactions.

Acknowledgements

This work was partly supported by Russian Fund for Basic Research, Grant # 12-03-00766a and by Siberian Branch of Russian Academy of Sciences (Interdisciplinary Integration Project # 47).

Author details

Vladimir I. Elokhin*

Address all correspondence to: elokhin@catalysis.ru

Boreskov Institute of Catalysis, Siberian Branch of Russian Academy of Sciences and Novosibirsk State University, Novosibirsk, Russian Federation

References

[1] Imbihl R. Oscillatory reactions at single-crystal surfaces. Progr. Surf. Sci. 1993; 44 185.

[2] Van Hove M.A., Somorjai G.A. Adsorption and adsorbate-induced restructuring: a LEED perspective. Surf. Sci. 1994; 299/300(1) 487-501.

[3] Nørskov J.K. Theory of adsorption and adsobate-induced restructuring. Surface Sci. 1994; 299/300(1) 690-705.

[4] Lapujoulade J. The roughening of metal surfaces. Surf. Sci. Rep. 1994; 20(4) 191- 294.

[5] Bracco J. Thermal roughening of the (110) surfaces of unreconstructed f.c.c. metals. Phys. Low-Dim. Struct. 1994; 8 1-22.

[6] Landau D.P., Binder K. A guide to Monte-Carlo simulations in statistical physics. Cambridge University Press: Cambridge, 2000.

[7] Temel B., Meskine H., Reuter K., Scheffler M., Metui H. Does phenomenological kinetics provide an adequate description of heterogeneous catalytic reactions? J. Chem. Phys. 2007; 126 204711.

[8] Sharifulina A., Elokhin V. Simulation of heterogeneous catalytic reaction by asynchronous cellular automata on multicomputer. Lectures Notes of Computer Science. 2011; 6873 204-209.

[9] Slinko M.G., Slinko M.M. Self-oscillations of heterogeneous catalytic reaction rates. Catal. Rev. Sci. Eng. 1978; 17 119-153.

[10] Razon L.F., Schmitz R.A. Intrinsically unstable behavior during the oxidation of carbon monoxide on platinum. Catal. Rev. Sci. Eng. 1986; 28 89-164.

[11] Ertl G. Oscillatory catalytic reactions on single-crystal surfaces. Adv. Catal. 1990; 37 213-277.

[12] Yablonskii G.S., Bykov V.I., Gorban' A.N., Elokhin V.I. Kinetic Models of Catalytic Reactions. In: Compton, R.G. (ed.) Comprehensive Chemical Kinetics, vol. 32, Amsterdam: Elsevier, 1991, chapt. 5 and 6.

[13] Schüth F., Henry B.E., Schmidt L.D. Oscillatory reactions in heterogeneous catalysis. Adv. Catal. 1990; 39 51-127.

[14] Eiswirth M., Ertl G. Pattern formation on catalytic surfaces. In: Kapral R., Showalter K. (eds.) Chemical Waves and Patterns, Understanding Chemical Reactivity, vol. 10, Dordrecht: Kluwer, 1994, p. 447-489.

[15] Slinko M.M., Jaeger N.I. Oscillating Heterogeneous Catalytic Systems. In: Delmon B., Yates J.T. (eds.) Studies in Surface Science and Catalysis, vol. 86, Amsterdam: Elsevier, 1994.

[16] Imbihl R., Ertl G. Oscillatory kinetics in heterogeneous catalysis. Chem. Rev. 1995; 95 697-733.

[17] Ertl G. Dynamics of reactions at surfaces. Adv. Catal. 2000; 45 1-69.

[18] Cobden P.D., Janssen N.M.H., van Breugel Y., Nieuwenhuys, B.E. Non-linear behavior in the NO-H_2 reaction over single crystals and field emitters of some Pt-group metals. Faraday Discuss. 1996; 105 57-72.

[19] Appendix: Oscillatory Heterogeneous Catalytic Systems. Catal. Today. 2005; 105 I-II.

[20] Zhdanov V.P. Monte-Carlo simulation of oscillations, chaos and pattern formation in heterogeneous catalytic reactions. Surf. Sci. Rep. 2002; 45; 231-326.

[21] Latkin E.I., Elokhin V.I., Gorodetskii V.V. Monte Carlo model of oscillatory CO oxidation having regard to the change of catalytic properties due to the adsorbate induced Pt(100) structural transformation. J. Molec. Catal. A: Chemical. 2001; 166(1) 23-30.

[22] Elokhin V.I., Gorodetskii V.V. Atomic scale imaging of oscillations and chemical waves at catalytic surface reactions: Experimental and statistical lattice models. In: A.M. Spasic, J.-P. Hsu, (eds.) Finely Dispersed Particles: Micro-, Nano-, and Atto-En-

gineering. Surfactant Science, vol. 130. Taylor & Francis, CRS Press: New York, 2005; Chapter 7, 159-189.

[23] Gorodetskii V.V., Elokhin V.I., Bakker J.W., Nieuwenhuys B.E. Field Electron and Field Ion Microscopy studies of chemical wave propagation in oscillatory reactions on platinum group metals. Catalysis Today 2005; 105(2) 183-205.

[24] Elokhin V.I., Matveev A.V., Kovalyov E.V., Gorodetskii V.V. From single crystals to supported nanoparticles in oscillatory behavior of $CO+O_2$ reaction on platinum and palladium surfaces: Experiment and stochastic models. Chem. Eng. Journal 2009; 154(1-3) 94-106.

[25] Gruyters M., Ali T., King D.A. Theoretical inquiry into the microscopic origin of the oscillatory CO oxidation reaction on Pt(100). J. Phys. Chem. 1996; 100 14417-14423.

[26] Imbihl R., Cox M.P., Ertl G., Müller H., Brenig W. Kinetic oscillations in the catalytic CO oxidation on Pt(110): Theory. J. Chem. Phys. 1985; 83 1578-1587.

[27] Gorodetskii V.V., Drachsel, W. Kinetic oscillations and surface waves in catalytic CO $+O_2$ reaction on Pt surface: FEM, FIM and HREELS studies. Appl. Catal., A: Gen. 1999; 188, 267-275.

[28] Gorodetskii V.V., Matveev A.V., Podgornov E.A., Zaera, F. Study of low-temperature reaction between CO and O_2 over Pd and Pt surfaces. Top. Catal. 2005; 32(1) 17-28.

[29] Sales B.S., Turner J.B., Maple, M.B. Oscillatory oxidation of CO over Pt, Pd and Ir catalysts: Theory. Surf. Sci., 1982; 114 381-394.

[30] Latkin E.I., Elokhin V.I., Matveev A.V., Gorodetskii V.V. The role of subsurface oxygen in oscillatory behaviour of $CO+O_2$ reaction over Pd metal catalysts: Monte Carlo model. J. Molec. Catal. A: Chemical 2000; 158(1) 161-166.

[31] Vishnevskii A.L., Latkin E.I., Elokhin V.I. Autowaves on catalyst surface caused by carbon monoxide oxidation kinetics: Imitation model. Surf. Rev. Lett. 1995; 2 459-469.

[32] Elokhin V., Kalgin K., Kovalyov E., Matveev A., Gorodetskii V. Specificity of oscillation performance over the flexible surfaces of the metal nanoparticles: Monte-Carlo approach. XIX International Conference on Chemical Reactors "ChemReactor-19", Vienna, Austria, September 5-9, 2010. Abstracts, OP-I-5, pp. 45-46.

[33] Elokhin V.I., Latkin E.I. Statistical model of oscillatory and wave phenomena on a catalyst surface in CO oxidation. Dokl. Akad. Nauk, 1995, vol. 344, p. 56-61.

[34] Latkin E.I., Elokhin V.I., Gorodetskii V.V. Spiral concentration waves in the Monte-Carlo model of CO oxidation over Pd(110) caused by synchronization via CO_{ads} diffusion between separate parts of catalytic surface. Chem. Eng. Journal, 2003; 91(2-3) 123-131.

[35] Matveev A.V., Latkin E.I., Elokhin V.I., Gorodetskii V.V. Turbulent and stripes wave patterns caused by limited CO_{ads} diffusion during CO oxidation over Pd(110) surface: Kinetic Monte-Carlo studies. Chem. Eng. Journal, 2005, V. 107, N 1, pp. 181-189.

[36] Elokhin V., Matveev A., Gorodetskii V., Latkin E. Hysteresis in Oscillatory Behaviour in CO Oxidation Reaction over Pd(110) Revealed by Asynchronous Cellular Automata Simulation. Lectures Notes of Computer Science. 2007; 4671 401-409.

[37] Matveev A.V., Latkin E.I., Elokhin V.I., Gorodetskii V.V. Manifestation of the adsorbed CO diffusion anisotropy caused by the structure properties of the Pd(110)-(1x2) surface on the oscillatory behavior during CO oxidation reaction – Monte-Carlo model. Chemistry for Sustainable Development. 2003; 11(1) 173-180.

[38] Elokhin V.I., Matveev A.V., Kovalyov E.V., Gorodetskii V.V. From single crystals to supported nanoparticles in oscillatory behavior of $CO+O_2$ reaction on platinum and palladium surfaces: Experiment and stochastic models. Chem. Eng. Journal. 2009; 154(1-3) 94-106.

[39] Jakubith S., Rotermund H.H., Engel W., von Oertzen A., Ertl G. Spatio-temporal concentration patterns in a surface reaction: Propagating and standing waves, rotating spirals, and turbulence. Phys. Rev. Lett. 1990; 65 3013–3016.

[40] Lauterbach J., Bonilla G., Fletcher T.D. Non-linear phenomena during CO oxidation in the mbar pressure range: a comparison between Pt/SiO_2 and Pt(110). Chem. Eng. Sci. 1999; 54 4501–4512.

[41] Yablonskii G.S., Elokhin V.I. Kinetic models of heterogeneous catalysis. In: Thomas J.M., Zamaraev K.I. (eds.) Perspectives in Catalysis. Blackwell Scientific Publications. Oxford. 1992. pp. 191-249

Chapter 9

Monte-Carlo Simulation of Particle Diffusion in Various Geometries and Application to Chemistry and Biology

Ianik Plante and Francis A. Cucinotta

Additional information is available at the end of the chapter

http://dx.doi.org/10.5772/53203

1. Introduction

The simulation of systems comprising different types of molecules is of great interest in several fields, notably in chemistry and biological sciences. The conventional approach to simulate biological networks is to write down macroscopic rate equations and solve the corresponding differential equations numerically to obtain the time evolution of molecules concentrations [1-3]. In this method, the system evolution is deterministic, and it is implicitly assumed that the concentrations are large. However, in most biological systems, the concentrations of molecules usually range from nanomolar to micromolar; therefore, the interactions of these molecules are highly stochastic. Recently, various techniques have been developed to take into account the spatial distribution of individual molecules and the stochastic character of reactions between them. Several of these techniques are based on the Green's functions of the Diffusion Equation (DE), and they offer the advantage of being able to follow all the particles in time and space. In this book chapter, this method is applied to simple systems in one, two, and three dimensions. Two applications are discussed. The first is the simulation of ligands molecules near a plane membrane comprising receptors with the possibility of dissociation and initiation of signal transduction. The second application of this theory is the simulation of partially diffusion-controlled chemical reactions.

2. Sampling of the Green's functions of the diffusion equation

The Green's functions of the DE in simple systems under different boundary conditions are known from the theory of heat propagation in solids [4], since the DE and the equation for the propagation of heat are the same. With few assumptions, these Green's functions can be used to model particle systems in specific environments.

INTECH
open science | open minds

© 2013 The Author(s). Licensee InTech. This chapter is distributed under the terms of the Creative Commons Attribution License http://creativecommons.org/licenses/by/3.0), which permits unrestricted use, distribution, and reproduction in any medium, provided the original work is properly cited.

2.1. Diffusion equation and boundary conditions

The DE can be written

$$\frac{\partial}{\partial t} p(\boldsymbol{r},t \mid \boldsymbol{r_0}) = D\nabla^2 p(\boldsymbol{r},t \mid \boldsymbol{r_0}), \tag{1}$$

where $\boldsymbol{r_0}$ is the initial position vector[1] of a particle and $\boldsymbol{r}$ is its position vector at time t. The diffusion coefficient of a particle (D) is used instead of the thermal diffusivity coefficient in the equation of the propagation of heat. In the model presented here, a particle is located at the position $\boldsymbol{r_0}$ at $t=0$. This is expressed mathematically as:

$$p(\boldsymbol{r},t=0 \mid \boldsymbol{r_0}) = \delta(\boldsymbol{r}-\boldsymbol{r_0}), \tag{2}$$

where $\delta(\boldsymbol{r}-\boldsymbol{r_0})=\delta(x-x_0)\delta(y-y_0)\delta(z-z_0)$ is the product of three Dirac's delta functions. To complete the description of the model the boundary conditions at the surfaces are specified. One important case is the *radiation* boundary condition at the surface $X=0$:

$$D\frac{\partial p(x,y,z,t \mid x_0,y_0,z_0)}{\partial x}\Big|_{x=0} = k_a p(0,y,z,t \mid x_0,y_0,z_0). \tag{3}$$

The limit $k_a \to \infty$ is known as the *absorbing* boundary condition. In this case, the boundary condition is written $p(0,y,z,t \mid x_0, y_0, z_0, t_0)=0$. The limit $k_a \to 0$ is the *reflecting* boundary condition. The condition $k_a>0$ implies that particles may bind at the surface; therefore, the Green's function of these systems are generally not normalized to 1. In all systems described in Sections 3 and 4 the boundary conditions on surfaces, if any, are reflecting ($k_a=0$). In Section 5 two applications of the theory for which the boundary conditions are different will be discussed.

2.2. Sampling of the Green's functions

To simulate the state of a particle system after one time step, the positions of each particle are calculated by sampling the Green's function for the position $\boldsymbol{r}$. The Green's function is written $p(\boldsymbol{r}, t \mid \boldsymbol{r_0})$ to emphasize that it represents the probability of a particle initially located at the position $\boldsymbol{r_0}$ to be found at the position $\boldsymbol{r}$ at time t. In the systems presented in Sections 3 and 4, there is no binding of particles to boundaries. Therefore, $p(\boldsymbol{r},t \mid \boldsymbol{r_0})$ is normalized as follows:

$$\int_{\Omega} p(\boldsymbol{r_1},t_1 \mid \boldsymbol{r_0}) d\boldsymbol{r_1} = 1, \tag{4}$$

---

1 Through the book chapter, variables written in bold are vectors.

where Ω is the domain where the particle can be found. Another important thing to consider is that the simulation of a particle trajectory can be done by using one or several time steps. This can be expressed mathematically as:

$$p\left(\boldsymbol{r}_2,\Delta t_1+\Delta t_2 \mid \boldsymbol{r}_0\right)=\int_{\Omega} p\left(\boldsymbol{r}_2,\Delta t_2 \mid \boldsymbol{r}_1\right) p\left(\boldsymbol{r}_1,\Delta t_1 \mid \boldsymbol{r}_0\right) d\boldsymbol{r}_1. \tag{5}$$

That is, the probability of a particle to be found at $\boldsymbol{r}_2$ after the time steps Δt_1 and Δt_2 is the same as going to the intermediate position $\boldsymbol{r}_1$ after Δt_1 and then the final position $\boldsymbol{r}_2$ at $\Delta t_1+\Delta t_2$. The integral over the domain Ω covers all intermediate positions. This is the Chapman-Kolmogorov equation, which hold in Markovian systems.

As seen in a previous paper [5], Equations (4) and (5) have to modified in systems where there is a possibility of binding of particles at the boundaries.

3. One-dimensional systems

One dimensional (1D) systems are simpler to study than those which are multi-dimensional. They are also of interest since several multi-dimensional systems can be approached as independent 1D systems [6]. In 1D, the DE is:

$$\frac{\partial p(x,t \mid x_0)}{\partial t}=D\frac{\partial^2}{\partial x^2}p(x,t \mid x_0). \tag{6}$$

The initial condition is $p(x,0 \mid x_0)=\delta(x-x_0)$. Three systems are described in this section: free diffusion, diffusion in the half-space $X>0$ and diffusion in the space between $X=0$ and $X=L$.

3.1. Free diffusion

The Green's function of the DE in 1D for a free particle, noted $p_{free}(x,t \mid x_0)$, is well known:

$$p_{\text{free}}\left(x,t \mid x_0\right)=\frac{1}{\sqrt{4\pi Dt}}\exp\left[-\frac{(x-x_0)^2}{4Dt}\right]. \tag{7}$$

This is a Gaussian distribution, with variance $\sigma^2=2Dt$. This distribution can be sampled by using, for example, the Box-Muller method [7].

Algorithm 1: Sampling algorithm for $p_{free}(x,\Delta t|x_0)$ (free 1D diffusion)

GENERATE N as a standard Normal

$X \leftarrow x_0 + \sqrt{D\Delta t}$

RETURN X.

The sampling algorithm is used to generate the positions of 1,000,000 particles after one time step. The results are stored in histograms and normalized. The Green's functions and the results of sampling are illustrated[2] in Figure 1.

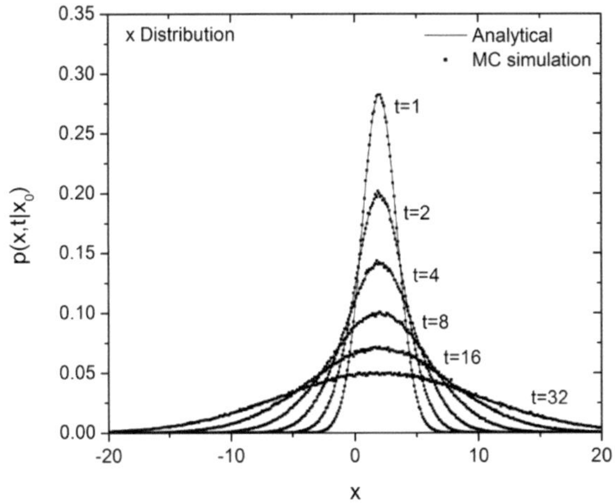

Figure 1. Green's functions $p_{free}(x,t|x_0)$ at $t=1$, 2, 4, 8, 16 and 32 time units, for a particle initially at $x_0=2$. The lines are analytical predictions; the points are the result of sampling from 1,000,000 particle histories.

Because the sampling algorithms use random numbers, the simulation results vary from one simulation to another. Usually, the larger the number of histories, the smaller the statistical fluctuation of the results. The algorithms presented in this book chapter are exact, i.e. the simulation results are expected to converge to the analytical Green's function at the limit of an infinite number of histories. In practice, 1,000,000 particle histories are usually sufficient to converge to the analytical Green's function and to confirm the validity of the algorithm. The time discretization property of the Green's function can also be used to validate the algorithm: since a simulation can be done in several time steps, the positions of the particles obtained after the first time step are used as the initial positions for the next step.

3.2. Diffusion in the half-space x>0

As it will be seen in the applications, this system may be used to represent the motion of particles near a membrane. The reflective boundary condition at $x=0$ is given by

2 Through this book chapter, the diffusion coefficient is set to $D=1$ in Figures.

$$D\frac{\partial p(x,t\mid x_0)}{\partial x}\Big|_{x=0}=0. \qquad (8)$$

The solution of the DE in 1D for this system, noted $p_{ref}(x,t\mid x_0)$, is given in ref. [8]:

$$p_{\text{ref}}\left(x,t\mid x_0\right)=\frac{1}{\sqrt{4\pi Dt}}\left\{\exp\left[-\frac{(x-x_0)^2}{4Dt}\right]+\exp\left[-\frac{(x+x_0)^2}{4Dt}\right]\right\}. \qquad (9)$$

This Green's function is the sum of two Gaussian distributions. It can be sampled by the method described in Algorithm 2 (given in ref. [8]):

Algorithm 2: Sampling algorithm for $p_{ref}(x,\Delta t\mid x_0)$ (free 1D diffusion with reflection at x=0)

SET $N_0 \leftarrow (1/2)\mathrm{Erfc}[-x_0/\sqrt{4D\Delta t}]$

GENERATE uniform [0,1] random variates U,V

IF ($U<N_0$) $\quad X \leftarrow x_0+\sqrt{4D\Delta t}\,\mathrm{Erfc}^{-1}[V\mathrm{Erfc}(-x_0/\sqrt{4D\Delta t})]$

ELSE $\quad X \leftarrow -x_0+\sqrt{4D\Delta t}\,\mathrm{Erfc}^{-1}[V\mathrm{Erfc}(x_0/\sqrt{4D\Delta t})]$

RETURN X

where *Erfc(x)* is the complementary error function [9]. The Green's functions and the result of sampling are illustrated in Figure 2.

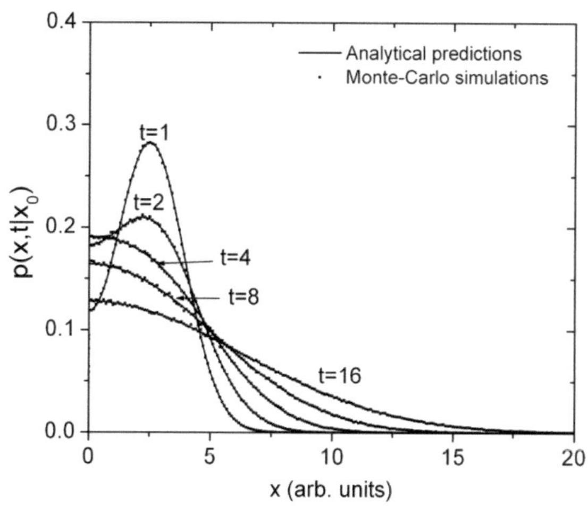

Figure 2. Green's functions $p_{ref}(x,t|x_0)$ at $t=1, 2, 4, 8, 16$ and 32 time units, for a particle in the half-space $x>0$ initially at $x_0=2.5$. The lines are analytical predictions; the points are the result of sampling from 1,000,000 particles histories.

3.3. Diffusion of a particle between *x=0* and *x=L*

This system is used to simulate the motion of particles in a confined space. In this case, the reflective boundary conditions at *x=0* and *x=L* are given by

$$D\frac{\partial p(x,t\mid x_0)}{\partial x}\Big|_{x=0}=0,\qquad D\frac{\partial p(x,t\mid x_0)}{\partial x}\Big|_{x=L}=0. \tag{10}$$

The Green's function of the DE in 1D for a particle between the boundaries, noted $p_{conf}(x,t\mid x_0)$, is [4]:

$$p_{\text{conf}}(x,t\mid x_0)=\frac{1}{L}\sum_{n=-\infty}^{\infty}\exp\left(-\frac{\pi^2 n^2 Dt}{L^2}\right)\cos\frac{n\pi x}{L}\cos\frac{n\pi x_0}{L}. \tag{11}$$

This function is complicated by an infinite sum. However, it is possible to use the following algorithm to generate trajectories of particles in this environment [10]. The algorithm is based on a series method, as described in [11]. For this section the functions $f(x)$ and $f_n(x)$ are defined:

$$f(x)=\frac{1}{L}+2\sum_{n=1}^{\infty}f_n(x),\qquad f_n(x)\overset{\text{def}}{=}\frac{1}{L}\exp\left(-\frac{\pi^2 n^2 Dt}{L^2}\right)\cos\frac{n\pi x}{L}\cos\frac{n\pi x_0}{L}. \tag{12}$$

The algorithm is:

Algorithm 3A: Generation of random variate X distributed as $p_{conf}(x,\Delta t\mid x_0)$ (particle between *x=0* and *x=L* in 1D)

```
DEFINE H ← 1/L + 1/√(πDΔt)
REPEAT
{
    GENERATE U,V uniform on [0,1] and X uniform on [0,L]
    SET Y ← VH
}
UNTIL Y≤f(X)
RETURN X
```

The verification of $Y \le f(X)$ is dose by using the second part of the algorithm:

http://dx.doi.org/10.5772/53203

Algorithm 3B: Verification of $Y<f(X)$

SET $S \leftarrow 1/L+2f_1(X)$, $k \leftarrow 1$ (S holds the approximation sum)

REPEAT FOREVER

{

$T=(L/\pi^2 kD\Delta t)exp(-\pi^2 k^2 D\Delta t/L^2)$

IF ($Y \geq S+T$) THEN RETURN "$Y \geq f(X)$" and EXIT

IF ($Y \leq S-T$) THEN RETURN "$Y \leq f(X)$" and EXIT

$k \leftarrow k+1$

$S \leftarrow S+2f_k(X)$

}

The Green's function and the result of sampling for 1,000,000 histories of particles initially located at x_0=5 are shown in Figure 3.

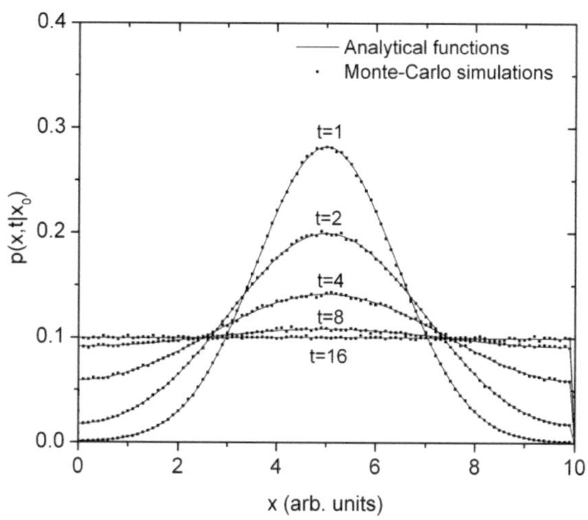

Figure 3. Green's functions $p_{conf}(x,t|x_0)$ at t=1, 2, 4, 8, 16 and 32 time units, for a particle initially at x_0=5, allowed to occupy the space between x=0 and x=10. The lines are analytical predictions; the points are the result of sampling of 1,000,000 particle histories.

When time evolves, as illustrated in Figure 3, the particles become uniformly distributed between $x=0$ and $x=10$.

4. Two-dimensional systems

Two dimensional (2D) systems are interesting, because the particles trajectories can be visualized in a plane. The DE in 2D can be written:

$$\frac{\partial p(x,y,t\,|\,x_0,y_0)}{\partial t}=D\left[\frac{\partial^2}{\partial x^2}+\frac{\partial^2}{\partial y^2}\right]p(x,y,t\,|\,x_0,y_0). \tag{13}$$

The initial condition is $p(x,y,t{=}0\,|\,x_0,y_0)=\delta(x-x_0)\delta(y-y_0)$. In several cases, the Green's function can be written as the product of the functions $p_x(x,t\,|\,x_0)$ and $p_y(y,t\,|\,y_0)$ (see ref. [6]):

$$p(x,y,t\,|\,x_0,y_0)=p_x(x,t\,|\,x_0)p_y(y,t\,|\,y_0). \tag{14}$$

This property of the Green's function allows the simulation of the motion of particles in the direction x and y independently.

4.1. Free diffusion

The solution of the DE is the product of two Gaussian functions:

$$p_{\text{free}}(x,y,t\,|\,x_0,y_0)=\frac{1}{4\pi Dt}\exp\left[-\frac{(x-x_0)^2+(y-y_0)^2}{4Dt}\right]\equiv p_{\text{free}}(x,t\,|\,x_0)p_{\text{free}}(y,t\,|\,y_0). \tag{15}$$

Therefore, sampling of this Green's function can be done by sampling two Gaussian functions:

Algorithm 4: Sampling algorithm for $p_{free}(x,y,\Delta t\,|\,x_0,y_0)$ (free 2D diffusion)

GENERATE N_1,N_2 as a standard Normals

$X \leftarrow x_0+\sqrt{D\Delta t}N_1$

$Y \leftarrow y_0+\sqrt{D\Delta t}N_2$

RETURN (X,Y).

Plotting the Green's functions in X and Y would give figures identical to Figure 1. However, in 2D, it is useful to use polar coordinates. That is, the following transformation is used:

$$\begin{aligned} x&=r\cos(\theta),\\ y&=r\sin(\theta). \end{aligned} \tag{16}$$

The same transformation is done with x_0 and y_0 to obtain r_0 and θ_0. The Green's function may be rewritten:

$$p_{\text{free}}(r,\theta,t\,|\,r_0,\theta_0)=\frac{1}{4\pi Dt}\exp\left[-\frac{r^2+r_0^2-2rr_0\cos(\theta-\theta_0)}{4Dt}\right]. \tag{17}$$

http://dx.doi.org/10.5772/53203

This form yields an alternate method to sample the Green's function in polar coordinates:

Algorithm 5: Sampling algorithm for $r^*p_{free}(r,\theta,\Delta t\,|\,r_0,\theta_0)$ (free 2D diffusion)

CALCULATE $\rho \leftarrow r_0 / \sqrt{2D\Delta t}$

REPEAT

GENERATE V,W uniform on [0,1], E_1 as standard exponential.

SET $\Theta \leftarrow 2\pi V$.

IF $W(1+\rho\sqrt{2\pi})<1$ THEN SET $R \leftarrow \rho + \sqrt{2E_2}$, where E_2 is standard exponential

ELSE SET $R \leftarrow \rho + N$, where N is standard normal

UNTIL $R>0$ and $\log(Max(R,\rho)/R)+R\rho(1-\cos(\Theta-\theta_0))<E_1$.

RETURN (R,Θ).

Algorithm 5 generates variates r and θ distributed as $r^*p_{free}(r,\theta,t\,|\,r_0,\theta_0)$. The factor r originates from the differential area in polar coordinates: $dxdy$ is replaced by $rdrd\theta$.

It is possible to obtain related distributions such as $p(r,t\,|\,r_0)$ and $p(\theta,t\,|\,\theta_0)$. They are found by integrating the Green's function:

$$p(r,t\,|\,r_0)=\frac{1}{4\pi Dt}\exp\left(-\frac{r^2+r_0^2}{4Dt}\right)\int_0^{2\pi}\exp\left[\frac{2rr_0\cos(\theta-\theta_0)}{4Dt}\right]d\theta=\frac{1}{2Dt}I_0\left(\frac{rr_0}{2Dt}\right), \tag{18}$$

where $I_0(x)$ is the Modified Bessel Function of the First Kind of order 0 (see ref. [9]). The angular distribution $p(\theta,t\,|\,\theta_0)$ is obtained by integrating over r:

$$p(\theta,t\,|\,\theta_0)=\frac{1}{4\pi Dt}\int_0^{\infty}\exp\left[-\frac{r^2+r_0^2-2rr_0\cos(\theta-\theta_0)}{4Dt}\right]r\mathrm{d}r. \tag{19}$$

The factor r is also included in the integral. The result is:

$$p(\theta,t\,|\,\theta_0)=\frac{1}{2\pi}\exp\left(-\frac{r_0^2}{4Dt}\right)+\exp\left[-\frac{r_0^2\sin^2(\theta-\theta_0)}{4Dt}\right]\frac{r_0\cos(\theta-\theta_0)}{4\pi\sqrt{Dt}}\left(1+\mathrm{Erf}\left[\frac{r_0\cos(\theta-\theta_0)}{\sqrt{4Dt}}\right]\right). \tag{20}$$

where $Erf(x)$ is the error function [9]. The distributions $p(r,t\,|\,r_0)$ and $p(\theta,t\,|\,\theta_0)$ for $x_0=2.5$ and $y_0=2.5$ are illustrated in Figure 4.

Similar results are found using either algorithm 4 or 5. In 2D, it is possible to represent the time evolution of the particle system (Figure 5).

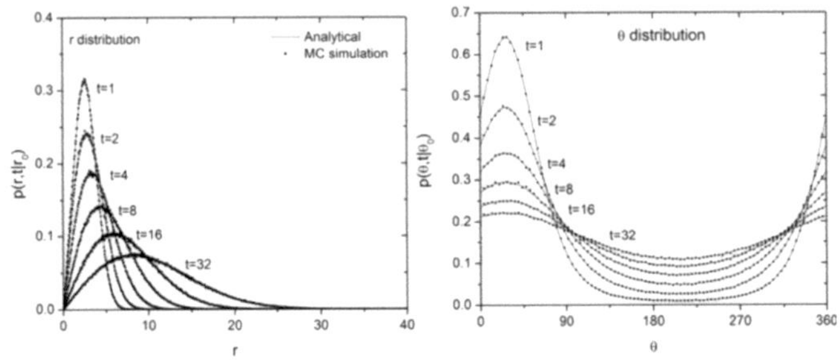

Figure 4. Distributions $p(r,t|r_0)$ and $p(\theta,t|\theta_0)$ for 1,000,000 particles initially located at $x_0=2.5$ and $y_0=2.5$ at t=1,2,4,8,16 and 32 units.

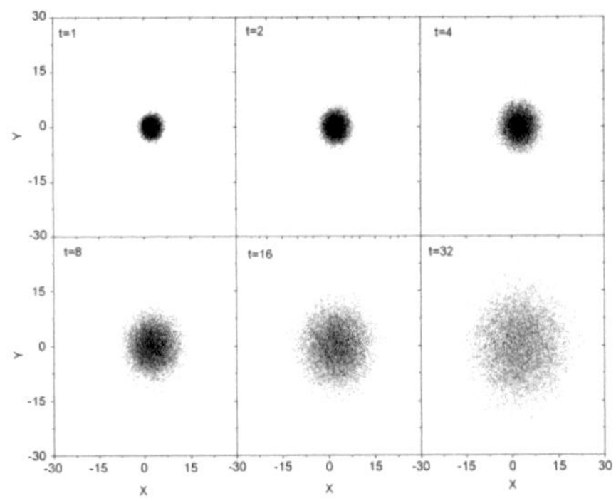

Figure 5. Positions of 1,000,000 particles initially located at $x_0=2.5$, $y_0=0$ at $t=1$, 2, 4, 8, 16 and 32 time units. The positions are obtained by sampling the Green's function as described in Algorithm 4 or 5.

4.2. The rectangular corner $x>0$, $y>0$

As in section 4.1, the solution of the DE is the product of two independent 1D reflective Green's functions:

$$p(x,y,t\,|\,x_0,y_0) = \\ = \frac{1}{4\pi Dt}\left\{\exp\left[-\frac{(x-x_0)^2}{4Dt}\right]+\exp\left[-\frac{(x+x_0)^2}{4Dt}\right]\right\}\left\{\exp\left[-\frac{(y-y_0)^2}{4Dt}\right]+\exp\left[-\frac{(y+y_0)^2}{4Dt}\right]\right\}. \tag{21}$$

The positions of the particles can be sampled by using two applications of Algorithm 2 (for X and Y). An example of the time evolution of 1,000,000 particles is illustrated in Figure 6.

4.3. The rectangle $0<x<a$, $0<y<b$

The solution of the DE is also the product of two independent 1D Green's functions:

http://dx.doi.org/10.5772/53203

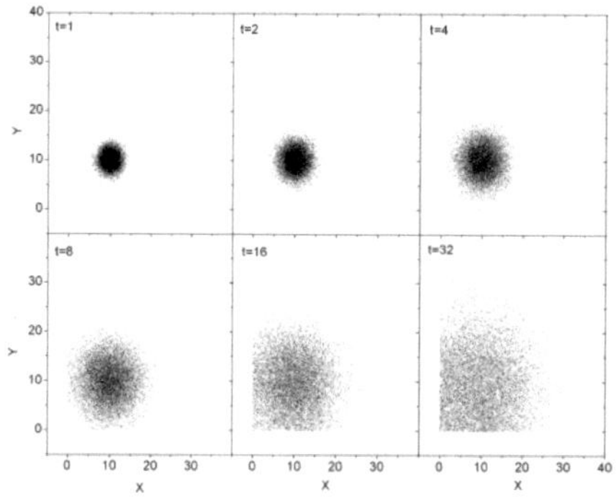

Figure 6. Positions of 1,000,000 particles initially located at $x_0=10$, $y_0=10$ at $t=1, 2, 4, 8, 16$ and 32 time units, assuming reflective boundaries at $X=0$ and $Y=0$. The positions are obtained by sampling the Green's function as described in Algorithm 2.

$$p(x,y,t \mid x_0,y_0) = \\ = \frac{1}{ab}\left[\sum_{m=-\infty}^{\infty} \exp\left(-\frac{\pi^2 m^2 Dt}{a^2}\right)\cos\frac{m\pi x}{a}\cos\frac{m\pi x_0}{a}\right]\left[\sum_{n=-\infty}^{\infty} \exp\left(-\frac{\pi^2 n^2 Dt}{b^2}\right)\cos\frac{n\pi y}{b}\cos\frac{n\pi y_0}{b}\right]. \tag{22}$$

Therefore the positions of the particles can be sampled by using Algorithm 3 for the coordinates x and y.

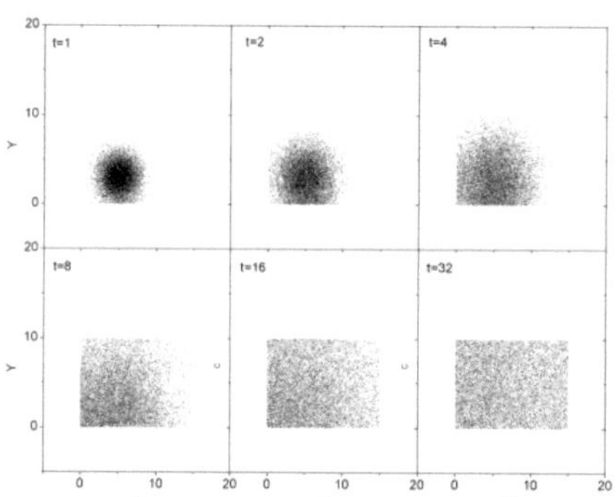

Figure 7. Positions of 1,000,000 particles initially located at $x_0=2.5$, $y_0=0$ in the rectangle of 10 units height and 15 units width at $t=1, 2, 4, 8, 16$ and 32 time units. The positions are obtained by sampling the Green's function as described in Algorithm 3.

The particle system depicted in Figure 7 illustrates how particles initially located in a given position will diffuse and eventually become uniformly distributed in the rectangular area.

4.4. The particles outside a disk of radius R

This problem is of interest to simulate how particles move and/or bind to curved cell membranes comprising receptors. In this section, only the case of the reflective boundary condition is discussed. In polar coordinates, the DE can be written

$$D\left[\frac{1}{r}\frac{\partial}{\partial r}\left(r\frac{\partial}{\partial r}\right)+\frac{1}{r^2}\frac{\partial^2}{\partial \theta^2}\right]p(\mathrm{r},\theta,\mathrm{t}\mid r_0,\ \theta_0)=\frac{\partial}{\partial t}p(\mathrm{r},\theta,\mathrm{t}\mid r_0,\ \theta_0). \tag{23}$$

The reflective boundary condition at $r=R$ is:

$$D\frac{\partial p(\mathrm{r},\theta,\mathrm{t}\mid r_0,\ \theta_0)}{\partial r}\bigg|_{r=R}=0. \tag{24}$$

The Green's function for a particle initially located at (r_0,θ_0) is:

$$p(\mathrm{r},\theta,\mathrm{t}\mid r_0,\ \theta_0)=\frac{1}{2\pi}\sum_{n=-\infty}^{\infty}\cos[n(\theta-\theta_0)]\int_0^{\infty}e^{-\mathrm{u}^2\mathrm{Dt}}\mathrm{u}C_n(\mathrm{u,r})C_n(\mathrm{u,r_0})\mathrm{du}, \tag{25}$$

where

$$C_n(u,r)=\frac{J_n(ur)Y_n^{'}(uR)-J_n^{'}(uR)Y_n(ur)}{\sqrt{J_n^{'}(uR)^2+Y_n^{'}(uR)^2}}. \tag{26}$$

$J_n(x)$ and $Y_n(x)$ are the Bessel Functions of the First and Second Kind, respectively (see ref. [9]). The parameters of this distribution are $R>0$, $0\leq\theta_0\leq 2\pi$, $r_0>R$ and $Dt>0$. The variates of this distributions are $r>R$ and $0\leq\theta\leq 2\pi$.

The normalization of this function is:

$$\int_0^{2\pi}\int_R^{\infty}p(\mathrm{r},\theta,\mathrm{t}\mid r_0,\ \theta_0)\mathrm{rdrd}\theta=1. \tag{27}$$

We have not been able so far to develop a sampling algorithm for the distribution function $p(r,\theta,t\mid r_0,\ \theta_0)$. An approximate algorithm to sample the positions can be done by using free diffusion and reflecting particles which are inside the disk ($r<R$). The results given by this simulation are illustrated in Figure 8.

In this example, since an approximate method is used to simulate the motion of particles, the distributions of r and θ do not verify the time discretization equations, as an exact sampling algorithm of $p(r,\theta,t\mid r_0,\ \theta_0)$ would (results not shown). Therefore, this example illustrate that the time discretization property of the Green's function is a very powerful way to verify the validity of the sampling algorithms.

http://dx.doi.org/10.5772/53203

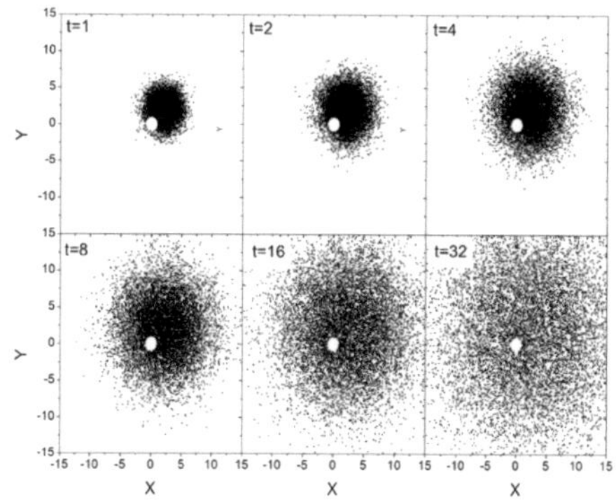

Figure 8. Positions of 1,000,000 particles initially located at x_0=2.5, y_0=2.5 near a reflective boundary at *R=1* at *t=1, 2, 4, 8, 16* and *32* time units.

It is interesting to note that for $R\to 0$, $C_n(u,r)\to J_n(ur)$; in this case, the integral can be evaluated by using Weber's formula (Watson P. 395 [12], Gradsteyn 6.633, Equation 2 [13]):

$$p_{\text{ref}}(\text{r},\theta,\text{t}\mid r_0,\ \theta_0)=\frac{1}{2\pi}\sum_{n=-\infty}^{\infty}\cos[n(\theta-\theta_0)]\frac{1}{2\text{Dt}}\exp\left(-\frac{r^2+r_0^2}{4\text{Dt}}\right)I_n\left(\frac{\text{rr}_0}{2\text{Dt}}\right). \tag{28}$$

The series which is obtained can be evaluated (http://functions.wolfram.com/03.02.23.0007.01):

$$p_{\text{ref}}(\text{r},\theta,\text{t}\mid r_0,\ \theta_0)=\frac{1}{2\pi}\frac{1}{2\text{Dt}}\exp\left(-\frac{r^2+r_0^2}{4\text{Dt}}\right)\exp\left[\frac{\text{rr}_0}{2\text{Dt}}\cos(\theta-\theta_0)\right]\equiv p_{\text{free}}(\text{r},\theta,\text{t}\mid r_0,\ \theta_0). \tag{29}$$

Thus, for $R\to 0$, $p_{ref}(r,\theta,t\mid r_0,\theta_0)\to p_{free}(r,\theta,t\mid r_0,\theta_0)$, as expected.

5. Three-dimensional systems

Three dimensional systems are more complex and harder to visualize. In 3D, the DE can be written in cartesian coordinates as:

$$\frac{\partial}{\partial t}p(\text{x,y,z,t}\mid x_0,\text{y}_0,\text{z}_0)=D\left[\frac{\partial^2}{\partial x^2}+\frac{\partial^2}{\partial y^2}+\frac{\partial^2}{\partial z^2}\right]p(\text{x,y,z,t}\mid x_0,\text{y}_0,\text{z}_0). \tag{30}$$

The initial condition is $p(x,y,z,t=0\mid x_0,\ y_0,\ z_0)=\delta(x-x_0)\delta(y-y_0)\delta(z-z_0)$. As in 2D, in several cases, the Green's function can be written as the product of the functions $p_x(x,t\mid x_0)$, $p_y(y,t\mid y_0)$ and $p_z(z,t\mid z_0)$:

$$p(x,y,z,t\mid x_0,y_0,z_0)=p_x(x,t\mid x_0)p_y(y,t\mid y_0)p_z(z,t\mid z_0). \tag{31}$$

5.1. Free diffusion

The solution of the DE for free particles is the product of three Gaussian functions:

$$\begin{aligned} &p_{\text{free}}(x,y,z,t\mid x_0,y_0,z_0)= \\ &=\frac{1}{(4\pi Dt)^{3/2}}\exp\left[-\frac{(x-x_0)^2+(y-y_0)^2+(z-z_0)^2}{4Dt}\right]\equiv p_{\text{free}}(x,t\mid x_0)p_{\text{free}}(y,t\mid y_0)p_{\text{free}}(z,t\mid z_0)\end{aligned} \tag{32}$$

Since the Gaussian functions are independent, the positions x, y and z can be obtained by sampling the Gaussian distribution for each variate$X$, Y and Z:

Algorithm 6: Sampling algorithm for $p_{free}(x,y,z,\Delta t\mid x_0,y_0,z_0)$ (free 3D diffusion)

GENERATE N_1, N_2, N_3 as a standard Normals

$X \leftarrow x_0+\sqrt{D\Delta t}N_1$

$Y \leftarrow y_0+\sqrt{D\Delta t}N_2$

$Z \leftarrow z_0+\sqrt{D\Delta t}N_3$

RETURN (X,Y,Z).

In 3D, it is useful to use spherical coordinates (r,θ,ϕ)[3]. That is, the following transformation is used:

$$\begin{aligned} x&=r\sin(\theta)\cos(\phi),\\ y&=r\sin(\theta)\sin(\phi),\\ z&=r\cos(\theta).\end{aligned} \tag{33}$$

The differential volume element is given by

$$dV=r^2\sin(\theta)drd\theta d\phi. \tag{34}$$

The DE can be written in spherical coordinates as:

$$\frac{\partial p(r,\theta,\phi,t\mid r_0,\theta_0,\phi_0)}{\partial t}=D\left[\frac{\partial^2}{\partial r^2}+\frac{2}{r}\frac{\partial}{\partial r}+\frac{1}{r^2\sin^2\theta}\frac{\partial^2}{\partial\phi^2}+\frac{1}{r^2\sin\theta}\frac{\partial}{\partial\theta}\left(\sin\theta\frac{\partial}{\partial\theta}\right)\right]p(r,\theta,\phi,t\mid r_0,\theta_0,\phi_0). \tag{35}$$

3 The following notation is used: (radial, azimutal, polar). r: $[0,\infty)$,θ: $[0,\pi]$,ϕ: $[0,2\pi)$.

Using the transformation to spherical coordinates, the Green's function of the DE for free particles can be rewritten as:

$$p_{\text{free}}(\mathrm{r},\theta,\phi,\mathrm{t}\,|\,r_0,\theta_0,\phi_0)= =\frac{1}{(4\pi \mathrm{Dt})^{3/2}}\exp\left\{-\frac{r^2+r_0^2-2\mathrm{rr}_0[\cos\theta\cos\theta_0+\sin\theta\sin\theta_0\cos(\phi-\phi_0)]}{4\mathrm{Dt}}\right\}. \tag{36}$$

The angle between the vectors (r,θ,ϕ) and (r_0,θ_0,ϕ_0) is given by $\cos(\gamma)$:

$$\cos(\gamma)=\cos\theta\cos\theta_0+\sin\theta\sin\theta_0\cos(\phi-\phi_0). \tag{37}$$

Therefore, Eq. (36) can be written in the compact form:

$$p_{\text{free}}(\mathrm{r},\theta,\phi,\mathrm{t}\,|\,r_0,\theta_0,\phi_0)=\frac{1}{(4\pi \mathrm{Dt})^{3/2}}\exp\left[-\frac{r^2+r_0^2-2\mathrm{rr}_0\cos\gamma}{4\mathrm{Dt}}\right]. \tag{38}$$

In spherical coordinates, as in 2D, it is possible to obtain related distributions such as $p(r,t\,|\,r_0)$. It is obtained by integrating the Green's function over the angles:

$$p(\mathrm{r},\mathrm{t}\,|\,r_0)=\int_0^{2\pi}\int_0^{\pi} r^2 p_{\text{free}}(\mathrm{r},\theta,\phi,\mathrm{t}\,|\,r_0,\theta_0,\phi_0)\sin(\phi)\,d\theta\, d\phi=\frac{r}{\sqrt{4\pi \mathrm{r}_0^2\mathrm{Dt}}}\exp\left(-\frac{r^2+r_0^2}{4\mathrm{Dt}}\right)\sinh\left(\frac{\mathrm{rr}_0}{2\mathrm{Dt}}\right). \tag{39}$$

5.2. The corner *x>0, y>0, z>0*

The Green's function is the product of three independent 1D Green's functions:

$$p(\mathrm{x,y,z,t}\,|\,x_0,\mathrm{y}_0,\mathrm{z}_0)=\frac{1}{(4\pi\mathrm{Dt})^{3/2}}\left[e^{-(\mathrm{x}-\mathrm{x}_0)^2/4\mathrm{Dt}}+e^{-(x+x_0)^2/4\mathrm{Dt}}\right] \left[e^{-(\mathrm{y}-\mathrm{y}_0)^2/4\mathrm{Dt}}+e^{-(y+y_0)^2/4\mathrm{Dt}}\right]\left[e^{-(\mathrm{z}-\mathrm{z}_0)^2/4\mathrm{Dt}}+e^{-(\mathrm{z}+\mathrm{z}_0)^2/4\mathrm{Dt}}\right]. \tag{40}$$

As it is the case in 2D, the coordinates x,y and z can be treated independently. Therefore, the positions of the particles can be generated by using Algorithm 2 for each of the coordinates.

5.3. The parallelipiped *0<x<a, 0<y<b, 0<z<c*

The Green's function is also the product of three independent 1D Green's functions:

$$p(\mathrm{x,y,z,t}\,|\,x_0,\mathrm{y}_0,\mathrm{z}_0)= \frac{1}{\mathrm{abc}}\sum_{\mathrm{m,n,l}=-\infty}^{\infty}\exp\left[-\pi^2\mathrm{Dt}\left(\frac{m^2}{a^2}+\frac{n^2}{b^2}+\frac{l^2}{c^2}\right)\right]\cos\frac{m\pi x}{a}\cos\frac{m\pi x_0}{a}\cos\frac{n\pi y}{b}\cos\frac{n\pi y_0}{b}\cos\frac{l\pi z}{c}\cos\frac{l\pi z_0}{c}. \tag{41}$$

Therefore, the positions of particles can be generated by using Algorithm 3 for each of the coordinates. This sampling algorithm can be used to simulate the trajectories of particles confined into a box of sides *a, b* and *c*. At equilibrium, as it is the case in 2D (Figure 7), the particles are uniformly distributed within the volume.

6. Applications

Two applications of the approach described in the previous sections are presented. The first is the simulation of particles near a membrane comprising receptors. The second one is the simulation of chemical reactions. These applications will eventually be used to study the evolution of the chemical species created by ionizing radiations in biological media [14].

6.1. Particle near a 1D membrane comprising receptors

To apply the theory described in the chapter to cell culture simulations, it is necessary to make some assumptions. The details of the model presented here and more results are given in ref. [5]. Similar models have been used to study autocrine and paracrine signals in cell culture assays [15], ligand accumulation in autocrine cell cultures [16] and the spatial range of autocrine signaling [17].

6.1.1. Model and assumptions

A particle is assumed to be located in the proximity of a plane membrane comprising receptors, corresponding to the plane *X=0*. The particle can move freely in the Y and Z directions, and can bind reversibly to receptors located on the membrane and initiate signal transduction. This is illustrated in Figure 9:

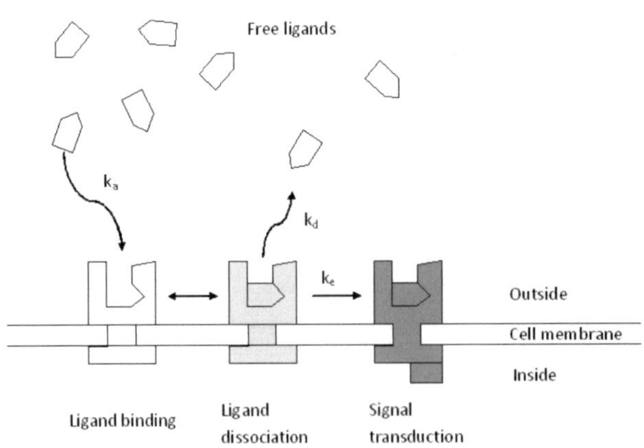

Figure 9. Ligands near a surface comprising receptors. The rate constants for association, dissociation and initiation of signal transduction are k_a, k_d and k_e, respectively.

The binding rate constant (k_a) is obtained from the ligand-receptor association rate constant and the density of receptors on the surface, which are assumed to be uniformly distributed on the membrane [16]. The ligand-receptor complex has the rate constants k_d for dissociation and k_e for initiation of signal transduction. As a first approximation, this is equivalent to the problem

$$A + B \underset{k_d}{\overset{k_a}{\rightleftarrows}} (AB) \xrightarrow{k_e} AB. \tag{42}$$

Since the particles are moving freely in the Y and Z direction, the Green's function can be written as the product of the independent functions $p_x(x,t|x_0)$, $p_y(y,t|y_0)$ and $p_z(z,t|z_0)$. But $p_y(y,t|y_0)$ and $p_z(z,t|z_0)$ are Gaussians functions, which can be sampled as described in section 4.1; therefore, only the sampling of $p_x(x,t|x_0)$ will be discussed here. For convenience, the index "x" will be omitted in this section.

A particle can be free at position $x>0$, in a reversible bound state (*) at $x=0$ or activating signal transduction (**). The boundary condition at $x=0$ can be written:

$$D\frac{\partial p(x,t|x_0)}{\partial x}\Big|_{x=0} = k_a p(0,t|x_0) - k_d p(*,t|x_0), \tag{43}$$

where $p(*,t|x_0)$ is the probability of a particle initially located at x_0 to be in the reversible bound state at time t. The time evolution of $p(*,t|x_0)$ is:

$$\frac{dp(*,t|x_0)}{dt} = k_a p(0,t|x_0) - (k_d + k_e)p(*,t|x_0). \tag{44}$$

Similarly, the time evolution of $p(**,t|x_0)$ is:

$$\frac{dp(**,t|x_0)}{dt} = k_e p(*,t|x_0). \tag{45}$$

6.1.2. Green's functions

This problem can be solved analytically by using Laplace Transforms [18]. The solutions are expressed using three coefficients α, β and γ. They are the roots of a cubic polynomial[4], for which the coefficients are given by the rate constants k_a, k_d and k_e as follows:

$$\begin{aligned} &\alpha+\beta+\gamma = k_a / D, \\ &\alpha\beta+\beta\gamma+\gamma\alpha = (k_e+k_d)/D, \\ &\alpha\beta\gamma = k_e k_a / D^2. \end{aligned} \tag{46}$$

4 At least one of the roots of a third-order polynomial is real, the two other roots being either real or complex conjugates.

The mathematical expressions of the Green's function for a particle in this system are quite long. To simplify the following expressions, the variables $\rho_x = x/\sqrt{4Dt}$, $\rho_0 = x_0/\sqrt{4Dt}$, $\alpha' = \alpha\sqrt{Dt}$, $\beta' = \beta\sqrt{Dt}$ and $\gamma' = \gamma\sqrt{Dt}$ are defined.

$$\begin{aligned} p(x,t \mid x_0) = {} & p_{ref}(x,t \mid x_0) + \frac{\alpha(\gamma+\alpha)(\alpha+\beta)}{(\gamma-\alpha)(\alpha-\beta)} W(\rho_x+\rho_0,\alpha') + \\ & + \frac{\beta(\alpha+\beta)(\beta+\gamma)}{(\alpha-\beta)(\beta-\gamma)} W(\rho_x+\rho_0,\beta') + \frac{\gamma(\beta+\gamma)(\gamma+\alpha)}{(\beta-\gamma)(\gamma-\alpha)} W(\rho_x+\rho_0,\gamma') \end{aligned} . \qquad (47)$$

where $p_{ref}(x,t \mid x_0)$ is the Green's function for a reflective membrane, given in Section 3.2. The functions $W(x,y)$ and $\Omega(x)$ are defined as:

$$\begin{aligned} & \Omega(x) = \exp(x^2)\mathrm{Erfc}(x), \\ & W(x,y) \equiv \exp(2xy + y^2)\mathrm{Erfc}(x+y) = \exp(-x^2)\Omega(x+y) \end{aligned} \qquad (48)$$

It is possible for two of the roots to be complex conjugates. Nevertheless, it is still possible to use the Green's function given in Equation (47) by implementing the numerical evaluation of W(x,y) for complex numbers [19].

The probability of survival for a free particle is obtained by integrating $p(x,t \mid x_0)$ on $[0,\infty)$:

$$\begin{aligned} Q(t \mid x_0) = {} & 1 - \frac{(\gamma+\alpha)(\alpha+\beta)}{(\gamma-\alpha)(\alpha-\beta)} W(\rho_0,\alpha') - \\ & - \frac{(\alpha+\beta)(\beta+\gamma)}{(\alpha-\beta)(\beta-\gamma)} W(\rho_0,\beta') - \frac{(\beta+\gamma)(\gamma+\alpha)}{(\beta-\gamma)(\gamma-\alpha)} W(\rho_0,\gamma') - \mathrm{Erfc}(\rho_0) \end{aligned} . \qquad (49)$$

The probability of a particle initially at $x_0>0$ to be reversibly bound at time t is:

$$p(*,t \mid x_0) = \frac{\alpha(\alpha+\beta+\gamma)}{(\gamma-\alpha)(\alpha-\beta)} W(\rho_0,\alpha') + \frac{\beta(\alpha+\beta+\gamma)}{(\alpha-\beta)(\beta-\gamma)} W(\rho_0,\beta') + \frac{\gamma(\alpha+\beta+\gamma)}{(\beta-\gamma)(\gamma-\alpha)} W(\rho_0,\gamma'). \qquad (50)$$

A particle initially at $x_0>0$ can also be found in an irreversibly bound state at time t. The probability to be found in this state is given by $p(**,t \mid x_0) = 1 - p(*,t \mid x_0) - Q(t \mid x_0)$, which can be written as:

$$\begin{aligned} p(**,t \mid x_0) = {} & \frac{\beta\gamma}{(\gamma-\alpha)(\alpha-\beta)} W(\rho_0,\alpha') + \\ & + \frac{\alpha\gamma}{(\alpha-\beta)(\beta-\gamma)} W(\rho_0,\beta') + \frac{\alpha\beta}{(\beta-\gamma)(\gamma-\alpha)} W(\rho_0,\gamma') + \mathrm{Erfc}(\rho_0) \end{aligned} . \qquad (51)$$

To obtain the Green's function of a particle in a reversibly bound state, the material balance condition $k_a p(x,t \mid *) = k_d p(*,t \mid x)$ (given in ref. [18,20]) is used. This yields the Green's function for the dissociation of a bound particle:

http://dx.doi.org/10.5772/53203

$$\frac{D}{k_d}p(x,t \mid *)=\frac{\alpha}{(\gamma-\alpha)(\alpha-\beta)}W(\rho_x,\alpha')+\frac{\beta}{(\alpha-\beta)(\beta-\gamma)}W(\rho_x,\beta')+\frac{\gamma}{(\beta-\gamma)(\gamma-\alpha)}W(\rho_x,\gamma'). \quad (52)$$

The probability of dissociation of a particle that was initially in a reversibly bound state $Q(t \mid *)$ is found by integrating $p(*,t \mid x)$ over $[0,\infty)$:

$$\frac{D}{k_d}Q(t \mid *)=-\frac{1}{(\gamma-\alpha)(\alpha-\beta)}\Omega(\alpha')-\frac{1}{(\alpha-\beta)(\beta-\gamma)}\Omega(\beta')-\frac{1}{(\beta-\gamma)(\gamma-\alpha)}\Omega(\gamma'). \quad (53)$$

The probability of a particle initially in a reversibly bound state to stay in this state is given by (ref. [18]):

$$p(*,t \mid *)=\frac{\alpha(\beta+\gamma)}{(\gamma-\alpha)(\alpha-\beta)}\Omega(\alpha')+\frac{\beta(\gamma+\alpha)}{(\alpha-\beta)(\beta-\gamma)}\Omega(\beta')+\frac{\gamma(\alpha+\beta)}{(\beta-\gamma)(\gamma-\alpha)}\Omega(\gamma'). \quad (54)$$

Finally, the probability of a particle initially in a reversibly bound state to activate signal transduction is:

$$p(**,t \mid *)=1+\frac{1}{\alpha+\beta+\gamma}\left[\frac{\beta\gamma(\beta+\gamma)}{(\gamma-\alpha)(\alpha-\beta)}\Omega(\alpha')+\frac{\alpha\gamma(\alpha+\gamma)}{(\alpha-\beta)(\beta-\gamma)}\Omega(\beta')+\frac{\alpha\beta(\alpha+\beta)}{(\beta-\gamma)(\gamma-\alpha)}\Omega(\gamma')\right]. \quad (55)$$

For some particular values of α, β and γ, the Green's functions of this section have singularities (0/0). In these cases, the Green's functions take slightly different forms, but it is still possible to use the approach described here (see ref. [5]).

6.1.3. Time discretization equations

A simulation is usually done by dividing the final simulation time in a finite number of time steps. If the simulation can be done in two time steps such as $t=\Delta t_1+\Delta t_2$, a particle initially located at position x_0 can:

i. go to position x_1 during Δt_1 and then go to its final x position during Δt_2,

ii. go to position x_1 during Δt_1 and reversibly bind to the membrane during Δt_2,

iii. go to position x_1 during Δt_1 and activate signal transduction during Δt_2,

iv. reversibly bind to the membrane during Δt_1 and stay in this state during Δt_2,

v. reversibly bind to the membrane during Δt_1 and dissociate during Δt_2,

vi. reversibly bind to the membrane during Δt_1 and activate signal transduction during Δt_2,

or

vii. activate signal transduction during Δt_1.

From this the following time discretization equations are obtained:

$$
\begin{aligned}
&p(\mathrm{x},\mathrm{t} \mid x_0)=\int_{\Omega} p(\mathrm{x},\Delta t_2 \mid x_1)p(x_1, \Delta t_1 \mid x_0)dx_1 + p(x, \Delta t_2 \mid *)p(*,\Delta t_1 \mid x_0),\\
&p(*,\mathrm{t} \mid x_0)=p(*,\Delta t_2 \mid *)p(*,\Delta t_1 \mid x_0)+\int_{\Omega} p(*,\Delta t_2 \mid x_1)p(x_1, \Delta t_1 \mid x_0)dx_1,\\
&p(**,\mathrm{t} \mid x_0)=p(**,\Delta t_1 \mid x_0)+p(**,\Delta t_2 \mid *)p(*,\Delta t_1 \mid x_0)+\int_{\Omega} p(**,\Delta t_2 \mid x_1)p(x_1, \Delta t_1 \mid x_0)dx_1.
\end{aligned}
\tag{56}
$$

The first of these equations is similar to the Chapman-Kolmogorov equation, to which a term has been added to account for the possibility of dissociation. Each term of these equations can be associated with the possibilities i-vii. Similarly, a particle initially in a reversibly bound state can:

i. dissociate to position x_1 during Δt_1 and go to its final position x during Δt_2,

ii. dissociate to position $x_1$during Δt_1 and re-bind reversibly during Δt_2,

iii. dissociate to position $x_1$during Δt_1 and initiate signal transduction during Δt_2,

iv. stay reversibly bound during Δt_1 and dissociate to position x during Δt_2,

v. stay reversibly bound during Δt_1 and Δt_2,

vi. stay reversibly bound during Δt_1 and initiate signal transduction during Δt_2, or

vii. initiate signal transduction during Δt_1.

This yields the time discretization equations for the bound particle:

$$
\begin{aligned}
&p(\mathrm{x},\mathrm{t} \mid *)=\int_{\Omega} p(\mathrm{x},\Delta t_2 \mid x_1)p(x_1, \Delta t_1 \mid *)dx_1 + p(x, \Delta t_2 \mid *)p(*, \Delta t_1 \mid *),\\
&p(*,\mathrm{t} \mid *)=p(*, \Delta t_2 \mid *)p(*, \Delta t_1 \mid *)+\int_{\Omega} p(*, \Delta t_2 \mid x_1)p(x_1, \Delta t_1 \mid *)dx_1,\\
&p(*,\mathrm{t} \mid *)=p(*, \Delta t_1 \mid *)+p(*, \Delta t_2 \mid *)p(*, \Delta t_1 \mid *)+\int_{\Omega} p(*, \Delta t_2 \mid x_1)p(x_1, \Delta t_1 \mid *)dx_1.
\end{aligned}
\tag{57}
$$

These equations are proven in the supplemental material of ref. [5].

6.1.4. Brownian dynamics algorithm

Using the Green's functions, it is possible to construct a Brownian Dynamics algorithm to simulate the motion and binding of the ligand and the possible initiation of signal transduction. First, it should be noted that $p(x,t \mid x_0)$ is a sub-density[5]. Since $p(x,t \mid x_0) \le p_{ref}(x,t \mid x_0)$, the rejection method can be used [21]. This yields the following algorithm:

Algorithm 7a: sampling of $p(x,\Delta t\,|\,x_0)$ (free particles)

```
REPEAT
{
    GENERATE U uniform on [0,1], X distributed as p_ref(x,Δt|x_0)
}
UNTIL p(X,Δt|x_0)≤U*p_ref(X,Δt|x_0)
RETURN X
```

There are also particles which are bound to the membrane. These particles may dissociate with probability $Q(\Delta t\,|\,*)$. If this is the case, the position x of the particle is distributed as $p(x,\Delta t\,|\,*)$, which can be written with a Gaussian factor in evidence:

$$p(x,\Delta t\mid *)=\frac{k_d}{D}\exp\left(-\frac{x^2}{4D\Delta t}\right)\left[\frac{\alpha}{(\gamma-\alpha)(\alpha-\beta)}\Omega\left(\frac{x}{\sqrt{4D\Delta t}}+\alpha\sqrt{D\Delta t}\right)+\frac{\beta}{(\alpha-\beta)(\beta-\gamma)}\Omega\left(\frac{x}{\sqrt{4D\Delta t}}+\beta\sqrt{D\Delta t}\right)+\frac{\gamma}{(\beta-\gamma)(\gamma-\alpha)}\Omega\left(\frac{x}{\sqrt{4D\Delta t}}+\gamma\sqrt{D\Delta t}\right)\right]. \quad (58)$$

This form is convenient because it is the product of a Gaussian function by a function $g(x)$ with three terms in $\Omega(x)$. Since $0\leq\Omega(x)\leq1$, $p(x,\Delta t\,|\,*)$ can be sampled by a rejection method:

Algorithm 7b: sampling of $p(x,\Delta t\,|\,*)$ (reversibly bound particles)

```
CALCULATE H = |α/(γ-α)(α-β)|+|β/(α-β)(β-γ)|+|γ/(β-γ)(γ-α)|
REPEAT
{
    GENERATE U uniform on [0,1], X = | N |√(2DΔt), where N is a standard Normal
}
UNTIL UH≤g(X)
RETURN X
```

6.1.5. Simulation results

A simulation has been done by using $k_a=6$, $k_d=10$ and $k_e=1$. The results are shown in Figure 10. It should also be noted that the time discretization equations (56) and (57) were used to validate the simulation results. In this case, it is possible to verify that the simulation results for free particles corresponds to $p(x,t\,|\,x_0)$, but also that the number of bound particles can be accurately predicted after several time steps.

---

5 A sub-density means that $P=\int_0^L f(x)dx\leq 1$, and f(x)≥0. In this case, a random variate with the density f/p is generated with probability P.

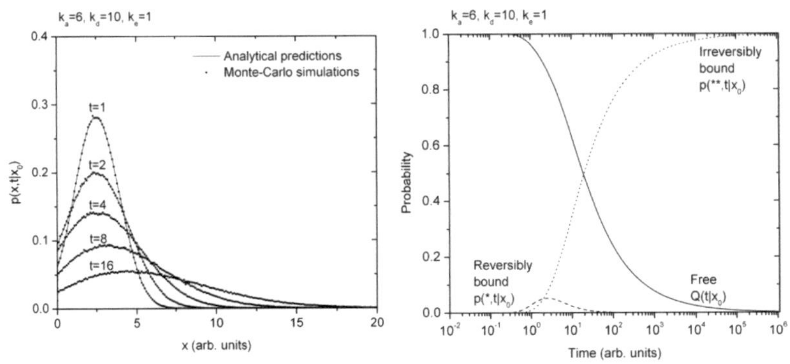

Figure 10. Left) Probability distribution of a particle near a partially absorbing and reflecting boundary with back reaction for x_0=2.5, k_a=6, k_d=10, k_e=1 and D=1 (α=1, β=2 and γ=3) at t=1, 2, 4, 8 and 16 time units. The lines are the analytical predictions $p(x,t|x_0)$. The dots are given by the simulation of 1,000,000 particle histories either with one or multiple time steps. (Right) Probability of a particle in these conditions to be free, reversibly bound or irreversibly bound as a function of time.

6.2. Bimolecular reactions

Bimolecular reactions are an important application of the theory described in the book chapter. Let the particles A and B initially at the positions $\boldsymbol{r}_{A0}$ and $\boldsymbol{r}_{B0}$. They can react with the reaction rate k_a:

$$A + B \xrightarrow{k_a} C. \tag{59}$$

6.2.1. Green's functions for the particles

The probability distribution is solution of the following equation [2]:

$$\frac{\partial}{\partial t} p(\boldsymbol{r}_A, \boldsymbol{r}_B, t \mid \boldsymbol{r}_{A_0}, \boldsymbol{r}_{B_0}) = \left[D_A \nabla_A^2 + D_B \nabla_B^2 \right] p(\boldsymbol{r}_A, \boldsymbol{r}_B, t \mid \boldsymbol{r}_{A_0}, \boldsymbol{r}_{B_0}). \tag{60}$$

It is convenient at this point to use a transformation of coordinates, similar to a center of mass transformation:

$$\begin{aligned} \boldsymbol{R} &= \sqrt{D_B / D_A}\, \boldsymbol{r}_A + \sqrt{D_A / D_B}\, \boldsymbol{r}_B, \\ \boldsymbol{r} &= \boldsymbol{r}_B - \boldsymbol{r}_A. \end{aligned} \tag{61}$$

The same transformation is done to $\boldsymbol{r}_{A0}$ and $\boldsymbol{r}_{B0}$ to obtain $\boldsymbol{r}_0$ and $\boldsymbol{R}_0$. The operators $\nabla_R=\partial/\partial\boldsymbol{R}$ and $\nabla \boldsymbol{r}=\partial/\partial\boldsymbol{r}$ are also defined. Using the transformation, Equation (60) can be rewritten as:

$$\frac{\partial}{\partial t}p(\boldsymbol{R},\boldsymbol{r},t\,|\,\boldsymbol{R_0},\boldsymbol{r_0}) = D\left[\nabla_{\boldsymbol{R}}^2 + \nabla_{\boldsymbol{r}}^2\right]p(\boldsymbol{R},\boldsymbol{r},t\,|\,\boldsymbol{R_0},\boldsymbol{r_0}). \tag{62}$$

where $D=D_A+D_B$, the sum of the diffusion coefficients of the particles. Therefore, $p(\boldsymbol{R},\boldsymbol{r},t\,|\,\boldsymbol{R_0},\boldsymbol{r_0})$ can be factorized as follows:

$$p(\boldsymbol{R},\boldsymbol{r},t\,|\,\boldsymbol{R_0},\boldsymbol{r_0}) = p^R(\boldsymbol{R},t\,|\,\boldsymbol{R_0})p^r(\boldsymbol{r},t\,|,\boldsymbol{r_0}). \tag{63}$$

Using this factorization, two DE are obtained in $\boldsymbol{r}$ and $\boldsymbol{R}$:

$$\begin{aligned}\frac{\partial}{\partial t}p^R(\boldsymbol{R},t\,|\,\boldsymbol{R_0}) &= D\nabla_{\boldsymbol{R}}^2 p^R(\boldsymbol{R},t\,|\,\boldsymbol{R_0}),\\ \frac{\partial}{\partial t}p^r(\boldsymbol{r},t\,|\,\boldsymbol{r_0}) &= D\nabla_{\boldsymbol{r}}^2 p^r(\boldsymbol{r},t\,|\,\boldsymbol{r_0}).\end{aligned} \tag{64}$$

This equation describes two independent random processes - diffusion in the coordinates $\boldsymbol{r}$ and $\boldsymbol{R}$. The initial condition for Equation (64a) is $p^R(\boldsymbol{R},t\,|\,\boldsymbol{R_0})=\delta(\boldsymbol{R}-\boldsymbol{R_0})$, and the boundary condition is $p^R(|\boldsymbol{R}|\to\infty,t\,|\,\boldsymbol{R_0})=0$. As seen in Section 5.1, Equation (64a) represents free diffusion in 3D:

$$p^R\left(\boldsymbol{R},t\,|\,\boldsymbol{R_0}\right) = \frac{1}{(4\pi \mathrm{D}t)^{3/2}}\exp\left[\frac{(\boldsymbol{R}-\boldsymbol{R_0})^2}{4\mathrm{D}t}\right]. \tag{65}$$

This function can be sampled for $\boldsymbol{R}$ as in Algorithm 3, by using three Gaussian random numbers. Equation (64b) is the diffusive motion of the separation vector between particles. The initial condition is $p^r(\boldsymbol{r},t\,|\,\boldsymbol{r_0},t_0)=\delta(\boldsymbol{r}-\boldsymbol{r_0})$, and the outer boundary condition is $p^r(|\boldsymbol{r}|\to\infty,t\,|\,\boldsymbol{r_0},t_0)=0$. The possibility of a chemical reaction is introduced as the inner boundary condition

$$4\pi\sigma^2 D\frac{\partial p^r(\boldsymbol{r},t\,|\,\boldsymbol{r_0})}{\partial \boldsymbol{r}}\Big|_{r=\sigma} = k_a p^r(|\boldsymbol{r}|=\sigma,t\,|\,\boldsymbol{r_0}), \tag{66}$$

where σ is the reaction radius. As it is the case for free particles, Equation (66) is the *radiation* boundary condition. The limit $k_a\to 0$ is the *reflecting* boundary condition (no reactions between particles), whereas the limit $k_a\to\infty$ is the *absorbing* boundary condition. In the latter case, the boundary condition is written $p^r(|\boldsymbol{r}|=\sigma,t\,|\,\boldsymbol{r_0})=0$.

The exact solution for this problem is given in ref. [4]:

$$p(\mathrm{r},\theta,\phi,t\,|\,r_0,\theta_0,\phi_0) = \frac{1}{4\pi\sqrt{\mathrm{r}\mathrm{r}_0}}\sum_{n=0}^{\infty}(2\mathrm{n}+1)P_n(\cos\gamma)\int_0^{\infty} e^{-\mathrm{u}^2\mathrm{D}t}\mathrm{u}F_{n+1/2}(\mathrm{u},\mathrm{r})F_{n+1/2}(\mathrm{u},\mathrm{r}_0)\mathrm{du}. \tag{67}$$

where $P_n(x)$ are the Legendre polynomials,

$$F_\upsilon(\mathrm{u,r})=\frac{(2\sigma\mathrm{k}_a+1)[J_\upsilon(\mathrm{ur})Y_\upsilon(u\sigma)-Y_\upsilon(\mathrm{ur})J_\upsilon(u\sigma)]-2\mathrm{u}\sigma[J_\upsilon(\mathrm{ur})Y_\upsilon^{'}(u\sigma)-Y_\upsilon(\mathrm{ur})J_\upsilon^{'}(u\sigma)]}{\sqrt{[(2\sigma\mathrm{k}_a+1)J_\upsilon(u\sigma)-2\mathrm{u}\sigma J_\upsilon^{'}(u\sigma)]^2+[(2\sigma\mathrm{k}_a+1)Y_\upsilon(u\sigma)-2\mathrm{u}\sigma Y_\upsilon^{'}(u\sigma)]^2}}. \quad (68)$$

and γ is the angle formed by (r,θ,ϕ), the origin and (r_0,θ_0,ϕ_0). In this expression, it is possible to evaluate $P_n(cos\gamma)$, knowing that

$$P_n(\cos\gamma)=P_n(\cos\theta)P_n(\cos\theta_0)+2\sum_{m=1}^{n}\frac{(\mathrm{n\text{-}m})!}{(n+m)!}P_n^m(\cos\theta)P_n^m(\cos\theta_0)\cos m(\phi-\phi_0). \quad (69)$$

where $P_n^m(x)$ are the associated Legendre polynomials (ref. [9]). For $\theta_0=0$ and $\phi_0=0$, $P_n(cos\gamma)=P_n(cos\theta)$. It is also interesting to note that for $k_a=0$ and $\sigma\to 0$, $F_{n+1/2}(u,r)\to J_{n+1/2}(ur)$. In this case, $p(r,\theta,\phi,t\,|\,r_0,\theta_0,\phi_0)$ can be written:

$$p(\mathrm{r},\theta,\ \phi,\mathrm{t}\,|\,r_0,\ \theta_0,\ \phi_0)=\frac{1}{4\pi\sqrt{\mathrm{rr}_0}}\sum_{n=0}^{\infty}(2\mathrm{n}+1)P_n(\cos\gamma)\int_0^\infty e^{-\mathrm{u}^2\mathrm{Dt}}\mathrm{u}J_{n+1/2}(\mathrm{ur})J_{n+1/2}(\mathrm{ur}_0)\mathrm{du}. \quad (70)$$

The integral can be evaluated using Weber's formula (ref. [13], section 6.633, eq 2):

$$p(\mathrm{r},\theta,\ \phi,\mathrm{t}\,|\,r_0,\ \theta_0,\ \phi_0)=\frac{1}{4\pi\sqrt{\mathrm{rr}_0}}\sum_{n=0}^{\infty}(2\mathrm{n}+1)P_n(\cos\gamma)\frac{1}{2\mathrm{Dt}}\exp\left(-\frac{r^2+r_0^2}{4\mathrm{Dt}}\right)I_{n+1/2}\left(\frac{\mathrm{rr}_0}{2\mathrm{Dt}}\right). \quad (71)$$

This equation can be further simplified by using $I_\upsilon(z)=e^{-i\upsilon\pi/2}J_\upsilon(e^{i\pi/2}z)$ (ref. [12], p. 77; ref. [13] section 8.406), $J_\upsilon(e^{im\pi}z)=e^{im\pi\upsilon}J_\upsilon(z)$ (ref. [12], p. 75; ref. [13], section 8.476) and the identity

$$\exp(iz\cos\gamma)=\sqrt{\frac{\pi}{2z}}\sum_{n=0}^{\infty}(2\mathrm{n}+1)i^nJ_{n+1/2}(z)P_n(\cos\gamma). \quad (72)$$

(ref. [12], p. 368; ref. [13], section 8.511). This yields the following equation:

$$p(\mathrm{r},\theta,\ \phi,\mathrm{t}\,|\,r_0,\ \theta_0,\ \phi_0)=$$
$$=\frac{1}{8\pi\mathrm{Dt}\sqrt{\mathrm{rr}_0}}\exp\left(-\frac{r^2+r_0^2}{4\mathrm{Dt}}\right)\sqrt{\frac{\mathrm{rr}_0}{\pi\mathrm{Dt}}}\exp\left(\frac{\mathrm{rr}_0\cos\gamma}{2\mathrm{Dt}}\right)\equiv\frac{1}{(4\pi\mathrm{Dt})^{3/2}}\exp\left[-\frac{r^2+r_0^2-2\mathrm{rr}_0\cos\gamma}{4\mathrm{Dt}}\right]. \quad (73)$$

Therefore, $p(r,\theta,\phi,t\,|\,r_0,\theta_0,\phi_0)$ is equivalent to free 3D diffusion (Equation 38) for $k_a=0$ and $\sigma=0$.

We were not able to develop a sampling algorithm for $p(r,\theta,\phi,t|r_0,\theta_0,\phi_0)$. However, it is possible to use the radial component of the DE in 3D:

$$\frac{\partial p(\mathrm{r,t}|r_0)}{\partial t}=\frac{D}{r^2}\frac{\partial}{\partial r}\left[r^2\frac{\partial}{\partial r}p(\mathrm{r,t}|r_0)\right], \tag{74}$$

with the boundary condition given by Equation 66. The solution is much simpler in this case:

$$4\pi \mathrm{r} r_0 p(\mathrm{r,t}|r_0)=\frac{1}{\sqrt{4\pi \mathrm{Dt}}}\left\{\exp\left[-\frac{(r-r_0)^2}{4\mathrm{Dt}}\right]+\exp\left[-\frac{(r+r_0-2\sigma)^2}{4\mathrm{Dt}}\right]\right\}+\alpha W\left(\frac{r+r_0-2\sigma}{\sqrt{4\mathrm{Dt}}},\ -\alpha\sqrt{\mathrm{Dt}}\right), \tag{75}$$

where $\alpha=-(k_a+4\pi\sigma D)/(4\pi\sigma^2 D)$. Therefore, this approximation is widely used in chemistry and biophysics [22]. The survival probability of a pair of particles, $Q(t|r_0)$, is well known and can be calculated by integrating $p(r,t|r_0)$ over space:

$$Q(t|r_0)=\int_\sigma^\infty 4\pi \mathrm{r}^2 p(\mathrm{r,t}|r_0)\mathrm{dr}=1+\frac{\sigma\alpha+1}{r_0\alpha}\left[W\left(\frac{r_0-\sigma}{\sqrt{4Dt}},\ \alpha\sqrt{Dt}\right)-Erfc\left(\frac{r_0-\sigma}{\sqrt{4Dt}}\right)\right]. \tag{76}$$

For this system, the time discretization equations takes the form:

$$\begin{aligned}
&p(r_2,\ \Delta t_1+\Delta t_2|r_0)=\int_\sigma^\infty 4\pi \mathrm{r}_1^2 p(r_2,\ \Delta t_2|r_1)p(r_1,\ \Delta t_1|r_0)\mathrm{dr},\\
&p(*,\Delta t_1+\Delta t_2|r_0)=p(*,\Delta t_1|r_0)+\int_\sigma^\infty 4\pi \mathrm{r}_1^2 p(*,\Delta t_2|r_1)p(r_1,\ \Delta t_1|r_0)\mathrm{dr},
\end{aligned} \tag{77}$$

where $\mathrm{p}(*,\mathrm{t}|\mathrm{r}_0)=1-\mathrm{Q}(\mathrm{t}|\mathrm{r}_0)$.

6.2.2. Sampling algorithm

The objective is to generate random variates from $f(r)=4\pi r^2 p(r,t|r_0)$ (ref. [23]). It can be noted that $f(r)$ is composed by the sum of two Gaussians and a negative term, since $k_a \geq 0$. Thus, $f(r) \leq h(r)$, where

$$h(r)=\frac{r}{r_0\sqrt{4\pi \mathrm{Dt}}}\left\{\exp\left[-\frac{(r-r_0)^2}{4\mathrm{Dt}}\right]+\exp\left[-\frac{(r+r_0-2\sigma)^2}{4\mathrm{Dt}}\right]\right\}. \tag{78}$$

Since $f(r)$ is bound by the sum of two Gaussian functions, it can be sampled by a rejection method. To do so, $h(r)$ is written as the sum of four terms, which, after rearrangement and truncation to the positive ranges, are:

$$
\begin{aligned}
h_1(r) &= \frac{\mathrm{r}-\mathrm{r}_0}{r_0\sqrt{4\pi \mathrm{Dt}}}\exp\left[-\frac{(\mathrm{r}-\mathrm{r}_0)^2}{4\mathrm{Dt}}\right]\times 1_{[r\geq r_0]},\\
h_2(r) &= \frac{r+r_0-2\sigma}{r_0\sqrt{4\pi \mathrm{Dt}}}\exp\left[-\frac{(r+r_0-2\sigma)^2}{4\mathrm{Dt}}\right]\times 1_{[r\geq \sigma]},\\
h_3(r) &= \frac{r_0}{r_0\sqrt{4\pi \mathrm{Dt}}}\exp\left[-\frac{(\mathrm{r}-\mathrm{r}_0)^2}{4\mathrm{Dt}}\right]\times 1_{[r\geq \sigma]},\\
h_4(r) &= \frac{2\sigma-\mathrm{r}_0}{r_0\sqrt{4\pi \mathrm{Dt}}}\exp\left[-\frac{(r+r_0-2\sigma)^2}{4\mathrm{Dt}}\right]\times 1_{[r\geq \sigma]}\times 1_{[r_0\leq 2\sigma]}
\end{aligned}
\tag{79}
$$

where $1_{[\text{condition}]}$ takes the value 1 when the condition is true, and 0 when it is false. A related function is also defined:

$$
h_4^{'}(r) = \frac{r_0}{r_0\sqrt{4\pi \mathrm{Dt}}}\exp\left[-\frac{(\mathrm{r}-\mathrm{r}_0)^2}{4\mathrm{Dt}}\right]\times 1_{[r\leq \sigma]}.
\tag{80}
$$

Thus, $f(r)\leq h(r) \overset{def}{=} \sum h_i(r)$. It is possible to generate a random variate with density proportional to $h(r)$, since $h(r)$ is a mixture of known probability distribution functions. To do so, the weight of the contributions of h_1, h_2 and h_3+h_4 are needed:

$$
\begin{aligned}
p_1 &= \int h_1(y)\mathrm{dy} = \sqrt{\frac{\mathrm{Dt}}{\pi r_0^2}},\\
p_2 &= \int h_2(y)\mathrm{dy} = \sqrt{\frac{\mathrm{Dt}}{\pi r_0^2}}\exp\left[-\frac{(\sigma-\mathrm{r}_0)^2}{4\mathrm{Dt}}\right],\\
p^{'} &= \int (h_3(y)+h_4(y))\mathrm{dy} = \Phi\left(\frac{r_0-\sigma}{\sqrt{2\mathrm{Dt}}}\right) + 1_{[r_0\leq 2\sigma]}\frac{2\sigma-r_0}{r_0}\Phi\left(\frac{\sigma-\mathrm{r}_0}{\sqrt{2\mathrm{Dt}}}\right).
\end{aligned}
\tag{81}
$$

where $\Phi(x)$ is the normal distribution function:

$$
\Phi(x\sqrt{2}) = 1-\mathrm{Erfc}(x)/2.
\tag{82}
$$

From this algorithm 8a is obtained:

Algorithm 8a

CALCULATE p_1, p_2 and p'. SET $s=p_1+p_2+p'$

GENERATE a uniform [0,1] random variate$U$

IF $sU\in[0,p_1]$, SET$X \leftarrow r_0+\sqrt{4\mathrm{DtE}}$, where E is standard exponential.

http://dx.doi.org/10.5772/53203

IF $sU \in (p_1,p_2]$, SET $X \leftarrow 2\sigma - r_0 + \sqrt{(r_0-\sigma)^2 + 4DtE}$, where E is standard exponential.

IF $sU \in [p_1+p_2,s]$, use algorithm 8b to generate X

RETURN X

The second part is given by Algorithm 8b:

Algorithm 8b

REPEAT

GENERATE N as standard normal, U uniform on [0,1]

Set $X \leftarrow r_0 + \sqrt{2Dt}N$

UNTIL $X>\sigma$, or jointly $X<\sigma$, $Dt<2\sigma^2$ and $U \leq (2\sigma - r_0)/r_0$

In the former case, RETURN X

In the latter case, RETURN 2σ-X

Algorithm 8 generates numbers with density probability proportional to $h(r)$. However, random numbers distributed as $f(r)$ are needed. Since $f(r)$ is bound by $h(r)$, a rejection method is used as the final step, i.e. the overall algorithm generate pairs of random numbers (X,U) with X having density distribution proportional to h and U uniform on [0,1] until $Uh(X) \leq f(X)$ and returns X. Results obtained by using this algorithm are shown in Figure 11.

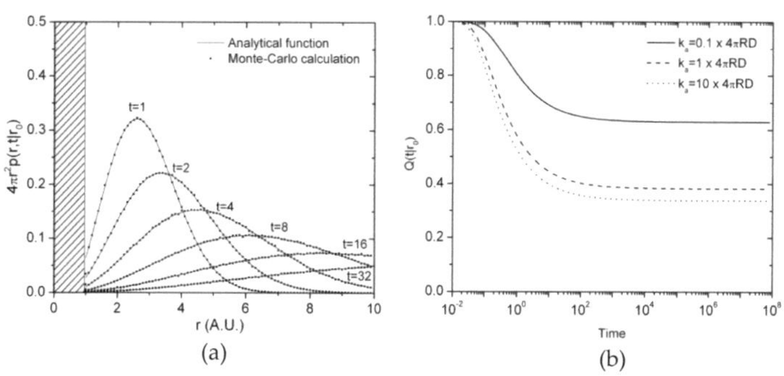

Figure 11. a) Green's function $4\pi r^2 p(r,t|r_0)$ for $D=1$, $R=1$, $r_0=1.5$ and $\alpha=-2$ at $t=1, 2, 4, 8, 16$ and 32. Analytical functions: (—); Result of sampling: (■). b) Survival probability $Q(t|r_0)$ as function of time for $D=1$, $R=1$, $r_0=1.5$ and $k_a=0.1 \times 4\pi RD$ (—), $4\pi RD$ (---) and $10 \times 4\pi RD$ ( ).

The time discretization property of the Green's functions (Equations 77) are also used to validate the simulation results and the sampling algorithm.

This algorithm is used to sample the length of the separation vector r. To fully caracterize the vector its direction should be specified by the angles θ and ϕ in a spherical coordinate system. An exact answer including the angles could be obtained by sampling the multi-variate Green's function given by Equation 67. An approximate method to obtain the deflection angles, which can be used here, is given by [24].

After sampling of the vectors $\boldsymbol{r}$ and $\boldsymbol{R}$, the new positions of the particles $\boldsymbol{r}_A$ and $\boldsymbol{r}_B$ are obtained by inverting the transformation given by Equation (61):

$$\begin{aligned} \boldsymbol{r}_A &= \frac{\sqrt{D_A / D_B}\boldsymbol{R} - D_A \boldsymbol{r}}{D_A + D_B}, \\ \boldsymbol{r}_B &= \frac{\sqrt{D_A / D_B}\boldsymbol{R} + D_B \boldsymbol{r}}{D_A + D_B}. \end{aligned} \tag{83}$$

6.2.3. Application to radiation chemistry

Ionizing radiation interacts with water molecules and creates radiolytic species, which react with cellular components and eventually lead to biological effects [14]. The precise location of the created radiolytic species are highly dependent of the type and energy of ionizing radiation. Therefore, considerable effort has been devoted to the Monte-Carlo simulation of ionizing radiation tracks, which provides such information [25]. After their formation, the radiolytic species react with each other and with other cellular molecules. Hence, radiation chemistry is a very important link between the radiation track structure and cellular damage and biological effects [26].

The simulation of radiation chemistry is difficult for several reasons. One important problem is the calculation time. Since the number of interactions between N particles is $N(N-1)/2$, the calculation time increases as $\sim N^2$. Therefore, simulation of systems comprising over 10000 particles is difficult, even in modern computers. For example, Uehara and Nikjoo [27] reported that the simulation of time-dependent yields of chemical species produced by five 1-MeV electron tracks comprising about 1,500 particles from 10^{-12} to 10^{-6} s requires about 250 h of calculation time. One promising approach is the new hardware called general purpose graphic processing units (GPGPU), which are special cards comprising a large number of processors designed to perform a large number of calculations simulaneously. Regarding this, the sampling algorithms proposed in this book chapter do not require much memory and could be implemented on a GPGPU, which could allow the simulation of large particle systems.

We conclude this section by showing a simulation result of water radiolysis by a $^{12}C^{6+}$ ion of 25 MeV/amu [28] in Figure 12. Briefly, the track structure and the position of all the radiolytic species ($^{\cdot}OH$, $H^{\cdot}$, e^-_{aq}, H_2, H_2O_2,..) at $\sim 10^{-13}$ s are calculated by the code RITRACKS, described in [25] and references therein. The time evolution of the radiolytic species are calculated by using a step-by-step Monte-Carlo simulation code of radiation chemistry [28-30]. Each dot in Figure 12 represents a radiolytic species. The changes in the colors of the dots indicates that chemical reaction occurs. The number of chemical reactions (the radiolytic yields) which are calculated by the program have been validated with experimental data [30].

http://dx.doi.org/10.5772/53203

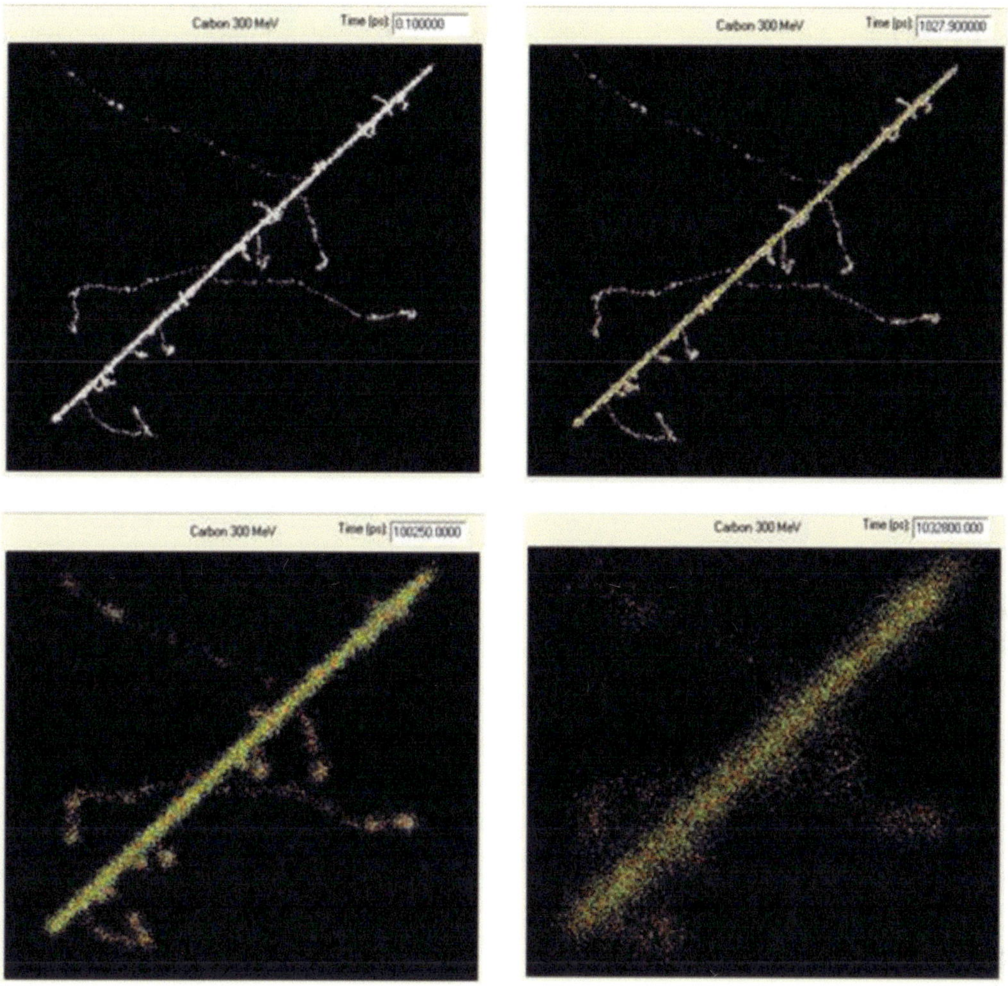

Figure 12. Time evolution of the radiolytic species created by a $^{12}C^{6+}$ ion track, 25 MeV/amu (LET~75 keV/μm) at 10^{-13}, 10^{-9}, 10^{-7} and 10^{-6} s.

7. Conclusion

The simulations based on the Green's function of the DE are able to accurately describe the evolution of particles in time and space in various geometries, even if the number of particles is small. In fact, this approach is now used in several fields. Of particular interest in radiobiology is the study of radiation chemistry, biochemical networks and bimolecular reactions.

The Green's functions and their respective sampling algorithms have been presented for simple systems in one, two and three dimensions. Obviously, it is difficult to develop sampling algorithm even for simple systems because of the complex mathematical form of the Green's functions. However, it is very useful to develop sampling algorithms for systems for which analytical solutions are known, because they can be used to validate future models which will be based on numerical solutions of the DE. The DE can be solved easily by numerical methods such as finite-difference schemes, but these techniques may have restrictions for computational stability and the boundary conditions are often difficult to implement [31]. The systems with complex boundary conditions are particularly relevant to study biological networks. However, as seen in the applications, since the Green's functions of systems with complex boundary conditions are often subdensities of the Green's functions for the corresponding system with reflective boundary conditions, the rejection method can be used.

The algorithms developed in this chapter are already used to simulate the radiation chemistyoccuring in liquid water [28-30]. In the future, they will allow the validation and verification of future calculations, which will use the numerical solution of the diffusion equation. Eventually, the approach depicted in this book chapter will be used to simulate the time evolution of radiolytic species created by ionizing radiation and their reactions with molecules in biological media [23].

Acknowledgements

This work was support by the NASA Space Radiation Risk Assessment Program. The help of Dr. Luc Devroye (McGill University) with sampling algorithms is greatly acknowledged.

Author details

Ianik Plante* and Francis A. Cucinotta

*Address all correspondence to: Ianik.Plante-1@nasa.gov

NASA Johnson Space Center, Houston, TX, USA

References

[1] Cucinotta FA, Pluth JM, Anderson JA, Harper JV, O'Neill P. Biochemical kinetics model of DSB repair and induction of γ-H2AX foci by non-homologous end joining. Radiation Research 2008; 169(2) 214-222. doi:10.1667/RR1035.1

[2] van Zon JS, ten Wolde PR. Green's-function reaction dynamics: A particle-based approach for simulating biochemical networks in time and space. Journal of Chemical Physics 2005; 123(23) 234910. doi: 10.1063/1.2137716

[3] Li Y, Wang M, Carra C, Cucinotta FA. Modularized Smad-regulated TGFβ signaling pathway. Mathematical Biosciences 2012; 240(2) 187-200. doi: 10.1016/j.mbs.2012.07.005

[4] Carslaw HS, Jaeger JC. Conduction of Heat in Solids. Oxford: Oxford University Press; 1959.

[5] Plante I, Cucinotta FA. Model of the initiation of signal transduction by ligands in a cell culture: Simulation of molecules near a plane membrane comprising receptors. Physical Review E 2011; 84(5) 051920. doi: 10.1103/PhysRevE.84.051920

[6] Selvadurai APS. Partial Differential Equations in Mechanics 1. New-York: Springer-Verlag; 2000.

[7] Press WH, Teukolsky SA, Vetterling WT, Flannery BP. Numerical Recipes in Fortran. 2nd Edition. Cambridge: Cambridge University Press; 1992.

[8] Lamm G, Schulten K. Extended Brownian Dynamics: II. Reactive, nonlinear diffusion. Journal of Chemical Physics 1983; 78(5) 2713-2734. doi: 10.1063/1.445002

[9] Abramowitz M, Stegun IA. Handbook of Mathematical Functions. New York: Dover Publications; 1964.

[10] Plante I, Devroye L, Cucinotta FA. Calculations of distance distribution and probabilities of binding by ligands between parallel plane membranes comprising receptors. Submitted to Computer Physics Communications.

[11] Devroye L. The series method in random variate generation and its application to the Kolmogorov-Smirnov distribution. American Journal of Mathematical and Management Sciences 1981; 1 359-379.

[12] Watson GN. A Treatise on the Theory of Bessel Functions. Cambridge: Cambridge University Press; 1922.

[13] Gradshteyn IS, Ryzhik IM. Table of Integrals, Series, and Products. New York: Academic Press; 1994.

[14] Muroya Y, Plante I, Azzam EI, Meesungnoen J, Katsumura Y, Jay-Gerin J-P. High-LET ion radiolysis of water: visualization of the formation and evolution of ion tracks and relevance to the radiation-induced bystander effect. Radiation Research 2006; 165(4): 485-491. doi: 10.1667/RR3540.1

[15] Batsilas L, Berezhkovskii AM, Shvartsman Y. Stochastic models of autocrine and paracrine signals in cell culture assays. Biophysical Journal 2003; 85(6) 3659-3665. doi: 10.1016/S0006-3495(03)74783-3

[16] Monine MI, Berezhkovskii AM, Joslin EJ, Wiley SH, Lauffenburger DA, Shvartsman SY. Ligand accumulation in autocrine cell cultures. Biophysical Journal 2005; 88(4) 2384-2390. doi: 10.1529/biophysj.104.051425

[17] Shvartsman SY, Wiley SH, Deen WH, Lauffenburger, DA. Spatial range of autocrine signaling: modeling and computational analysis. Biophysical Journal 2001; 81(4) 1854-1867. doi: 10.1016/S0006-3495(01)75837-7

[18] Kim H, Shin KJ, Agmon N. Excited-state reversible geminate recombination with quenching in one dimension. Journal of Chemical Physics 1999; 111 (9) 3791-3799. doi: 10.1063/1.479682

[19] Poppe, GP, Wijers CMJ. Algorithm 680: evaluation of the complex error function. ACM Trans Math Software 1990; 16(1) 47. doi:10.1145/77626.77630

[20] Edelstein AL, Agmon N. Brownian dynamics simulations of reversible reactions in one dimension. Journal of Chemical Physics 1993; 99(7) 5396-5404. doi: 10.1063/1.465983

[21] Devroye L. Non-Uniform Random Variate Generation. New York: Springler-Verlag; 1986. luc.devroye.org/rnbookindex.html

[22] Krissinel EB, Agmon N. Spherical symmetric diffusion problem. Journal of Computational Chemistry 1996; 17(9) 1085-1098. doi: 10.1002/(SICI)1096-987X(19960715)17:9<1085::AID-JCC1>3.0.CO;2-O

[23] Plante I, Devroye L, Cucinotta FA. Random sampling of the Green's functions for reversible reactions with an intermediate state. Article in press, Journal of Computational Physics. doi: 10.1016/j.jcp.2013.02.001

[24] Clifford P, Green NJB, Oldfield M, Pilling MJ, Pimblott SM. Stochastic models of multi-species kinetics in radiation-induced spurs. Journal of the Chemical Society Faraday Transactions 1 1986; 82(9) 2673-2689. doi:10.1039/f19868202673

[25] Plante I, Cucinotta FA. Monte-Carlo simulation of ionizing radiation tracks. In: Mode C. (ed.) Monte Carlo Methods in Biology, Medicine and Other Fields of Science. Rijeka: InTech; 2011. p 315-356. doi: 10.5772/15674

[26] O'Neill P, Wardman P, Radiation chemistry comes before radiation biology. International Journal of Radiation Biology 2009; 85(1) 9-25. doi: 10.1080/09553000802640401

[27] Uehara S, Nikjoo H. Monte Carlo simulation of water radiolysis for low-energy charged particles. Journal of Radiation Research 2006; 47(1) 69-81. doi: 10.1269/jrr.47.69

[28] Plante I. Développement de codes de simulation Monte-Carlo de la radiolyse de l'eau par des électrons, ion lourds, protons et neutrons. Applications à divers sujets d'intérêt expérimental. PhD thesis. University of Sherbrooke; 2009.

[29] Plante I. A Monte-Carlo step-by-step simulation code of the non-homogeneous chemistry of the radiolysis of water and aqueous solutions. Part I: theoretical framework and implementation. Radiation and Environmental Biophysics 50(3) 389-403. doi: 10.1007/s00411-011-0367-8

[30] Plante I. A Monte-Carlo step-by-step simulation code of the non-homogeneous chemistry of the radiolysis of water and aqueous solutions - Part II: calculation of radiolytic yields under different conditions of LET, pH, and temperature. Radiation Environmental Biophysics 2011; 50(3) 405-415. doi: 10.1007/s00411-011-0368-7

[31] Carrier GF, Pearson CE. Partial Differential Equations. New York: Academic Press; 1988.

Chapter 10

Kinetic Monte Carlo Simulation in Biophysics and Systems Biology

Subhadip Raychaudhuri

Additional information is available at the end of the chapter

http://dx.doi.org/10.5772/53709

1. Introduction

Generation of large amount of biological data has provided us with some of its unique challenges in modeling of biological systems. Recent advances in imaging techniques, such as confocal, FRET, multi-photon among others, led systems level information for biological processes and accumulation of even more biological data. There is a clear need for quantitative (mathematical and computational) tools that are capable of analyzing such large amount of information. Equally pressing is the need for theoretical models that can elucidate the cellular and molecular mechanisms of complex biological processes. Systems biology modeling (differential equations, stochastic simulations, agent based models) is emerging as a powerful tool that can provide mechanistic insight into workings of complex biological systems as well as allow analysis of large datasets. Such computational models can be validated using synergistic experiments (in an iterative manner) and also possess predictive power. Monte Carlo (MC) simulation is a stochastic modeling approach that can be utilized to carry out *in silico* studies of biological problems.

Monte Carlo simulation is now an established technique to solve problems in a wide variety of disciplines. It is an essential tool in statistical mechanics and has been frequently used for problems in material science and engineering. Monte Carlo method relies on selecting an initial configuration state and then iterate through a series of steps during which one or more moves are selected and evaluated for acceptance. The number of moves per step is often taken to be the number of available degrees of freedom in that step so as to ensure probing (*on the average*) of each degree of freedom once per step. However, other types of implementations (such as a rejection-free algorithm) are also possible. Use of Monte Carlo method to solve biological problems has its unique challenges, but if successfully addressed, it can become a powerful tool. Monte Carlo models (for biological systems) can be developed based

INTECH
open science | open minds

© 2013 The Author(s). Licensee InTech. This chapter is distributed under the terms of the Creative Commons Attribution License http://creativecommons.org/licenses/by/3.0), which permits unrestricted use, distribution, and reproduction in any medium, provided the original work is properly cited.

on statistical mechanics and thus it is expected that it would work well for probing the underlying biophysics of a complex biological process. Of particular interest is a class of Monte Carlo simulations that are based on a set of pre-defined probabilistic rate constants and can be called kinetic Monte Carlo models. Probabilistic rate constant based kinetic Monte Carlo simulations can be developed for a wide variety of biological processes that span multiple length and time scales. We demonstrate that controlled kinetic Monte Carlo experiments are capable of revealing fundamental regulatory mechanisms in a complex biological system.

The organization of the chapter is as follows. We begin with a discussion of the random walk problem in section 2. It elucidates the theoretical basis of Monte Carlo simulations in terms of master equations. It is also an instructive example problem to elucidate some key features, such as the concept of probabilistic simulation parameters (constants), of the kinetic Monte Carlo method. In section 3 Monte Carlo simulation is discussed in the context of physical sciences and materials engineering. This allowed us to discuss how Monte Carlo models can be developed based on statistical mechanics (detailed balance and ergodicity). We also briefly discuss implicit and explicit free energy based implementations of Monte Carlo simulations as applied in physical sciences and materials engineering. In section 4 we describe how Monte Carlo simulations can be used to solve problems in biophysics and biology. A probabilistic rate constant based kinetic Monte Carlo algorithm is discussed in detail. We developed this algorithm to solve the following biological problems: (i) the problem of B cell affinity discrimination and B cell activation (section 5), (ii) systems biology of apoptotic cell death signaling (section 6). We conclude with a discussion on emergence of Monte Carlo simulation as a tool to solve problems of biomedical relevance (section 7). The discussion is focused on our recent efforts to address some key issues in cancer biology and cancer therapy.

2. Monte Carlo simulation of random walk

Random walk is a probabilistic process that is analytically tractable and can also be easily simulated on a computer. Analytical approach is based on master equations that describe the system by equations in probability space. Computer simulation for a random walk is carried out using a set of pre-defined probability constants that are taken from the master equation [1-2]. Random walk based kinetic Monte Carlo simulations can be developed that can describe diffusion and trafficking in biological systems. Below we discuss a simple one-dimensional random walk for which results obtained from Monte Carlo simulations can be readily compared with exact results obtained by analytically solving random walk master equations.

2.1. Master equation description for one-dimensional random walk

At each step, a random walker executing a one-dimensional random walk (on a lattice) jumps to one of the two neighboring lattice sites. One-dimensional random walk is described by a master equation (discrete time and discrete space formulation) of the form: $P_{n,N+1} =$

(1/2) $P_{n-1,N}$ + (1/2) $P_{n+1,N}$. $P_{n,N}$ is the probability of finding the random walker at site n at time step N [1]. The above master equation describes probability conservation for a symmetric random walk having equal (=1/2) probability of moving left or right. The random walker can reach the site n (at time N+1) from either of the two neighboring sites n-1 or n+1.

Random walk master equation can be solved by defining a characteristic function G = $\Sigma P_{n,N} e^{ins}$ (the sum is over all possible values of n $[-\infty,\infty]$) [1]. By making this change in variable n → s (through the function G), the random walk master equation becomes an algebraic equation G(s,N) = α G(s,N-1), where $\alpha = (e^{is} + e^{-is})$. The equation in G can be solved recursively G(s,N) = α^N G(s,0). For a random walk starting at the origin (n=0 at N=0), G(s,0) = 1, leading to G(s,N) = $(e^{is} + e^{-is})^N$. The probability function for the random walker $P_{n,N}$ can then be obtained by expanding G(s,N) in a power series (binomial expansion) and comparing with the starting definition G = $\Sigma P_{n,N} e^{ins}$. Various moments of the random walk, such as $\langle n \rangle = 0$ and $\langle n^2 \rangle = N$ can be obtained directly from G(s,N).

A more general form of the random walk master equation is: $P_{n,N+1} = p_r P_{n-1,N} + p_l P_{n+1,N} + p_w P_{n,N}$; p_r, p_l, and p_w are right jump, left jump, and waiting (at site n) probabilities respectively. This equation is still amenable to exact solution through the characteristic function G(s,N).

2.2. Monte Carlo simulation of a one-dimensional random walk

First, we need to decide on the allowed moves, which are called Monte Carlo moves, in the simulation. For a simple one-dimensional random walk there are two possible Monte Carlo moves: right and left jumps. At each Monte Carlo time step, those two moves are sampled with equal probability and then the chosen move is performed by increasing or decreasing the position, n, by unit length (n → n+1 or n → n-1). We store the information for the position of the random walker in a pre-defined variable (memory location on a computer). The process is then repeated many times by the use of a loop (such as the *for* loop). Position data (n) is recorded at every time-step or every M (integer) number of MC time steps. Often data is stored in a separate output file location that can be processed later for analyzing simulation data.

Sampling of a probability distribution, such as the equal probability sampling of right / left jumps, can be carried out on a computer using pseudo random number generators. Standard uniform random number generators in a programming platform, such as the rand function in the C library, are often used for this purpose. Uniform random number generators provide a number by sampling a uniform probability density function in the interval (0,1). Equal sampling in case of a one-dimensional symmetric random walk can be achieved by diving the interval (0,1) into two equal parts. At each MC step, the random number is called once, and right / left jump is chosen depending on whether the random number is > or < 0.5 (Head or Tail). Other types of probability distributions can be sampled by utilizing the uniform random number generator.

We can run the random walk simulation many times by generating a different sequence of random numbers in each run. Thus each simulation run corresponds to a distinct random walk trajectory. One can solve the random walk problem by calculating $P_{n,N}$ from many runs of such random walk simulations; statistical quantities such as $\langle n \rangle$ or $\langle n^2 \rangle$ can also be estimated. A computer program for simulating two-dimensional random walk is provided in the Appendix. Results from simulations should agree with the exact results obtained from the solution of the random walk master equation. For a slightly generalized random walk, having asymmetric right and left jumps and also a waiting probability, the uniform distribution in (0,1) is sampled accordingly (based on P_r, P_l, and P_w). The probability constants P_r, P_l, and P_w can be taken as an input of the simulation. This type of random walk simulations provides a simple example of the probabilistic constant based kinetic Monte Carlo method. Each Monte Carlo step in such a simulation can be assigned a physical time (depending on the system under study); the probability constants P_r, P_l, and P_w would vary with the physical time-scale assigned to a MC step. Periodic boundary conditions can be used to avoid finite size effects.

3. Monte Carlo simulation in physical sciences and materials engineering

Monte Carlo simulation is now an established method in statistical mechanics having wide applicability [2-4]. Monte Carlo moves in such systems typically correspond to changes in configuration space and hence the total energy of the system under consideration. The two key requirements for this class of simulations are ergodicity (of the MC moves) and the detailed balance condition of the acceptance criteria [3].

3.1. Ergodicity and detailed balance

Ergodicity demands that any state in the configuration space of the system can be reached in a finite number of Monte Carlo moves starting from an arbitrary initial state. Such a condition ensures that the configuration space of the system is adequately explored in a given time.

Detailed balance maintains the equilibrium probability distribution for different states by setting a condition for equilibrium. The requirement of detailed balance can be elucidated by considering a two state system. Suppose N_1 is the number of particles in state 1 (or the number of one particle system in state 1 for an ensemble of systems) and N_2 is the same for state 2. $S_{1\to2}$ represents the probability that state 1 is proposed to move to state 2 (similarly define $S_{2\to1}$ for $2 \to 1$) and $P_{1\to2}$ represents the acceptance probability (similarly $P_{2\to1}$ for $2 \to 1$). The condition of detailed balance ensures equilibrium in the following manner: $N_1 S_{1\to2} P_{1\to2} = N_2 S_{2\to1} P_{2\to1}$. Assuming each degree of freedom is sampled once (on average) per Monte Carlo step: $S_{1\to2} = S_{2\to1}$. In equilibrium, the particles (or the ensemble) should be distributed according to the Gibbs-Boltzmann distribution so that $N_i \sim \exp(-E_i/K_BT)$. Hence $P_{1\to2} / P_{2\to1} = \exp\{-(E_2 - E_1)/K_BT\}$. In the Metropolis Monte Carlo algorithm, $P_{2\to1} = 1$ (assuming $E_2 > E_1$). Thus for any move that results in an increase in free energy the acceptance probability is given by $P_{1\to2} = \exp\{-(E_2 - E_1)/K_BT\}$.

3.2. Various implementations of Monte Carlo algorithm

i. Explicit free energy simulations: Algorithms with explicit consideration of thermodynamic free energy, such as the Metropolis acceptance criteria, have been widely used to calculate physical properties of a system at equilibrium [2-6]. For systems that are not analytically tractable, such as the Ising model in 3 dimensions and certain disordered systems, Monte Carlo simulation remains a powerful approach. For systems that are driven out-of-equilibrium, Monte Carlo simulation is an essential tool to study the approach-to-equilibrium dynamics in such systems [3].

ii. Implicit free energy simulations: Various types of discrete particle based simulations have been employed to study physical properties of systems that remain out-of-equilibrium. Examples of such non-equilibrium systems include surface growth models that show kinetic roughening [7-8]. Non-equilibrium condition is generated in a wide variety of systems such as in molecular beam epitaxy where a surface is grown by vapor deposition. The discrete particle based simulations that are developed to study surface growth and kinetic roughening in non-equilibrium systems can be considered as atomistic (or discrete particle based) kinetic Monte Carlo simulations. These simulations are often based on a set of rules for Monte Carlo moves and any consideration of free energy (if needed) remain implicit. Some of the initial simulations were developed to study universal properties of out-of-equilibrium systems; such universal properties were also studied utilizing coarse-grained field theoretic models [7-10]. However, more complex Monte Carlo models can be developed for realistic simulations of systems in material science, engineering, and nanotechnology [11-15].

4. Monte Carlo simulations in biology

Metropolis Monte Carlo, an algorithm based on explicit consideration of free energy and detailed balance, has been utilized in the past to simulate biological processes such as receptor clustering and cellular signaling. One of the early examples include a model for TNFR1 receptor clustering that is induced by ligand binding [16]. In that study, a Hamiltonian was constructed with a linear chemical energy and binding energy term for each lattice site, as well as an interaction term involving molecules present in adjoining lattice sites. The interaction energy considered in their model was similar to the energy function used in lattice gas models in statistical mechanics [3]. Another study modeled more complex receptor clustering at the T cell synapse [17], in which two types of receptor-ligand pairs cluster at the cell-cell contact but also known to segregate driven by receptor-ligand pair length differences [18-23]. These two types of receptor-ligand pairs, which possess different equilibrium bond lengths, cause membrane bending and tension; thus the Hamiltonian is a sum of elastic energy from the membrane plus the interaction energies of receptors and ligands. In a separate study, the functional role of T cell synapse was explored by a Monte Carlo model of membrane proximal signaling events in T cells [24]. An internal spin state {0 or 1} dependent energy term was considered in the Hamiltonian to model phosphorylation-dephosphorylation type signaling reactions. Examples of Monte Carlo modeling include rolling and adhesion of leukocytes [25] and dynamics of G-protein activation [26].

Another type of Monte Carlo approach, known as Gillespie's stochastic simulation algorithm (SSA), has been widely used to simulate biochemical signaling networks, especially for spatially homogeneous systems [27-28]. Several attempts have been made to introduce diffusion into Gillespie's SSA [29]. Some of the initial works that explored stochastic fluctuations in genetic regulatory networks used the SSA for its efficient sampling scheme [28, 30-31]. A similar approach, known as continuous time Monte Carlo, has been employed to study low temperature systems [3, 32]. The advantage of this type of rejection-free algorithms arises from frequent sampling of high probability reaction moves (not wasting computational time by repeatedly rejecting low probability events). When large numbers of signaling reactions are present, such as in a complex cell signaling network, Gillespie's SSA method might become computationally expensive.

4.1. Study of complex systems in biology: Probabilistic rate constant based kinetic Monte Carlo simulations

Probabilistic rate constant based kinetic Monte Carlo simulations are emerging as a powerful tool to solve biological problems. Though similar implicit free energy simulations have been used in random walk problems as well as in non-equilibrium statistical physics, solving complex biological problems by the Monte Carlo method pose its unique challenges. Finding a suitable parameter mapping scheme, between experimentally measured rate constants and simulation parameters, is an example of such issues that needs to be addressed when simulating biological systems [33]. Below we discuss a kinetic Monte Carlo method that has been developed by us to solve the following problems: (i) antigen affinity discrimination by B lymphocytes, (ii) systems biology of cell death (apoptosis) signaling [34].

In our developed kinetic Monte Carlo method a set of MC moves are carried out with predefined probabilistic rate constants. All possible moves are randomly sampled by first randomly sampling individual objects (or agents). Once a move is selected, acceptance / rejection for that move is determined by a pre-defined probability constant. In this method it is possible to satisfy the conditions of detailed balance and ergodicity, thus the model can be placed on a firm basis of statistical mechanics (necessary when thermodynamic considerations are relevant). A parameter mapping scheme was designed that can be used to obtain the probabilistic simulation parameters from known rate constants. Assigning physical time to a MC step is part of this parameter mapping scheme. For lattice simulation, individual nodes are occupied by discrete particles (cells / molecules / agents); such explicit simulation of individual objects (in a temporal model) can be considered agent-based simulations. In our simulations, lattice size and lattice spacing are defined by relevant length scales of the problem. For cell-signaling problems in biology, lattice size will be set by the size of a cell and lattice spacing by size of protein molecules. Our simulation method can be modified, when necessary, to perform off-lattice simulations. At the beginning of the simulation, molecules are either (i) uniformly and randomly distributed, or, (ii) distributed according to their

http://dx.doi.org/10.5772/53709

known spatial localization. Even when the molecules are randomly distributed initially, spatial heterogeneity can emerge during the course of simulation.

4.2. Monte Carlo in biophysics and systems biology: Simulation method

i. Random sampling of all possible MC moves and acceptance / rejection criteria: This can be implemented in the following manner. After an object (*e.g.* molecule) is first randomly sampled, all possible diffusion / reaction moves (degrees of freedom) for that object are randomly sampled to choose one particular move, which is then accepted / rejected based on pre-defined probability constants. Thus the effective probability for a Monte Carlo move is given by $P_{eff} = S\ P_{reaction}$, where $S = 1/N$ is the sampling probability for N number of allowed Monte Carlo moves and $P_{reaction}$= acceptance / rejection probability for the chosen reaction. If we decide to attempt N Monte Carlo moves in a MC step (Δt), then $S = 1$.

ii. Detailed balance and ergodicity: The probabilistic constants (for reaction / diffusion moves) contain the information for free energy changes, associated with a reaction or a diffusion move, in an implicit manner. Let us first consider a bi-molecular reaction of the type $A + B \rightarrow C$. We need two probability constants, P_{on} and P_{off}, corresponding to the forward and the backward reactions respectively. The ratio P_{on} / P_{off} should be equal to $\exp(-\beta\Delta E)$to satisfy the detailed balance condition at each spatial point. $\beta = 1/K_BT$ and ΔE is the free energy change associated with the reaction move ($\Delta E = E_{bound} - E_{free}, E_{bound} < E_{free}$). Clearly, the reaction probabilities $P_{on}$and P_{off} should be connected to the kinetic reaction rate constants $K_{on}$and K_{off}, the exact relation for which is discussed later in the parameter mapping section. For a class of problems in systems biology, thermodynamic considerations are not necessary and the detailed balance condition to achieve Gibbs-Boltzmann equilibrium distribution need not be satisfied. Rather direct estimation of reaction probabilities ($P_{reaction}$) from known rate constants ($K_{reaction}$) is more important in such systems biology problems. Ergodicity is satisfied as any state in the configuration space can be reached in a finite number of MC steps starting from an arbitrary initial state of the system.

iii. Parameter mapping scheme: Time-scale of the simulation is estimated by considering the time-scale for diffusive motion in the system. We associate $P_{diffusion} = 1$ for the fastest diffusing species and determine Δt (MC time step) by matching the diffusion constant (for that species) to the experimentally measured diffusion co-efficient. An approximate estimate for the diffusion constant $D \sim P_{diffusion} (\Delta x)^2 / (\Delta t)$ can be used, where $P_{diffusion}$ is the diffusion probability of a given species, (Δx) is the lattice spacing, and, (Δt) is the MC time-step used in the simulation. Reaction probabilities are then estimated using t.

For the $A + B \rightarrow C$ type reaction, the dissociation reaction probability P_{off} can be calculated directly from the backward reaction rate constant K_{off} by using $P_{off} = K_{off}\ \Delta t$. Such a mapping would work for a class of reaction rates (expressed in sec^{-1} unit) such as the degradation rate or the catalytic conversion rate. Estimation of the association reaction probability P_{on} (for A + B → C type reaction) is not straightforward as the forward reaction rate K_{on} has the unit [area sec^{-1}]. Note, the on rate K_{on} has two components to it, one of it captures the association rate for two free reactant molecules and a second factor corresponds to the reaction probability [35]. One can use simulations to find a relation between the ratios (P_{on} / P_{off}) and (K_{on} / K_{off}). Typically, P_{off} can be varied in a simulation keeping P_{on} fixed, and the affinity constant K_A (= K_{on} / K_{off}) can be obtained from the average steady-state (or equilibrium) value of the reactant molecules. A linear relationship in the form of (P_{on} / P_{off}) = α (K_{on} / K_{off}) was found, which provides an estimation for the association reaction probability P_{on}. The constant α captures the effect of diffusion-limited association of free reactant molecules and clearly its value should depend on the spatial dimension of the system. If the value obtained for P_{on} or P_{off} turns out to be >1, the MC time-step (Δt) needs to be readjusted accordingly.

iv. Simulating complexity in biological systems: Complexities involved in biological processes, such as complex rules of cellular signaling, are handled well by Monte Carlo simulations. In contrast, increasing complexity of a biological system can make developing the correct set of differential equations for that system increasingly difficult. Other examples of such complexity will include formation of multi-molecular complexes (hetero-oligomers) such as the assembly of an apoptosome during apoptotic cell death activation. Our previous studies have shown the effectiveness of kinetic Monte Carlo methods in capturing the complexities of a biological system. In addition, such probabilistic rate constant based methods can be successfully combined with other types of simulation or differential equation based models. We could combine the dynamical equation for membrane shape fluctuations with a kinetic Monte Carlo method describing receptor-ligand binding at the cell-cell contact region [36].We can also couple our probabilistic rate constant based method to explicit free energy based Monte Carlo techniques (such as the Metropolis scheme). Such a hybrid simulation technique was found to be key to developing a Monte Carlo model for receptor-lipid raft formation during B lymphocyte activation.

v. Boundary conditions: Appropriate boundary conditions, depending on the biological problem under consideration, need to be employed in the Monte Carlo simulation code. For example, when simulating an intra-cellular signaling pathway signaling molecules are restricted to diffuse within the cellular volume. Such no flux boundary conditions are implemented by reflective boundary conditions in a lattice simulation. Linear dimensions of the simulation lattice are determined by the size of a cell. Scaled-down versions with smaller lattice sizes are also used in the cases of computationally expensive simulations.

5. B lymphocyte activation and antigen affinity discrimination

Only a few specific lymphocytes (T and B cells), out of billions of such cells, are known to get activated and mount a successful immune response against a particular type of pathogen. How the adaptive immune system carry out such a task remains a problem of considerable interest. B lymphocytes have an ability to adapt to the changing pathogenic load by continuously generating diversity in the variable region of the receptor (somatic hypermutation leading to variations in antigen binding affinity) and selecting the high affinity clones, a feature known as affinity maturation. It is a strategy by which B lymphocytes optimize the immune response given a pathogenic load. Affinity maturation is also key to design of vaccines that rely on B cell mediated antibody production. Earlier studies indicated factors such as competition for antigens could lead to selection of high affinity receptors during the process of affinity maturation. More recent observations, however, focus on antigen affinity discrimination at the level of single cell activation [37-42]. In B cells, affinity discrimination implies increasing level of signaling response as the affinity (K_A=K_{on} /K_{off}) for antigen is increased. Such a monotonically increasing response, however, is not obvious as low affinity antigens clearly have the ability to quickly dissociate from a B cell receptor and serially activate a large number of such receptors in a small amount of time. We use Monte Carlo simulations to explore the molecular mechanism of B cell affinity discrimination [36, 43-46].

Mathematical and computational modeling, often in synergy with biological experiments, has been increasingly utilized to solve immunological problems. Previous studies in T cells assumed a series of conformational changes in the T cell receptor upon antigen binding, a concept known as kinetic proofreading, to explain affinity discrimination in T cells [47-49]. Kinetic proofreading was thought to compete against loss in serial triggering (the ability of a single antigen to serially trigger many T cell receptors [50]), as the affinity for antigen is increased. Our initial Monte Carlo studies also utilized such kinetic proofreading requirements in an ad hoc manner. However, explicit simulation of molecular level events, such as B cell receptor oligomerization and lipid raft formation, can allow kinetic proofreading to emerge naturally from simulations. Monte Carlo models seem to be particularly suitable for simulating such molecular level details and biological complexity. Affinity discrimination can be studied in a controlled manner as only the BCR-antigen binding affinity can be varied in our simulations by keeping other parameters fixed.

5.1. Brief description of simulation set up

B cell receptors are placed on a two-dimensional lattice that mimics the B cell surface. Anitgens are also placed on a two-dimensional lattice that represents a lipid bilayer (surrogate for an antigen presenting cell). Diffusion move consists of moving a molecule to one of its four nearest neighbor nodes thus displacing the molecule by unit lattice spacing. Reaction between a B cell receptor and an antigen molecule may take place when they are at the same spatial location (x,y coordinates) on two opposing lattices. The probability of binding / unbinding between a BCR and an antigen should depend on the spatial location of the molecule to take into account the spherical curvature of a B cell. The center of the cell-cell contact region is assumed to adjust itself to the equilibrium bond length of the BCR-antigen pair; thus the probability for the association reaction at that point is maximal. Below we discuss how increasing level of biological complexity can be simulated by our Monte Carlo model:

a. Simulating formation of B cell receptor (BCR) oligomers and oligomerization mediated signaling [46]

i. We allow two types of MC moves: diffusion and reaction. Once a molecule is sampled randomly, diffusion or reaction is chosen with equal probability. Reaction moves include binding / unbinding between two molecules (such as between a BCR and an antigen), BCR-BCR oligomer formation, phosphorylation by signaling kinases. Simulation procedure is similar to that described in section #.4.2.

ii. Two antigen bound BCRs, when in sufficient spatial proximity, can form dimers and dimerization can eventually lead to formation of higher order oligomers. It is simulated based on the recent experimental observation that BCRs oligomerize due to opening of their Cμ4 domains upon antigen binding [51-52]. We also allow dissociation of such oligomers such as due to antigen dissociation from a dimerized BCR.

iii. In our model, the tyrosine residues in the signaling chains (ITAMs) of BCRs can get phosphorylated only when they are part of an oligomer; Signaling kinase Lyn can then bind and phosphorylate the tyrosine residues. Such a requirement for oligomerization introduces a delay time before activating signal can propagate downstream and thus provides a basis for kinetic proofreading.

iv. Syk (Spleen tyrosine kinase) can only bind to phosphorylated signaling chains of BCR molecules and get phosphorylated. Syk phosphorylation propagates the activation signal downstream.

v. We are also able to simulate diffusion of various types of molecules (free and antigen bound) in a realistic manner by varying the probability of diffusion move. BCR oligomers, for example, are assumed to be immobile.

vi. Affinity discrimination can be studied by running Monte Carlo experiments where BCR-antigen affinity is varied but all the other parameters remain constant. Simulation results indicate that formation of BCR oligomers is affinity dependent in a manner that can lead to enhanced signaling with increasing affinity.

The complexity of lipid-mediated interactions cannot be captured by the oligomerization model, however, such interactions are instrumental to understanding how signaling kinase Lyn can access antigen bound BCRs (upon antigen stimulation). Lipid rafts are sphingolipid and cholesterol enriched membrane microdomains [53]. Large (> 100 nm) and stable BCR-lipid rafts are known to form upon antigen binding [54-57], whereas in resting B cells lipid rafts are small and transient.

b. Simulating lipid mediated interactions and formation of BCR-lipid rafts

i. BCR-antigen binding is simulated by the probabilistic rate constant based kinetic Monte Carlo model. We couple the kinetic MC model with an explicit free-energy based model for lipid mediated interactions [58].

ii. In the explicit free-energy based model, we simulate BCR-BCR and BCR-lipid interactions through two energy-based parameters BB and BL. BB captures pairwise BCR-BCR interaction energy such as that is needed to form BCR oligomers. BL denotes the interaction between a BCR molecule and a raft-forming sphingolipid. We can increase the strength of those parameters upon antigen binding and follow the dynamics of BCR-BCR and BCR-lipid cluster formation. Variations in BB and BL parameters, which depend on the state of antigen binding, create a coupling between the implicit free-energy and explicit free-energy Monte Carlo models.

iii. For antigen bound BCRs, origin of large BB lies in the opening of the Cμ4 domains of BCRs upon antigen binding. As for increased BL (upon antigen binding), in addition to energetics and entropy, effects of membrane curvature can be important.

iv. Lipid-lipid interactions, such as one that arises due to hydrophobic mismatch, are captured by an energy-based parameter LL.

v. In resting B cells, Lyn is already in sphingolipid rich regions due to its dual acyl chains. We can explicitly simulate the spatial localization of Lyn kinase in sphingolipid rich regions through a KL parameter. When there is no antigen, BB and BL are small, and BCRs partition into non-raft regions of the membrane. Thus BCR and Lyn are segregated into distinct spatial regions in resting B cells. This provides a mechanism for inhibition of spontaneous activation in resting B cells.

vi. Antigen binding leads to enhanced BB and BL, generation of BCR-sphingolipid rafts, and co-localization of BCRs with signaling kinase Lyn. The delay in BCR-Lyn association, upon antigen binding, provides a key step in kinetic proofreading mechanism. Thus selective partitioning and recruitment of signaling molecules, in different spatial regions on the B cell membrane, emerge as a basis for kinetic proofreading. Interestingly, the requirement of kinetic proofreading time decreases with increasing affinity thus favoring increasingly higher affinity for antigens.

It becomes evident that Monte Carlo simulations can handle spatial heterogeneity and clustering, a key aspect of biological complexity, in a rigorous manner. In addition, complex regulatory mechanisms of B cell signaling, such as the signal transduction through distinct phosphorylation sites on Syk, can be incorporated in a Monte Carlo simulation. Monte Carlo method is also suitable for capturing stochastic effects that are unavoidable when antigen concentration is low. Such antigen limiting conditions might arise, for example, during the initial phase of an infection. Stochastic effects are also going to be important when BCR concentration is low, such as in pre-plasma cells. Moreover, Monte Carlo models can be used to probe the underlying biophysics of BCR-lipid raft domain formation (such as phase separation, scaling behavior in domain growth, and the nature of criticality).

5.2. Analysis of single cell data

Phosphorylation of BCR signaling chains (pBCR) and Syk (pSyk) are measured in our simulations as readouts for membrane proximal signaling. Each run of Monte Carlo simulations provide us activation data at the level of single cells and thus can be readily compared with data obtained from single cell experiments. Standard statistical measures, such as the average and the second moment (or standard deviation), can be calculated for relevant variables from many runs of the simulation. If simulation data for large number of runs is available, then the full probability distribution for a physical variable can be calculated and compared with experimental histograms obtained from, for example, flow cytometric measurements. In our analysis, probability distributions for pBCR (Figure 1) and pSyk are generated for various affinity values and affinity discrimination is obtained from the separation of probability distributions.

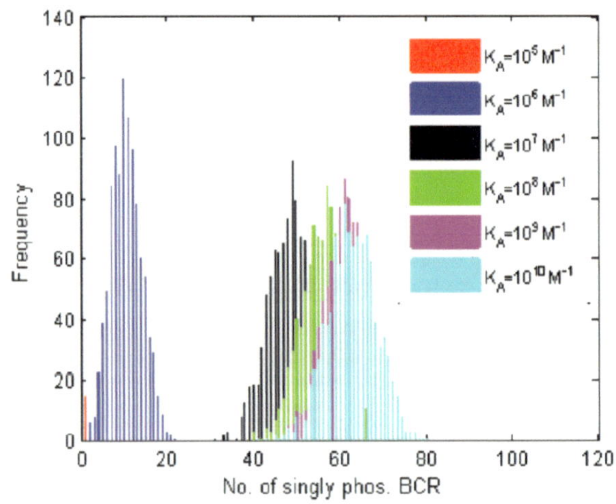

Figure 1. Histogram plots of the number of BCR molecules with at least one ITAM phosphorylated by Lyn (figure re-produced from our earlier published article in Journal of Theoretical Biology 2012;307: 174-182; reference [46]). Data from one thousand single cell runs were used (at t =, 10^5 MC step); simulation parameters are listed in Table 2 of [46]. The number of Lyn-phosphorylated BCRs, a measure of early-time membrane proximal signaling, increases with affinity.

We proposed the following metric that can be used to analyze the probability distributions obtained from simulation data and quantitatively characterize affinity discrimination: Δ = overlap area / ($m_1 - m_2$); the area of overlap between the histograms for two affinity values is divided by m_1 and m_2, the histograms' mean values for those two affinities. Lower Δ values correspond to better affinity discrimination, with the best discrimination occurring at Δ=0 (no overlap between histograms). When Δ=0, it becomes necessary to compare the mean values of the histograms. From Fig. 1, significant affinity discrimination is obtained even between affinity values $K_A = 10^8 M^{-1}$ and $K_A = 10^9 M^{-1}$ (Δ values are provided in Fig. 6 of reference [46]). The quantitative metric Δ can also be used to analyze single cell experimental data for B cell activation (such as the pSyk data in fig 8 in reference [42]).

5.3. Hybrid simulation methods

Our probabilistic rate constant based kinetic Monte Carlo method has the advantage that it can be coupled to other types of Monte Carlo or differential equation based models. Monte Carlo simulations can be computationally expensive, especially when large-scale intracellular signaling pathways are considered. For many such signaling pathways, presence of large number of molecules make stochastic fluctuations less significant and differential equation based approaches are often sufficient to describe such systems [24, 59]. It is also assumed that differential equation based approaches would be able to handle the biological complexity. Whether differential equation based models are valid descriptions also depends on the biological question one wants to address. In situations where membrane proximal events activate the downstream signaling, such as antigen binding mediated activation of B cell intracellular signaling pathways, spatial heterogeneity and other complexities might demand application of Monte Carlo type approaches for the membrane events but differential equations might be sufficient for describing the intracellular signaling processes. In such cases, a hybrid simulation method, which combines a Monte Carlo simulation with an ODE / PDE based model, can be an efficient modeling approach. We have developed two hybrid simulations in the context of studying B cell activation:

1. Modeling membrane deformation as a result of receptor-ligand binding: A time dependent Landau-Ginzburg type equation, which describes membrane shape fluctuations, was coupled to a probabilistic rate constant based kinetic MC model that simulates receptor-ligand binding dynamics. The most widespread approach for modeling membrane deformation due to receptor-ligand binding is based on modeling the free energy of the membrane as a function of receptor-ligand bond stretching and mechanical restitution forces [17, 20-23].The change in the local intermembrane membrane separation distance can be assumed to evolve (towards the free-energy minimum) according to a time-dependent Landau-Ginzburg formulation. A random noise term in the equation captures the effect of thermal fluctuations (variance of noise ~ K_BT). For the purpose of calculating local concentrations of receptor-ligand complexes, the membrane surface is discretized into square subdomains over which membrane separation remains approximately constant. The spatially averaged concentration of receptor-ligand complexes in each of these subdomains is then calculated from the kinetic Monte Carlo model and entered in the discrete form of the membrane equation [44-45]. In our Monte Carlo model, memebrane separation is updated at the end of each MC time step by solving the membrane equation.

2. Modeling lipid mediated interactions and BCR-lipid raft (microcluster) formation:Here, a kinetic MC model (for receptor-ligand binding) is linked to an explicit free-energy based MC model for lipid mediated interactions [58]. B cell receptors (BCRs) need to be modeled as a two-layer structure: (i) the bivalent Fab domains move in the first layer where it can bind monovalent antigens and (ii) the transmembrane part diffuse in the second layer with lipids and other proteins. Diffusion moves in this second layer is accepted / rejected based on an explicit free-energy based mechanism (such as the Metropolis scheme). Src family kinase Lyn is also simulated in a manner that can interact with lipids. The hybrid Monte Carlo simulation proceeds as follows:

i. At the beginning of the simulation, all the protein molecules and lipids are distributed uniformly and randomly on their respective 2d lattice grids. Any clustering of proteins and lipids emerges from our simulation and MC simulations are well suited to capture such spatial heterogeneity.

ii. Lipids are placed on a smaller sized lattice grid than that for protein molecules such as BCRs. Lipids, however, are going to be sampled n times more frequently than protein molecules (n is determined by relative diffusion). Diffusion constants for lipids and BCRs (or other proteins) will be used to set the time-step Δt of MC simulations. Lipid diffusion moves are determined by lipid-lipid and lipid-protein free energy of interactions.

iii. Diffusion of antigen molecules is carried out only with the constraint of mutual physical exclusion. Diffusion of BCRs, however, has additional free energy considerations arising from BCR-BCR and BCR-lipid interactions.

iv. Diffusion of Lyn molecules is also governed by free energy changes associated with Lyn's affinity to raft forming sphingolipids. Lyn prefers to cluster with spingolipids due to increased hydrophobicity caused by its doubly acylated (palmitoylation and myristoylation) form. We assume interdigitation between the two leaflets will allow Lyn to get associated with BCR-lipid raft domains [60].

v. It is technically challenging to simulate two disparate size objects (lipids and BCRs) on the same 2-dimensional lattice. Two possible ways to implement the simulation:

   a. One BCR and a significantly larger number of lipids will be placed on a relatively large lattice block (approximately, 20 nm x 20 nm). We assume the lone BCR in a lattice block will get a chance to interact with all other lipids in the same block through short-time ($<\Delta T$ of MC step) rotational/translational displacements.

   b. Another potential solution is to define BCR and lipids blocks (approximately 10 nm x 10 nm) on a 2-d lattice and allow exchange of blocks (Monte Carlo moves) in a manner that will (i) allow one BCR molecule to interact with several lipid molecules and (ii) satisfy detailed balance. Such an approximation is justified by noting that the relevant length scale of the problem, namely the size of generated raft domains (> 100 nm), is significantly larger than size of the unit blocks (~ 10 nm). A schematic of the simulation is provided on the right. Initial results from simulations of two distinct affinity values ($K_A = 10^7\ M^{-1}$ and $K_A = 10^9\ M^{-1}$) are shown in Fig 2.

The underlying physics of BCR-lipid raft formation is similar to the phase separation process in a two liquid system. BCRs and raft forming lipids can be treated as one type of liquid molecules that phase separates from other lipids and proteins. In the case of two liquids, phase separation is typically driven by a low temperature quench that initially drives the system out-of-equilibrium. Some aspects of the out-of-equilibrium dynamics (towards an equilibrium state) studied in the context of liquid-liquid phase separations [3] can be useful here. However, complexity of the BCR-lipid raft formation makes any simulation and its analysis more challenging. Here, antigen binding drives the system out of its steady state (small unstable rafts). As long as we do not consider any active processes, the problem of BCR-lipid raft formation can be considered as out-of-equilibrium dynamics towards an effective equilibrium state. BCRs are assumed to have significantly increased mutual attractive interactions (BB) upon antigen binding, presumably due to opening of the Cμ4 domains, introducing affinity into the problem of raft formation. As expected, the phase diagram is also affinity dependent elucidating the physical basis for early-time affinity discrimination in B cells.

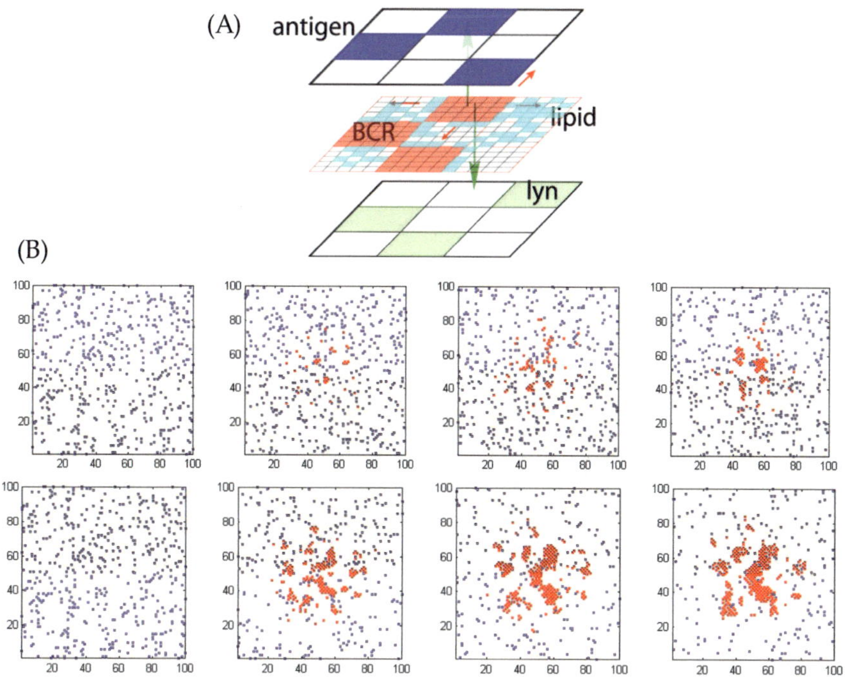

Figure 2. (A) Schematic of the BCR-lipid raft formation simulation. (B) Time-course of BCR-lipid raft formation is simulated for two affinity values, low affinity (top): $K_A = 10^7$ M^{-1} ($P_{on} = 10^{-3}$ and $P_{off}=10^{-6}$) and high affinity (bottom): $K_A = 10^9$ M^{-1} ($P_{on} = 10^{-2}$ and $P_{off}=10^{-7}$). Affinity discrimination has been studied experimentally for similar affinity values: $K_A = 9.9 \times 10^6$ M^{-1} (B1-8-Low antibody) and $K_A = 5.2 \times 10^8$ M^{-1} (B1-8-High antibody) for the antigen hapten NIP [42]. We use the following energy-based parameter values in our simulation: BB = 3.0, BL = 2.0 and LL = 2.0 (in K_BT); BB and BL values are for antigen bound BCRs. Both unbound (blue) and bound BCRs (red) are shown at the cell-cell contact region. Raft forming lipids (not shown) are co-clustered with the B cell receptors. Significantly larger amount of BCRs are clustered in the high affinity case.

5.4. Simulating B cell affinity discrimination: Role of spatial heterogeneity

Recent work by us and others have demonstrated that early time (~ 100 seconds) membrane proximal events, BCR oligomerization, BCR-lipid raft formation, and B cell immune synapse formation, hold the key to B cell affinity discrimination problem. BCR-lipid raft structures start forming within tens of seconds after antigen binding and precede the formation of B cell immune synapse (~ 100 seconds). Synaptic structure consists of a central cluster of BCR-antigen complexes surrounded by a peripheral ring of integrin complexes (LFA1 –ICAM1) [61-62]. Spatial clustering and heterogeneity, in the form of lipid rafts or immunological synapses, presumably modulate serial activation (serial triggering) and kinetic proofreading effects and determine the nature of affinity discrimination in B cells. It is apparent that Monte Carlo models can capture the relevant details of spatial clustering and spatial heterogeneity, even when antigen or receptor concentration is low. We discussed how to combine implicit and explicit free energy MC models in a hybrid simulation scheme to simulate BCR-lipid raft formation. Detailed method for simulating B cell immune synapses can be found in our earlier work [36, 43-44]. We showed that, a directed transport (of antigen bound receptors) based mechanism is needed for synaptic pattern formation, as the size difference between BCR-antigen (at least for IgM) and integrin complexes is not significant. Further work needs to done that can link BCR-lipid raft formation to immunological synapse formation in B cells. Whether affinity dependent signaling through rafts, as found in our simulations, can generate an affinity dependent directed transport mechanism remains to be explored.

6. Systems biology of apoptotic cell death signaling

Programmed cell death, apoptosis, is one of the most important cellular processes. Apoptotic death is critical to a wide variety of cellular and physiological phenomena ranging from the normal development of multicellular organisms to maintaining homeostasis [63-64]. Dysregulated apoptosis has been implicated in a large number of diseases including in cancer and degenerative disorders. Targeting the apoptosis pathway is emerging as a new frontier in the therapeutic approaches for those diseases. Large number of signaling species and an intricate network structure generate complexity in the apoptotic cell death signaling pathway and make any computational study of apoptosis a challenging task. Apoptosis pathway has evolved to sense and respond to a wide variety of stimuli through structurally similar signaling molecules having similar pro- or anti- apoptotic functions. The system level regulation of apoptosis signaling is achieved through a loop network structure that combines two distinct pathways known as Type 1 (extrinsic) and Type 2 (intrinsic or mitochondrial) pathways (Figure 3). In addition, several smaller loop network structures exist within the Type 2 pathway that seem capable of generating nonlinear effects in the signaling response. Such loop networks are different from well studied feed forward and feed back loops that are frequently encountered in signaling pathways. Additional complexity in the apoptotic pathway arises due to the formation of multi-molecular complex apoptosome. Translocation of pro- and anti- apoptotic proteins to the mitochondrial membrane, such as that happen for activated Bax dimers, generate spatial heterogeneity in the system.

6.1. Monte Carlo model for the apoptosis signaling pathway

We developed a fairly detailed Monte Carlo model to study the systems biology of apoptotic cell death signaling [65]. We simulate a single cell using a cubic lattice in which all the molecules were placed at different nodes of the lattice. Membrane bound molecules such as the death inducing signaling complex (DISC) are confined to one surface of the cubic box and allowed to diffuse only in two dimensions. Intracellular signaling molecules are allowed to diffuse inside the cubic box when they are in free state; multi-molecular complexes are assumed to be immobile.

We simulate the signaling network shown in Fig. 3. Our model considers apoptotic signaling through two distinct pathways: direct activation of caspase 3 by caspase 8 (type 1) and activation of caspase 3 through mitochondrial cytochrome c release and apoptosome formation (type 2) (Fig. 3). In our model, intracellular apoptosis signalling was triggered by the activation of caspase 8 molecules (at the cell surface) that, in turn, diffused in the cytosol and activated both pathways of apoptosis signaling. In the type 1 pathway, caspase 8 molecules directly catalyze the cleavage reaction of procaspase 3 to generate active form of caspase 3. In the type 2 pathway, caspase 8 binds with Bid and catalyzes its truncation to form tBid that, in turn, binds to Bax to generate Bax2 homodimers. Bcl2, an antiapoptotic molecule, can inhibit both tBid and Bax, thus creates a local loop structure in the type 2 signaling cascade. Formation of the active Bax2 complex leads to cytochrome c release from mitochondria and formation of multi-molecular Cytochorme c-Apaf1-ATP complex apoptosome, which ultimately induces activation of caspase 3. Hence, caspase 3 activation at the end of both the type 1 and the type 2 pathways creates a global loop structure in apoptosis signaling. Values for kinetic rate constants and molecular concentrations are taken from previous measurements (and/or used in previous theoretical studies) [66-69].

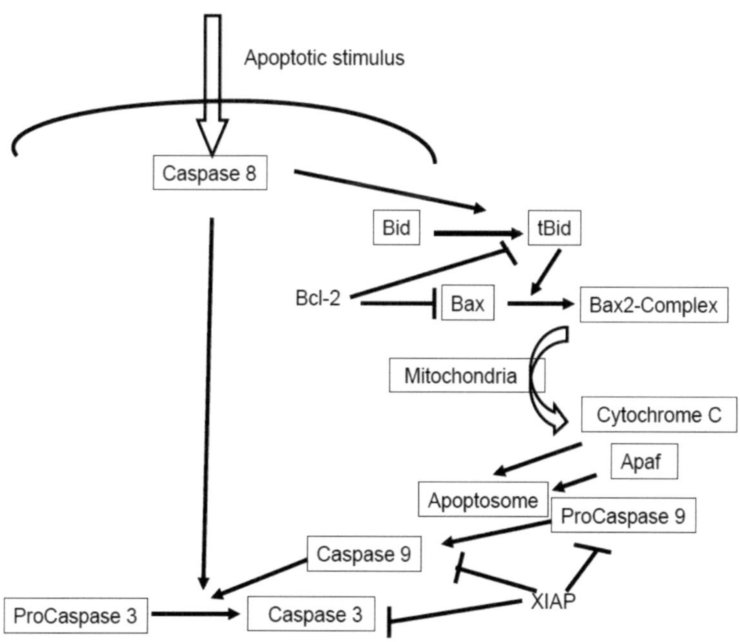

Figure 3. Schematic of a simplified signalling network for the apoptotic cell death pathway.

6.2. Simulation code for apoptosis signaling

We define several generalized functions to carry out diffusion or reaction moves. Those functions are called when a molecule is randomly sampled and a MC move (diffusion or reaction) is attempted. Separate diffusion functions are defined depending on, for example, whether a molecule is diffusing in the intracellular space (within cytosol) or on the mitochondrial surface. Similarly, separate functions are assigned for distinct reaction types such as for binding and unbinding reactions. When a given molecule is known to stay bound with more than one molecule (of the same type or different types), we assign multiple binding sites for that molecule. Ability to bind to multiple partners (at the same time) allows us to simulate oligomeric complexes such as the apoptosome. At each MC time step, N random sampling of molecules are carried out, where N is the total number of molecules in the system; hence, on average one molecule is sampled once within a MC time step. We define separate functions for each molecular species. Once a molecule is randomly chosen, diffusion or reaction move is attempted by calling the function for that molecule. As an example, we provide the function for Caspase 8 molecule in the Appendix.

Simulating the type 2 pathway can be computationally expensive due to the presence of low probability reactions, such as the Bid-Bax reaction or the formation of apoptosome. One potential modification to improve the speed of the simulation is to partition the signaling network into groups of fast and slow reactions and then sample the slow reactions less frequently than the fast reactions [70-71].

6.3. *In silico* experiments of apoptosis signaling

We wanted to study the mechanism of system level regulations in apoptosis signaling. In silico experiments were designed to address the following biological question: how do the two distinct apoptotic pathways get activated? A related question is why two very distinct time-scales are observed in biological experiments of apoptosis [72]. In order to address these questions we designed three sets of experiments

- **i.** Study the type 1 pathway only (set the rate constant for the type 2 pathway to zero).
- **ii.** Study the type 2 pathway only (set the rate constant for the type 1 pathway to zero).
- **iii.** Keep both the pathways open for activation but vary the strength of apoptotic stimuli (by varying the level of pro-caspase 8 or caspase 8).

One of the advantages of the Monte Carlo simulation approach is that clean experiments can be carried out *in silico*, such as selective activation of one of the two pathways of apoptosis (by simply setting the rate constant for other pathway to zero) to study its signaling behavior. In silico experiments revealed some of the fundamental regulatory mechanisms in apoptosis biology [65].

Pure type 1 activation: For the type 1 pathway, population averaged (over many cells) activation data could capture the fast (seconds – minutes) caspase 3 activation observed for all the cells in our simulations. Decreasing strength of stimuli, i.e. decreasing caspase 8 concentrations, leads to slower activation of caspase 3 (Figure 4A). Stochastic fluctuations are starting to be seen for very low (< nanomolar) caspase 8 concentrations.

Pure type 2 activation: In contrast to type 1 behavior, caspase 3 activation in individual cell simulations for type 2 showed slow activation with large cell-to-cell stochastic variability. Such stochastic variability in type 2 apoptosis activation was characterized by all-or-none type activation (of capsase 3) at the level of single cells with large variability in the activation time (minutes – hours) (Figure 4B). Stochastic fluctuations in type 2 activation is caused by (i) Bcl2 inhibition of tBid-Bax reaction and (ii) low probability of apoptosome formation. When caspase 8 concentration is low, stochastic fluctuations are more pronounced due to additional stochastic variability arising from the reaction Bid truncation to tBid. Population average (over many cells) behavior cannot capture the all-or-none type rapid caspase 3 activation observed at the level of single cells. Also note, the information of the strength of apoptotic stimuli is lost at the level of single cell capsase3 activation, but could be captured by the probability distribution of the time-scale of caspase 3 activation.

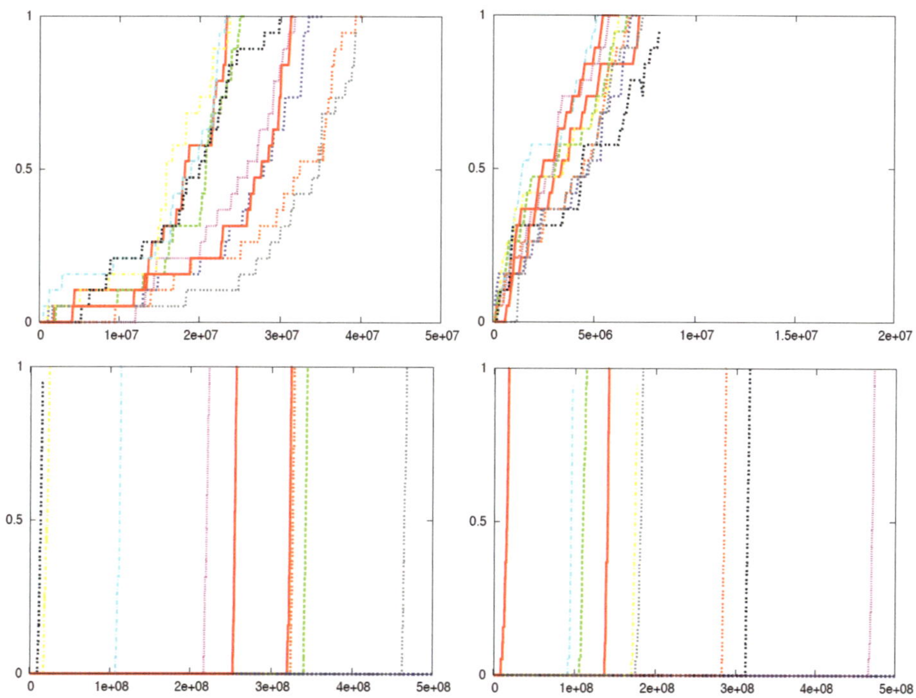

(A) (B)

Figure 4. Time course of caspase 3 activation, as readout for apoptotic activation, is shown for single cells. Data is shown for simulation of the pure type 1 activation (4A) and the pure type 2 activation (4B). 1 Monte Carlo step = 10^{-4} sec. Normalized data is shown for caspase-8 = 1 (left) and caspase-8 = 10 (right). Nano-molar concentration is obtained by multiplying the number of molecules with 1.67. Data is shown for 10 individual single cell runs. Data is similar to our earlier published result (Figure 2) in Biophysical Journal 2008;95: 3559-3562 [65].

Combined type 1 and 2 activation: Under weak apoptotic stimuli, such as for very low concentrations of active caspase 8, stronger binding affinity between caspase 8 and Bid, compared with that between caspase 8 and pro-caspase 3 in the type 1 pathway, leads to selective activation of the type 2 pathway with its characteristic slow activation and large cell-to-cell variability (as seen in pure type 2 activation). Clearly, the all-or-none type behavior in caspase 3 activation, and its rapid completion, shows that the type 2 pathway is designed to amplify an initially weak signaling. However, type 1 activation (accompanied by partial activation of the type 2 pathway) is observed in our simulations, even for low caspase 8 concentrations, if the following conditions are met: [1] active caspase 3 can feedback its activation by directly activating caspase9, (ii) Xiap is inhibited by Smac released in the type 2 pathway, (iii) rate of multi-molecular complex apoptosome formation is very slow. How these cellular factors impact the value of caspase 8 at which the type2 → type 1 transition occurs (depending on the cell type) needs to be explored further. For example, presence of apoptosome inhibiting anti-apoptotic proteins in certain cell types (such as neuroglobin in neural cells [73]) and the cytosolic condition (such as the oxidative condition or the pH level) would affect the rate of apoptosome formation and hence type 2 activation. For strong apoptotic stimuli, large number of available caspase 8 molecules (even after binding with Bid) directly binds and activates pro-caspase 3 to active capsase 3 in a fast deterministic manner. For intermediate strength of apoptotic stimuli, initial slow and gradual activation of capsase 3 through the type 1 pathway can suddenly change to a mode of rapid activation through the type 2 pathway (once the apoptosome has formed). Time-scale of apoptotic activation, as emerges from our single cell simulations, is comparable to that observed in biological experiments. Better estimates can be obtained as quantitative information for the kinetic rate constants and the expression levels of signaling proteins are gathered.

Thus, *in silico* experiments reveal a unique system level design mechanism for apoptosis signaling; weak apoptotic stimuli activates the type 2 pathway in a slow stochastic manner, whereas under strong stimuli the type 1 pathway gets activated in a fast deterministic manner. We also used a minimal network based approach, to provide further insight into the fundamental design mechanism of apoptosis signaling, and to demonstrate robustness of some of our results [74]. Previously it was thought that DISC (death-inducing-signaling-complex) formation and caspase 8 activation could lead to activation of either the type 1 or the type 2 pathway in a cell type intrinsic manner; cells were labeled either as a type 1 cell or as a type 2 cell depending on their mode of activation [72]. More recent observations, however, indicate that both the pathways can be activated irrespective of cell types [75], as observed in our earlier Monte Carlo studies [65] and clearly elucidated by a minimal network based analysis [74]. Cell type specificity (in type 1 / type 2 choice) arises from differential expression of death receptors in different cell types [75], which presumably modulates the activation level of caspase 8, a key determinant of type2-type1 switch [65,72,74-75]. Whether variations in the concentration of death ligands, even when the death receptor expressions are comparable, can determine the mode of activation (type 1 or type 2), needs to be investigated. Additional complexities (in type 1 / type 2 choice) are generated due to, for example, variations in cellular protein levels such as the Xiap concentration (depending on cell types and cellular conditions) [69]. Lipid mediated interactions can also be important in determining the cell type specificity of type 1 / type 2 choice in apoptosis signaling. These additional complexities are currently being incorporated into our Monte Carlo model. Stochastic type 2 to deterministic type 1 transition has important ramifications for cancer biology and cancer therapy [76] and will be discussed further in the next section.

6.4. Analysis of single cell simulation data for apoptosis signaling

Probability distributions, such as that for activated caspase 3, are obtained from many runs of single cell simulations. Interestingly, probability distributions for type 1 and type 2 signaling show two distinct functional behaviors. For signaling through the type 1 pathway, probability distribution shows a single peak that shifts towards larger caspase 3 value as time increases. The value of caspase 3 corresponding to the peak of the probability distribution indicates the average level of caspase 3 activation. For type 2 signaling, large cell-to-cell variability coupled with rapid all-or-none type activation of caspase 3 leads to a bi-modal distribution [65].

Assuming a perfect bi-modal distribution for caspase 3, the ratio variance/average for capsase 3 activity can be estimated by the metric C3[1-f(e,t), where C3 is the initial number of pro-caspase 3 molecules and f(e,t) is the fraction of cells in which caspase 3 has undergone complete activation within a given time t [77-78]. Another quantitative measure that can be used to assess the single cell variability in apoptotic activation is cell-to-cell variability in time-to-death. Such a quantitative measure is also useful in estimating the relative contributions of inherent stochastic variability and stochastic variability arising from cellular variations in protein levels. Cellular variability in protein levels can arise due to genetic and/or epigenetic variations. Stochastic gene expression can also generate cellular variability in protein levels.

7. Applications of Monte Carlo simulation in systems biology and systems medicine

Systems level approaches can be utilized to study complex biological processes and have been increasingly used in the recent past. Additional impetus to develop such systems level models comes from the recent generation of large amount of biological data and an urgent need for systems level computational models that are capable of analyzing this huge amount of biological data. Monte Carlo models are suitable for handling large number of degrees of freedom in a system and it is becoming an essential tool in systems biology. Monte Carlo simulations could capture the following key aspects of a biological process: (i) stochastic variability, (ii) spatial heterogeneity, and (iii) biological complexity (as demonstrated for the problems discussed in the previous section). For a class of systems biology problems that do not require consideration of free energy, instead a coarse-grained phenomenological approach is more appropriate, suitable kinetic Monte Carlo simulations can be developed for such systems. Examples of such problems would include multi-cell simulations in a tissue, and, some of the diffusion and trafficking problems in biology (such as trafficking of immune cells). Probabilistic rate constants that need to be used in such type of Monte Carlo models can be extracted from biological data. For problems in systems biology, Monte Carlo technique can also be used for rapidly carrying out parametric variation study once the MC model has been calibrated against experimental data. Such parametric variation analysis is also essential in cases where the kinetic rate constants are only approximately known.

7.1. Cancer biology and cancer therapy: Insights from Monte Carlo studies

Modeling diseases, as well as designing therapeutic approaches, is an area where systems level approaches and Monte Carlo simulation will become increasingly important. As a prominent example, here, we discuss the impact of systems level computational modeling in cancer biology and cancer therapy. It is now established that a hallmark of cancer is loss of apoptotic regulation in cancerous cells (along with aberrant growth signaling). Thus it is expected that the system level regulatory mechanisms and cell-to-cell stochastic variability in apoptosis, as emerged from recent studies by us and other labs, will have significant ramifications in cancer biology. Major findings from our Monte Carlo modeling of apoptosis and cancer are summarized below.

Bcl-2 overexpression increases cell-to-cell stochastic variability in apoptotic activation: This is an example of parametric variation study that can be carried out using Monte Carlo simulations. Increase in Bcl-2 concentration leads to increasing inhibition of both tBid and Bax, and leaves only a few number of available reactant molecules for the tBid-Bax reaction; such low reactant concentrations generates stochastic fluctuations and slow activation in the pre-mitochondrial signaling module of the type 2 pathway. In addition, simulation results indicate non-linear effect of Bcl-2 variation due to its simultaneous inhibition of tBid and Bax through the tBid-Bax-Bcl2 loop network. Such slow activation of the death pathway under Bcl-2 inhibition, as well as its non-linear effect, explains apoptosis resistance of cancer cells equipped with higher levels of Bcl-2 proteins [77]. Bcl-2 over-expression has been observed in a variety of cancer cells and is a marker for poor prognosis [79-80]. Increase in cell-to-cell variability in apoptotic activation, due to increased expression of Bcl-2, might allow a normal cell (out of many such cells) that is particularly slow to activate the apoptotic pathway to acquire tumor initiating features. In a similar manner, a cancer cell equipped with higher Bcl-2 level might acquire additional mutations to generate a more malignant genetic subclone.

A low probability Bid-Bax reaction can allow selective killing of cancer cells: Finding the mechanisms for inducing selective apoptotic death of cancer cells, which would leave normal cells unharmed, can be key to designing successful anti-cancer therapy. Monte Carlo models can simulate activation of the apoptotic death pathway, under the action of a chemotherapeutic agent (such as a Bcl-2 inhibitor), for both (i) normal cells and (ii) cancer cells. Such simulations can provide information regarding specificity (selective killing of cancer cells); simulation results can also be used to determine the optimal dose for a specific anti-cancer agent. We have studied the mechanism of BH3 mimetic Bcl-2 inhibitors that are considered as potential anti-cancer agents [81-82]. Monte Carlo simulations indicate a low-probability for the direct Bid-Bax type reaction could allow selective killing of cancer cells, which are presumably equipped with higher levels of Bid and Bax molecules, under the action of a Bcl-2 inhibitor (Figure 5). Such a low probability Bid-Bax reaction is also a mechanism for generating cell-to-cell variability in apoptotic activation and highly relevant for apoptotic death of cancer cells.

http://dx.doi.org/10.5772/53709

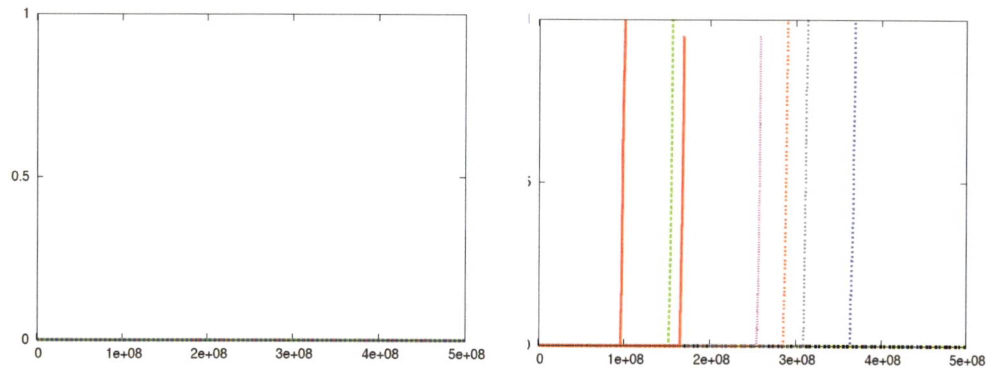

Figure 5. Apoptotic activation, under the action of 3 μm HA14-1 (a BH3 mimetic Bcl-2 protein inhibitor [77-78]) is shown for normal (left) and cancer (right) cells. Time course of caspase 3 activation, as readout for downstream apoptotic activation, is shown for single cells. 1 Monte Carlo step = 10^{-4} sec. Nano-molar concentration is obtained by multiplying the number of molecules with 1.67. Data is shown for 10 individual single cell runs (only a fraction of cells show activation within the given simulation time).

Simultaneous inhibition of Bcl-2 and Xiap in cancer therapy: This is an example of applying systems level computational approaches in designing cancer therapy. A key challenge that cancer therapy needs to address is the issue of cell-to-cell stochastic variability in apoptotic death of cancer cells. Cell-to-cell variability is linked to the apoptosis resistance of cancer cells and modulated by key anti-apoptotic proteins such as Bcl-2 (pre-mitochondrial) and Xiap (post-mitochondrial). Thus combinatorial targeting of the apoptotic pathway at different signaling modules can be a novel strategy in cancer therapy, and, systems level approaches can elucidate potential options. We carried out Monte Carlo simulations of apoptotic activation for various combinations of Bcl-2 and Xiap inhibitor concentrations. Such a study can provide us with an estimate of optimal inhibitor concentrations for reducing (i) cell-to-cell stochastic variability (in the type 2 pathway) and (ii) toxicity to healthy cells [78].

7.2. Systems level Monte Carlo modeling: a tool to determine optimal strategies in cancer therapy

Monte Carlo simulation is a tool to determine optimal strategies to perturb the apoptotic network at a system level; controlled Monte Carlo experiments of cancer cell death can be carried out *in silico*. The following key issues needs be addressed:

1. How to maximize specificity (maximize selectivity for cancer cells and minimize toxicity to healthy cells)
2. How to minimize inherent cell-to-cell variability
3. Compare various potential options

Our recent studies indicate that a stochastic to deterministic transition can be achieved selectively for cancer cells, which are equipped with over-expressed pro-apoptotic proteins, in the type 2 pathway of apoptosis. Alternatively, switching the activation from type 2 to type 1 can also lead to deterministic activation of the apoptotic pathway (in cancer cells), as revealed by our earlier systems level studies of apoptosis signaling. In both cases, inherent cell-to-cell variability would protect normal cells from harmful toxicity. Cell-to-cell stochastic fluctuations in the type 2 pathway can also be exploited to protect cells in degenerative disorders. In cancer therapy, it is also important to compare among various possible options and the optimal strategy might depend on the cancer type under consideration. For example, type 2 to type 1 transition in TRAIL resistant cancer cells can be achieved by hedgehog inhibition [76] or possibly by a Xiap inhibitor. Monte Carlo simulations can be carried out for various possible options to determine the optimal one.

Appendix

Simulation code for 2-dimensional random walk

```
/* diffusion2D.c simulates a random walk in 2 dimensions using Monte Carlo method

#include <stdio.h>
#include <stdlib.h>
#include <math.h>
#include <time.h>


#define NUM_RUNS 10000  // number of runs for the random walk (to generate distinct random walk trajectories)
#define TIME 1000  // Monte Carlo time-step over which the simulation is run
#define L 1000 // lattice spacings ~ 10 nm  => 100 lattice size = 1000 nm
#define Molecule_Total 10  // total number of moleucles / particles / agents in the system



main()     // the main program
{

        double r;
        int nx,ny,mx,my;
        int count,run,molecule,trial,move,pick;

        int up(int),down(int);

        int coor[L+1][L+1];
        int Xcor[Molecule_Total+1],Ycor[Molecule_Total+1];
        int Xcorinitial[Molecule_Total+1],Ycorinitial[Molecule_Total+1];

        int rsquaredisplace[TIME+1],xdisplace[TIME+1],ydisplace[TIME+1];

        FILE *fp1, *fopen();  // open a file

        srand (time(NULL));  // the seed for the rundom number generator is calculated using the current time

        /* initialize rsquaredisplace to zero */
        for (count=1;count<=TIME;count++){
          rsquaredisplace[count] = 0;
          xdisplace[count] = 0;
          ydisplace[count] = 0;
        }


        for(run=1;run<=NUM_RUNS;run++){  // runs for different realizations of random walks
          printf("run: %d\n", run);  // print to screen - number of runs

          /*  initially none of the sites are occupied */
          for(nx=1;nx<=L;nx++){
                    for(ny=1;ny<=L;ny++){
                              coor[nx][ny] = 0;  // keep track if a site is occupied
                    }
          }
```

http://dx.doi.org/10.5772/53709

```
/* assign initial x and y coordinates to molecules */
        molecule = 1;
        while (molecule <= Molecule_Total){
                nx = 1 + rand() % L;
                ny = 1 + rand() % L;

                if(coor[nx][ny] != 1){  // occupy only when site is open
                        Xcor[molecule] = nx;
                        Ycor[molecule] = ny;
                        Xcorinitial[molecule] = nx;
                        Ycorinitial[molecule] = ny;
                        coor[nx][ny] = 1;  // assign coor[][] = 1 if there is a molecule
                        molecule = molecule + 1;
                }
        }


for(count= 1; count<= TIME; count++){   // loop over total time (MC steps)


        for(trial=1;trial<= Molecule_Total;trial++){  // In one MC step --> number of attempts to move = number of molecules


                        pick = 1 + rand() % Molecule_Total;     // picking up a molecule randomly
                        /* coordinates of "pick" molecule */
                        mx = Xcor[pick];
                        my = Ycor[pick];


                        move = 1 + rand() % 4;  // generates a number between 1 and 4

                        switch (move) {

                        case 1:   // attempt to move down

                        if (coor[mx][down(my)] != 1){  // check if down(my) is not already occupied => accept move

                                        Xcor[pick] = mx;
                                        Ycor[pick] = down(my);
                                        coor[mx][my] = 0;
                                        coor[mx][down(my)] = 1;

                                }
                                break;


                         case 2:   // attempt to move up

                         if (coor[mx][up(my)] != 1){  // check if up(my) is not already occupied => accept move

                                        Xcor[pick] = mx;
                                        Ycor[pick] = up(my);
                                        coor[mx][my] = 0;
                                        coor[mx][up(my)] = 1;
                                }
                                break;
```

```
case 3:   // attempt to move left

if (coor[down(mx)][my] != 1){  // check if down(mx) is not already occupied => accept move

                Xcor[pick] = down(mx);
                Ycor[pick] = my;
                coor[mx][my] = 0;
                coor[down(mx)][my] = 1;
        }
        break;


case 4:   // attempt to move right

if (coor[up(mx)][my] != 1){  // check if up(mx) is not already occupied => accept move

                Xcor[pick] = up(mx);
                Ycor[pick] = my;
                coor[mx][my] = 0;
                coor[up(mx)][my] = 1;
        }
        break;
}


} // end loop over trial ~ 1 MC step



/* data analysis: mean displacement and mean square displacememnt */
for (molecule=1;molecule<= Molecule_Total;molecule++){
rsquaredisplace[count] = (Xcor[molecule]-Xcorinitial[molecule])*(Xcor[molecule]-Xcorinitial[molecule]) +
                (Ycor[molecule]-Ycorinitial[molecule])*(Ycor[molecule]-Ycorinitial[molecule]) + rsquaredisplace[count];
        xdisplace[count] = (Xcor[molecule] - Xcorinitial[molecule]) + xdisplace[count];
        ydisplace[count] = (Ycor[molecule] - Ycorinitial[molecule]) + ydisplace[count];
                }



        } // end loop over count ~ total time (MC steps)


    } // end loop over run



    /* writing data to an output file */
    fp1= fopen("diffuse2D.dat", "w");
    for(count=1; count<=TIME; count++){

fprintf(fp1,"%d %f %f
%f\n",count,(1.0*rsquaredisplace[count])/(NUM_RUNS*Molecule_Total),(1.0*xdisplace[count])/(NUM_RUNS*Molecule_Total),(1
.0*ydisplace[count])/(NUM_RUNS*Molecule_Total));
    }
    fclose(fp1);



}
```

http://dx.doi.org/10.5772/53709

```
/********************************* Function up (down) **************************************/

int up(m)

{
   int u;
   if (m >= L)
      u = L; // reflective boundary (no flux)
   else
           u = m + 1;
   return u;
}

int down(m)
{
   int d;
   if (m <= 1)
           d = 1; // reflective boundary (no flux)
   else
           d = m - 1;
   return d;
}

/*************************************************************************************************/
```

Caspase-8 function (Apoptosis cell signaling simulation)

```
/* Function for handling move when Casp8 is chosen */
   void Casp8function(int w){

        int partner;
        if (randNum(1) < .5){ // reaction move is chosen
          if ((*MOLECULES)[w].status == UNBOUND){ //if unbound, then bind to Bid or Caspase3
                  partner = generalBindingMove(w, Bid, Pon_Casp8_Bid, ProCasp3, Pon_Casp8_ProCasp3, 1);
                 /* The function generalBindingMove is for handling binding reaction moves */

                  if (partner==1) {
                          NumCasp8--;   // NumCasp8: counter for number of Caspase8 molecules
                          NumBid--;     // NumBid: number of Bid
                          NumCasp8Bid++;  // NumCasp8Bid: number of Caspase8-Bid complexes
                  } else if (partner==2) {
                          NumCasp8--;   // NumCasp8: number of Caspase8
                          NumProCasp3--;  // NumProCasp3: number of ProCaspase3
                          NumCasp8ProCasp3++; // NumCasp8ProCasp3: number of Caspase8-ProCaspase3 complexes
                  }

          } else   if ((*MOLECULES)[w].status == BOUND){ //if bound, then might dissociate or cleaves partner
                  int b = (*MOLECULES)[w].partner[1];

                  if ((*MOLECULES)[b].name == Bid){ //if bound to Bid
                          long double p = randNum(1);
                          if (p < Poff_Casp8_Bid){ //dissociates from Bid
                                  NumCasp8++;
                                  NumBid++;
                                  NumCasp8Bid--;
                                  unbindTwoMolecules(w,b);
                   /* The function unbindTwoMolecules is for handling unbinding reaction moves */
```

```
                    } else if (p < (Poff_Casp8_Bid + Pcat_Casp8_Bid )){ //cleaves Bid to tBid
                              (*MOLECULES)[b].name = tBid;
                              NumCasp8++;
                              NumtBid++;
                              NumCasp8Bid--;
                              unbindTwoMolecules(w,b);
                    }
          } else if ((*MOLECULES)[b].name == ProCasp3){ //if bound to ProCasp3
                    long double p = randNum(1);
                    if (p < Poff_Casp8_ProCasp3){ //dissociates from ProCasp3
                              NumCasp8++;
                              NumProCasp3++;
                              NumCasp8ProCasp3--;
                              unbindTwoMolecules(w,b);


                    } else if (p < (Poff_Casp8_ProCasp3 + Pcat_Casp8_ProCasp3 )){ //cleaves ProCasp3 to Casp3
                              (*MOLECULES)[b].name = Casp3;
                              NumCasp8ProCasp3--;
                              NumCasp3++;
                              NumCasp8++;
                              Type1++; // keep track of Type1 activation
                              unbindTwoMolecules(w,b);
                    }
          }
}

}else{ // diffusion move is chosen
          diffusionCytosol(w);
     }
}
```

Acknowledgements

The author acknowledges Somkanya C. Das (for Bid-Bax work in apoptosis) and Paul Yu-Yang (for BCR-lipid raft simulations in B cell affinity discrimination). Work carried out by former lab members and rotation students is also acknowledged.

Author details

Subhadip Raychaudhuri*

Address all correspondence to: raychaudhuri@ucdavis.edu, subraychaudhuri@gmail.com

Department of Chemistry, University of California, Davis, USA

References

[1] Gardiner CW. Handbook of stochastic methods for Physics, Chemistry and the Natural Sciences. Berlin Hydelberg: Springer-Verlag; 1990.

[2] Binder K and Heermann DW. Monte Carlo Simulation in Statistical Physics. Berlin Hydelberg: Springer; 2002 .

[3] Newman MEJ and Barkema GT. Monte Carlo Methods in Statistical Physics. Oxford: Oxford University Press; 1999.

[4] Frenkel D, Smit B. Understanding molecular simulation. Burlington, MA, USA: Academic Press; 2001.

[5] Metropolis N, Rosenbluth AW, Rosenbluth MN, Teller AH, Teller E. Equations of state calculations by fast computing machines. J ChemPhys 1953;21: 1087-1092.

[6] Hastings WK. Monte Carlo sampling methods using Markov chains and their applications. Biometrika 1970;57: 97-8.

[7] Barabasi AL, Stanley HE. Fractal concepts in surface growth. Cambridge, UK: Cambridge University Press; 1995.

[8] Halpin-Healy T, Zhang YC. Kinetic roughening phenomena, stochastic growth directed polymers and all that. Amsterdam, Holland: Elsevier; 1995.

[9] Raychaudhuri S, Cranston M, Przybyla C, Shapir Y. Maximal height scaling of kinetically growing surfaces. Phys Rev Lett 2001, 87:136101.

[10] Schehr G, Majumdar SN. Universal asymptotic statistics of maximal relative height in one-dimensional solid-on-solid models. Phys Rev E 2006;73: 056103.

[11] Vézian S, Natali F, Semond F, Massies J. From spiral growth to kinetic roughening in molecular-beam epitaxy of GaN(0001) Phys Rev B 2004;69: 125329.

[12] Chatterjee A, Vlachos DG. An overview of spatial microscopic and accelerated kinetic Monte Carlo methods. J Computer-Aided Mater Des 2007;14: 253–308.

[13] Kratzer P. Monte Carlo and kinetic Monte Carlo methods - a tutorial. Multiscale Simulation Methods in Molecular Sciences. In: J. Grotendorst, N. Attig, S. Blugel, D. Marx (eds.), Institute for Advanced Simulation, ForschungszentrumJulich, NIC Series, 2009. Vol. 42, p51-76.

[14] Caspersen KJ, Liu D-J, Bartelt MC, Stoldt CR, Layson AR, Thiel PA and Evans JW. Nanostructure Formation and Relaxation in Metal(100) Homoepitaxial Thin Films: Atomistic and Continuum Modeling. In: Curtiss LA, Gordon MS (eds.) Computational Materials Chemistry. Netherlands: Springer; 2005; p91-124,

[15] Juvenil S. Filho O, Tiago, Oliveira J, Redinz JA. Surface and bulk properties of ballistic deposition models with bond breaking. http://arxiv.org/pdf/1208.1547v1.pdf (2012).

[16] Guo C, Levine H. A statistical mechanics model for receptor clustering. Biophys J 2000;26: 219-234.

[17] Weikl TR, Lipowsky R. Pattern formation during T-cell adhesion. Biophys J 2004;87: 3665-3678.

[18] Monks CR, Freiberg BA, Kupfer H, Sciaky N, Kupfer A. Three-dimensional segregation of supramolecular activation clusters in T cells. Nature 1998;395: 82-86.

[19] Grakoui A, Bromley SK, Sumen C, Davis MM, Shaw AS, Allen PM, et al. The immunological synapse: A molecular machine controlling T cell activation. Science 1999;285: 221-227.

[20] Qi SY, Groves JT, Chakraborty AK. Synaptic pattern formation during cellular recognition. ProcNatlAcadSci USA 2001;98: 6548-6553.

[21] Burroughs NJ, Wülfing C. Differential segregation in a cell-cell contact interface: The dynamics of the immunological synapse. Biophys J 2002;83: 1784-1796.

[22] Raychaudhuri S, Chakraborty AK, Kardar M. Effective membrane model of the immunological synapse. Phys Rev Lett 2003;91: (208101-1)-(208101-4).

[23] Coombs D, Dembo M, Wofsy C, Goldstein B. Equilibrium thermodynamics of cell-cell adhesion mediated by multiple ligand-receptor pairs. Biophys J 2004;86: 1408-1423.

[24] Lee KH, Dinner AR, Tu C, Campi G, Raychaudhri S, Varma R, et al. The immunological synapse balances T cell receptor signaling and degradation. Science 2003;302: 1218-1222.

[25] Hammer D and Apte S. Simulation of cell rolling and adhesion of surfaces in shear flow: general results and analysis of selectin mediated neutrophil adhesion. Biophys J 1991;63:35–57.

[26] Mahama PA and Linderman JJ. Monte Carlo simulations of membrane signal transduction events: effect of receptor blockers on G-protein activation. Ann Biomed Eng 1995;23: 299–307.

[27] Gillespie DT. Exact stochastic simulation of coupled chemical reactions. J PhysChem 1977;81:2340-2361.

[28] Gillespie DT. Stochastic simulation of chemical kinetics. Annu Rev PhysChem 2007;58 35-55

[29] Erban R, Chapman J, Maini PK. A practical guide to stochastic simulations of reaction-diffusion processes. http://xxx.lanl.gov/pdf/0704.1908 (2007).

[30] McAdams HH, Arkin A. It's a noisy business! Genetic regulation at the nanomolar scale. Trends Genet 1999;15:65-69.

[31] Ozbudak EM, Thattai M, Kurtser I, Grossman AD, van Oudenaarden A. Regulation of noise in the expression of single gene. Nat Genet 2002;31:69-73.

[32] Bortz AB, Kalos MH, Lebowitz JL. J Comp Phys 1975;17:10.

[33] Goldstein B, Faeder JR, Hlavacek WS. Mathematical and computational models of immune-receptor signaling. Nat Rev Immunol 2004;4:445-456.

[34] Raychaudhuri S, Tsourkas P, Willgohs E. Computational modeling of receptor-ligand binding and cellular signaling processes. In: Jue T (ed.) Handbook of Modern Biophysics, Volume I: Fundamentals. New York: Humana Press, 2009: 41-61.

http://dx.doi.org/10.5772/53709

[35] Nudelman G, Weigert M, Louzoun Y. In-silico cell surface modeling reveals mechanism for initial steps of B-cell receptor signal transduction. MolImmunol 46 (2009) 3141–3150.

[36] Tsourkas PK, Baumgarth N, Simon SI, Raychaudhuri S. Mechanisms of B cell synapse formation predicted by Monte Carlo Simulation. Biophys J 2007;92:4196-4208.

[37] Kouskoff V, Famiglietti S, Lacaud G, Lang P, Rider JE, et al. Antigens varying in affinity for the B cell receptor induce differential B lymphocyte responses, J Exp Med 1998;188: 1453-1464.

[38] Batista FD, Neuberger M. B cells extract and present immobilized antigen: Implications for affinity discrimination, EMBO J 2000;19: 513-520.

[39] Shih TA, Meffre E, Roederer M, Nussenzweig MC. Role of antigen receptor affinity in T cell-independent antibody responses in vivo. Nat Immunol 2002;3: 399-406.

[40] Shih TA, Meffre E, Roederer M, Nussenzweig MC. Role of BCR affinity in T cell dependent responses in vivo. Nat Immunol 2002;3: 570-575.

[41] Fleire SJ, Goldman JP, Carrasco YR, Weber M, Bray D, Batista FD. B cell ligand discrimination through a spreading and contracting response. Science 2006;312: 738-741.

[42] Liu W, Meckel T, Tolar P, Sohn HW, Pierce SK. Antigen affinity discrimination is an intrinsic function of the B cell receptor. J Exp Med 2010; 207: 1095-1111.

[43] Tsourkas PK, Longo M, and Raychaudhuri S. Monte Carlo study of single molecule diffusion can elucidate the mechanism of B cell synapse formation. Biophys J 2008; 95: 1118-1125.

[44] Tsourkas PK, Raychaudhuri S. Modeling of B cell synapse formation by Monte Carlo simulation shows that directed transport of receptors is a potential formation mechanism. Cell MolBioeng 2010; 3:256-268.

[45] Tsourkas PK, Raychaudhuri S. Monte Carlo investigation of diffusion of receptors and ligands that bind across opposing surfaces. Ann Biomed Eng. 2011; 39:427-442.

[46] Tsourkas PK, Das SC, Yu-Yang P, Liu W, Pierce SK, Raychaudhuri, S. Formation of BCR oligomers provides a mechanism for B cell affinity discrimination. Journal of Theoretical Biology 2012; 307:174-182.

[47] McKeithan TW. Kinetic proofreading in T-cell receptor signal-transduction, ProcNatlAcadSci USA 92 (1995) 5042–5046.

[48] Coombs D, Kalergis AM, Nathenson SG, Wofsy C, Goldstein B. Activated TCRs remained marked for internalization after dissociation from pMHC. Nat Immunol 2002; 3: 926-931.

[49] Kalergis AM, Boucheron N, Doucey MA, Palmieri E, Goyarts EC, Vegh Z. Efficient cell activation requires an optimal dwell-time of interaction between the TCR and the pMHC complex. Nat Immunol 2001;2: 229–234.

[50] Valitutti S, Lanzavecchia A. Serial triggering of TCRs: A basis for the sensitivity and specificity of antigen recognition. Immunol Today 1997;18: 299–304.

[51] Tolar P, Hanna J, Krueger PD, Pierce SK. The constant region of the membrane immunoglobulin mediates B cell-receptor clustering and signaling in response to membrane antigens. Immunity 2009;30: 44–55.

[52] Tolar P, Sohn HW, Liu W, Pierce SK. The molecular assembly and organization of signaling active B-cell receptor oligomers. Immunol Rev 2009;232: 34–41.

[53] Simons K, Ikonen E. Functional rafts in cell membranes. Nature. 1997;387: 569-572.

[54] Cheng PC, Dykstra ML, Mitchell RN, Pierce SK. A role for lipid rafts in B cell antigen receptor signaling and antigen targeting. J Exp Med. 1999;190(11): 1549-1560.

[55] Pierce SK. Lipid rafts and B-cell activation. Nat Rev Immun. 2002;2: 96-105.

[56] Gupta N, DeFranco AL. Visualizing lipid raft dynamics and early signaling events during antigen receptor-mediated B-lymphocyte activation. MolBiol Cell 2003;14: 432-444.

[57] Sohn HW, Tolar P, Pierce SK. Membrane heterogeneities in the formation of B cell receptor-Lyn kinase microclusters and the immune synapse. J Cell Biol 2008;182(2): 367-370.

[58] Yu-Yang PP. Development of a Monte Carlo Simulation of Early Events in B Cell Activation. PhD thesis. University of California Davis. 2012.

[59] Lauffenburger DA, Linderman JJ. Models for binding, trafficking and signaling. Oxford, England: Oxford University Press; 1993.

[60] Kusumi A, Koyama-Honda I, Suzuki K. Molecular dynamics and interactions for creation of stimulation-induced stabilized rafts from small unstable steady-state rafts. Traffic. 2004;5: 213-30.

[61] Batista FD, Iber D, Neuberger MS. B cells acquire antigen from target cells after synapse formation. Nature 2001;411: 489-494.

[62] Carrasco YR, Fleire SJ, Cameron T, Dustin ML, Batista FD. LFA- 1/ICAM-1 interaction lowers the threshold of B cell activation by facilitating B cell adhesion and synapse formation. Immunity 2004;20: 589-599.

[63] Gewies A. ApoReview Introduction to Apoptosis. 2003. http://www.celldeath.de/encyclo/aporev/aporev.htm.

[64] Green DR, Reed JC, editors. Apoptosis: Physiology and Pathology. Cambridge University Press; 2011.

[65] Raychaudhuri S, Willgohs E, Nguyen T-N, Khan EM, Goldkorn T. Monte Carlo simulation of cell death signaling predicts large cell-to-cell stochastic fluctuations through the type 2 pathway of apoptosis. Biophys J 2008;95:3559-62.

[66] Hua F, Cornejo MG, Cardone MH, Stokes CL, Lauffenburger DA. Effects of Bcl-2 Levels on Fas signaling induced caspase-3 activation: molecular genetic tests of computational model predictions. J Immunol 2005;175:985-995.

[67] Eising TH, Conzelman ED, Allgower F, Bullinger E, Scheurich P. Bistability analysis of a caspase activation model for receptor-induced apoptosis. J BiolChem 2004;279: 36892-36897.

[68] Bagci EZ, Vodovotz Y, Billiar TR, Ermentrout GB, and Bahar I. Bistability in apoptosis: roles of Bax, Bcl-2, and mitochondrial permeability transition pores. Biophys J 2006;90: 1546-1559.

[69] Sun X, Bratton SB, Butterworth M, MacFarlane M, and Cohen GM. 2002. Bcl-2 and Bcl-xL inhibit CD95-mediated apoptosis by preventing mitochondrial release of Smac/DIABLO and subsequent inactivation of x-linked Inhibitor-of-apoptosis protein. J BiolChem 277, 11345-11351.

[70] Samant A, Ogunnaike BA, Vlachos DG. A hybrid multiscale Monte Carlo algorithm (HyMSMC) to cope with disparity in time scales and species populations in intracellular networks. BMC Bioinformatics. 2007;8: 175.

[71] Burrage K, Tian T, Burrage P. A multi-scaled approach for simulating chemical reaction systems.ProgBiophysMolBiol 2004;85 (2-3):217-34.

[72] Scaffidi C, Fulda S, Srinivasan A, Friesen C, Li F, Tomaselli KJ, Debatin KM, Krammer PH, Peter ME. Two CD95 (APO-1/Fas) signaling pathways. EMBO J. 1998;17(6): 1675-87.

[73] Raychaudhuri S, Skommer J, Henty K, Birch N, Brittain T. Neuroglobin protects nerve cells from apoptosis by inhibiting the intrinsic pathway of cell death. Apoptosis 2010;15:401-11.

[74] Raychaudhuri, S. Minimal model of a signaling network elucidates cell-to-cell stochastic variability in apoptosis. PLoS One 2010; 5:e11930.

[75] Meng XW, Peterson KL, Dai H, Schneider P, Lee SH, Zhang JS, Koenig A, Bronk S, Billadeau DD, Gores GJ, Kaufmann SH. High cell surface death receptor expression determines type I versus type II signaling. J BiolChem 2011;286(41): 35823-33.

[76] Kurita S, Mott JL, Cazanave SC, Fingas CD, Guicciardi ME, Bronk SF, Roberts LR, Fernandez-Zapico ME, Gores GJ. Hedgehog inhibition promotes a switch from Type II to Type I cell death receptor signaling in cancer cells. PLoS One 2011;6(3): e18330.

[77] Skommer J, Brittain T, Raychaudhuri S. Bcl-2 inhibits apoptosis by increasing the time-to-death and intrinsic cell-to-cell variations in the mitochondrial pathway of cell death. Apoptosis 2010;15: 1223-1233.

[78] Skommer J, Das S, Nair A, Brittain T, Raychaudhuri S. Nonlinear regulation of commitment to apoptosis by simultaneous inhibition of Bcl-2 and XIAP in leukemia and lymphoma cells. Apoptosis 2011;16: 619-26.

[79] Letai A, Sorcinelli MD, Beard C, Korsmeyer SJ.Antiapoptotic Bcl-2 is required for maintenance of a model leukemia.Cancer Cell 2004;6: 241-249.

[80] Skommer J, Wlodkowic D, Deptala A. Larger than life: Mitochondria and the Bcl-2 family.Leuk Res 2007;31: 277-86.

[81] Letai A, Bassik MC, Walensky LD, Sorcinelli MD, Weiler S, Korsmeyer SJ. Distinct BH3 domains either sensitize or activate mitochondrialapoptosis, serving as prototype cancer therapeutics. Cancer Cell 2002;2: 183-192.

[82] Chonghaile TN, Letai A. Mimicking the BH3 domain to kill cancer cells.Oncogene. 2008;Suppl 1: S149-157.

Chapter 11

Detection of Breast Cancer Lumps Using Scattered X-Ray Profiles: A Monte Carlo Simulation Study

Wael M. Elshemey

Additional information is available at the end of the chapter

http://dx.doi.org/10.5772/52787

1. Introduction

The difference in the position of the main scattering peak of adipose and soft tissue has been utilized by many authors for the purpose of differentiating between healthy and malignant excised breast tissue samples. Evans et al 1991 [3] measured the x-ray scattering profiles of nineteen samples of healthy and diseased human breast tissues. They reported that while large differences were found in the shapes of scattered photon distributions between adipose and fibroglandular tissues, only small differences existed between carcinomas and fibroglandular tissue.

Kidane et al 1999 [2] measured the diffraction patterns of one hundred excised breast tissue samples. They found that breast tissue types could be characterized on the basis of the shape of scattered spectrum (from 1.0 to 1.8nm^{-1}) and the relative intensities of the adipose and fat free peaks at 1.1 and 1.6nm^{-1} respectively.

Poletti et al 2002a [4] found that the scattered photon distribution of healthy and cancerous breast tissues were considerably different. They also found differences in the scattered photon distributions of human breast tissue & breast equivalent materials. They pointed out that the scattered photon distribution of adipose tissue was similar to corresponding commercial breast-equivalent materials and that of glandular tissue was equivalent to water.

Using x-ray from a synchrotron, Ryan and Farquharson 2004 [5] showed the well documented differences between the scattering profiles of adipose and diseased (malignant) tissue while Castro et al 2004 [6] measured scattering distributions at six different sites in breast tissue sample and showed that the fat content decreased as the tumor infiltrated the tissue.

INTECH
open science | open minds

© 2013 The Author(s). Licensee InTech. This chapter is distributed under the terms of the Creative Commons Attribution License http://creativecommons.org/licenses/by/3.0), which permits unrestricted use, distribution, and reproduction in any medium, provided the original work is properly cited.

Geraki et al 2004 [7] presented averaged diffraction spectra of one hundred and twenty specimens of healthy and tumor breast tissue samples measured using Energy Dispersive X-ray Diffraction (EDXRD) system. Their averaged profiles clearly showed the characteristic diffraction peaks of adipose and fibrous tissues.

Ryan and Farquharson 2007 [8] presented averaged and smoothed x-ray scattering profiles of five different breast tissue classifications measured using an EDXRD system which also measured Compton scattering in order to provide additional information about the electron density of samples. The collected information was utilized by a proposed model that was capable to differentiate between malignant and non-malignant breast tissue samples.

Theodorakou and Farquharson 2008 [9] summarized a collection of contributions by different authors about the application of x-ray diffraction to breast tissue characterization.

Elshemey and Elsharkawy 2009 [10] presented a Monte Carlo simulation code capable of simulating x-ray scattering profiles from breast tissue samples, where breast tissue was considered as a mixture of two main components (e.g. adipose and glandular or adipose and cancer tissues). The Monte Carlo code inputs which resulted in the best fitted simulated profile to a measured profile of an excised breast tissue sample were used to identify and estimate the percentages of the two main breast tissue components in the measured sample.

Bohndiek et al 2009 [11] used an active pixel sensor x-ray diffraction (APXRD) system in order to measure scatter profiles from biopsy-equivalent samples of different compositions (from 100% fat to 100% fibrous tissue). The measured profiles were used to build a model that was capable of accurately predicting the fat content of a series of unknown samples.

Elshemey et al 2010 [12] evaluated the diagnostic capability of x-ray scattering parameters (the full width at half maximum FWHM and area under the x-ray scattering profile of breast tissue in addition to the ratio of scattering intensities $I_2 / I_1\%$ at 1.6 nm^{-1} to that at 1.1 nm^{-1} corresponding to scattering from soft and adipose tissues, respectively) for the characterization of breast cancer. They reported high sensitivity, specificity and diagnostic accuracy of the examined parameters for the probing of breast cancer in excised tissue samples.

In spite of the wide research work aiming to differentiate between healthy and malignant breast tissues in excised samples using the pronounced differences in their x-ray scattering profiles, yet performing a research work to investigate the applicability of this technique for the detection of breast cancer in a whole breast of a patient would probably face many difficulties: First, the data obtained from the small-sized excised breast tissue samples do not account for multiple scattering effects which would probably affect the shape of scattered photon distribution in case of whole breast of normal dimension. Second, it is not acceptable (for many known reasons) to perform test measurements directly on patients. Even if this were possible, still there will be a great difficulty in correlating the measured profiles to a specific histopathology in breast tissue. Third, an alternative approach may be performing research on breast phantoms. Unfortunately, the available breast phantom materials are only excellent in mimicking the attenuation properties of breast tissue rather than producing an x-ray scattered photon distribution equivalent to scattering from breast tissue [4]. Moreover, what would be the tissue-equivalent material that produces a scattered photon distribution similar to breast cancer?

For these reasons, the present work introduces Monte Carlo simulation of photon transport inside a model breast in the presence and in the absence of breast cancer lump as a suggested means to examine the possibility of characterizing breast cancer in patient breast using the angular distribution of scattered x-ray photons.

2. Theoretical background

At the energy range (15 to 40 keV) encountered in mammography [13, 14], an incident x-ray photon will interact with breast tissue either by photoelectric absorption, Compton (inelastic, incoherent) scattering or Rayleigh (elastic, coherent) scattering.

If photoelectric absorption takes place, the incident photon energy will be absorbed by bound atomic electrons leading to the removal of such photons from the incident beam. The attenuation of an x-ray beam in mammography is due to all three interaction processes.

For a biological sample of known composition, its mass attenuation coefficient μ/ρ can be approximately evaluated from the tabulated coefficients μ_i / ρ_i for the constituent elements according to the weighted average w_i of each element, where:

$$\frac{\mu}{\rho} = \sum_i \frac{w_i \mu_i}{\rho_i} \quad or \quad \mu = \rho . \sum_i \frac{w_i \mu_i}{\rho_i} \tag{1}$$

μ_i and ρ_i are respectively, the attenuation coefficient and density of element i, while μ and ρ are respectively, the linear attenuation coefficient and density of the biological sample [15].

If Compton scattering takes place, the incident photons will impart some of their energy to a loosely bound electron which then leaves the atom while incident photons will be deflected from its initial direction by a scattering angle θ. At low photon energies, incoherent scattering shows small angular variations compared to coherent scattering and as such it would not affect the characterization of tissues based on the angular distribution of coherently scattered photons [1].

The differential cross section of incoherent scattering including electron binding effects can be given as the product of Klein–Nishina differential cross section $d\sigma_{KN,e}/d\Omega$ (for Compton collision between a photon and a free electron) and the incoherent scattering function of an atom $S(x, Z)$ where $x = \sin(\theta/2)/\lambda$ is the momentum transfer variable, Z is the atomic number and λ is the wave length of incident photon. $S(x, Z)$ represents the probability that an atom will be raised to any excited or ionized state when a photon imparts a recoil momentum to an atomic electron. The differential cross section of a molecule for incoherent scattering determines the new direction of photon after incoherent scattering and can be written as:

$$\frac{d\sigma_{incoh,m}}{d\Omega} = \frac{d\sigma_{KN,e}}{d\Omega} S_m(x) = \frac{r_o^2}{2}(\frac{E^{/}}{E})^2(\frac{E^{/}}{E} + \frac{E}{E^{/}} + \cos^2\theta - 1) S_m(x) \quad (2)$$

Where $S_m(x)$ is the incoherent scattering function of a molecule; considering that atomic cross sections for incoherent scattering combine independently. *E & E′* are the energies of incident and scattered photons, respectively [10].

If Coherent scattering takes place, an incident photon will interact with bound atomic electrons where the struck electron is neither ionized nor excited as there is no energy transfer from the incident photon to the electron. The scattered photon attains a new direction with no loss of energy [9]. Coherent scattering is dominant over incoherent scattering at the energy range of mammography.

The differential coherent scattering cross-section per atom for unpolarized radiation determines the new direction of photon after coherent scattering and can be expressed approximately as:

$$\frac{d_a\sigma_{coh}}{d\Omega} = \frac{r_o^2}{2}\left(1+\cos^2\theta\right).\left[F(x,Z)\right]^2 \quad (3)$$

Where; r_o is the classical electron radius, θ is the photon scattering angle and,

$$\frac{r_o^2}{2}\left(1+\cos^2\theta\right) \quad (4)$$

is the energy independent Thomson differential cross-section per electron, $(d_e\sigma_T / d\Omega)$. The variable *F(x, Z)* is called the atomic form factor which is the sum of electronic form factors and represents the ratio of the amplitude of the coherently scattered radiation by an entire atom to that by a single free electron. The square of this form factor is the probability that Z electrons of the atom take up a recoil momentum, (*q*), without absorbing any energy. Similar to the incoherent scattering function of an atom *S(x, Z)*, the atomic form factor *F(x, Z)* also depends on the momentum transfer variable (*x*), defined before in this section [16].

When considering a molecule, the molecular coherent differential scattering cross-section can be utilized to calculate the scattered photons distribution and is given by:

$$\frac{d_m\sigma_{coh}}{d\Omega} = \frac{r_o^2}{2}\left(1+\cos^2\theta\right).F_m^2(x) \quad (5)$$

Where $F_m^2(x)$is the square of molecular form factor.

Due to the interference of photons after coherent scattering, the molecular form factors calculated using the independent atomic model employing the sum rule [17] are considerably different from the measured molecular form factors at low values of momentum transfer. Several authors have presented measured molecular form factors for a wide variety of biological tissues (17, 18, 19, 16, 20, 21).

The present work aims at examining the validity of characterizing breast cancer lumps in a breast model. This is based on the idea that the presence of a lump would result in an increase in the amplitude of the x-ray scattering peak due to soft tissue at 1.6 nm^{-1} relative to the breast adipose peak at 1.1 nm^{-1}. Moreover, it is expected that an increase in the size of the lump would result in more photons interacting with the lump and consequently an increase in the amplitude of the scattering peak at 1.6nm^{-1} relative to the 1.1 nm^{-1} peak. A linear dependence of the ratio of amplitudes of these two peaks on lump size would be considered a proper evidence of the validity of the suggested method.

A main challenge which faces the ability to characterize a breast lump in a normal breast using the proposed method would probably be the multiple scattering effects. Photons carrying more than one scattering event inside the breast would affect the expected angular distribution of photons exiting the breast. Fortunately, multiple scattering at mammographic energies is considerably low. Chan & Doi 1986 [22] showed that the mean number of interactions for an incident photon inside a water phantom strongly depended on incident photon energy and phantom thickness. They reported a mean number of interactions of 1.2 for photon energy of 15keV incident on a phantom of thickness 5cm in the direction of the beam. These conditions are comparable to those investigated in the present work. For a 20 cm phantom and 100 keV incident photon energy, Chan & Doi 1986 [22] reported a mean number of interactions equal to a maximum of 5.

3. Monte Carlo simulation

The present Monte Carlo simulation is a modification of older versions of the Monte Carlo simulations by Elshemey et al 1999 [23] and Elshemey and Elsharkawy 2009 [10]. All three versions represent a step by step tracing of the sampling procedures described in detail by Chan and Doi 1983 [24] with modifications in the algorithm in order to reach different simulation goals. Figure 1 shows a block diagram illustrating the main steps of the simulation algorithm used in this study.

The proposed setup includes a pencil beam of highly collimated monoenergetic photons of known energy (either 20 or 40keV) from a stationary source is allowed to fall on the center of a rectangular uncompressed model breast of fixed average dimension; a thickness of 6cm in the direction of the beam, a width of 18cm and a breadth of 8cm [25, 26]. A cubic model breast cancer lump centered in the direction of the beam may be also present. The size of the lump is selectable ranging from 0.1 up to 3cm^3, while the depth is either 2 or 4cm below the surface of breast. Similar to the work of Bohndiek et al 2008 [11] and Elshemey & Elsharkawy 2009 [10], pork muscle data is used to simulate breast cancer lump tissue [19, 27]. The attenuation coefficients for breast tissue and pork muscle are calculated using the sum rule from their elemental composition as shown in the theoretical background section. This work uses the elemental composition of breast tissue used by Peplow and Verghese 1998 [19] in the calculation of their tabulated molecular form factors (H 0.115, C 0.387 and O 0.498) with a breast tissue density of 0.960 g/cm^3. The elemental composition of pork muscle is obtained from Kosanetzky et al 1987 [1], (H 0.1, C 0.107, N 0.0275, O 0.75, Cl 7.8 x 10^{-4}) with a density of 1.066 g/cm^3. The data for Cl is not included in the calculation of the attenuation coefficient of pork muscle as its proportion is extremely low.

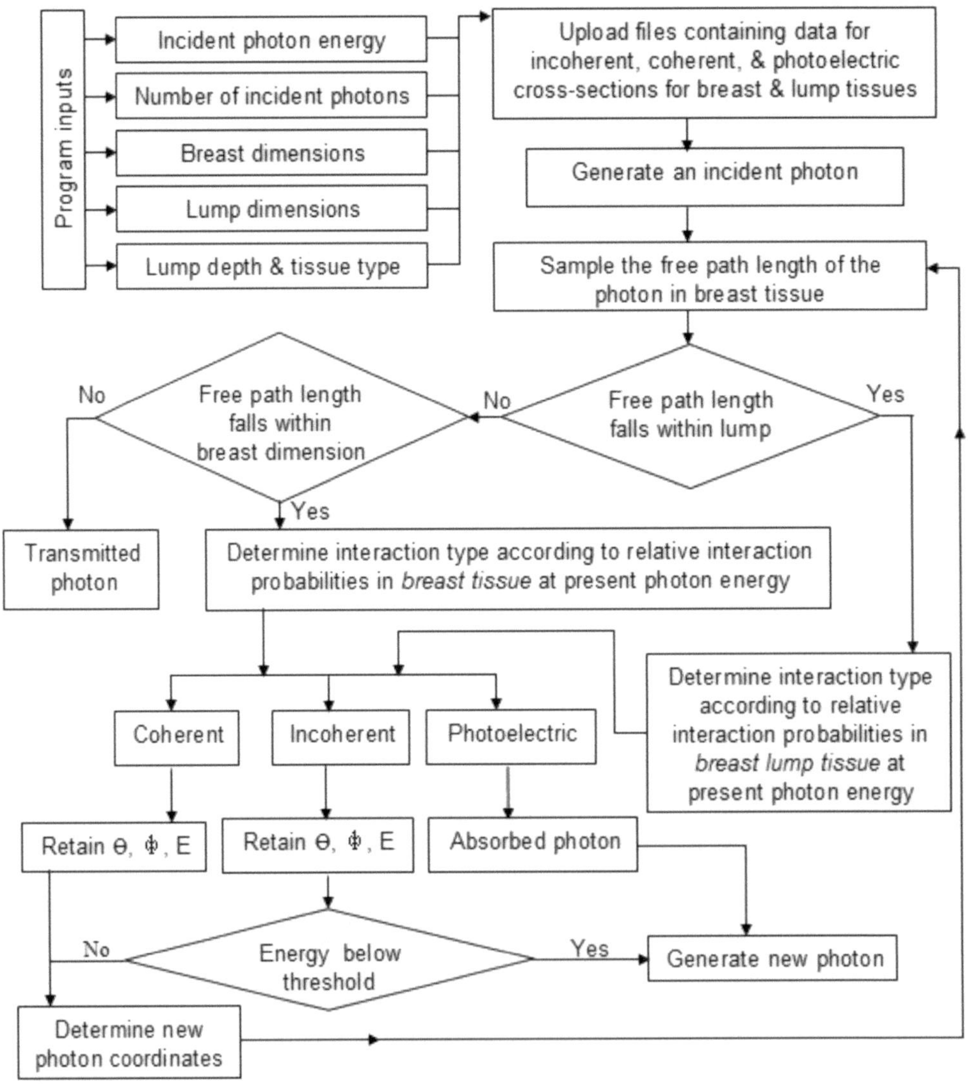

Figure 1. Block diagram of the present Monte Carlo simulation steps.

http://dx.doi.org/10.5772/52787

The proposed detector is probably a highly collimated Hyper-pure Germanium or NaI(Th) detector of maximum possible energy resolution and sensitivity. The detector would be able to scan the breast phantom from the direction opposite to the source with high precision.

For each incident photon, the first step is to calculate its free path t in order to predict the first interaction site. This is carried out by sampling from the exponential probability density function: $p(t) = \mu e^{-\mu t}$, such that $t = 1/(\mu \ln r)$, where r is a random number uniformly distributed in the interval [0, 1] and μ is the total linear attenuation coefficient of breast tissue at the energy of incident photon [24].

If the interaction site falls within the dimension of the lump, then the interaction mechanism of photon in the lump is determined from the relative probabilities of interaction at the given photon energy. A random number is drawn, and according to its value an interaction mechanism is selected [24].

The photon is either absorbed (photoelectric effect) and consequently the program will generate a new photon, or it will be coherently scattered thus the program will continue tracing the photon by calculating the new photon coordinates, new free path length and interaction site taking into consideration the photon scattering angle (θ) and simulated azimuthal angle (ϕ). If the photon is incoherently scattered, the program will follow the same steps as coherent scattering except that it will take into consideration the change in scattered photon energy.

If the new interaction site falls outside the lump and inside the dimension of the breast, the type of interaction will be determined in a way similar to the case of breast lump but in this case using the photon interaction probabilities in breast tissue at the energy of interacting photon. The new photon coordinates; new free path length and interaction site will be determined and so on.

If the free path length of photon at any step falls outside the dimensions of the breast, all photon information including energy and scattering angle will be saved in a file for the development of the x-ray photon scattering profile. All forward scattered photons exiting from the model breast at an angle between 0^0 (i.e. in the direction of the incident beam) up to 90^0 are recorded. The data are binned into angles with an increment of 0.5^0.The program will keep on generating photons up to a pre-defined maximum number of photons. A single run takes only few minutes.

In the present simulation 9 x 10^6 photons are generated in each run of the program. For each simulated condition, the code is run three times in order to calculate the standard error in parameters calculated from the scattered photon distribution. Values of incoherent scattering function are obtained from Hubbell et al 1975 [28] and values of measured coherent scattering form factors accounting for molecular interference effects are obtained from Peplow and Verghese 1998 [19], where as values of photon attenuation coefficients are obtained from Hubbell 1977 [29].

4. Results and discussion

Figure 2 (a & b) presents simulated x-ray scattering profiles from model breast in the presence and in the absence of a breast cancer lump of different sizes at a depth of 2cm for incident photon energies of 20keV (figure 2a) and 40keV (figure 2b) respectively. For both energies, there is an apparent decrease in the total number of scattered photons with increase in breast lump size. The scattered photon distributions in case of 20keV photons looked noisy where it is hard to resolve the x-ray scattering profiles in the presence of breast lumps of small size variations. This would be attributed to the fact that 20keV photons suffer more attenuation than 40keV photons, where as for the same number of incident photons 9 x 10^6, the scattered count in case of 20keV photons is about one order of magnitude less than the case of 40keV photons. On the other hand, the scattered photon distributions of 40keV photons are smooth and even small differences in lump size result in distinguishable differences in the scattering profiles. The adipose peak at 1.1nm^{-1} and the soft tissue peak at 1.6nm^{-1} are well represented in the scattering profiles of 40keV photons compared to a noisy appearance in case of 20keV photons.

The simulated x-ray scattering profiles from model breast in the presence and in the absence of a breast cancer lump of different sizes at a depth of 4cm for incident photon energies of 20 and 40keV are presented in figure 3 (a & b) respectively. The maximum chosen lump size for breast lumps located at a depth of 4cm is 2cm^3 because otherwise the tumor will exceed the maximum dimension of the breast in the direction of the incident beam (6 cm). In other words, the tumor will be budding outside the selected model breast dimensions. Almost all of the comments on the x-ray scattering distributions in case of breast lumps located at 2cm still apply on the scattering profiles in case of breast lumps located at 4cm below the surface of breast. The 40keV photons produce scattering profiles which are smoother and more informative than 20keV photons.

In order to test the validity of characterization of cancer lumps inside a breast of normal dimensions using the differences in relative scattered photon intensities at 1.6 to 1.1nm^{-1} ($P_2/P_1\%$), a plot of $P_2/P_1\%$ versus lump size is presented in figure 4a for 20 keV incident photons and lump depth of 2cm ($P_2/P_1\%$ on the right hand axis, data represented by unfilled circles). The graph show a weak linear relationship ($R^2 = 0.6176$) in addition to a small slope reflecting a poor dependence of the $P_2/P_1\%$ parameter on breast lump size in the model breast. The same poor dependence was also reported for other investigated lump depths and photon energies and as such they are not presented in the other three graphs (b, c & d) in figure 4. One would expect that multiple scattering is the main reason for the ratio $P_2/P_1\%$ to produce weak correlation towards breast cancer lump size in case of model breast. Multiple scattering may cause a shift in the adipose or soft tissue peak positions which will directly affect the value of the $P_2/P_1\%$ ratio.

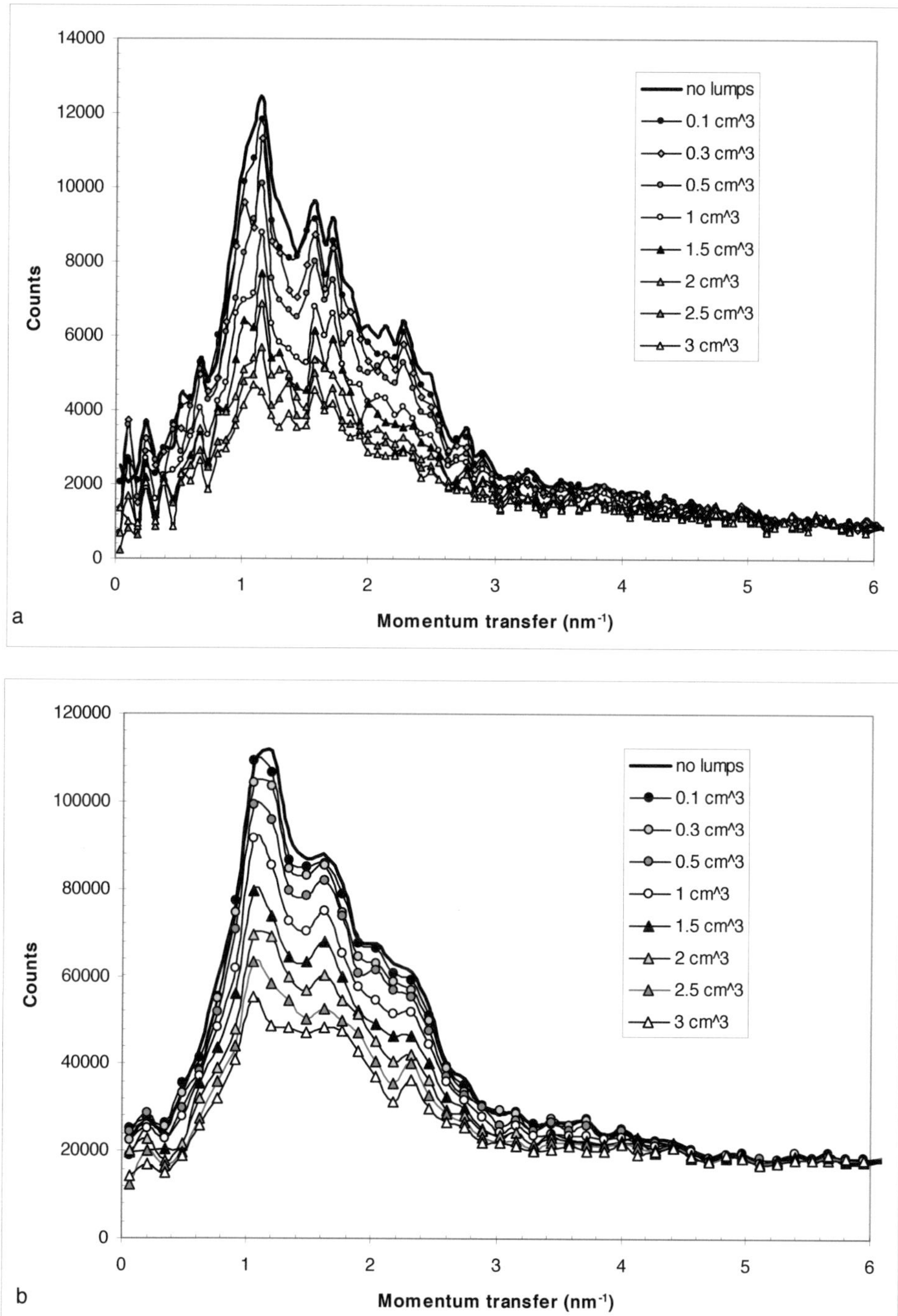

Figure 2. X-ray scattering from a model breast containing a breast cancer lump of different sizes at a depth of 2cm and incident photon energies of (a) 20keV and (b) 40keV.

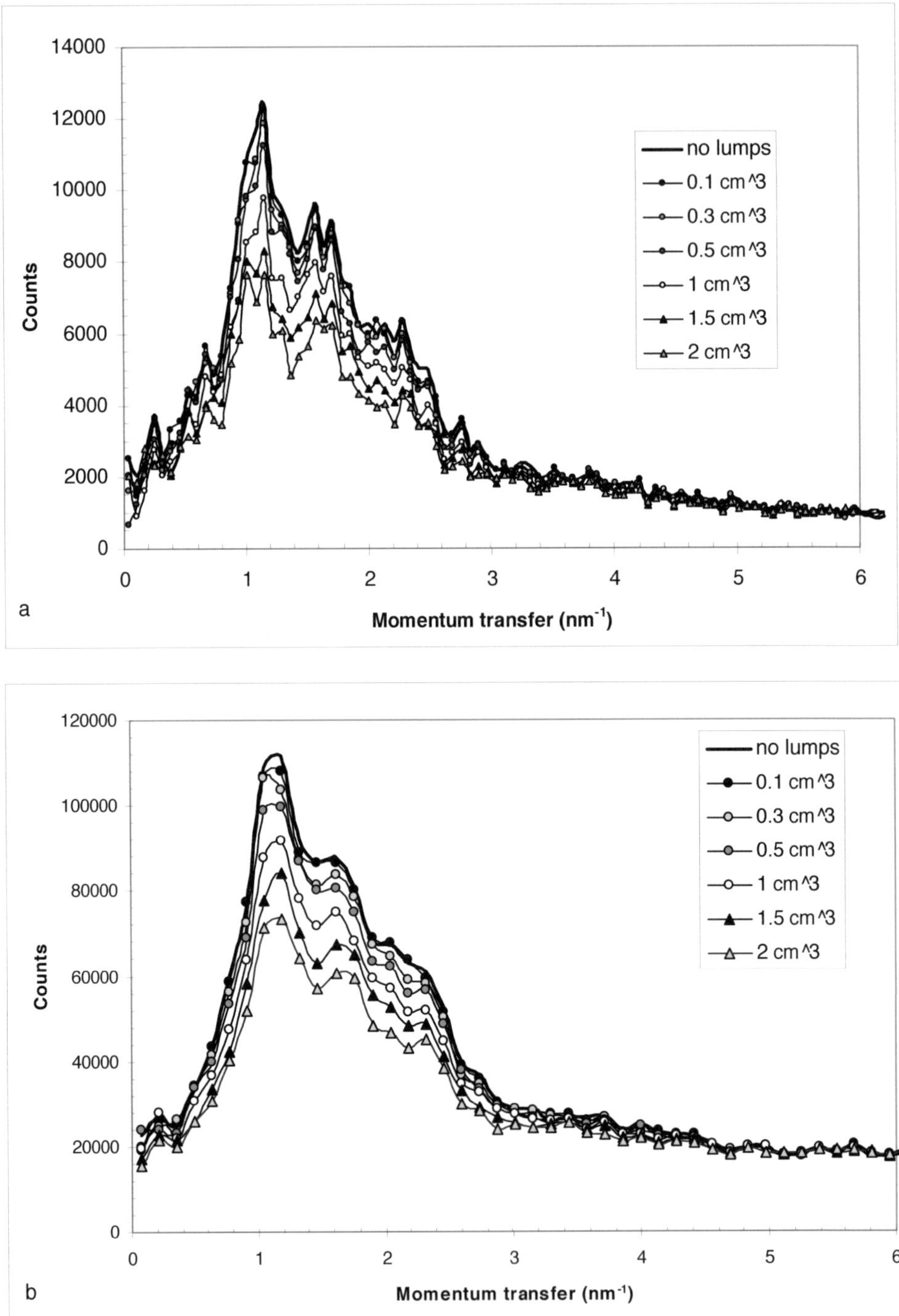

Figure 3. X-ray scattering from a model breast containing a breast cancer lump of different sizes at a depth of 4cm and incident photon energies of (a) 20keV and (b) 40keV.

http://dx.doi.org/10.5772/52787

Nevertheless, a plot of the area under the 1.6nm^{-1} peak relative to the area under the 1.1nm^{-1} peak (A_2/A_1%) versus lump size yielded much better data linearity (R^2 = 0.9684) and a sharp slope (figure 4a) reflecting a degree of dependence of this parameter on breast lump size variations for lumps located at 2cm and incident photon energy of 20keV. The area under the 1.1nm^{-1} peak is determined as the region starting from minimum momentum transfer value up to a momentum transfer value of 1.4nm^{-1}, which corresponds to the trough of the valley between the two peaks. The area under the 1.6nm^{-1} peak is calculated as the region starting from the trough up to a momentum transfer value of 5nm^{-1}, where the halo due to molecular interference of coherently scattered photons apparently ends.

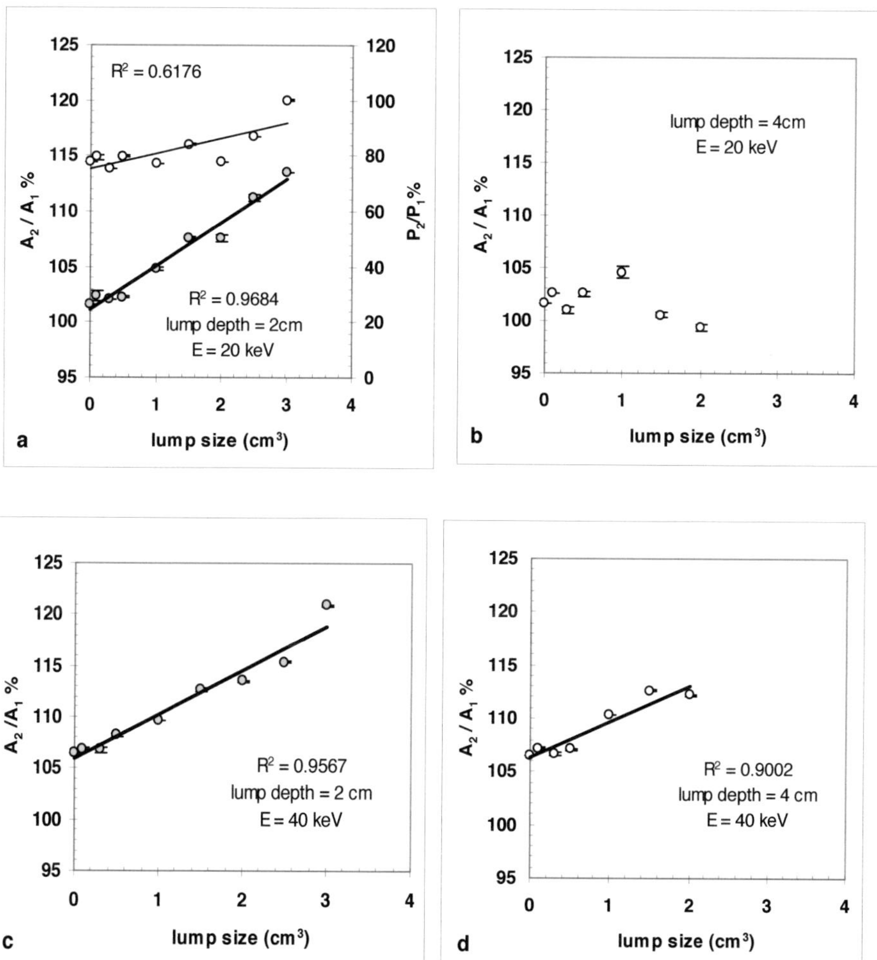

Figure 4. Variation of the ratio of areas (A_2/A_1%) under the x-ray scattering peaks at 1.6nm^{-1} and 1.1 nm^{-1} respectively with breast cancer lump size for 20 keV incident photons (a) lump depth 2 cm & (b) lump depth 4 cm, and for 40 keV incident photons (c) lump depth 2 cm & (d) lump depth 4 cm. Figure 4a also presents the variation of the P_2/P_1% ratio with lump size (right vertical axis, unfilled circles).

For breast cancer lumps located at 4cm and incident photon energy of 20keV, the variation of relative area under peak ratio ($A_2/A_1\%$) with lump size produced scattered values which are far from being correlated to a linear behavior ($R^2 = 0.2006$). This result is probably due to the sharp decrease in the proportion of 20keV photons reaching the detector after interacting with the breast cancer lump located at 4cm from breast surface compared to the proportion of 20keV photons reaching the detector after interacting with the overlying tissue. This is further explained in figure 5 which shows the distribution of simulated free path lengths from the surface of the model breast of 20 and 40keV photons. While the proportion of 20 and 40keV incident photons reaching a depth of 2cm below the surface of breast are considerably high, at a depth of 4cm, the proportion of 20keV photons is substantially reduced compared to the 40keV photons reaching the same depth. This will affect the ability of characterizing the breast lump based on the distribution of scattered photons.

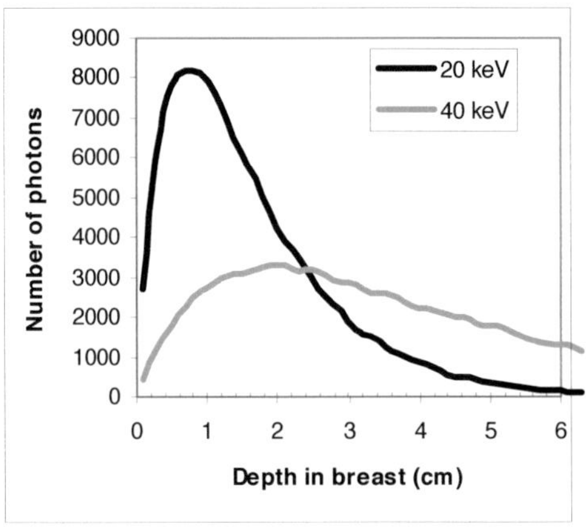

Figure 5. Simulated free path lengths of 20 and 40keV photons inside a model breast.

For 40keV incident photons the $A_2/A_1\%$ ratio varies linearly with lump depth, where the linearity and resolution of breast lumps of small sizes (up to $0.5cm^3$) is much better for breast lumps located at 2cm ($R^2 = 0.9567$) compared to that located at 4cm ($R^2 = 0.9002$) below model breast surface (figure 4c & 4d respectively).

The angular distributions of scattered photons presented in figures 2 and 3 show that for all of the investigated photon energies, lump depths and lump sizes, there exists a noticeable decrease in the total number of scattered photons with increase in lump size.

Figure 6 (a, b, c & d) presents the variation in the attenuation ($\ln I_o/I$) due to breast cancer lump measured from the total number of scattered photons in the absence (I_o) and in the presence (I) of breast lump of different sizes. For all of the investigated situations, there is a strong linear dependence of the $\ln I_o/I$ parameter on breast lump size. The linearity is slightly higher ($R^2 = 0.9941$ & 0.9995 for breast lumps at 2cm & 4cm depths respectively) at 40keV incident photons (figure 6 c & d) compared to the linearity ($R^2 = 0.9792$ & 0.9962 for breast lumps at 2cm & 4cm depths respectively) at 20keV incident photons (figure 6 a & b). All four graphs in figure 6 show better fit to a straight line compared to the graphs in figure 4 which would be considered an advantage for the ln I_o/I parameter compared to the $A_2/A_1\%$ parameter in the determination of lump size. Moreover, breast lumps of small sizes (up to 0.5cm^3) are much better differentiated using the ln I_o/I parameter compared to the $A_2/A_1\%$ parameter (figures 6 & 4 respectively).

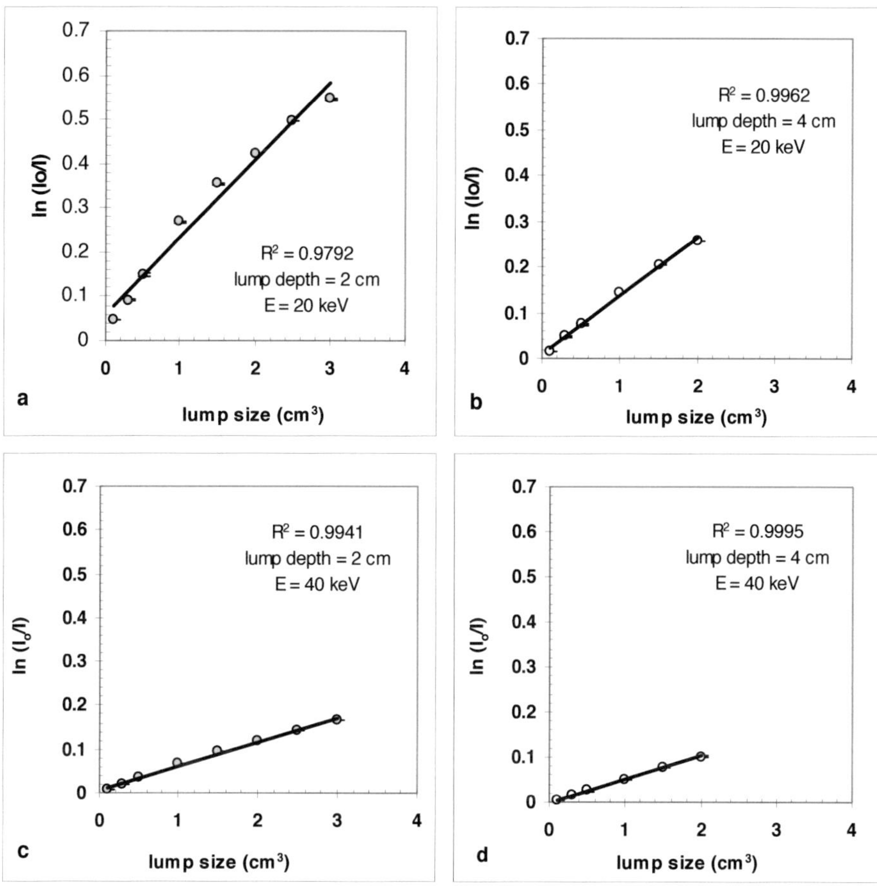

Figure 6. Variation of the attenuation (ln I_o/I) due to breast cancer lump measured from the variation in scattered photons in the absence and in the presence of breast lump of different sizes for 20keV incident photons (a) lump depth 2cm & (b) lump depth 4cm and for 40keV incident photons, (c) lump depth 2cm & (d) lump depth 4cm.

5. Conclusion

It has been shown that it would be possible to characterize breast cancer lumps inside a model breast of dimensions comparable to average breast dimensions using the relative difference in areas of the soft tissue to adipose peak instead of the relative intensities at a single momentum transfer value for each peak. It has also been shown that it would be even more informative to characterize breast cancer lumps using the variation in the attenuation in scattered photons due to breast cancer lump. The data obtained at 40keV incident photon energy was always better than that obtained at 20keV. The present results show a possibility of extending the application of x-ray scattering from the detection of breast cancer in excised tissues to the detection of cancer in patients' breasts. Some possible difficulties should be overcome for applying the proposed method on patients; the availability of a monoenergetic photon source for energies between 20-40keV (a Synchrotron would be a possible solution), the design of new breast scanning system for practical testing of the present results and the development of a software specially dedicated for the analysis of acquired data and printing a user-friendly diagnostic report for the physician.

Author details

Wael M. Elshemey

Address all correspondence to: waelelshemey@yahoo.com

Biophysics Department, Faculty of Science, Cairo University, Giza, Egypt

References

[1] Kosanetzky J, Knoerr B, Harding G and Neitzel U 1987 X-ray diffraction measurement of some plastic materials and body tissues *Med. Phys.* 14 526–32.

[2] Kidane G, Speller R D, Royle G J and Hanby A M 1999 X-ray scatter signatures for normal and neoplastic breast tissues. *Phys. Med. Biol.* 44 1791–1802.

[3] Evans S H, Bradley D A, Dance D R, Bateman J E and Jones C H 1991. Measurement of small-angle photon scattering for some breast tissues and tissue substitute materials. *Phys. Med. Biol.*, 36, 7-18.

[4] Poletti M E, Goncalves O D and Mazzaro I 2002a Coherent and incoherent scattering of 17.44 and 6.93 kev x-ray photons scattered from biological and biological-equivalent samples: characterization of tissues. *X-Ray Spectrom*. 31, 57–61.

[5] Ryan E, and Farquharson M J 2004. Angular dispersive X-ray scattering from breast tissue using synchrotron radiation. *Radiat. Phys. Chem.* 71, 971–972.

[6] Castro C R F, Barroso R C, Anjos M J, Lopes R T, and Braz D 2004 Coherent scattering characteristics of normal and pathological breast human tissues *Radiat. Phys. Chem.* 71 649–651.

[7] Geraki K, Farquharson M, Bradley D 2004 X-ray fluorescence and energy dispersive X-ray diffraction for the characterisation of breast tissue *Radiation Physics and Chemistry* 71 969–970.

[8] Ryan Elaine A and Farquharson Michael J 2007. Breast tissue classification using x-ray scattering measurements and multivariate data analysis. *Phys. Med. Biol*. 52 6679–6696.

[9] Theodorakou C And Farquharson M J 2008 Human Soft Tissue Analysis Using X-Ray Or Gamma-Ray Techniques. *Phys. Med. Biol.* 53 R111–R149.

[10] Elshemey W M and Elsharkawy W B 2009 Monte Carlo simulation of x-ray scattering for quantitative characterization of breast cancer *Phys. Med. Biol*. 54 3773–84.

[11] Bohndiek Sarah E, Cook Emily J, Arvanitis Costas D, Olivo Alessandro, Royle Gary J, Clark Andy T, Prydderch Mark L, Turchetta Renato and Speller Robert D 2008 A CMOS active pixel sensor system for laboratorybased x-ray diffraction studies of biological tissue. *Phys. Med. Biol*. 53 655–672.

[12] Wael M Elshemey, Omar S Desouky, Mostafa M Fekry, Sahar M Talaat and Anwar A Elsayed 2010. The diagnostic capability of x-ray scattering parameters for the characterization of breast cancer, *Med. Phys* 37 4257-4265.

[13] Boone John M, Yu Tong and Seibert Anthony 1998 Mammography spectrum measurement using an x-ray diffraction device *Phys. Med. Biol.* 43 2569

[14] Ducote, Justin L. and Molloi Sabee 2010 Quantification of breast density with dual energy mammography: An experimental feasibility study *Med. Phys.* 37, 793-801.

[15] Hubbell J H 1969 Photon cross sections, attenuation coefficients, and energy absorption coefficients from 10 keV to 100 GeV *NSRDS-NBS* 29 (Washington, DC: National Bureau of Standards).

[16] Johns P C and Wismayer M P 2004 Measurement of coherent x-ray scatter form factors for amorphous materials using diffractometers *Phys. Med. Biol.* 49 5233–50

[17] Tartari Agostino, Casnati Ernesto, Bonifazzi Claudio and Baraldi Claudio 1997. Molecular differential cross sections for x-ray coherent scattering in fat and polymethyl methacrylate. *Phys. Med. Biol*. 42, 2551–2560.

[18] Tartari A, Taibi A, Bonifazzi C and Baraldi C 2002. Updating of form factor tabulations for coherent scattering of photons in tissues. *Phys. Med. Biol.* 47 163–175.

[19] Peplow Douglas E and Verghese Kuruvilla 1998. Measured molecular coherent scattering form factors of animal tissues, plastics and human breast tissue. *Phys. Med. Biol.* 43 2431–2452.

[20] Poletti M E, Goncalves O D, Schechter H, Mazzaro I 2002b Precise evaluation of elastic differential scattering cross-sections and their uncertainties in X-ray scattering experiments. *Nucl. Instrum. Methods Phys. Res. B* 187, 437–446.

[21] King B W and Johns P C 2010 An energy-dispersive technique to measure x-ray coherent scattering form factors of amorphous materials *Phys. Med. Biol.* 55 855-871

[22] Chan H P and Doi K 1986 Some properties of photon scattering in water phantoms in diagnostic radiology *Med. Phys.* 13 824–30.

[23] Elshemey Wael M, Elsayed Anwar A and El-Lakkani Ali 1999. Physical characteristics of X-ray scattering in fat and blood *Radiat. Meas.* 30 715–723.

[24] Chan H P and Doi K 1983 The validity of Monte Carlo simulation in studies of scattered radiation in diagnostic radiology *Phys. Med. Biol.* 28 109–29.

[25] Dance D. R., Skinner C. L., Carlsson G. Alm 1999 Breast dosimetry *Applied Radiation and Isotopes*, 50, 85-203

[26] Highnam R, Jeffreys M, McCormack V, Warren R, Smith G Davey and Brady M2007 comparing measurements of breast density Phys. Med. Biol. 52 5881

[27] Griffiths J A, Royle G J, Hanby A M, Horrocks J A, Bohndiek S E and Speller R D 2007 Correlation of energy dispersive diffraction signatures and microCT of small breast tissue samples with pathological analysis. *Phys. Med. Biol.* 52 6151–6164.

[28] Hubbell J H, Veigele Wm J, Briggs E A, Brown R T, Cromer D T and Howerton R J 1975 Atomic form factors, incoherent scattering functions and photon scattering cross-sections *J. Phys. Chem. Ref. Data* 4 471–538.

[29] Hubbell J H 1977 Photon mass attenuation and mass energy-absorption coefficients for H, C, N, O, Ar and seven mixtures from 0.1 keV to 20 MeV *Radiat. Res.* 70 58–81.